Belize

John Noble
Susan Forsyth

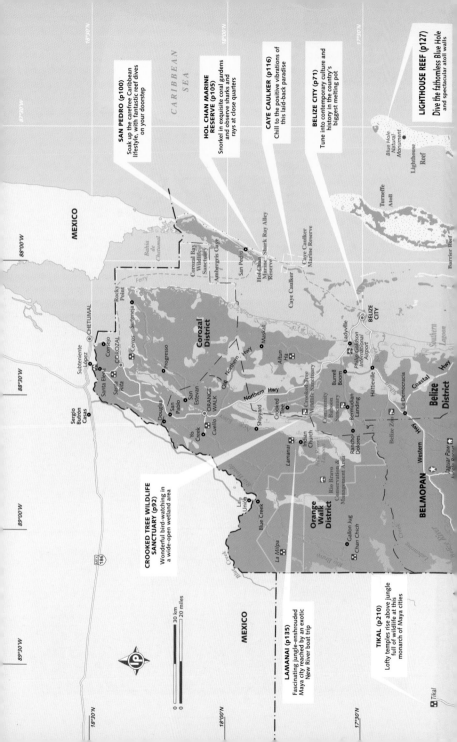

SAN PEDRO (p100)
Soak up the carefree Caribbean lifestyle, with fantastic reef dives on your doorstep

HOL CHAN MARINE RESERVE (p105)
Snorkel in exquisite coral gardens and observe sharks and rays at close quarters

CAYE CAULKER (p116)
Chill to the positive vibrations of this laid-back paradise

BELIZE CITY (p71)
Tune into contemporary culture and history in the country's biggest melting pot

LIGHTHOUSE REEF (p127)
Dive the fathomless Blue Hole and spectacular atoll walls

CROOKED TREE WILDLIFE SANCTUARY (p92)
Wonderful bird-watching in a wide-open wetland area

LAMANAI (p135)
Fascinating jungle-enshrouded Maya city reached by an exotic New River boat trip

TIKAL (p210)
Lofty temples rise above jungle full of wildlife at this monarch of Maya cities

MEXICO

CARIBBEAN SEA

MEXICO

0   30 km
0   20 miles

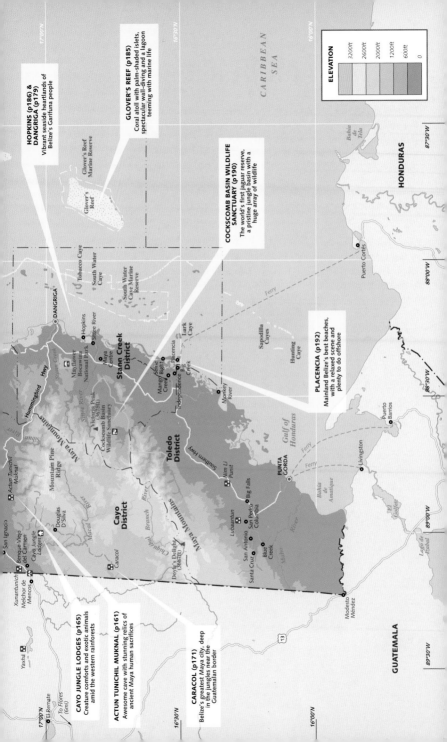

HOPKINS (p186) & DANGRIGA (p179)
Vibrant seaside heartlands of Belize's Garífuna people

GLOVER'S REEF (p185)
Coral atoll with palm-shaded islets, spectacular wall-diving and a lagoon teeming with marine life

COCKSCOMB BASIN WILDLIFE SANCTUARY (p190)
The world's first jaguar reserve, a pristine jungle basin with a huge array of wildlife

PLACENCIA (p192)
Mainland Belize's best beaches, with a relaxed scene and plenty to do offshore

CAYO JUNGLE LODGES (p165)
Creature comforts and exotic animals amid the western rainforests

ACTUN TUNICHIL MUKNAL (p161)
Awesome cave with stunning relics of ancient Maya human sacrifices

CARACOL (p171)
Belize's greatest Maya city, deep in the jungles near the Guatemalan border

ELEVATION

3200ft
2600ft
2000ft
1200ft
600ft
0

CARIBBEAN SEA

HONDURAS

GUATEMALA

Destination Belize

Modern Belize has emerged from centuries of domination by pirates, loggers and British imperial rule as one of the planet's most environmentally progressive and harmoniously multicultural nations. Great swaths of rainforest and the world's second-longest barrier reef remain intact, while the sparse human populace is celebrated for its relaxed and welcoming lifestyle.

With one foot planted in Central America's jungles and the other dipped in the Caribbean, Belize almost invented ecotourism. Offshore, you'll kayak from one sandy, palm-dotted islet to another and swim through translucent seas gazing on a kaleidoscope of corals, tropical fish, dolphins, turtles and rays.

Inland, boat along a jungle river to the roars of howler monkeys and the flash of toucans, climb Maya temples, discover relics of ancient sacrifices deep underground, and spotlight kinkajous and crocodiles on a nocturnal jungle walk. Wake next morning to the sounds and sights of a rainforest full of tropical birds.

Yes, this is Belize. And you'll experience it all in a climate that's always warm, amid the smiles of one of the planet's least numerous but most amiable populations, speaking English with a uniquely charming lilt. This is a place where people still have the time and space not just to say 'Hi' and hurry on, but to stop, chat and get to know strangers; a country where even immigration officers may wear Rasta plaits and greet you, smiling, by your first name.

Sounds like an ad. But get on down there – as they say in Belize, seein' is Belizin'!

GREG JOHNSTO

Beneath the Caribbean

A diver explores the vibrant underwater garden at Half Moon Caye (p128)

Dive the unique Blue Hole (p127), one of Belize's natural wonders

OTHER HIGHLIGHTS

- Shark Ray Alley (p105) is unmissable for its captivating marine life.
- With an ocean floor that plummets away to 2700ft, Glover's Reef (p185) is a superb site for divers.
- Coral-dotted Hol Chan Marine Reserve (p105) is the longest-established marine reserve in Belize.

Discover the mysteries of the deep at Ambergris Caye (p100)

Mainland Marvels

Hang out with black howler monkeys (p48)

OTHER HIGHLIGHTS

- Attention bird-watchers! Grab your binoculars and head for the rural delights of Crooked Tree Wildlife Sanctuary (p92).
- The Belize Zoo (p95) boasts an amazing array of wildlife, including jaguars, pumas, ocelots, monkeys, crocodiles and a magnificent harpy eagle.

Make a splash in the Rio On Pools (p171)

Greet sunrise on the banks of the serene New River (p135)

LUKE HUNTER

Lose yourself in the lush, tropical surrounds of the Cockscomb Basin Wildlife Sanctuary (p190)

Admire the vivid red ginger flower, found along the New River in Orange Walk (p131)

If you're lucky you might spot a jaguar at Cockscomb Basin Wildlife Sanctuary (p190)

GREG JOHNSTON

JOHN ELK III

Catch a glance of a green iguana (p49)

LUKE HUNTER

Monumental Maya

ERIC L WHEATER

Walk among the lofty Maya ruins at Tikal (p210), in Guatemala

OTHER HIGHLIGHTS

- Impressive, jungle-enshrouded Caracol (p171) is Belize's biggest ancient city.
- An excursion into Actun Tunichil Muknal (p161) will expose ancient Maya cave rituals…including human sacrifice!
- The ancient Maya religious and ceremonial center of Nim Li Punit (p205) is fascinating for its stelae and tombs.

Examine the intricate sculptural friezes at Xunantunich (p163)

DEBRA MILLER

Marvel at the grandeur of Jaguar Temple (p136) at Lamanai

JOHN ELK

Adventure!

Deep-sea adventures reveal bountiful marine life (p50)

Kayakers glide through the waters of the barrier reef (p53)

OTHER HIGHLIGHTS

- For an exhilarating river-tubing adventure, try the Caves Branch River (p153) near Jaguar Paw Jungle Resort.

- The brilliant turquoise waters around San Pedro (p100) invite you to windsurf, kayak, snorkel, sail or just splash about!

- With a 12-mile network of trails, Cockscomb Basin Wildlife Sanctuary (p190) is a fantastic place for a relaxing wander or energizing hike.

Hike the invigorating rainforests of Punta Gorda (p200)

Melting Pot

JEFFREY BECOM

Share a smile with a local from the Maya Mountains

WAYNE WALTON

Take time out in the Maya village of San Antonio (p206)

Chill out with the locals on Caye Caulker (p116)

ANDREW MARSHALL & LEANNE WALK

OTHER HIGHLIGHTS

- The town of Dangriga (p179) is a great place to visit if you're interested in learning about Garifuna culture and history.

- For urban vibes and ethnic diversity, get out on the streets of colorful Belize City (p71).

Heavenly Lodgings

Nature abounds at Lamanai Outpost Lodge (p137)

OTHER HIGHLIGHTS

■ Get away from it all on Ambergris Caye, where Mata Chica Beach Resort (p111) and Victoria House (p111) offer luxury and seclusion.

■ With its remote jungle setting, exotic wildlife and atmospheric thatched cabanas, Chan Chich Lodge (p139) is a spectacular place to stay.

Sample rustic beachfront living on Caye Caulker (p122)

Pick a palm and camp under the stars on Half Moon Caye (p128)

Beach & Breeze

MARK WEBSTER

Find paradise on Long Caye (p128)

Art imitates life in a mural on Caye Caulker (p116)

WAYNE WALTON

OTHER HIGHLIGHTS

- With some of the best beaches in all of Belize, Placencia (p192) is a perfect place to laze away the days.
- San Pedro (p100), with its palm-fringed beaches, Caribbean-style wooden houses and laid-back atmosphere, is half a mile from the stunning barrier reef.

Linger over the colors of the Caribbean from the shores of Caye Caulker (p116)

JOHN ELK

Contents

Regional Map Contents

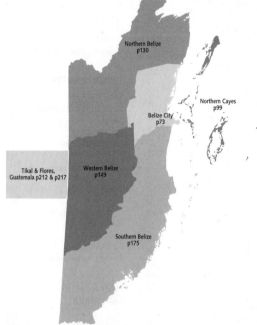

Northern Belize
p130

Northern Cayes
p99

Belize City
p73

Tikal & Flores,
Guatemala p212 & p217

Western Belize
p149

Southern Belize
p175

The Authors

JOHN NOBLE
Coordinating Author, Belize City, Northern Belize, Western Belize, Southern Belize

John has been drawn to Belize ever since someone told him on an early Central American backpacking trip: 'It's the kind of place you might settle when you've been round the world seven times and seen everything.' John is based in Spain now, but he loves to visit Belize for a host of reasons, especially the people's unhurried lifestyle and all those little oddities that make a destination unique: place names like Scotland Half Moon, business names like Hokey Pokey Water Taxi, and the bus driver who soothes the agitated crowds on his vehicle by playing Bob Marley: 'Well there's no need, there's no need, to get jumpy...'

The Coordinating Author's Favorite Trip

I actually like Belize City (p71). Along with its seamy side it has character, history, good restaurants and good lodgings. So I'll begin my trip here, then I'll take the canals-and-rivers route south to Gales Point Manatee (p176), spot some manatees and move on to Hopkins (p186) to soak up some Garifuna rhythm. I'll visit the Garifuna 'capital' Dangriga (p179) and walk the trails of Mayflower Bocawina National Park (p186) and Cockscomb Basin Wildlife Sanctuary (p190). Then I'll take a boat to Glover's Reef (p185) and live the desert-island life for a few days before returning for a spell in relatively urbane Placencia (p192). Finally I'll move on down to the untrammeled far south to explore its little known national parks, wildlife sanctuaries, marine reserves and Maya villages.

SUSAN FORSYTH
Northern Cayes, Tikal & Flores

Susan has had one foot in the Maya world for over a decade due to travel and work in the region. In Belize she enjoys being able to converse in English rather than Spanish with the Maya. Susan has been addicted to islands since her teens, when she began visiting Australian-island surfing spots, and likes nothing better than the smell of the ocean – a taste perfectly satisfied by Belize's cayes and atolls. She is enchanted by the islands' beauty and an enduring penchant for reggae helps her to feel right at home here. As for Tikal, the place is supernatural!

LONELY PLANET AUTHORS

Why is our travel information the best in the world? It's simple: our authors are independent, dedicated travelers. They don't research using just the Internet or phone, and they don't take freebies in exchange for positive coverage. They travel widely, to all the popular spots and off the beaten track. They personally visit thousands of hotels, restaurants, cafés, bars, galleries, palaces, museums and more – and they take pride in getting all the details right, and telling it how it is. For more, see the authors section on www.lonelyplanet.com.

CONTRIBUTING AUTHORS

Dr Allen J Christenson wrote The Ancient Maya World chapter. He earned both his MA and PhD in Pre-Columbian Maya Art History at the University of Texas at Austin, and now works as an associate professor in the Humanities, Classics and Comparative Literature department of Brigham Young University in Provo, Utah. He is the author of *Art and Society in a Highland Maya Community* (2001), which is about the art and culture of the Maya community of Santiago Atitlan, Guatemala, as well as a critical edition and new translation of the great K'iche'-Maya epic, the *Popol Vuh*, published in 2003.

Dr David Goldberg MD wrote the Health chapter. He completed his training in internal medicine and infectious diseases at Columbia-Presbyterian Medical Center in New York City, where he has also served as voluntary faculty. At present, he is an infectious diseases specialist in Scarsdale, New York State, and the editor-in-chief of the website MDTravelHealth.com.

Mark Webster wrote the Diving & Snorkeling section of the Belize Outdoors chapter. Mark works both as a photojournalist and a diving consultant in the oil industry. He writes regularly for scuba-diving magazines and his work has featured in many diving, photographic and wildlife publications. Mark's other books include Lonely Planet's *Diving & Snorkeling Belize, The Art and Technique of Underwater Photography* and *The Blue (Unesco)*. Mark has achieved many international competition successes, including third place overall in the CMAS World Championships of Underwater Photography.

Getting Started

A little advance planning definitely helps you make the most of your time and money in Belize. Our Itineraries and Highlights chapters will give you a start. Most travelers opt for what's called a surf-and-turf vacation: some time on the cayes, atolls or mainland coast, plus a bit of time inland. The good thing is that despite all of its variety, Belize is a tiny place and it's relatively easy to get anywhere within half a day, especially if you're willing to fly. You can easily enjoy all three of Belize's main fields of interest – sea, jungle and ruins – in a week.

Only over the Christmas–New Year's and Easter holiday periods might you face any difficulties in finding a room, but it still pays to book ahead for any particular places you're keen to stay in, and make inquiries about the necessity of booking for any activities, such as diving and dive courses.

Budget travelers need to be aware that Belize is not the low-budget paradise that neighboring Guatemala is. All you've got to do is get used to the idea that a US$20 double room is very cheap.

WHEN TO GO

The best months to visit Belize are the drier ones: December through May. The rainy season (June to November) isn't so wet that you can't do anything (except at times in the south, which has two to three times as much rain as the rest of the country), but it generally makes things less fun. The biggest tourist influx is in the couple of weeks each side of Christmas and Easter. Some of the most popular accommodations get fully booked at these times.

For more information, see Climate Charts (p222)

Many accommodations, especially the more expensive ones, have high- and low-season prices: high-season is usually from December to May, low-season covers the rest of the year (the prices given in this book are for the high season). But some accommodations also have 'extra' seasons covering the Christmas, New Year's and Easter periods, when their prices go above normal high-season rates. If you're using top-end or some mid-range accommodations, you'll certainly save money by avoiding these 'extra' seasons. See p220 for more on accommodations in Belize.

DON'T LEAVE HOME WITHOUT...

- Checking your foreign ministry's travel information on Belize (see p224)
- Any necessary immunizations or medications (see p239) and special toiletries you may require, including contact lens solution
- A flashlight (torch) for those not-so-well-lit Belizean streets, pathways, stairs – and caves!
- A compact pair of binoculars
- A small padlock
- A sun hat
- Waterproof sunscreen
- Adequate insurance (see p227)
- A sweater for unexpected cool days
- Light, long-sleeved pants and shirt for protection against bugs and sun

COSTS & MONEY

Though a poor country, Belize is at least as expensive as Mexico, and much more costly than Guatemala. High taxes, many imports and the fact that much of its tourism industry is geared to North Americans on fairly short vacations help to keep prices high. Whereas US$40 to US$50 will buy you a solidly comfortable midrange double in Guatemala and most of Mexico, in Belize it's likely to bring you a room that is little more than perfunctory. For anything above the ordinary you're often looking at a minimum of US$70, and the top end of the market goes above US$300. A good two- or three-course meal with a couple of drinks in a pleasant restaurant will average US$15 to US$25 (more if you have lobster!). Prices are highest on Ambergris Caye and in the more upmarket jungle lodges and resorts. Budget travelers can make their money last longer by hanging out in places like Caye Caulker, San Ignacio and Placencia.

Traveling by public bus is dirt cheap, but car hire, taxis, boats and hotel transfers are not. Expect a day's auto rental to cost between US$80 and US$100. Tours and excursions mostly run US$60 to US$100 per person for a day (more for diving trips).

Overall, a comfortable midrange budget per person is US$100 to US$150 per day. Staying in some of the country's better accommodations, enjoying plenty of tours and activities, and traveling by rented car, plane or hotel transfer can easily add up to US$300 a day. Budget travelers might get away with US$30 a day if they're particularly frugal, but you need to spend more like US$50 or US$60 to enjoy yourself.

The simplest way to cut costs is to share rooms, transport and tours with other people.

Belize's currency is the Belize dollar (BZ$), which has hovered at or around a rate of BZ$2=US$1 for several years, but since talk of a devaluation is never far beneath the surface, prices in this book are given in US dollars. We also include taxes and any obligatory service charges in the prices we provide. See p228 for more on Belizean money matters.

See p228 for more on Belizean money matters.

HOW MUCH?

Three-dive trip to Lighthouse Reef from San Pedro: US$185

Comfortable midrange double room by the sea, on Ambergris Caye: US$100

Lobster main course: US$12-25

One day's car rental: US$80-100

One hour of Internet access: US$3

TRAVEL LITERATURE

Belizean character Emory King wrote *Hey Dad, This is Belize* and *I Spent it All in Belize*, though they are not exactly travel books, but more collections of amusing and insightful articles on the many quirks of a country that King has been chronicling since he bumped into it (after being shipwrecked) one night in 1953.

Richard Timothy Conroy's *Our Man in Belize* is a fun, engaging memoir of his stint as US vice-consul to the impoverished British Honduras of the early 1960s, a period marked by the devastating Hurricane Hattie.

Thor Janson's *Belize: Land of the Free by the Carib Sea* captures Belize in pictures – all the color of its forests, islands, wildlife, festivals and ruins, and the smiles of its people.

Most travel writers have given Belize just one or two chapters in books of wider compass. One such was Aldous Huxley in the 1930s in *Beyond the Mexique Bay*, a book with plenty of interesting material on the Maya, but which puts down Belize as 'of no strategic value,' 'all but unpopulated' and 'not on the way from anywhere to anywhere else.'

Ronald Wright's *Time Among the Maya* is an acutely observed account of travels through Belize, Guatemala and Mexico in the troubled 1980s, delving into the past and present of the Maya and the profound importance they attach to their calendar and the passing of time. Peter Canby, too, focuses on Maya culture in his insightful 1990s book *The Heart of the Sky: Travels Among the Maya,* which has one chapter on Belize.

TOP TENS

WATER ADVENTURES
Even inland, you'll be taking to the water for fun! See the Belize Outdoors chapter (p57) for more information.

- Snorkeling or diving Hol Chan Marine Reserve (p106)
- Diving with whale sharks at Gladden Spit (p194)
- Kayaking Glover's Reef (p185)
- Diving Long Caye Wall, Glover's Reef (p185)
- Diving the Elbow, Turneffe Atoll (p126)
- Diving the Blue Hole (p127)
- Canoeing through Barton Creek Cave (p162)
- River-tubing the Caves Branch River (p152)
- Cruising the cayes and atolls by yacht (p63)
- Snorkeling Half Moon Caye (p128)

LAND ADVENTURES
There's plenty of dry-land excitement to be had (see the Belize Outdoors chapter, p57).

- Caving Actun Tunichil Muknal (p161)
- Experiencing the Black Hole Drop (p179)
- Spotting countless birds at Crooked Tree Wildlife Sanctuary (p92)
- Taking night jungle walks at Cockscomb Basin Wildlife Sanctuary (p191)
- Exploring the jungle-shrouded Maya ruins at Lamanai (p135)
- Horseback riding at Banana Bank (p153)
- Hiking the waterfall trails at Mayflower Bocawina National Park (p186)
- Watching scarlet macaws at Red Bank (p195)
- Walking the trails of Cockscomb Basin Wildlife Sanctuary (p191)
- Hiking around Black Rock River Lodge (p165)

FESTIVALS & EVENTS
These are the times when Belize lets loose even more than usual (see p225 for more).

- Belize International Film Festival (Belize City; p81) Last week of February
- La Ruta Maya Belize River Challenge (canoe race from San Ignacio to Belize City; p157) Four days ending on Baron Bliss Day (on or near March 9)
- Cashew Festival (Crooked Tree; p93) First weekend in May
- Lobsterfest (Placencia; p196) Last weekend of June; (Caye Caulker; p121) First weekend of July
- Feast of San Luis (San Antonio; p206) Around August 15 to 25
- September Celebrations (Belize City; p81) September 10 to 21
- Garifuna Settlement Day (Dangriga; p181) November 19
- Toledo Fish Fest (Punta Gorda; p201) Weekend near Garifuna Settlement Day
- Wilfrid Peters Brok Dong Competition (Belize City; p81) Mid- to late December
- Christmas and New Year's season festivities (Dangriga; p181) Around December 24 to January 6

INTERNET RESOURCES

Belize (www.travelbelize.org) The Belize Tourism Board's site is a fine place to start for almost any Belize-related travel topic.

Belize by Naturalight (www.belizenet.com) Belize portal with hosts of travel and business links.

Belize Forums (www.belizeforum.com) Great message and discussion board covering just about everything under the Belizean sun.

Lonely Planet (www.lonelyplanet.com) Succinct summaries on Belize travel; the popular Thorn Tree bulletin board and travel news.

News5 (new.channel5belize.com) Transcripts and archives of Belizean TV news.

Itineraries

CLASSIC ROUTES

TROPICAL DREAMS
Two to Three Weeks / San Pedro to San Ignacio

Launch your trip at **San Pedro** (p100) on Ambergris Caye, Belize's holiday central. Soak up the sun on the beaches, swim from the docks, snorkel or dive among coral gardens and the sharks and stingrays of **Shark Ray Alley** (p105), indulge in gourmet meals at Capricorn, Mambo or Caramba restaurants, and boogie at Fido's Courtyard Bar. San Pedro is the best-equipped launching pad for dives at **Blue Hole** (p127) and other atoll sites. From San Pedro, sail a few miles south to unwind on **Caye Caulker** (p116). After dark, absorb the positive vibrations at Herbal Tribe or I&I Reggae Bar.

Make for dry land and stop in **Belize City** (p71) for the Museum of Belize and Government House, then head for birding at **Crooked Tree Wildlife Sanctuary** (p92) and the trip along the New River to **Lamanai** (p135). To complete the mainland part of your trip go west to Belize's jungles and back country. Base yourself at a lodge in **Cayo District** (p159) – or, for slimmer budgets, at a hotel in **San Ignacio** (p154). Explore caves loaded with ancient remains, such as **Actun Tunichil Muknal** (p161), take hikes by day or night, travel by canoe or river-tube along jungle rivers, dip beneath the waterfalls of the **Mountain Pine Ridge** (p170) and explore Belize's greatest Maya site, **Caracol** (p171).

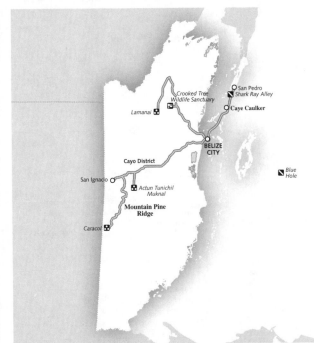

You'll travel around 500 miles on water and land on this great 'surf-and-turf' trip, absolutely the best recipe for introducing yourself to Belize's multifarious attractions. You'll need your swimsuit, sunglasses, sun hat, binoculars and long sleeves and pants for the jungle.

SOUTHERN SENSATIONS   Two to Three Weeks / Belize City to Punta Gorda

There's so much to do and experience in southern Belize that you could devote a whole trip to it. From **Belize City** (p71) head westward just as far as the start of the beautiful Hummingbird Hwy, which carries you across the thickly forested northern foothills of the Maya Mountains to the Garifuna capital of Dangriga. En route, stop at **Ian Anderson's Caves Branch Adventure Company** (p178) for some active excitement in the form of cave exploration, jungle expeditions and abseiling down bottomless sinkholes. Hang out in **Dangriga** (p179) or the nearby coastal village of **Hopkins** (p186) to absorb some Garifuna rhythms and make trips out to watch manatees at **Gales Point Manatee** (p176) and hike the beautiful jungle trails at **Mayflower Bocawina National Park** (p186) or **Cockscomb Basin Wildlife Sanctuary** (p190). Head seaward from Dangriga or Hopkins to indulge your tropical-island fantasies at **Tobacco Caye** (p183) or **South Water Caye** (p184) – or, best of all, from nearby **Sittee River** (p189) to **Glover's Reef** (p185), the most southerly and most complete of Belize's three offshore atolls.

Move on down to **Placencia** (p192) for some mainland holiday time, with its lovely sandy beaches, lively bars, accommodations from luxury resorts to budget guesthouses and an array of water sports from sailing, fishing and kayaking to snorkeling and diving around idyllic cayes.

Further down, the southernmost town in Belize, **Punta Gorda** (p200), has yet to see tourism on a serious scale and for that reason has the appeal of an unspoiled multicultural Belizean town. From here head out for a day or two on the equally unspoiled **Sapodilla Cayes** (p200) and inland to explore the lagoons, caves, waterfalls, forests, ancient Maya archaeological sites and modern Maya villages of the **Toledo District** (p203).

Your trip through the Belizean south will carry you 600 or 700 miles on land and water. Giving it three, or even four, weeks instead of two will let you truly soak up the culture, the climate and the textures of this region that not so long ago was little known and even less traveled.

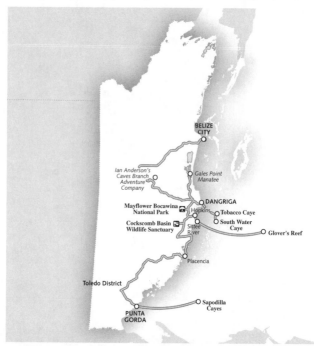

ISLAND HOPPING

A COCKTAIL OF CAYES   Three Weeks / Ambergris Caye to Sapodilla Cayes

Saltwater junkies need hardly set foot on mainland soil as they roam from one idyllic sandy island to another. Out on Belize's cayes and atolls you can truly devote yourself to the sun and sea in whatever form takes your fancy – swimming, snorkeling, diving, kayaking, sailing, fishing… Though regular island-to-island transportation is rare, you can (at a price) charter small launches for most hops (see p235 for information on boat services).

Ease your way into the island life on **Ambergris Caye** (p100), where comfortable to luxurious lodgings and fine restaurants will pamper you between water activities. Smooth away any lingering symptoms of stress with a few days on **Caye Caulker** (p116), then head to **Lighthouse Reef** (p127) or **Turneffe Atoll** (p126) for a spell of more remote island life with as much top-class diving, snorkeling and fishing as you can take. Accommodations range from camping on Half Moon Caye to the luxuries of Lighthouse Reef Resort.

South of Turneffe Atoll, **Tobacco Caye** (p183), with a cluster of midrange accommodations, and **South Water Caye** (p184), with just three lodges, pop their heads up off the barrier reef. Further out is possibly the most idyllic of Belize's three atolls, **Glover's Reef** (p185), with the only true budget resort on Belize's outer islands as well as a couple of more expensive places.

Continue by visiting beautiful reef islands such as the **Silk Cayes** (p194) and **Ranguana Caye** (p194), and to round off your peregrinations on Belize's southernmost offshore gems, the unspoiled **Sapodilla Cayes** (p200).

If you can charter boats to hop you direct from island to island, you'll cover around 220 miles in this ramble of Belize's most idyllic offshore spots from north to south. Using the more usual routes back and forth from Belize City, Dangriga and Placencia might double your distance and add a couple of days to your time.

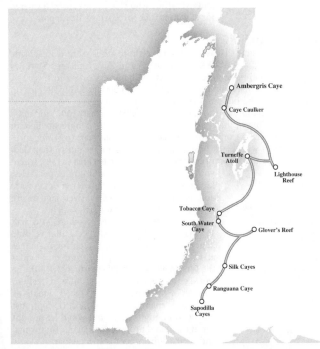

TAILORED TRIPS

BELIZE FOR KIDS

Belize provides enough to keep anyone busy throughout their stay. Most kids love the brightly colored tropical fish they'll see while snorkeling at places such as **Laughing Bird Caye** (p194), **Tobacco Caye** (p183) and **Glover's Reef** (p185), and older ones can kayak or even learn to dive in places such as **San Pedro** (p100) and **Placencia** (p192).

Start with **Old Belize** (p95), a quick introduction to Belizean history and culture in one handy, reasonably entertaining package, and **Belize Zoo** (p95), where you are guaranteed to see all the requisite colorful and furry beasties.

The generation of the future finds jungle walks, Maya ruins and long drives less exciting than canoeing or river-tubing, or taking a guided night hike where guides pick out crocodiles and kinkajous by flashlight. But all ages get a buzz out of venturing into caves, and if you can canoe, as at **Barton Creek Cave** (p162) or river-tube, as at **Jaguar Paw** (p152) through them, so much the better!

Ian Anderson's Caves Branch Adventure Company (p178) on the Hummingbird Hwy packs many of Belize's most exciting land adventures together in one handy package and is particularly popular among families with children who are 11 years and over. Kids who ride horses are well catered for at **Banana Bank** (p153), near Belmopan.

WILDLIFE WATCHING

The waters of Belize's barrier reef and offshore atolls teem with marine life. Ambergris Caye's **Shark Ray Alley** (p105) and Caye Caulker's **Shark Ray Village** (p119) guarantee close encounters with nurse sharks and stingrays. Awesome whale sharks up to 60ft long frequent **Gladden Spit** (p194) for up to 10 days after the full moon, March through June.

On the mainland, head to **Crooked Tree Wildlife Sanctuary** (p92) for some of the best birding in the country. Giant jabiru storks congregate here in April and May. Move on to the **Community Baboon Sanctuary** (p94) for sure-fire encounters with black howler monkeys. Try to get out to **Chan Chich Lodge** (p139) or the **Rio Bravo Conservation & Management Area** (p138), where your chances of seeing coatimundis, peccaries, kinkajous and spider or howler monkeys are among the highest in Belize. Even jaguars are regularly sighted around Chan Chich.

Do visit **Belize Zoo** (p95), where you will see many of Belize's most spectacular wildlife kept in good conditions. Watch for manatees at **Gales Point Manatee** (p176) and don't miss the **Cockscomb Basin Wildlife Sanctuary** (p190), the world's first jaguar reserve. You're unlikely to see any of the sanctuary's 40 or 50 jaguars or other large mammals in the flesh (except, just maybe, on a night tour), but you'll learn a lot about them and probably see jaguar footprints, and their environment is spectacular.

TREASURES OF THE MAYA

Arguably the most spectacular, if not quite the most important, of Belize's many ancient Maya sites is **Lamanai** (p135), for its superb jungle setting beside New River Lagoon and the river trip by which most people approach it. Also in the north of the country, don't miss the important Classic Period trading town of **Altun Ha** (p89), featured on Belizean beer labels, and do your best to fit in **Cerros** (p144), probably once a seaside dependency of Lamanai, and **La Milpa** (p138), a large site in the remote jungles of the Rio Bravo Conservation & Management Area.

Caracol (p171), way out west in the jungles near the Guatemalan border, was the biggest and most powerful ancient city in Belize (bigger than Belize City is today) and mustn't be missed.
Access to it has become a lot easier thanks to road improvements. Also out west, don't miss **Xunantunich** (p163), an impressive hilltop site that once commanded the Belize River valley, and be sure to visit the Maya underworld – caves such as **Actun Tunichil Muknal** (p161), **Barton Creek Cave** (p162) or **Che Chem Ha** (p167), where the relics of offerings, sometime human sacrifices, to the ancient gods have lain undisturbed for centuries.

Southern Belize was out of the ancient Maya mainstream but still left us **Nim Li Punit** (p205) and **Lubaantun** (p204), two medium-sized centers on fine hilltop sites.

NATURAL WONDERS

Belize's World Heritage–listed **barrier reef** (p47) is the second longest barrier reef in the world (after Australia's) – a 160-mile-long coral buttress, with precipitous walls along much of its seaward edge and strung with idyllic little islands of sand and palms. Beyond the reef, Belize is home to three of only four atolls in the Western Hemisphere – **Lighthouse Reef** (p127), **Glover's Reef** (p185) and **Turneffe Atoll** (p126).

Inland, large swaths of tropical rainforest in areas such as the **Rio Bravo Conservation & Management Area** (p138), the **Gallon Jug Parcel** (p139), **Cockscomb Basin Wildlife Sanctuary** (p190) and the **Caracol Archaeological Reserve** (p171) are incomparable funds of biodiversity and a delight for botanists, birders and wildlife spotters. A trip along one of the many beautiful jungle rivers – the **New River**, **Belize River**, **Macal River** or **Mopan River** to name but a few – is always a highlight. In the central west, the tropical broadleaf ecosystem gives way to pines on the **Mountain Pine Ridge** (p169), a broad upland area speckled with spectacular waterfalls and mountain rivers.

Underground, the action of water on limestone has produced well-developed cave systems, such as **Che Chem Ha** (p167), **Barton Creek Cave** (p162), **Actun Tunichil Muknal** (p161) and **Jaguar Paw** (p152), through which today we can walk, crawl, scramble and even canoe or river-tube along underground rivers. Many of them still hold the relics of ancient Maya ceremonies and sacrifices.

Snapshot

Belizeans have a happy habit of making the best of things, but they get upset about two things: their government and crime. How is it, people ask, that a government that espouses low taxation actually raises taxes and still gets Belize's finances into a mess? The answer that many would give: by lending too much public money to too many private companies. In 2005, when the government announced new tax increases on businesses, beer and tobacco, yet proposed to postpone a wage increase for public servants, it provoked rare riots in the capital, Belmopan, and widespread strikes. After negotiations the wage increase was reinstated.

FAST FACTS

Population (2004): 282,600

Population density: 31 people per sq mile

GDP per person (2004): US$3751

Inflation (2004): 3.1%

Unemployment rate (2004): 11.6%

Cruise-ship tourist visitors (2004): 851,436

Other tourist visitors (2004): 230,848

Banana production (2003): 75,000 metric tons

Orange production (2003): 165,000 metric tons

Literacy (2000): 77%

A few months later, worse riots and looting broke out in Belize City amid strikes by telecommunications workers, teachers and public-service workers. The ostensible issue this time was a delay in a promised share issue to communications workers, but the strikers and protesters, in their demands for the resignation of Prime Minister Said Musa and his government, were also expressing the anger of many Belizeans over the government's financial mismanagement and perceived corruption. The preceding year had brought one piece of negative financial news after another – a series of bad loans by the government, a burgeoning foreign debt and a downgrading of Belize's credit rating internationally.

Musa and his People's United Party (PUP) had won a second successive landslide election in 2003, but despite solid economic growth things soon started to turn sour, with a series of scandals around major companies and government finances, which showed an alarming gap between revenue and expenditure.

As a visitor, the issue that you may hear most about is cruise-ship tourism, which has mushroomed from nearly nothing in the late 1990s to nearly a million arrivals a year – almost four times the number of conventional tourists. Large North American cruise ships anchor off Belize City and discharge boatloads of day-trip passengers to snorkel around Belize's islands or head inland to Maya ruins and wildlife sanctuaries. Environmentalists and conventional 'overnight' tourism businesses fear the effects of large groups descending on fragile environments, and also the potential damage to Belize's image as a country that takes conservation seriously. Strong voices argue for stricter controls over cruise tourism and for its economic benefits to be spread more widely.

As for crime, you only have to look at any Belizean newspaper to read about a new handful of murders. Certainly press sensationalism makes the most of these crimes, but no-one can pretend that they don't happen. Many of them are drug-trade related, and the worst-hit area is Belize City's impoverished, underemployed and underprivileged Southside district.

But don't imagine for a minute that this is a country of gloom and doom. The aforementioned problems grab the headlines because they're out of the ordinary. Day-to-day life for the great majority of Belizeans is still very much a thing to be enjoyed. A satisfying meal, good company, friendly communication, an unhurried pace, music, dancing and the ocean breeze – most Belizeans know their country has rare gifts and are very content to make the most of them.

History

Belize lies on the eastern edge of the territory that was occupied by the most sophisticated ancient civilization in the Western Hemisphere – that of the Maya, a people who still form a sizable component of Belize's population today.

THE EARLY MAYA

The first stirrings of Maya civilization came with the emergence of farming villages in what are now Guatemala, Belize, Mexico's Yucatán Peninsula and northern Honduras between 2000 and 1000 BC. Cuello (p132), near Orange Walk in northern Belize, was one of the very first settlements in the Maya world, dating back to around 2400 BC.

Historians normally divide Maya chronology into three periods: Preclassic (around 2000 BC to AD 250), Classic (about AD 250 to 900) and Postclassic (around AD 900 to the arrival of the Spanish, which in Belize was probably 1508). Key Maya trade routes ran across northern and central Belize, connecting the Yucatán, the coast of Central America and some Caribbean islands with the Petén, Guatemala's Pacific Coast and central Mexico. The New River, Rio Hondo and Belize River were all important arteries, and the towns that mattered stood beside or close to rivers.

The earliest known site in the Belize River valley, Cahal Pech (p156), was settled between 1500 and 1000 BC. Lamanai (p135), beside the New River, surged in importance around 200–100 BC, when its core became a major ceremonial center. Lamanai remained an important city until at least the 8th century AD and at its peak had an estimated population of 35,000.

Joyce Kelly's *An Archaeological Guide to Northern Central America* offers the best descriptions of the Maya sites of Belize, along with those in Guatemala and Mexico.

THE CLASSIC MAYA

It was in the Classic Period that the Maya attained the peaks of intellectual, architectural and artistic achievement that set them apart. Maya civilization was not an empire, more a scattering of city states sharing a common culture (see The Ancient Maya World chapter on p40 for details of the Maya's lifestyle and their sophisticated mathematics, writing, religion and mythology). The greatest city of the Classic Period was Tikal (p210) in Guatemala. Though Belize was on the fringe of the Classic Period heartland (centered on the Petén and the south of Mexico's Yucatán Peninsula), cities in Belize were still politically and commercially important. Maya civilization in Belize, as in the Petén and the southern Yucatán, reached its peak between the 6th and 9th centuries AD.

In AD 562 the greatest of Belize's Maya cities, Caracol (p171), conquered Tikal, some 50 miles northwest. Caracol appears to have been allied with Calakmul in the Yucatán, Tikal's rival in the Classic Maya world. The following decades saw a surge of construction and population at Caracol, which by 650 may have had a population approaching 150,000, far bigger than Belize City today. Caracol declined in importance after a defeat by Naranjo (Guatemala) in 680, but remained locally influential.

Numerous other Maya cities and towns in Belize – among them Altun Ha (p89), La Milpa (p138), Xunantunich (p163), Nim Li Punit (p205) and

Belize: A Concise History by PAB Thomson, a former British High Commissioner to Belize, tells the country's story right up to the 21st century in a comprehensive but not overly lengthy form.

TIMELINE	600–400 BC	AD 550–850
	First monumental Maya temples in Belize built at Cahal Pech	Maya civilization at its Classic Period peak

Lubaantun (p204) – enjoyed their finest moments at one time or another between 550 and 850. The 9th and 10th centuries, however, were the time of the mysterious Classic Maya collapse, when many once-flourishing settlements were abandoned. Research points to a series of devastating droughts as the major culprits for this disaster. Archaeologists have discovered that ritual activity in Belize's many caves – believed by the Maya to be residences of important deities, including the rain god, Chac – increased after about 750, doubtless in supplication for a reversal of whatever crisis was overwhelming Maya civilization. Chilling evidence of sacrifices can still be seen in caves such as Actun Tunichil Muknal (p161).

The palace-temple called Caana at Caracol is still, at 141ft high, the tallest building in the entire country!

The Classic Maya heartland reverted to a far more primitive cultural level, with a much-reduced population living away from their great Classic-era cities, but Maya civilization continued in the Yucatán and the highlands of Guatemala and Chiapas. By the 15th century the Yucatán and northern Belize were divided among a number of small, often quarrelsome, city states. One, called Chetumal, occupied the west side of Chetumal Bay, where Belize meets Mexico. Its capital was probably Santa Rita (p141). The other statelet on Belizean territory was Dzuluinicob, occupying approximately the rest of what's now the northern half of Belize, with its capital at Tipu, whose ruins lie close to the Macal River in western Belize.

THE SPANISH ARRIVE

The Spanish arrived in the Caribbean in 1492 and soon began poking around the American landmass to the west. The number of Maya in Belize at this time has been estimated at 200,000. The first Spanish ships may have visited Belize's coast in 1508, possibly already bringing diseases such as smallpox, yellow fever and measles, which were to decimate the Maya population. In 1544 a notoriously cruel Spanish expedition from southeast Mexico succeeding in conquering Maya settlements as far south as Tipu. The Spanish set up Christian missions, including at Lamanai and Tipu, under the supervision of a priest at Bacalar in southeastern Yucatán, but the Maya rebelled frequently, destroying the churches. A major rebellion originating from Tipu in 1638 expelled the Spanish from most of Belize, and attacks on Bacalar by Caribbean pirates in 1642 and 1648 effectively ended Spanish efforts to control Belize.

Unlike logwood, which could be cut into small blocks and transported by canoe or raft, mahogany trunks had to be floated downriver whole.

PIRATES, LOGGERS & SLAVES

The pirates, who were by now terrorizing places like Bacalar and Spanish ships in the Caribbean, were a multinational bunch, but it was the British among them who were to start the next chapter in the history of Belize. As well as slaves and silver, one of the prizes the pirates liked to loot from Spanish ships was logwood, a dye-yielding timber much in demand by the European wool industry. Some of the pirates soon worked out that cutting this wood themselves would probably be at least as profitable as stealing it on the high seas – and definitely less dangerous. The British pirate/woodcutters ended up congregating in Belize, where (unlike in Mexico and the rest of Central America) Spain exercised no effective control. Most of the Baymen, as they became known, based themselves on St George's Caye (see p30), an island a few miles off the site of Belize City – which itself began life as a few huts at the mouth of a river that

Caracol defeats Tikal

Spanish expedition conquers Maya settlements in northern Belize

BURNABY'S CODE

Belize's first 'laws' were known as Burnaby's Code. In 1765 Admiral Sir William Burnaby, the British naval commander on Jamaica, visited Belize and persuaded the settlers to agree to a code to govern their society. The code was a practical one with 12 articles and regulations. Most of these were aimed at preventing the theft of servants or property, but the code also established systems for collecting taxes, settling disputes and determining punishments (usually fines). It exhibited unexpected touches of gentility, too: 'Whoever shall be found guilty of profane cursing and swearing in disobedience of God's Commands [shall] forfeit and pay for every such Offence the sum of Two shillings and six pence...' Burnaby's Code remained in effect till the mid-19th century.

gave the loggers access to the interior. The Baymen were an infamously rude and drunken lot who, legend tells, laid down a foundation of rum bottles and woodchips for the future Belize City to be built on.

But Spain did not allow the Baymen free rein, launching a series of attacks on them through the 18th century. By the Treaty of Versailles in 1783, Spain permitted them to cut logwood from the Rio Hondo to the Belize River (essentially the northern half of Belize). This area was extended south to the Sibun River by the Convention of London (1786), which also permitted the British to cut another type of timber – mahogany, a hardwood that was highly valued in Europe for making furniture (and, later, railroad carriages). In return Britain agreed to abandon the Mosquito Shore of Nicaragua, from which 2214 new settlers came to Belize, quadrupling its non-Maya population. Three-quarters of the newcomers were slaves of African origin, which was convenient for the loggers since the extraction of mahogany, a larger tree than logwood and more scattered in the forests, required more labor. Thus it was that mahogany played a key role in the creation of the Afro-Belizean population. As the loggers moved inland up the rivers, they met with sporadic attacks from the depleted Maya still living in remote forest settlements.

The number of slaves in the colony was between 2000 and 3000 – half to three-quarters of the total population (except for the Maya) – until slavery was abolished in the British empire in 1833. Most of the male slaves worked in logging, while the women did domestic work. Some of the slaves were given, or managed to buy, their freedom, becoming what were known as 'free blacks' and 'free coloureds' (people of mixed European and African ancestry – the first Creoles).

> Even after the abolition of slavery in 1833, Belize's freed slaves had to work for nothing for a further four years as 'apprentices.'

> Emory King's *The Great Story of Belize* is a fun read, and quite detailed, even if it has come under criticism for glamorizing the swashbuckling ways of the early British settlers.

> For lots on Ambergris Caye and some great stuff on the rest of Belize, including a hugely detailed Maya Sites in Belize section, go to www .belizehistory.com.

THE WAR OF THE CASTES

Mexico and Spain's Central American colonies won their independence in the 1820s, but this didn't improve the lot of the Maya in the Yucatán and Guatemala, where they still formed large percentages of the population. In the Yucatán the Maya were treated as third-class citizens, after the Yucatecos (people of Spanish descent) and the Mestizos (people of mixed Spanish and Maya descent). In 1847 they finally rose up in rebellion. The ensuing conflict is known as the War of the Castes. In little more than a year the Maya had driven their oppressors from every part of the peninsula except the cities of Mérida and Campeche. But the tide of war turned when the rebels saw the annual appearance of the winged ant, which to the Maya

1638–40	1638
Maya rebellion drives out the Spanish	First British settlement in Belize

---

THE BATTLE OF ST GEORGE'S CAYE

As the Napoleonic Wars enveloped Europe, and Spain and Britain found themselves on opposing sides, the Spanish prepared for one more attempt to evict the British from Belize. The attack on St George's Caye came on September 10, 1798, but the settlers had had time to bring in weapons, soldiers and a sloop of war from Jamaica, and with the aid of their own more maneuverable shallow-draft boats, they repulsed the 31-vessel Spanish fleet in a few hours. Spain never again tried to wrest control of Belize.

The Battle of St George's Caye was later played up by the British colonial authorities as an occasion on which slaves had fought alongside their British masters against the Spanish enemy – supposedly evidence of the slaves' loyalty to their masters and even of some kind of preference for British rule. Though the slaves did indeed fight, they clearly didn't have much choice about it, and the 'shoulder-to-shoulder' myth was debunked by Belizean nationalists during the independence movement of the mid-20th century. Nevertheless the anniversary of the battle is still a holiday in Belize, celebrated as National Day.

---

meant it was time to plant corn. They abandoned their attack on Mérida and went home to plant the corn. The counterattack against the Maya was vicious in the extreme. Between 1848 and 1855 the Yucatán's indigenous population was halved. Nevertheless, localized resistance, especially in the southeast, continued, and it wasn't until the early 20th century that Mexican troops finally subdued the last Maya resistance.

All of this had significant consequences for Belize. Not only did some Belizean residents make a lot of money by selling arms to the Cruzob (a group of Maya rebels inspired by a 'talking cross' in the village of Santa Cruz, modern Felipe Carrillo Puerto, in the southeastern Yucatán), but large numbers of refugees from both sides of the conflict fled into Belize. Yucateco and Mestizo refugees founded the towns of Corozal and Orange Walk, while Maya refugees moved into the forests and countryside. The conflict itself spilled into Belize chiefly in the shape of a group called the Icaiché Maya, who claimed lands in northwest Belize where British loggers were starting to penetrate. The defeat of a British force near the Icaiché village of San Pedro in western Belize in 1866 led the British to burn down San Pedro and several neighboring villages the following year. In 1872, in what's considered the last significant armed Maya resistance to the British in Belize, the Icaiché attacked Orange Walk and were only repulsed after a day of fierce fighting.

The Caste War refugees helped to swell Belize's population from less than 10,000 in 1845 to more than 25,000 in 1861. They gave the north a strong Mestizo and Maya character, which it retains today.

Assad Shoman's 13 Chapters of a History of Belize is a detailed, readable, anticolonialist account up to the 1990s; the author has helped make modern history himself as a pro-independence activist and People's United Party cabinet minister.

COLONIAL RULE

The 1840s saw a slump in mahogany exports and an economic depression in the colony. Property belonging to old settler families was mopped up by London merchants to which they were indebted, and by the mid-century two London firms, Young Toledo & Co and the British Honduras Company, owned most of the privately held land in Belize. In 1875 the British Honduras Company became the Belize Estate & Produce Company (BEC) and when Young & Toledo went broke in 1880, the BEC bought up some

1765	1798
Burnaby's Code bans swearing	Battle of St George's Caye – the last Spanish attempt to control Belize

of its lands. The BEC, with its huge landholdings and timber operations, had enormous influence on Belizean affairs right up to the 1970s. The late 19th century saw a dramatic swing away from Britain and toward the USA in British Honduras' external trade. The US was the main importer of Belizean mahogany from 1900 onwards, and by 1927 82% of all Belizean exports were bound for the States.

Early Belizean democracy, such as it was, consisted of the Public Meeting, a gathering controlled by a few wealthy male woodcutters. In 1853 this was replaced by a legislative assembly whose members were elected by the leading male property owners. In 1871 Britain switched British Honduras (as Belize was then known) to Crown Colony status, meaning that all members of its legislature would be nominated by the crown or the governor. Such tinkerings did little for the great majority of the inhabitants, however, and in 1894 mahogany workers rioted in Belize City over a currency devaluation that halved the value of their pay. More riots occurred in 1919 when Belizean soldiers returned from WWI. Their protest over racist treatment by the British – who had not deemed it suitable to deploy them against a European enemy – turned into a riot by 3000 people over living standards and high prices.

TOWARDS INDEPENDENCE

Organized political action against colonialism did not begin until after the Great Depression, and the first leader was Antonio Soberanis, who started out as one of the 'Unemployed Brigade' who marched to the governor's residence in 1934 demanding employment. Soberanis began to organize regular public meetings at Battlefield Park in Belize City (see p79) demanding work for the unemployed and attacking the injustices of colonial society. He led pickets and boycotts against 'bloodsucking' merchant houses, and founded the Labour and Unemployed Association (LUA), which organized a strike at the BEC sawmill in Belize City. This led to Soberanis' arrest, and while he was in jail the LUA split and never recovered. But Soberanis had launched the Belizean nationalist movement by taking his struggle to the people and to the regions.

By 1950 the Belizean economy was severely depressed. A currency devaluation on December 31, 1949, made things worse. Violent anti-British demonstrations ensued, the authorities declared a state of emergency, and in September 1950 Belize's pro-independence People's United Party (PUP) was formed. A national strike followed in 1952, and in 1954 the PUP won a campaign for universal adult suffrage and then won the elections to the new legislative assembly. In 1964 British Honduras became an internally self-governing British colony, and the PUP, led by George Price, won the elections of 1965, 1969, 1974 and 1979.

In 1971 the government announced that a new capital was to be built at Belmopan, in a symbolically central location and away from the threat of hurricanes on the coasts. In 1973 the name of the country was changed from British Honduras to Belize, and on September 21, 1981, Belize finally became an independent nation, with a bicameral legislature comprising a popularly elected house of representatives and an appointed senate similar in function to the British House of Lords. The British monarch remains the official head of state.

Belize switched to driving on the right in the 1960s, partly because Hurricane Hattie (1961) had wiped out most of the lefty cars.

A History of Belize (www .belizenet.com/history/toc .html) is an online version of a Belizean school textbook – quite a good read, with some excellent illustrations.

A Country Study: Belize (lcweb2.loc.gov/frd/cs /bztoc.html) is the US Library of Congress' comprehensive view not just of Belize's history, but of politics, the economy and more.

1847	1950
War of the Castes begins	Pro-independence movement launched under the leadership of People's United Party (PUP)

THE GUATEMALA CLAIM

Belizean music star Andy Palacio once commented that in multicultural Belize just three things united all sectors of the nation: punta rock music, rice and beans, and fear of Guatemala.

When Guatemala gained independence from Spain in 1821, it considered itself the inheritor of a Spanish claim to southern Belize, based on the fact that Spain had agreed in 1786 to British loggers operating north of the Sibun River (which enters the Caribbean south of Belize City) but had never made any concessions about the area south of the Sibun. The Anglo-Guatemalan Treaty of 1859 defined the Belize–Guatemala border which still exists today, while also obliging Britain to build a road linking Guatemala to the Caribbean. But because Guatemala was involved in a war with El Salvador at the time, its government never signed the agreement, and Britain never built the road, allowing Guatemala to maintain a claim on Belize, something it asserts most strongly during times of domestic strife as a distraction from interior problems.

In 1945 a new Guatemalan constitution declared Belize to be part of Guatemala, and through the 1970s, as Belize waited for independence from Britain, Guatemala threatened to invade. The stationing of increasing numbers of British troops in Belize restricted the dispute to diplomatic dimensions (the British troops finally left in 1994). In 1991 Guatemala recognized Belize as a sovereign, independent state, but without relinquishing a territorial claim. Intermittent border flare-ups continued, but with the help of mediation by the Organization of American States (OAS) in 2000 the two countries signed an Agreement on Confidence Building Measures, providing a framework for managing disagreements and preventing border incidents. OAS-sponsored facilitators made concrete proposals for resolving the issue in 2002. These were accepted by Belize but rejected by Guatemala, which cited constitutional difficulties. An OAS-established 'Group of Friends' is now attempting to bring Belize and Guatemala back to the negotiating table.

INDEPENDENT BELIZE

Post-independence, the PUP did not manage to deliver the economic prosperity Belizeans had hoped for. This was partly due to world market conditions, but the PUP was also seen as having been in power too long and was accused of complacency and corruption.

At the time it was bought by Belizean businessman Barry Bowen in 1982, the Belize Estate & Produce Company still owned one-eighth of the country.

The right-of-center United Democratic Party (UDP) won the 1984 elections under the slogan 'It's time for a change,' and Manuel Esquivel replaced Price as prime minister. Price turned the tables again in 1989, then suffered a shock defeat in 1993 when the PUP's electoral victory seemed such a foregone conclusion that many of its supporters didn't bother to vote. Price retired in 1996 and the ensuing noisy power struggle among his lieutenants was won by Said Musa. Musa led the PUP to landslide victories in 1998 and 2003.

Belize's economy today is based primarily on the agro-industries of sugar (see the boxed text on p134), citrus fruit and bananas (crops that are always susceptible to price fluctuations and hurricane damage beyond their producers' control), with tourism and construction also important. The PUP under Musa campaigns with rather dreamy promises of lower taxes, more jobs and better education, but by midway through Musa's second term his government had run into problems over allegations of corruption and a growing national debt, something it was trying to tackle by raising taxes without managing to rein in expenditure (see p26).

1981	2003
Belize becomes an independent nation, with George Price (PUP) as prime minister	Said Musa leads PUP to landslide election victory

The Culture

THE NATIONAL PSYCHE

Belizeans have elevated 'taking it easy' to an art form (where else will you be told that checkout time is 'Whatever time you like'?) Shopkeepers will close early if they feel they've made enough money for the day, and hammock swinging is pretty much a national pastime. Most people here realize that a sane pace, and time to communicate with fellow human beings make life much more worth living than constantly stressing to go one more mile for the sake of an extra bit of profit. Not that they don't work, of course – but they know when they have done enough. As a visitor, you too will find yourself slowing down to the Belizean pace and relearning some of the forgotten art of human communication.

Because of the mix of ethnicities and cultures in Belize, its people are very open, tolerant and accepting of the differences of others. Not that everything in the garden is completely rosy. Poverty is still widespread, crime is almost a way of life in some sectors of Belize City, and widespread corruption in the middle and upper levels of government has left most Belizeans with a deep cynicism about politicians. The gap between rich and poor doesn't make them think much better of the leaders of the private sector.

Some feel that citizens' feelings of powerlessness to effect change, even in their immediate communities, are a legacy of Belize's colonial past. On the other hand, many Belizeans feel that in other ways they are better off than other Central American countries that were colonized by Spain. The positives include socialized medicine, mandatory and free education and a pretty clean record on human rights. Most Belizeans are proud, and happy, to be Belizean.

While Yucatec and Mopan speakers can more or less understand each other, Kekchi is mutually unintelligible with both of the other Mayan languages.

LIFESTYLE

With compulsory education, a relatively stable democracy, some classy tourism offerings and an economy that is, on the surface of things, doing nicely, you would expect Belize to be doing all right by its citizens. Unfortunately, for many people, this is not the case. The country has never been rich, and while a few have made big money from arcane financial dealings, and a small middle class does OK from business, tourism and other professions, many other Belizeans live in fairly basic circumstances. You can admire lovely, large, breezy, two-story, old Caribbean–style wooden houses in parts of Belize City, but most Belizeans live in smaller dwellings, and new houses are often small, cinder-block boxes, while old ones may be composed of warped and rotting wood that has seen much better days.

Labor – whether washing dirty hotel sheets, cutting sugarcane or packing bananas – is poorly paid (most workers earn between US$10

BELIZEANS BUILD HOUSES ON STILTS BECAUSE...

- they avoid floods
- they get more breeze
- they get less ground heat
- it's easier to control termites
- it keeps other bugs and rodents out
- it provides shelter for dogs, cats etc
- it permits infilling if the family gets bigger
- it's tradition!

THE GARIFUNA

Southern Belize is one home of the Garifuna (plural Garinagu, also called Black Caribs), a people of mixed American and African heritage who originated on the eastern Caribbean island of St Vincent in the 17th century, when shipwrecked African slaves mixed with the indigenous population of Caribs and Arawaks. France claimed possession of St Vincent in the early 18th century but ceded it to Britain in 1763. In the face of prolonged resistance, Britain decided to deport most of the Black Caribs in 1796. After being shuffled around various spots in the Caribbean for a year or so, with many dying from malnutrition and disease, 1465 of the original 4338 deportees arrived at the Honduran coastal town of Trujillo. From there, they eventually spread along the Caribbean coast of Central America.

The first Garifuna had arrived in Belize by 1802, but the biggest migration took place in 1832, when on November 19, some 200 Garifuna reached Belize in dugout canoes from Honduras, having backed the wrong side in a revolt there.

Most Garifuna in Belize still live in the south of the country, from Dangriga to Punta Gorda. The Garifuna excelled at growing food and became a significant element in the colonial economy. By the 1850s they numbered over 2000. Today the Belize Garifuna are around 16,000 people, 6% of Belize's population.

The Garifuna language is a combination of Arawak and African languages with bits of English and French thrown in, and the Garifuna maintain a unique culture with a strong sense of community and ritual, in which drumming and dancing play important roles. The *dügü* ('feasting of the ancestors' ceremony) involves several nights and days of dancing, drumming and singing by an extended family. Its immediate purpose is to heal a sick individual, but it also serves to reaffirm community solidarity. Some participants may become 'possessed' by the spirits of dead ancestors. Other noted Garifuna ceremonials include the *beluria* (ninth-night festivity), for the departure of a dead person's soul, attended by entire communities with copious drumming, dancing and drinking; and the *wanaragua* or *jonkonu* dance, performed in some places during the Christmas-to-early-January festive season (see p181).

Belize is perhaps the country where Garifuna culture is most respected and celebrated. The anniversary of the Garifuna arrival on November 19, 1832 is celebrated as Garifuna Settlement Day, a national holiday; Garifuna culture has been enjoying a revival since the 1980s, with no small part played by the punta rock phenomenon (see p36). In 2001 Unesco declared Garifuna language, dance and music in Belize to be a 'Masterpiece of the Oral and Intangible Heritage of Humanity' – one of the initial selections for what is intended to become the cultural equivalent of the World Heritage list.

Garifuna History, Language & Culture of Belize, Central America & the Caribbean, by Sebastian Cayetano, gives an easily understood overview of the Garifuna people and their culture.

and US$20 a day) and the cost of living is high in comparison. It is estimated that one third of the population lives below the poverty line, and that's why tens of thousands of Belizeans live in the USA these days. The saving grace of life in Belize is that the folk here know how to make the best of things. Check out any karaoke bar on a Friday night and you'll see enough Belikin beer consumption and smiling faces to know that, for some at least, things aren't as bad as they look on paper.

Among the blessings of Belize are its tiny population and tiny area. It's said that everyone here knows everyone else, and it is true that many people will have supportive networks of family and friends, not only in their local neighborhood, but also quite likely in other parts of the country. Belize's different ethnic groups socialize and mix primarily among themselves, but the different groups certainly get along pretty well with each other.

Education in Belize is free and compulsory up to the age of 14. After that, instruction is free, but students are required to buy their own books, which is a deterrent against higher education. Most schools are state-subsidized church schools, mainly run by Catholics, Methodists and

Anglicans, although recently evangelical religions such as the Seventh Day Adventists have opened schools.

Except among the middle class, women in Belizean society have some way to go to achieve genuine equality. Women who work outside the home are mostly concentrated in female-dominated occupations with low status and low wages. Though there are no laws against women owning land or property, they often find it harder than men to obtain business or agricultural financing. In politics, the 29-seat house of representatives contained only two women at the last count.

Belize doesn't have much of a gay scene, but this does not imply that in this tolerant land people are secretive, just that they are low-key.

MULTICULTURALISM

For such a tiny country (population around 282,600), Belize enjoys a fabulous, improbable ethnic diversity, and inter-ethnic tensions are minor. Creoles – descendants of British loggers, colonists and African slaves – now form only about 25% of Belize's population, but theirs remains a sort of paradigm culture. Racially mixed and proud of it, Creoles speak a fascinating and unique version of English that, though it sounds familiar at first, is not at all easily intelligible to a speaker of standard English. Most of the people you'll encounter in Belize City and the center of the country will be Creole.

Over the last couple of decades, Mestizos (people of mixed Spanish and Amerindian descent) have become Belize's largest ethnic group, now at 53%. The first Mestizos arrived during the War of the Castes in the mid-19th century, when refugees from the Yucatán flooded into northern and western Belize. Their modern successors have been thousands of political refugees from troubled neighboring Central American countries. While English remains Belize's official language, Spanish is spoken by over half of the population, which has caused some resentment among the Creoles, who for the most part are fiercely proud of their country's Anglo roots.

The Maya of Belize make up 10% of the population and are divided into three linguistic groups. The Yucatec Maya live mainly in the north, the Mopan Maya in the southern Toledo District and in western Belize, and the Kekchi Maya, who also live in the Toledo District. Use of both Spanish and English is becoming more widespread among the Maya. Traditional Maya culture is perhaps strongest among the Maya of the south.

Southern Belize is also the main home of the Garifuna (see opposite), who account for 6% of the population. The remaining 6% of the population is composed of several groups: 'East Indians' (people of Indian subcontinent origins), Chinese, Arabs (generally known as Lebanese), the small but influential group of Mennonites (p36) and North Americans and Europeans who have settled here in the last couple of decades.

RELIGION

Belizeans are a pretty religious lot, with most people adhering to one faith or another. A large percentage of the population are Christians, and most of these are Catholics. Ethnicity is a big determinant of religion, with most Mestizos, Maya and Garifuna espousing Catholicism as a result of their ethnic origins in Spanish- or French-ruled countries or colonies. Catholicism among Creoles increased with the work of North American missionaries in the late 19th and early 20th centuries. Perhaps a quarter of Belizeans are Protestants, chiefly Anglicans, Methodists and, today, Pentecostalists, Adventists and Mennonites. Among the Garifuna, and to a lesser extent Belize's Maya and Creoles, Christianity coexists

There are many Garifuna in Honduras (100,000 to 150,000) and the USA (90,000 to 100,000), plus small communities in Guatemala, Nicaragua and St Vincent.

The folklore collection *If Di Pin Neva Ben: Folktales and Legends of Belize* demonstrates the vibrancy and cultural strength of Belize's ethnic jigsaw.

Belize Kriol (www.kriol .org.bz), the website of the National Kriol Council of Belize, has interesting info on Creole history, culture, language and more.

THE MENNONITES

It almost seems like an aberration, an odd sight inspired by the hot sun, or maybe just a blurry result of too much sweat dripping in your eyes. But the vision of women in bonnets and wintry frocks, and blond men with blue eyes, denim overalls and straw cowboy hats is not something your imagination has conjured up: you're looking at Belizean Mennonites.

The Mennonites stem from an enigmatic Anabaptist group that dates back to 16th-century Netherlands. Like the Amish of Pennsylvania, the Mennonites have strict religion-based values that keep them isolated in agricultural communities. Speaking mostly Low German, they run their own schools, banks and churches. Traditional groups reject any form of mechanization or technology, which is why they're often seen riding along in horse-drawn buggies.

Mennonites are devout pacifists and reject most of the political ideologies (including paying taxes) that societies down the centuries have tried to thrust upon them, so they have a long history of moving about the world trying to find a place where they could be left in peace. They left the Netherlands for Prussia and Russia in the late 17th century. In the 1870s, when Russia insisted on military conscription, the Mennonites living there upped and moved to Canada. They built communities in isolated parts of Saskatchewan, Alberta and British Columbia. But after WWI the Canadian government demanded that English be taught in Mennonite schools, and the Mennonites' exemption from conscription was being reconsidered. Again, the most devout Mennonites moved, this time to northern Mexico and South America. But by the 1950s Mexico wanted the Mennonites to join its social security program, so once again the Mennonites packed up.

The first wave of about 3500 Mennonites settled in Belize (then called British Honduras) in 1958. Belize was happy to have them and their industriousness and farming expertise.

Today, Belize has both progressive and traditional Mennonite communities. The progressives, many of whom came from Canada, speak English and have no qualms about using tractors to clear their land, or pickup trucks to shuttle their families about. These (wealthy) groups are found in Blue Creek, west of Orange Walk, or at Spanish Lookout in Cayo District. Strongly conservative groups, such as the ones at Shipyard near Orange Walk or Barton Creek in Cayo District, still ride in horse-drawn buggies and shun electricity.

Belize has been good to the Mennonites and in turn the Mennonites have been good to Belize. Mennonite farms now supply most of the country's dairy products, eggs and poultry. Furniture-making is another Mennonite specialty and you'll often see them selling their goods at markets.

Some Mennonites are open to the rest of the world and don't mind a good chat. Others don't want contact, so treat them with respect and do ask permission if you want to take a photo.

with other beliefs. Maya Catholicism has long been syncretized with traditional beliefs and rites that go back to pre-Hispanic times, while some Creoles (especially older people) have a belief in obeah, a form of witchcraft.

Belize's tradition of tolerance also encompasses Hindus, Muslims, Baha'i, Jehovah's Witnesses and a small (but eye-catching!) number of Rastafarians.

ARTS
Music

Music – often for dancing – is definitely the most developed art form in Belize, and you'll hear a variety of pan-Caribbean musical styles, including calypso (of which Belize has its own star in Gerald 'Lord' Rhaburn), *soca* (an up-tempo fusion of calypso with Indian rhythms) and, of course, reggae.

But much of the music you'll hear is specifically Belizean – especially the phenomenon known as punta rock, which has attained the status of Belize's national music. Punta rock is a combination of punta – a trad-itional Garifuna drumming style – with the electrified instruments of rock, invented by Dangriga's Pen Cayetano in 1981 after travels in other Central American countries, which made him aware that Garifuna traditions were in danger of withering away. Punta rock can be frenetic or it can be a little more mellow, but at its base are always fast rhythms designed to get the hips swiveling. The dance is strongly sexually suggestive, with men and women gyrating their pelvises in close proximity to each other. Cayetano's Turtle Shell Band spread the word, and the rhythm, to neighboring Guatemala, Honduras (both with their own Garifuna populations), Mexico and even the USA (where there are sizable Belizean and Garifuna communities), and have been followed by a host of other performers.

Andy Palacio has been a leading ambassador of punta rock, but the most recent sensation is Supa G, who provides a fusion between punta rock, techno and even a spot of Mexican balladeering. Also look out for Mohobub Flores, Myme Martinez (both members of the Turtle Shell Band and still going strong), Aziatic (who has blended punta with R&B, jazz and pop), Lloyd and Reckless, and the Coolie Rebels, a popular 'East Indian' punta rock group from Punta Gorda. For more traditional Garifuna drumming, keep an eye open for Luqua and the Laribeya Drummers.

Another great Garifuna style is *paranda*, which grew out of the meld of African percussion and chanting with Spanish-style acoustic guitar and Latin rhythms that occurred when the Garifuna reached Spanish-dominated parts of Central America. *Paranda's* Belizean master is Paul Nabor from Punta Gorda, born in the 1920s, and its bright young light is Aurelio Martínez, a Honduran who is often in Belize. The title of Martínez' album *Garifuna Soul* gives a good idea of what *paranda* is about. Its rhythms are fairly fast, but it has a lyrical tone too.

The Creoles have given us *brukdown*, traditionally played by an ensemble of accordion, banjo, harmonica and a percussion instrument – usually the jawbone of a pig, its teeth rattled with a stick. Nowadays a drum and/or electric guitar or two might be added. Deeply African-rooted with its layered rhythms and call-and-response vocals, *brukdown* developed in the logging camps during the 18th and 19th centuries and its heartland is the Belize River valley. Wilfred Peters, with his band Mr Peters' Boom and Chime, is still the preeminent *brukdown* artist after many years. But also watch out for singer Leela Vernon from Punta Gorda.

Bredda David & Tribal Vibes are the creators of *kungo* music, a fast-paced fusion of Creole styles with other African rhythms.

The Maya of Belize have their own favored instruments. Top artists include flautist Pablo Collado and harpist Florencio Mess. In the north you'll hear plenty of Mexican styles popular with the Mestizo people.

Hearing live music in Belize is a matter of keeping your eyes open for posters and press announcements of coming events. Gig organizers make sure the public knows what's cooking.

You can take classes in Garifuna drumming in Hopkins (see p187), and in Creole drumming at Gales Point Manatee (p177).

> Listen to a great sampling of Belizean music at the website of Stonetree Records (www.stonetreerecords.com), which produces many of the best artists.

Literature

Belizean writer Zee Edgell has won international attention with three novels treating different aspects of Belizean society and history. *Beka Lamb* (1982) tells of adolescence at a Belize City girls' school amid the political upheavals of the mid-20th century, with detailed pictures of life in the city during that time. *In Times Like These* (1991) delves into the independence-era political and social landscapes through the experience of a woman returned from studies in London, and *The Festival of*

San Joaquin (1997) focuses on a Mestizo woman's painful clashes with machismo, poverty and class discrimination.

Another talented writer is Zoila Ellis, whose *On Heroes, Lizards and Passion* brings together seven short stories that demonstrate an acute perception of Belize and Belizeans.

Carlos Ledson Miller's *Belize* is the closest you'll get to a Belizean bodice-ripper. The story begins in 1961 with Hurricane Hattie, and tells the tale of a Belizean-American man and his two sons, with a realistic portrayal of Belize's recent history, including the mahogany industry, drug smuggling, hurricanes, the move to independence and the development of ecotourism. It's fun to walk through neighborhoods in Belize City and Ambergris Caye that are described in the book.

While you're in Belize, look for titles in the Belizean Writers Series, which includes anthologies of poetry, plays and short fiction.

The best-known movie shot in Belize is *Mosquito Coast* (1986), starring Harrison Ford. Belize stood in for Africa in *Heart of Darkness* (1993), with John Malkovich, and *The Dogs of War* (1980), starring Christopher Walken.

Cinema

Belize doesn't have a film industry but it does stage the admirable Belize International Film Festival (www.belizefilmfestival.com) in Belize City every February, which showcases films from Central America and the Caribbean. The launching of the festival in 2003 was an achievement of Belize's Film Commissioner, its best known American expat and indefatigable character, Emory King (www.emoryking.com).

Painting & Sculpture

Belizean art started to emerge in the 1970s. Today, a distinct Belizean style has emerged, focusing on flora and fauna, landscapes, seascapes and ethnic groups. Pen Cayetano (www.cayetano.de) and Benjamin Nicholas (see p181) paint colorful scenes from Garifuna folklore, history and culture. Nicholas has a primitivist style, with flat perspective, bright colors and stylized figures, while Cayetano's oils are more realistic in approach. Cayetano is a polymathic figure who also started the punta rock musical phenomenon; a native of Dangriga, he now lives in Germany but usually returns to Belize around November or December each year. Also look out for the street scenes of Teryl Godoy. In western Belize, art lovers should make an effort to visit the avant-garde rainforest sculpture park, Poustinia (p167).

The annual Sidewalk Art Festival in Placencia, held on the weekend nearest to Valentine's Day, provides an excellent shop window on Belizean art.

Belizean wood-carvers work chiefly with the hardwoods zericote and mahogany. Ignatius Peyrefitte Jr has developed a distinctive personal style with Madonnas, abstracts and family scenes. The García sisters, of San Antonio, Cayo (see p163), carve some finely worked figures from Maya mythology and Belizean wildlife out of local black slate – a craft that has spawned a host of imitators.

SPORTS

Like any Central American country worth its stripes, Belize is a soccer-playing nation and has national tournaments contested by a number of semi-pro clubs. The Regent Insurance Cup competition runs from about January to June, and the Prime Minister's Cup starts in August. Leading clubs include Kulture Yabra of Belize City, Juventus of Orange Walk, Sagitún of Independence and San Pedro Seahawks. Games are played on Saturday and Sunday. The stadiums are easy enough to find in each town: you'll be in a crowd of a few hundred at most.

Softball, basketball and cricket are also played (cricket mainly in Belize District, from February to June), and horse races and long-distance cycling races occur at times such as New Year's Day and the Easter weekend. Burrell Boom, 18 miles west of Belize City, is the main horse-racing venue. Belize's most unique sporting event is La Ruta Maya Belize River Challenge, a four-day canoe race down the Belize River from San Ignacio to Belize City that takes place in March (see p157).

Newspapers report and advertise upcoming sports events.

MEDIA

Belizean newspapers are small in size and circulation, and present news by party line. The twice-weekly, left-wing *Amandala* (www.amandala .com.bz) has the largest circulation. Its Sunday edition comes out on Thursday or Friday and its Tuesday edition comes out on Tuesday but is datelined Wednesday. Other papers are Sunday only: the *Belize Times* (www.belizetimes.bz) represents the People's United Party (PUP) perspective, while the *Guardian* (www.guardian.bz) is the voice of the United Democratic Party (UDP). The *Reporter* (www.reporter.bz) presents the most independent coverage.

For links to most of Belize's main media, including online radio, visit belizenews.com.

Most TV you'll see in Belize will be international cable channels, but there are a couple of local stations: Channel 5 ('Great Belize TV'; new .channel5belize.com), Channel 7 ('The Nation's Station'; www.7news belize.com) and Channel 11 ('The Family Channel'). This is a country where the national news can contain items such as 'There will be a fireworks display on the football field in Hattieville at 7pm tonight'.

Love FM (www.lovefm.com) is the most widely broadcast radio station in Belize, with spots at 95.1 mHz and 98.1 mHz. It's a charming mix of local news, public-service announcements and the world's best love songs. KREM FM (www.krem.bz), at 96.5 mHz, plays a more modern selection of music.

The Ancient Maya World

Dr Allen J Christenson

Dr Allen J Christenson has a MA and PhD in Pre-Columbian Maya Art History, and works as an associate professor in the Humanities, Classics and Comparative Literature department of Brigham Young University in Provo, Utah.

The ancient Maya patterned their lives according to precedents set by their first ancestors. Nearly all aspects of Maya faith begin with their view of the creation, when the gods and divine forebears established the world at the beginning of time. From their hieroglyphic texts (see p43) and art carved on stone monuments and buildings, or painted on pottery, we can now piece together much of the Maya view of the creation. We can even read the precise date of when the creation took place.

In AD 775, a Maya lord with the high-sounding name of K'ak' Tiliw Chan Yoat (Fire Burning Sky Lightning God) set up an immense stone monument in the center of his city, Quirigua, in Guatemala. The unimaginative archaeologists who discovered the stone called it Stela C. This monument bears the longest single hieroglyphic description of the creation, noting that it took place on the day 13.0.0.0.0, 4 Ahaw, 8 Kumk'u, a date corresponding to August 13, 3114 BC on our calendar. This date appears over and over in other inscriptions throughout the Maya world. On that day the creator gods set three stones or mountains in the dark waters that once covered the primordial world. These three stones formed a cosmic hearth at the center of the universe. The gods then struck divine new fire by means of lightning, which charged the world with new life.

This account of the creation is echoed in the first chapters of the *Popol Vuh*, a book compiled by members of the Maya nobility soon after the Spanish conquest in 1524, many centuries after the erection of Quirigua Stela C. Although this book was written in their native Mayan language, its authors used European letters rather than the more terse hieroglyphic script. Thus the book gives a fuller account of how they conceived the first creation:

For a lively discussion of Maya religion and the creation, pick up a copy of *Maya Cosmos* by David Freidel, Linda Schele and Joy Parker.

This is the account of when all is still, silent and placid. All is silent and calm. Hushed and empty is the womb of the sky. These then are the first words, the first speech. There is not yet one person, one animal, bird, fish, crab, tree, rock, hollow, canyon, meadow, or forest. All alone the sky exists. The face of the earth has not yet appeared. Alone lies the expanse of the sea, along with the womb of all the sky. There is not yet anything gathered together. All is at rest. Nothing stirs. All is languid, at rest in the sky. Only the expanse of the water, only the tranquil sea lies alone. All lies placid and silent in the darkness, in the night.

All alone are the Framer and the Shaper, Sovereign and Quetzal Serpent, They Who Have Borne Children and They Who Have Begotten Sons. Luminous they are in the water, wrapped in feathers…They are great sages, great possessors of knowledge…

Then they called forth the mountains from the water. Straightaway the great mountains came to be. It was merely their spirit essence, their miraculous power, that brought about the conception of the mountains.

The oldest known copy of the *Popol Vuh* was made around 1701–03 by a Roman Catholic priest named Francisco Ximénez in Guatemala. The location of the original from which Ximénez made his copy, if it still survives, is unknown.

The Maya saw this pattern all around them. In the night sky, the three brightest stars in the constellation of Orion's Belt were conceived as the cosmic hearth at the center of the universe. On a clear night in the crisp mountain air of the Maya highlands, one can even see what looks like a wisp of smoke within these stars, although it is really only a far-distant string of stars within the M4 Nebula.

MAYA CITIES AS THE CENTER OF CREATION

Perhaps because the ancient Maya of northern Belize didn't have real mountains as symbols of the creation, they built them instead in the form of plaza-temple complexes. In hieroglyphic inscriptions, the large open-air plazas at the center of Maya cities are often called *nab'* (sea) or *lakam ja'* (great water). Rising above these plastered stone spaces are massive pyramid temples, often oriented in groups of three, representing the first mountains to emerge out of the 'waters' of the plaza. The tiny elevated sanctuaries of these temples served as portals into the abodes of gods that lived within. Offerings were burned on altars in the plazas, as if the flames were struck in the midst of immense three-stone hearths. Only a few elite persons were allowed to enter the small interior spaces atop the temples, while the majority of the populace observed their actions from the plaza below. The architecture of ancient Maya centers thus replicated sacred geography to form an elaborate stage on which rituals that charged their world with regenerative power could be carried out.

Many of the earliest-known Maya cities were built in Belize, including Cuello (p132), Lamanai (p135), Cerros (p144), Caracol (p171) and Altun Ha (p89), all of which were founded at some point during the Middle and late Preclassic Periods (in the first millennium BC). The earliest temples at these sites are often constructed in this three-temple arrangement, grouped together on a single platform, as an echo of the first three mountains of creation. The ancient name for the site known today as Caracol was Oxwitza' (Three Hills Place), symbolically linking this community with the three mountains of creation and thus the center of life. The Caana (Sky Place) is the largest structure at Caracol and consists of a massive pyramid-shaped platform topped by three temples that represent these three sacred mountains.

The Belizean site of Lamanai is one of the oldest and largest Maya cities known. It is also one of the few Maya sites that still bears its ancient name (which means Submerged Crocodile). While other sites were abandoned well before the Spanish Conquest in the 16th century, Lamanai continued to be occupied by the Maya centuries afterward. For the ancient Maya the crocodile symbolized the rough surface of the earth, newly emerged from the primordial sea that once covered the world. The name of the city reveals that its inhabitants saw themselves as living at the center of creation, rising from the waters of creation. Its massive pyramid temples include Structure N10-43, which is the second-largest pyramid known from the Maya Preclassic Period and represents the first mountain and dwelling place of the gods.

THE MAYA CREATION OF MANKIND

According to the *Popol Vuh*, the purpose of the creation was to give form and shape to beings who would 'remember' the gods through ritual. The Maya take their roles in life very seriously. They believe that people exist as mediators between this world and that of the gods. If they fail to carry out the proper prayers and ceremonies at just the right time and place, the universe will come to an abrupt end.

The gods created the first people out of maize (corn) dough, literally from the flesh of the Maize God, the principal deity of creation. Because of their divine origin, they were able to see with miraculous vision:

Recent translations of the *Popol Vuh* from the original Maya text are *Popol Vuh: The Sacred Book of the Maya* (2003), translated by Dr Allen Christenson; and *Popol Vuh* (1996), translated by Dennis Tedlock.

A good introduction to Maya art is Mary Ellen Miller's *Maya Art and Architecture*. For a more complete overview of Maya cities and culture, try *The Ancient Maya* by Robert J Sharer.

For up-to-date articles on archaeological discoveries as well as essays on Maya theology and ritual practices, visit www.mesoweb.com.

For a beautiful and searchable collection of photographs of vases, monuments and other works of ancient Maya art, visit the Kerr Archives at www.famsi.org /research/kerr/index.html.

Perfect was their sight, and perfect was their knowledge of every-thing beneath the sky. If they gazed about them, looking intently, they beheld that which was in the sky and that which was upon the earth. Instantly they were able to behold everything…Thus their knowledge became full. Their vision passed beyond the trees and the rocks, beyond the lakes and the seas, beyond the mountains and the valleys. Truly they were very esteemed people.

In nearly all of their languages, the Maya refer to themselves as 'true people' and consider that they are literally of a different flesh than those who do not eat maize. They are maize people, and foreigners who eat bread are wheat people. This mythic connection between maize and human flesh influenced birth rituals in the Maya world for centuries.

No self-respecting Maya, raised in the traditional way, would consider eating a meal that didn't include maize. They treat it with the utmost respect. Women do not let grains of maize fall on the ground or into an open fire. If it happens accidentally, as I saw once, the woman picks it up gently and apologizes to it. The Maya love to talk and laugh, but are gen-erally silent during meals. Most don't know why, it's just the way things have always been done. I once asked an elder about it and he said, 'for us tortillas are like the Catholic sacramental bread, it is the flesh of god. You don't laugh or speak when taking the flesh of god into your body. The young people are beginning to forget this. They will someday regret it.'

MAYA KINGSHIP

But the creation wasn't a one-time event. The Maya constantly repeated these primordial events in their ceremonies, timed to the sacred calendar. They saw the universe as a living thing. And just like any living thing, it grows old, weakens and ultimately passes away. Everything, including the gods, needed to be periodically recharged with life-bearing power or the world would slip back into the darkness and chaos that existed before the world began. Maya kings were seen as mediators. In countless wall carvings and paintings, monumental stone stelae and altars, painted pottery and other sacred objects, the Maya depicted their kings dressed as gods, repeating the actions of deities at the time of creation.

Like the ancient Greeks, there was no unified Maya empire. Each city had its own royal family and its own patron gods. Warfare was often conducted not for conquest, but to obtain captives who bore within their veins royal blood to be sacrificed.

A common theme was the king dressed as the Maize God himself, bearing a huge pack on his back containing the sacred bits and pieces that make up the world, while dancing them into existence. A beautiful example of this may be seen on the painted *Buena Vista Vase,* one of the true masterpieces of Maya art – discovered at Buenavista el Cayo, a small site in the Cayo District of Belize, right on the river (north side) close to the border with Guatemala – and now one of the gems of the Maya collection housed in the Department of Archaeology, Belize City. These rituals were done at very specific times of the year, timed to match calendric dates when the gods first performed them. For the Maya, these ceremonies were not merely symbolic of the rebirth of the cosmos, but a genuine creative act in which time folded in on itself to reveal the actions of the divine creators in the primordial world.

In Maya theology, the Maize God is the most sacred of the creator de-ities because he gives his very flesh in order for human beings to live. But this sacrifice must be repaid. The Maya as 'true people' felt an obligation to the cosmos to compensate for the loss of divine life, not because the gods were cruel, but because gods cannot rebirth themselves and need the intercession of human beings. Maya kings stood as the sacred link between their subjects and the gods. The king was thus required to periodically give that which was most precious – his own blood, which was believed to contain the essence of godhood itself. Generally, this meant that members of the royal family bled themselves with stingray spines or stone lancets. Males did their bloodletting from the genital area, literally birthing gods from the penis. Women most often drew blood from their tongues. This royal blood was collected on sheets of bark paper and then burned to release its divine essence, opening a portal to the other world and allowing the gods to emerge to a new life. At times of crisis, such as the end of a calendar cycle, or upon the death of a king and the succession of another, the sacrifice had to be greater to compensate for the loss of divine life. This generally involved obtaining noble or royal captives through warfare against a neighboring Maya state in order to sacrifice them.

Altar 23 from Caracol shows two captive lords from the Maya cities of B'ital and Ucanal, on the Guatemala–Belize border, with their arms bound behind their backs in preparation for sacrifice, perhaps on that very altar. If this were not done, they believed that life itself would cease to exist.

The beauty of Maya religion is that these great visions of creation mirror everyday events in the lives of the people. When a Maya woman rises early in the morning, before dawn, to grind maize for the family meal, she replicates the actions of the creators at the beginning of time. The darkness that surrounds her is reminiscent of the gloom of the primordial world. When she lights the three-stone hearth on the floor of her home, she is once again striking the new fire that generates life. The grains of maize that she cooks and then forms into tortillas are literally the flesh of the Maize God, who nourishes and rebuilds the bodies of her family members. This divine symmetry is comforting in a world that often proves intolerant and cruel.

> The Maya hieroglyphic writing system is one of only five major phonetic scripts ever invented – the others being cuneiform (used in ancient Mesopotamia), Egyptian, Harappan and Chinese.

MAYA HIEROGLYPHIC WRITING

More than 1500 years prior to the Spanish Conquest, the Maya developed a sophisticated hieroglyphic script capable of recording complex literary compositions, both on folded screen codices made of bark paper or deer skin, as well as texts incised on more durable stone or wood. The importance of preserving written records was a hallmark of Maya culture, as witnessed by the thousands of known hieroglyphic inscriptions, many more of which are still being discovered in the jungles of Belize and other Maya regions. The sophisticated Maya hieroglyphic script is partly phonetic (glyphs representing sounds tied to the spoken language) and partly logographic (glyphs representing entire words), making it capable of recording any idea that could be thought or spoken.

> If you are curious about how scholars unlocked the secrets of Maya hieroglyphics, read Michael Coe's *Breaking the Maya Code*. It reads like a detective novel.

Ancient Maya scribes were among the most honored members of their society. They were often important representatives of the royal family, and as such were believed to carry the seeds of divinity within their blood. Among the titles given to artists and scribes in Maya inscriptions of the Classic Period were *itz'aat* (sage) and *miyaatz* (wise one).

> When the Spaniards arrived, Christian missionaries zealously burned all the Maya hieroglyphic books they could find. Only four are known to have survived and are held in Dresden, Madrid, Paris and Mexico City.

COUNTING SYSTEM

Maya arithmetic was elegantly simple: dots were used to count from one to four, a horizontal bar signified five, a bar with one dot above it was six, a bar with two dots was seven etc. Two bars signified 10, three bars 15. Nineteen, the highest common number, was three bars stacked up and topped by four dots.

The Maya didn't use a decimal system (which is based on the number 10), but rather a vigesimal system, that is, a system that has a base of 20. The late Mayanist Linda Schele used to suggest that this was because

Right: Bars and dots formed the basis of the Maya counting system

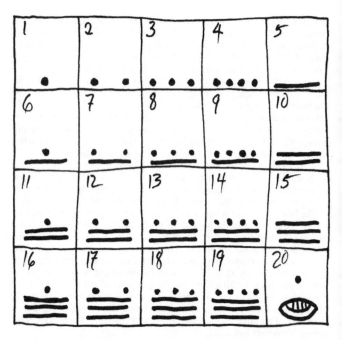

The Maya likely used their counting system by writing on the ground, the tip of the finger creating a dot. By using the edge of the hand they could make a bar, representing the entire hand of five fingers.

they wore sandals and thus counted not only their fingers but their toes as well. This is a likely explanation, since the number 20 in nearly all Mayan languages means 'person.'

To signify larger sums the Maya used positional numbers – a fairly sophisticated system similar to the one we use today and much more advanced than the crude additive numbers used in the Roman Empire. In positional numbers, the position of a sign as well as the sign's value determine the number. For example, in our decimal system the number 23 is made up of two signs: a 2 in the 'tens' position and a 3 in the 'ones' position; two tens plus three ones equals 23.

In the Maya system, positions of increasing value went not right to left (as ours do) but from bottom to top. So the bottom position showed values from one to 19 (remember that this is a base-20 system so three bars and four dots in this lowest position would equal 19); the next position up showed multiples of 20 (for example four dots at this position would equal 80); the next position represents multiples of 400; the next, multiples of 8000 etc. By adding more positions one could count as high as needed.

Such positional numbers depend upon the use of zero, a concept that the Romans never developed but the Maya did. The zero in Maya numbering was represented by a stylized picture of a shell or some other object – but never a bar or a dot.

CALENDAR SYSTEM

The Maya counting system was used by merchants and others who had to add up many things, but its most important use – and the one you will most often encounter during your travels – was in writing calendar dates. The ancient Maya calendar was a way of interpreting the order of the universe itself. The sun, moon and stars were not simply handy ways of measuring the passage of time, but living beings that influenced the world in fundamentally important ways. Even today, the Maya refer to days as 'he.' The days and years were conceived as being carried by gods, each with definite personalities and spheres of influence that colored the experience of those who lived them. Priests carefully watched the sky to watch for the appearance of celestial bodies that would determine the time to plant and harvest crops, celebrate certain ceremonies, or go to war. The regular rotation of the heavens served as a comforting contrast to the chaos that characterizes our imperfect human world.

In some ways, the ancient Maya calendar – still used in parts of the region – is more accurate than the Gregorian calendar we use today. Without sophisticated technology, Maya astronomers were able to ascertain the length of the solar year as 365.2420 days (a discrepancy of 17.28 seconds per year from the true average length of 365.2422 days). The Gregorian calendar year works out to be 365.2425 days. Thus the Maya year count is 1/10,000 closer to the truth than our own modern calendar.

Maya astronomers were able to pinpoint eclipses with uncanny accuracy, a skill that was unknown among the brightest scholars in contemporary medieval Europe. The Maya lunar cycle was a mere seven minutes off today's sophisticated technological calculations. They calculated the Venus cycle at 583.92 days. By dropping four days each 61 Venus years and eight days at the end of 300 Venus years, the Maya lost less than a day in accuracy in 1000 years!

How the Calendar Worked

The ancient Maya actually used three calendars. The first was a period of 260 days, known as the Tzolkin, likely based on the nine months it takes

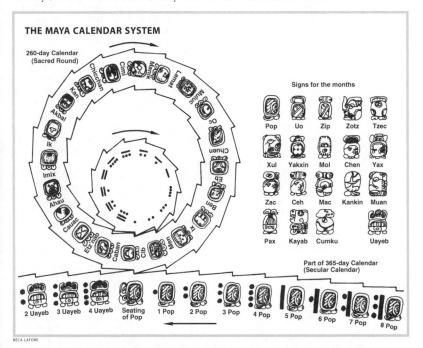

BECA LAFORE

for a human fetus to develop prior to birth. Traditionalist Maya priests still undergo a 260-day period of training before they are 'reborn' as priests worthy to interpret the ancient calendar on behalf of petitioners. The second Maya calendar system was a solar year of 365 days, called the Haab. Both the Tzolkin and Haab were measured in endlessly repeating cycles. When meshed together, a total of 18,980 day-name permutations are possible (a period of 52 solar years) called the Calendar Round.

Though fascinating in its complexity, the Calendar Round has its limitations, the greatest being that it only goes for 52 years. After that, it starts again and so provides no way for Maya ceremony planners (or modern historians) to distinguish a day in this 52-year Calendar Round cycle from the identically named day in the next cycle, or in the cycle after that, or a dozen cycles later. Thus the Maya developed a third calendar system that we call the Long Count, which pinpoints a date based on the number of days it takes place after the day of creation on August 13, 3114 BC.

If you would like to convert a modern Gregorian date, such as your birthday or anniversary, to the Maya Long Count and Calendar Round calendars, you could use the Maya Date Calculator found at www.halfmoon.org.

Let's use the example of the day on which I am writing this chapter. The Maya Long Count date corresponding to today, Saturday, April 10, 2004, is 12.19.11.3.3, 12 Akbal 4 Men. The first number, '12', of this Long Count date represents how many *baktuns* (400 x 360 days or 144,000 days) that have passed since the day of creation (thus 12 x 144,000 = 1,728,000 days). The second number, '19', represents the number of *katuns* (20 x 360 or 7200 days) that have passed, thus adding another 19 x 7200 = 136,800 days. The third number, '11' is the number of *tuns* (360 days), or 3960 days. The fourth number, '3' is the number of *uinals* (20 days), or 60 days. Finally the fifth number, '3' is the number of whole days. Adding each of these numbers gives us the sum of 1,728,000 + 136,800 + 3960 + 60 + 3 = 1,868,823 days since the day of creation.

To further nail down this date, although it isn't really necessary, the Maya added the Tzolkin date (12 Akbal) and the Haab date (4 Men). If that weren't precise enough, the Maya would also often mention the dates from various planetary cycles, which lord of the night was in place etc.

The ancient Maya believed that the Great Cycle of the present age would last for 13 *baktun* cycles in all (each *baktun* lasting 144,000 days), which according to our calendar will end on December 23, AD 2012. By my count we have 2825 days left. By the time you read this, it will be less. The Maya saw the end of large cycles of time as a kind of death, and they were thus fraught with peril. But both death and life must dance together on the cosmic stage for the succession of days to come. Thus the Maya conducted ceremonies to periodically 'rebirth' the world and keep the endless march of time going. These ceremonies continue today among traditionalist Maya, so likely we have nothing to fear.

The Maya never expected the end of this Great Cycle to be the last word for the cosmos, since the world regularly undergoes death and rebirth. Koba Stela 1 (the first stela from the site of Koba) records a period of time equivalent to approximately 41,341,050,000,000,000,000, 000,000,000 of our years! (In comparison, the Big Bang that is said to have formed our universe is estimated to have occurred a mere 15,000,000,000 years ago.)

Environment

With Belize's sparse human population and history of relatively low-key human impact, more than 70% of the country still has natural vegetation cover, a much higher proportion than in most other Central American countries. The hot, mostly moist climate and varied topsoils have yielded a vast diversity of animal and plant species, many of which are able to live on undisturbed in their natural habitats. Thanks to an admirable conservation agenda pursued by governments and nongovernmental organizations (NGOs) since Belizean independence in 1981, more than 40% of the national territory is under environmental protection. All of this makes Belize a particularly fascinating destination for anyone interested in nature, be it the marine life of the coral reefs, the vegetation and animal life of the forests or the hundreds of bird species that soar, flutter and swoop through the skies.

The best all-in-one wildlife guide is *Belize & Northern Guatemala: The Ecotravellers' Wildlife Guide* by Les Beletsky, offering helpful descriptions along with full-color drawings and photographs.

THE LAND

Belize is certainly a small country – at 8866 sq miles, only slightly bigger than Massachusetts or Wales – but it harbors great variety. If you were a magnificent frigate bird flying in westward over the Caribbean toward Belize, the first breaks you'd notice in the surface of the waters would be the three offshore atolls, Lighthouse Reef (p127), Glover's Reef (p185) and Turneffe Atoll (p126). These broken rings of coral reef, dotted with low islands, surround shallow inner lagoons. They're the tips of tall, steep, underwater mountains pushed up by the action of the Caribbean tectonic plate (to their south) sliding past the North American plate on which Belize sits. The sea floor drops away rapidly to great depths around the atolls – to 6000ft within 5 miles east of Lighthouse Reef, for instance.

West of the atolls you'll see Belize's barrier reef breaking the water surface for 160 miles parallel to nearly the entire coastline of the country, ranging between 10 and 25 miles off the mainland. Like the atolls, the reef sits atop geological fault blocks, with steep drop-offs on its eastern side but shallow waters inshore, where the sea floor is a continuation of the continental shelf and rarely more than 15ft deep. The reef itself and the area between it and the mainland are dotted with hundreds of islands known as cayes (pronounced 'keys'). Cayes inshore of the reef tend to be mangrove-lined; those on and beyond the reef are generally sandy with palm trees.

On the mainland, low-lying plains spread across the northern half of the country and the coastal areas of the south. Belize's uplands, stretching southwest from the center of the country to just across the Guatemalan border, are the Maya Mountains. Their highest peak is Doyle's Delight (3687ft) in the southwest, although Victoria Peak (3675ft), on the fringe of the Cockscomb Basin on the northeast side of the mountains, is a much better known landmark. Numerous rivers drop down off the mountains to snake their way south, east or north across the plains to the Caribbean. None of them is of huge magnitude, but all the country's bigger towns lie on or at the mouths of rivers, which have always been key trade and transportation routes. The biggest is the Belize River, running west to east across the middle of the country from San Ignacio to Belize City.

While the central core of the Maya Mountains is hard granite, laid down 125 million or more years ago, the range's northern, western and southern fringes – such as Belize's northern plains – are limestone, laid down more recently and evidence that these areas were once under warm, shallow seas. The erosive action of water on the relatively soft limestone has produced numerous underground rivers and caves. Many of the caves were ritual sites for the ancient Maya and they can be visited today.

The interior of the country, including most of the Maya Mountains, is still to a large extent covered in moist, tropical broadleaf forests, which are highly diverse and shelter a great range of wildlife. Pines and savannah break out west of Belize City and on Mountain Pine Ridge, a northwestern spur of the Maya Mountains. Nearer the coast you'll find littoral forests with tougher-leaved, salt-tolerant trees.

Fiona Reid's booklet Mammals of Belize *and her comprehensive* The Mammals of Central America and Southeast Mexico *are tops in their field.*

WILDLIFE

Belize's animal and plant life are among the country's major attractions, thanks to the conservation of its forests and reefs. Getting to see the animals and identify and understand the plant life is in large measure a matter of having a good guide. Resorts, lodges, hotels and tour agencies throughout the country offer a range of tours, nature walks, birding trips, botanical trails and other activities for nature lovers.

A good guide (of which there are many in Belize) will show you a surprising variety of creatures and plants, many of which you would never spot otherwise. Night forest walks can be especially (and literally) illuminating, as you use flashlights to check out kinkajous, crocodiles and all manner of other nocturnal creatures. Birds, of course, are everywhere, but again guides will spot and identify far more than you likely would alone.

While most jaguars have yellow-brown fur with 'rosettes' of black spots, a few (known as black panthers) are all black.

Animals

MAMMALS

Felines

Everyone dreams of seeing a jaguar in the wild but even though Belize has healthy numbers of this biggest feline in the Western hemisphere (up to 6ft long and 250lb in weight), your best chance of seeing one, as with many other species, is still at the Belize Zoo (p95). They're widely distributed, living almost anywhere that has large expanses of thick forest. The biggest populations and most frequent reported sightings are in the Chan Chich area (p139) and Rio Bravo Conservation & Management Area (p138). You stand a good chance of seeing their tracks and maybe the remains of their meals in Cockscomb Basin Wildlife Sanctuary (p190), which was established as a jaguar reserve in the 1980s, when the then highly endangered jaguar became protected in Belize.

Belize has four smaller wildcats, all elusive like the jaguar: the puma (aka mountain lion or cougar), almost as big as the jaguar but a uniform gray or brown color (occasionally black); the ocelot, spotted similarly to the jaguar but a lot smaller; the margay, smaller again and also spotted; and the small, brown or gray jaguarundi.

The howler monkey's eerie dawn and evening cries – can carry two miles across the treetops.

Monkeys

The endangered black howler monkey exists only in Belize, northern Guatemala and southern Mexico. Its population has made a comeback in several areas, especially in the Community Baboon Sanctuary (p94), set up in the 1980s specifically to protect this noisy animal and now home to some 3000 individuals. Other places where you stand a good chance of seeing them are the Lamanai ruins (p135), Cockscomb Basin Wildlife Sanctuary (p190), Chan Chich Lodge (p139) and the Rio Bravo area (p138).

Less common, though you may still spot some in similar areas, are the smaller, long-tailed, spider monkeys.

Other Land Mammals

Related to the horse but with shorter legs and tail, a stouter build and small eyes, ears and intellect, the Baird's tapir (or mountain cow) eats plants, bathes daily and runs like mad when approached. It's shy and seldom seen in the forest.

Resembling a large spotted guinea pig, up to 2ft long and weighing up to 22lb, the nocturnal gibnut (or paca) is a rodent that often lives in pairs. The agouti is similar but diurnal and more closely resembles a rabbit, with strong back legs.

The tayra (or bushdog) is a member of the weasel family and has a dark brown body, yellowish neck and 1ft-long tail. The coatimundi (or quash) is a rather cute-looking, rusty brown, raccoon-like creature with a long nose and striped tail that it often holds upright when walking. You stand a chance of seeing a coatimundi in daylight on the sides of roads or trails. Also in the raccoon family is the nocturnal kinkajou (or nightwalker), mainly a tree-dweller.

You may well see a peccary – a sort of wild pig that weighs 50lb or more, is active by day and tends to travel in groups. There are two types, whose names – white-lipped peccary and collared peccary – define their differences.

Aquatic Mammals

The West Indian manatee can be seen at the mouths of rivers, in coastal lagoons and around the cayes. The most sure-fire places to spot these gentle, slow-moving creatures are Southern Lagoon, near Gales Point Manatee village (p176), and Swallow Caye off Belize City (p119). Also called sea cows, manatees are the only vegetarian sea mammals in existence. Just a few hundred manatees survive in Belizean waters. They are threatened by increased boat traffic (you'll see some with scars from propellers) and erosion that threatens their feeding areas. Typically 10ft long and weighing 1000lb, adults eat 100 to 150lb of vegetation, especially sea grass, daily. For more on manatees see p120.

REPTILES

The protected green iguana is a dragon-like vegetarian lizard that can grow to 6ft in length and is often spotted in trees along riverbanks. You can also see it in iguana houses at Monkey Bay Wildlife Sanctuary (p96) and the San Ignacio Resort Hotel (p156).

Of Belize's two crocodile species, the American crocodile can live in both saltwater and freshwater, while the smaller Morelet's crocodile lives only in freshwater. Both are on the endangered species list. The American usually grows to 13ft, the Morelet's to 8ft. Belizean crocs tend to stick to prey that's smaller than the average adult human. Still, it's best to keep your distance.

Hawksbill, loggerhead, leatherback and green sea turtles can be seen in the waters of Belize. They live at sea and the females come ashore only to lay their eggs. Sea turtles are victims of poaching and egg-hunting, as their eggs are believed by the uninformed to be an aphrodisiac. However, while all sea turtles are endangered, the hawksbill, which was hunted for its shell, is the only one currently protected in Belize. Turtle-viewing trips are organized in the May to October laying season from Gales Point Manatee village (p176).

Male green iguanas turn browny-orange in the mating season (around December to January).

Up to 60 species of snake inhabit the forests and waters of Belize and, of these, only a handful are dangerous (see p244). The nasties include the (sometimes fatally) poisonous fer-de-lance (commonly known as the yellow-jaw tommygoff), which is earth toned and a particular threat to farmers when they're clearing areas of vegetation; the coral snake, banded with bright red, yellow and black stripes; the tropical rattlesnake; and the boa constrictor, which kills by constriction but can also give you a mean (but venomless) bite.

The Belize Zoo's website, www.belizezoo.org, is a good resource on Belizean animals.

OTHER MARINE LIFE

Whale sharks can be seen in Belizean waters – notably Gladden Spit (p195) – between March and June, most commonly during the 10 days after the full moon, when these filter-feeding behemoths come in close to the reef to dine on spawn. These are the world's largest fish (yes, they're sharks not whales), growing up to a whopping 60ft and weighing up to 15 tons – although the average length is 25ft – and can live up to 150 years. They're gray with random light-yellow spots and stripes, and are quite harmless to humans.

Other sharks – nurse, reef, lemontip and hammerhead – and a variety of rays often make appearances around the reefs and islands. They tend to leave divers and snorkelers alone.

Sharing the coral with the larger animals is a kaleidoscope of reef fish, ranging from larger barracuda and groupers to parrotfish, angelfish, butterfly fish and clown fish (they're the ones who like to nestle into the anemones). Belizean waters host nearly every species of fish and coral found in the Caribbean, plus an amazing variety of sponges. The total number of fish and invertebrate species is around 600, and there are over 40 species of coral, from hard elkhorn and staghorn coral (named because they branch like antlers) to gorgonian fans and other soft formations that sway with the current.

Just in case you're wondering what you've just seen, most dive and snorkel boats have laminated fish-identifier cards on board.

BIRDS

Almost 600 bird species have been identified in Belize, 20% of them winter migrants from North America. Even if you don't consider yourself

---

TOP TEN BIRDING DESTINATIONS

- Chan Chich Lodge (p139)
- Cockscomb Basin Wildlife Sanctuary (p190)
- Crooked Tree Wildlife Sanctuary (p92)
- El Pilar (p169)
- Hidden Valley Inn (p173)
- Lodges around San Ignacio, in particular Pook's Hill Lodge (p161), Crystal Paradise Resort (p163), duPlooys' Jungle Lodge (p165), Black Rock River Lodge (p165) and the Lodge at Chaa Creek (p166)
- Lodges near Southern Hwy around Punta Gorda (p208)
- Lamanai and New River (p135)
- La Milpa Field Station (p138)
- Sittee River (p189)

SPOTTING WILDLIFE

Nature viewing with a guide can be thrilling, but it's even more exciting when you start to develop the skills to spot animals on your own.

Birds and other animals will ignore you if you stay fairly still and don't make too much noise: move slowly, avoid sudden movements and keep your voice low. Most animals are well camouflaged, so they're not going to stand out against their natural background. Look for unusual movement in trees, on the ground or on the surface of water. Keep your binoculars around your neck – they're useful only if you can get to them quickly and with little movement. With or without binoculars, a good trick is to scan the horizon rather than peer at one spot.

Listen carefully, because noises in the forest can be very telling. Your best chance of spotting most birds and animals is early in the morning when they're having their early meal. Don't overlook the little things like bugs, ants, small reptiles or small birds and crabs – they can be some of the most interesting and accessible wildlife on any excursion.

a bird enthusiast, you'll be amazed by the unusual and colorful species that guides will show you on any trip.

You're likely to see interesting birds almost anywhere at any time, although February to May are particularly good months in many places. Wetlands, lagoons, forested riverbanks and forest areas with clearings (the setting of many jungle lodges and Maya ruins) are propitious for observing a variety of birds. Some lodges proudly announce how many hundreds of species have been spotted in their areas: these are likely to be places with a focus on birding, that provide reference materials and good guides.

Following are a few of the highlight Belizean birds. You'll also have the chance to see (among others) many colorful hummingbirds, kingfishers, motmots, parrots, woodpeckers, tinamous, tanagers and trogons.

Belize finally got its own birding guide with the publication in 2004 of the comprehensive *Birds of Belize* by H Lee Jones, well illustrated by Dana Gardner.

Sea Birds

Magnificent frigate birds are constantly soaring over the coastline on pointed, prehistoric-looking wings with a span of up to 6ft. They have difficulties taking off from the ground, so their method of hunting is to swoop down and catch fish as they jump from the sea. They often hang out around fisherfolk and other birds so that they can swoop in on discarded or dropped catch. Males have red throats that are displayed during courtship.

Sharing a habitat with the frigate birds is a colony of red-footed boobies living out at Half Moon Caye (p128). They dive from great heights deep into the sea to catch fish. The frigate birds often try to snatch their catch away as they resurface.

Efforts are being made to reintroduce the enormous harpy eagle, which eats, among other things, monkeys, kinkajous and anteaters, to the Rio Bravo area.

Raptors & Vultures

Raptors usually hunt rodents and small birds. The most commonly seen species in Belize include the osprey (look for their huge nests atop houses and telephone posts), the peregrine falcon, roadside hawk and the American kestrel. Most of these birds of prey are territorial and solitary. Don't pass up any chance to spot an ornate hawk eagle, a beautiful large raptor with a black crest, striped tail and mottled breast.

Inland along the sides of the road and flying overhead you'll see large turkey, black and king vultures. Their job is to feast on dead animals. The turkey vulture has a red head; the king has a black-and-white color scheme with a red beak; and the black vulture appears in black and shades of gray.

Other Well-Known Birds

The beautiful scarlet macaw, a member of the parrot family, is highly endangered. Belize's small population – possibly under 200 – lives most of the year in remote jungles near the Guatemalan border, but from January to March scarlet macaws can be seen at the southern village of Red Bank (p196), where they come to eat fruit.

The jabiru stork is the largest flying bird in the Americas, standing up to 5ft tall and with wingspans of up to 12ft. Many of the 100 or so remaining Belizean jabirus gather in Crooked Tree Wildlife Sanctuary (p92) in April and May. They feed by wading in shallows, enjoying fish, frogs, snails and the occasional snake.

Belize's national bird, the keel-billed toucan, is black with a yellow face and neck and is widely distributed around the country. Its huge multicolored bill is very light and almost hollow, enabling it to fly with surprising agility and to reach berries at the end of branches. Toucans like to stay at treetop level and nest in holes in trees.

Biodiversity in Belize (www.biological-diversity.info) has an enormous wealth of information about Belizean fauna, flora, ecosystems and more, including lots of species lists.

Plants

Belize is home to over 4000 species of flowering plant, including some 700 trees (similar to the total of the USA and Canada combined) and 250 orchids. Nonspecialists can usefully distinguish three chief varieties of forest in the country: coastal forests (19%), moist, tropical broadleaf forest (68%), and pine and savannah (13%). The tropical broadleaf is often called rainforest, although technically only far southwestern Belize receives enough rain to officially support rainforest.

COASTAL FORESTS

Coastal forests comprise both the mangrove stands that grow along much of the shoreline and the littoral forests slightly further inland. Mangroves serve many useful purposes as fish nurseries, hurricane barriers and shoreline stabilizers, and they are credited with creating the cayes: when coral grows close enough to the water surface, mangrove spores carried by the wind take root on it. Mangrove debris eventually creates solid ground cover, inviting other plants to take root and eventually attracting animal life. There are four common species of mangrove: red, button-wood, white and black.

Trees of the littoral forests typically have tough, moisture-retaining leaves. They include the coconut palm, the Norfolk Island pine, the sea grape and the poisonwood, whose sap causes blistering, swelling and itching of the skin, as well as (happily) the gumbo-limbo, with its flaky, shredding bark that acts as an antidote to poisonwood rashes! These forests often provide a key refuge for migrating birds.

TROPICAL BROADLEAF FOREST

Tropical broadleaf grows on thin clay soils where the principal nutrients come not from the soil but from the biomass of the forest – that is, debris from plants and animals. Buttressed trunks are a common phenomenon here. These forests support huge diversity not only of plants but of animal life.

One of the fascinating elements of these forests is their natural layering. Most have at least three layers: ground cover (a ground or herb layer); a canopy layer formed from the crowns of the forest's tallest trees; and, in between, shorter sub-canopy or understory trees. Throughout the layers grow hanging vines and epiphytes, or 'air plants,' such as orchids, moss and ferns, which live on other trees but aren't parasites.

BELIZE'S WORLD HERITAGE SITE

In 1996 Unesco designated the Belize Barrier Reef Reserve System as a World Heritage site. The World Heritage listing covers seven separate reef, island and atoll areas, not all of which include bits of the barrier reef. The seven sites (listed below) were recognized for demonstrating a unique array of reef types (fringing, barrier and atoll) and a classic example of reef evolution; for their exceptional natural beauty and pristine nature; and for being an important habitat for internationally threatened species, including marine turtles, the West Indian manatee and the American crocodile.

- Bacalar Chico National Park & Marine Reserve (p108)
- Blue Hole Natural Monument (p127)
- Half Moon Caye Natural Monument (p128)
- Glover's Reef Marine Reserve (p185)
- South Water Caye Marine Reserve (p184 and p183)
- Laughing Bird Caye National Park (p195)
- Sapodilla Cayes Marine Reserve (p200)

Trees of the tropical broadleaf forest include the ceiba (the sacred tree of the Maya), with its tall gray trunk and fluffy kapok down around its seeds; the broad-canopied guanacaste (or tubroos), another tree that can grow over 100ft high, with a wide, straight trunk and light wood used for dugout canoes (its broad seed pods coil up into what looks like a giant, shriveled ear); the strangler fig, whose tendrils and branches surround a host tree until the unfortunate host dies; and the majestic mahogany, of which sadly few full-size specimens remain.

PINE & SAVANNAH

In the drier lowland areas inland of Belize City and the sandy areas of the north grow Honduran and Caribbean pine, along with savannah grasses, giant stands of bamboo and some oak and calabash.

The pine forest of western Belize's Mountain Pine Ridge (p169) is a fascinating phenomenon. As you ascend to these uplands the forest changes abruptly from tropical broadleaf to pine (mainly Caribbean), brought on by a transition to drier, sandier soils.

NATIONAL PARKS & PROTECTED AREAS

Just over 40% of Belizean territory, a little over 3600 sq miles, is under official protection of one kind or another. Belize's protected areas fall into six main categories:

Forest reserve Protects forests, controls timber extraction and conserves soil, water and wildlife resources.

Marine reserve Protects, and controls extraction of, marine and freshwater species; also focuses on research, recreation and education.

National park Preserves nationally significant nature and scenery for the benefit of the public.

Natural monument Protects special natural features for education, research and public appreciation.

Nature reserve Maintains natural environments and processes in an undisturbed state for scientific study, monitoring, education and maintenance of genetic resources; not usually open to the general public.

Wildlife sanctuary Protects nationally significant species, groups of species, biotic communities or physical features.

Jaguar: One Man's Struggle to Establish the World's First Jaguar Preserve is American zoologist Alan Rabinowitz' story of his efforts to set up what has become the Cockscomb Basin Wildlife Sanctuary – a good read.

Protected Area	Features	Activities	Best Time to Visit
Actun Tunichil Muknal Natural Monument (p161)	spectacular cave with ancient Maya sacrificial remains	caving	year-round
Bacalar Chico National Park & Marine Reserve (p108)	northern Ambergris Caye & surrounding barrier reef & waters	diving, snorkeling, birding, wildlife spotting	year-round
Blue Hole Natural Monument (p127)	400ft-deep ocean-filled sinkhole, home to sharks	diving, snorkeling	Dec-Aug
Caracol Archaeological Reserve (p171)	Belize's biggest & greatest ancient Maya city	exploring ruins, birding	year-round
Caye Caulker Marine Reserve (p118)	barrier reef reserve with plentiful marine life	diving, snorkeling	year-round
Cockscomb Basin Wildlife Sanctuary (p190)	large rainforest reserve, established for jaguars, with huge range of wildlife	hiking, wildlife & plant observation, river-tubing	Dec-May
Community Baboon Sanctuary (p94)	forest sanctuary for black howler monkeys	wildlife viewing, birding, horseback riding	year-round
Crooked Tree Wildlife Sanctuary (p92)	wetland area with huge bird population	birding, walking, canoeing, horseback riding	Feb-May
Gales Point Wildlife Sanctuary (p176)	inland lagoons with Belize's biggest manatee colony & much other wildlife	manatee- & turtle-watching, birding, fishing, sailing	year-round
Gladden Spit & Silk Cayes Marine Reserve (p194)	barrier reef & island reserve visited by whale sharks	diving, snorkeling, kayaking	Mar-Jun
Glover's Reef Marine Reserve (p185)	beautiful atoll with coral-filled lagoon & seas swarming with marine life	diving, snorkeling, swimming, fishing, sailing, kayaking	Dec-Aug
Guanacaste National Park (p152)	small forest park centered on huge guanacaste tree	birding, plant identification, swimming	year-round
Half Moon Caye Natural Monument (p128)	lush bird-sanctuary atoll island with spectacular underwater walls offshore	diving, snorkeling, birding, kayaking	Dec-Aug
Hol Chan Marine Reserve (p105)	waters off Ambergris Caye with the famous Shark Ray Alley	diving, snorkeling	year-round
Laughing Bird Caye National Park (p195)	island on unusual faro reef in waters full of marine life	diving, snorkeling	Dec-Aug

ENVIRONMENTAL ISSUES

The Belize Audubon Society's website, www .belizeaudubon.org, is a fine resource on protected areas and other environmental topics.

While the Baymen (see p28) and later Belizean loggers weren't by any stretch of the imagination conservationists, their methods of selectively pulling logwood and mahogany from forests meant that clear-cutting practices never caught on in Belize, and vegetation that was less of a commodity was allowed to survive. Because they relied on waterways to transport their logs, a road system never cleared the way for further settlement of the forests.

After Belizean independence in 1981, governments adopted a strongly conservationist policy, developing a large network of protected areas in the awareness that not only was Belize's huge terrestrial and marine biodiversity a treasure that needed to be preserved, but also that it was a key factor in attracting tourism. Ecotourism was practically born here, and in Belize's jungle lodges you'll meet some of the pioneers of the

Protected Area	Features	Activities	Best Time to Visit
Mayflower Bocawina National Park (p186)	rainforest park with hills, waterfalls, howler monkeys & hundreds of bird species	hiking, birding, swimming	year-round
Monkey Bay Wildlife Sanctuary (p96)	small private sanctuary on savannah & tropical forest	birding, wildlife viewing, canoeing, caving	year-round
Mountain Pine Ridge Forest Reserve (p169)	upland area with rare pine forests & many waterfalls	walking, birding, swimming, horseback riding	year-round
Nohoch Che'en Caves Branch Archaeological Reserve (p153)	stretch of Caves Branch River running through caverns	river-tubing	year-round
Port Honduras Marine Reserve (p200)	inshore islands & coastal waters important for marine life	diving, snorkeling	Dec-May
Rio Bravo Conservation & Management Area (p138)	large rainforest reserve with great wildlife diversity	birding, wildlife viewing, trail hikes, canoeing	year-round
St Herman's Blue Hole National Park (p178)	small rainforest park with cave & swimming hole	swimming, caving, hiking, birding	year-round
Sapodilla Cayes Marine Reserve (p200)	beautiful barrier reef islets with healthy coral, abundant marine life	diving, snorkeling, swimming, fishing, kayaking	Dec-May
Shipstern Nature Reserve (p145)	wetlands & rare semi-deciduous hardwood forests, with diverse wildlife, including wood-stork colony	wildlife viewing	year-round
South Water Caye Marine Reserve (p183 & p184)	large reserve encompassing parts of barrier reef & inshore islands	diving, snorkeling, fishing, swimming, birding, kayaking	Dec-May
Swallow Caye Wildlife Sanctuary (p120)	small island with permanent manatee population in surrounding waters	manatee-watching	year-round
Temash-Sarstoon National Park (p207)	rainforests, wetlands & rivers with huge variety of wildlife	wildlife viewing, walks, boat trips	Dec-May

sustainable tourism movement. Today over 40% of the national territory is under official protection and Belize has one of the most eco-conscious populaces you'll find anywhere on the planet.

Not everything is as rosy as it might seem, however. Protection requires money and even at the best of times Belizean governments are short of cash. Underfunding means a lack of vigilance, which in turn leads to poaching and illegal extraction. The conservation fee of US$3.75 that every visitor pays when leaving Belize goes to the **Protected Areas Conservation Trust** (PACT; www.pactbelize.org), which helps to provide funding for protected areas. But nongovernment money and initiatives are essential to the success of environmental protection in Belize. Many protected areas are jointly managed by government and local or international NGOs, and it's often the involvement of NGOs that makes the crucial difference between a genuinely protected area and a 'paper park' that exists only in name.

RESPONSIBLE TOURISM

Belize's natural environment, though under an admirable degree of official and local protection, is still a fragile and globally valuable organism which it is in everyone's interest to help protect. Here are some ways in which you can assist:

■ Don't remove coral or shells from the sea and avoid purchasing any items made from turtle shell or coral.

■ Don't swim with manatees or attempt to piggyback a sea turtle. You may like it, but they find it very stressful.

■ Use air-con judiciously. It's expensive and a strain on local energy reserves. If you just move around a bit more slowly than normal and use fans, you'll find that you adjust to the heat in a couple of days.

■ In the jungle, stay on trails to avoid trampling fragile plants. Appreciate wildlife from a distance. Never feed wild animals, including those in the sea.

■ Do not order lobster, crab or fresh shrimp in their closed seasons (lobster February 15 to June 14; conch July 1 to September 30; shrimp April 15 to August 14).

■ Don't fish in protected areas and always check up on seasons and other regulations concerning the place and the species that you're planning to fish. Catch-and-release is obligatory for some species.

■ Dispose of trash properly, even if it means carrying it with you until you find a trash bin.

■ For tips on responsible diving and snorkeling see p61.

To date the single biggest environment-related issue of the 21st century is cruise-ship tourism. Cruise liners anchoring off Belize City brought 850,000 passengers to the country in 2004, up from almost zero five years previously, and the shore excursions made by these visitors are a highly lucrative business for some in Belizean tourism. However, those who are involved in smaller scale and more ecologically aware forms of tourism fear that large groups of cruise tourists threaten not only to damage the archaeological and natural sites they visit but also seriously to impair Belize's image as an environmentally responsible country. Influential organizations including the **Belize Tourism Industry Association** (www.btia.org) and **Belize Eco-Tourism Association** (www.bzecotourism.org) have mounted a challenge to unchecked cruise tourism.

Programme for Belize's website, www.pfbelize .org, has a great set of environmental links.

Environmental activists lost a battle in 2004 when the Chalillo hydroelectric dam project on the upper Macal River in western Belize was finally given the go-ahead, despite a long campaign of opposition from those who opposed flooding a beautiful valley and important habitat for species such as the endangered scarlet macaw.

Environmental organizations of interest to travelers:

Belize Audubon Society (www.belizeaudubon.org) Prominent NGO involved in the management of eight protected areas and campaigning on environmental issues. Based in Belize City (see p79).

Friends of Nature (☎ 523-3377) Placencia-based NGO co-managing Laughing Bird Caye National Park (p195) and Gladden Spit & Silk Cayes Marine Reserve (p194).

Programme for Belize (www.pfbelize.org) Owns and manages Rio Bravo Conservation & Management Area (p138).

Toledo Institute for Development & Environment (TIDE; www.tidebelize.org) Punta Gorda-based organization involved in managing the Port Honduras Marine Reserve (p200) and other projects.

Wildlife Conservation Society (www.wcs.org) US-based international conservation body involved in research and conservation at Glover's Reef (p185).

Belize Outdoors

Belize is the perfect destination for the active and adventurous. Of course if your idea of the outdoors is sunbathing and occasionally dabbling a toe in warm Caribbean waters, that's cool. But if you like to be more energetic, at least some of the time, Belize is waiting for you to select your idea of fun. World-famous since the days of Jacques Cousteau for the spectacular diving and snorkeling along its 160-mile barrier reef and around its coral atolls, Belize has blossomed in recent years as a great place to pursue other activities too. Not surprisingly, saltwater features in many of them: kayaking, sailing or windsurfing across the surface of those crystal-clear Caribbean waters is just as much fun as gazing upon their depths, and Belize's amazing stocks of big fish in the sea, rivers, estuaries and lagoons are just starting to become known to anglers worldwide.

The site www.belize explorer.com has a wealth of information, including lots of useful links to dive operators, resorts and dive-site descriptions.

Even inland, water is the source of much of the best fun: Belize's many rivers don't just provide plenty of refreshing swimming holes but are also great for canoeing and – the latest rage – river-tubing. Out of the water, you can ride horses or bicycles, walk jungle trails, watch birds or wildlife (see p47) and explore some unique caves. Then of course there are caves with underground rivers, where you'll combine caving with canoeing or cave-tubing!

Most of this can be done year-round, although some times of year are better for some activities, and in general it's preferable to avoid the wettest months (June to October in most parts of the country). The Belizean tourism industry is well geared to making it as easy as possible for visitors to enjoy the country's excitements, with plenty of capable, knowledgeable and amiable guides and a number of lodges and resorts specifically devoted to adventure and sports. These range from diving, fishing and kayaking places out on the cayes to the highly popular Ian Anderson's Jungle Lodge (p179), with its array of cave, river and jungle adventures.

Dedicated to diving in Belize, www.scubadiving belize.com is very useful for detailed information about specific areas and dive sites.

DIVING & SNORKELING

For divers and snorkelers Belize is truly a world-class destination. The barrier reef here is the world's second longest and follows the entire coastline from north to south. Although tourism is big business in Belize, the development of the diving industry has been lower key than in other Caribbean destinations. This equates to fewer divers and unspoilt reefs scattered among more than 450 cayes and small islands, which provide an amazing variety of diving. Here you will find dazzling coral reefs, some of the most spectacular walls in the Caribbean region and the sensational Blue Hole (p127), first made famous on TV by Jacques Cousteau and the *Calypso*.

Diving & Snorkeling Belize by Mark Webster (Lonely Planet) describes 66 of the best dive and snorkeling sites in the Northern Cayes, Middle Cayes, Southern Cayes and offshore atolls.

The diving and snorkeling in Belize can be divided into four main areas – the Northern Cayes, Middle Cayes, Southern Cayes and offshore atolls – each of which offer something a little different. Some sites are particularly suited to snorkeling and free diving but, whatever your level of experience or taste, you are likely to find a location that will allow you to do both. The majority of dive sites are accessible only by boat although a few dives can be reached from the shore on Tobacco Caye, South Water Caye and the atolls. Most operators offer two-tank dive trips in the morning and afternoon, which means three or four dives a day are possible from your island base. Choosing a live-aboard boat gives you the opportunity for up to five dives a day if you have the energy.

TOP TEN SNORKELING SITES IN BELIZE

Northern Cayes
- Hol Chan Cut (p105)
- Shark Ray Alley (p105)
- The Split, Caye Caulker (p120)

Southern Cayes
- Laughing Bird Caye (p195)
- Silk Cayes (p194)
- Pompion Caye (p194)

Middle Cayes
- South Water Caye (p184)
- Tobacco Caye (p183)

Offshore Atolls
- Half Moon Caye (p128)
- Glover's Reef (p185)

Northern Cayes

The two main centers in this northern sector of the barrier reef are Ambergris Caye (p106) and Caye Caulker (p119), both of which are a short flight or boat ride from Belize City. Ambergris Caye is the largest offshore island and the most developed, so it attracts most of the visiting divers. Many choose it for the variety of accommodations and nightlife, though it is pretty laid-back as well. The hub of diving activity is the town of San Pedro, at the southern end of the island, and many of the hotels and accommodations are located along the shoreline. Caye Caulker, a few miles to the south, is smaller, less developed and a popular choice with travelers on a budget.

The barrier reef is only a few minutes by boat from both these islands and you will find the dive shops all offer diving in similar areas in addition to dives at the offshore atolls. Reef topography here is dominated by spur-and-groove formations until you get further offshore to the atolls. Don't miss the opportunity to visit the Hol Chan Marine Reserve and Shark Ray Alley (p105). Although these are very popular spots, the fish life is profuse, and snorkeling with dozens of nurse sharks and southern stingrays close enough to touch is a real buzz.

It is also possible to dive these reefs and the atolls on a daily basis from a base in Belize City (p79), where there are currently two major dive operators.

Middle Cayes

The central location of Dangriga (p179) is the key to the increase in its popularity as a tourist destination. If your interest is purely in diving, then it is the best departure point for the offshore resorts at Tobacco Caye, South Water Caye and Glover's Reef. Alternatively, Dangriga, Hopkins (p186) and Sittee River (p189) provide a very good shore base for exploring a range of dive sites on a daily basis.

If you are in search of a low-key and relaxed experience, try Tobacco Caye (p183), a tiny 5-acre island only 10 miles from Dangriga, which is dotted with rustic hotels and guesthouses. This caye sits right on the edge of the barrier reef, provides excellent snorkeling and is one of the few beach-diving locations in Belize. From here you can reach a wide range of dive sites as well as those around the atoll of Glover's Reef (p185) further offshore to the east. There is a variety of reef topographies to be explored, ranging from shallow-water coral gardens to spur-and-groove formations, and of course the drop-offs from the reef edge. A little further south, toward South Water Caye (p184), the spur and

There is only one decompression chamber in Belize, on Ambergris Caye. You will be asked to support it by donating $1 for every tank used. Be sure to use a decompression computer and dive well within safe limits.

Part of a set of three, *Reef Creature Identification and Reef Fish: Florida, Caribbean, Bahamas* by Paul Humann and Ned Deloach is invaluable to snorkelers or divers wishing to identify marine life.

grooves change to what is locally known as a double-wall reef system. Here there are two separate systems, the first of which slopes sharply seaward from depths of 40ft down to 100ft to 120ft. This is followed by a wide sand channel with isolated coral outcrops and pillars and then a second coral reef rising to 60ft before it plunges sheer over the wall beyond scuba diving depths.

The reef systems in this area are considered unique, and Tobacco Caye has been the base for an Earthwatch (www.earthwatch.org) reef-study project for several years; in fact, both Tobacco Caye and South Water Caye are designated as marine reserves. South Water Caye is a little larger and offers more expensive accommodations, but also sits on the crest of the barrier reef, offering beach diving and spectacular snorkeling.

Southern Cayes

Placencia (p192) lies in the far south of Belize on its own peninsula. Until recently it had a reputation as a backpackers' destination, but now upscale resorts have been developed to the north of the main town. The budget hotels and guesthouses are still on the beachfront and you will find dive centers both in town and tied to the resorts. The reef table here is much wider and so it takes a little longer to reach the barrier reef by boat, however the bonus is the numerous islands with large expanses of coral reef and connecting channels between them, which provide a host of alternative dive and snorkeling sites on the way to/from the reef.

Some of the islands have stunning diving, most notably the faro-reef system around Laughing Bird Caye. When you reach the reef the diving is equally spectacular. At the edge of the reef table the topography varies from scattered coral heads leading immediately to sheer walls to the familiar spur-and-groove formation that terminates at the drop-off. The northernmost point of this reef area is Gladden Spit (p195), which is gaining a worldwide reputation as the place in Belize to encounter whale sharks and manta rays.

There are fleets of fast boats to whisk you out to the reef in the morning, back to an idyllic island for a lunch break and then you can choose between more diving on the reef or exploring one of the shallow sites around the islands.

For listings of dive centers, hotels and resorts in Placencia see p192.

Gladden Spit (p195) is the best place to see whale sharks and manta rays. From March through June huge schools of cubera snapper spawn here at full moon, and whale sharks and mantas come to feed on their eggs.

LEARNING TO DIVE

Have you ever wondered what it would be like to swim along a spur-and-groove reef system or peer over a drop-off into the blue and watch schools of fish or cruise by? You can by taking the opportunity to learn to dive during your visit to Belize. It's not as difficult as you might think, and most of the larger dive centers offer 'try dives' to see if the sport appeals to you. The PADI system is now the most popular worldwide and the first step is the basic Open Water qualification.

If you already have the basic qualification then perhaps you could extend your training to Advanced Open Water or one of the specialty qualifications, such as Nitrox diving, deep diving, night diving etc. Another option is to undertake your basic theory training close to home and complete your open-water dives in Belize under the PADI referral system. You can hire everything from fins and mask to a full scuba kit, which saves on baggage weight and provides the opportunity to test different equipment before investing in your own.

Three live-aboard boats operating here (see the boxed text, p63) also offer PADI specialty courses on board. The *Nekton Pilot* offers the complete beginner's referral package, providing basic training with an operator close to your home, followed by your open-water dives when you join the cruise.

LAUGHING BIRD CAYE FARO REEF SYSTEM

Laughing Bird Caye earned its name from the colonies of laughing gulls that nest here, but the reason that it is unique lies below the water. The island sits on top of a faro reef system that has a similar composition to an atoll but has developed on a reef shelf or table. Laughing Bird Caye (p195) is one of Belize's national parks and a part of the Belize Barrier Reef Reserve System World Heritage site (see p53), which includes the island and surrounding reefs.

Within the faro is a system of patch reefs and coral ridges boasting luxuriant hard-coral growth and a variety of sponges and soft corals. The tremendous diversity of fish and invertebrate life in the inshore waters around the island make them ideal for both snorkeling and diving.

There is a definite day and night shift on the reef. By night, most of the fish hide in the reef and sleep, while crabs, shrimps, lobsters and octopuses come out to hunt, and coral polyps emerge to feed.

Offshore Atolls

There are only four atolls in the Caribbean and three of them are right here in Belize. All three – Turneffe Atoll, Lighthouse Reef and Glover's Reef – lie offshore from the barrier reef, rising from great depths to just a few feet above sea level. You can dive them on day trips from the main islands, choose one of the atoll-based resorts or take a live-aboard boat, which concentrates on diving the atolls.

The deep water around the atolls guarantees the best visibility and some of the most thrilling wall-diving you could wish for. Turneffe Atoll (p126) is the largest of the atolls and comprises a series of islands that run north–south. Being the closest to the coast, it is quickly reached by the day boats from Ambergris Caye and Caye Caulker, although there are resorts on a few of the islands. If the conditions are right, try to dive at the southern end of the atoll, where there are frequently schools of pelagic fish and pods of dolphins.

Galapagos, Titicaca, the Blue Holes: The Undersea Discoveries of Jacques-Yves Cousteau is a classic. The book is out of print, but is available through www.amazon.com.

Lighthouse Reef (p127) lies furthest offshore to the east and includes one of the 'must do' sites on any diver's itinerary. This is the famous Blue Hole (p127), which offers a truly thrilling dive experience swimming among prehistoric stalactite formations. Close by is Half Moon Caye (p128), which also boasts some of the best snorkeling sites on this atoll.

SAFETY GUIDELINES FOR DIVING

Before embarking on a scuba diving or snorkeling trip, carefully consider the following points to ensure you have a safe and enjoyable experience:

- If scuba diving, make sure you have a current diving certification card from a recognized instructional agency.
- Be sure you are healthy and feel comfortable diving.
- Obtain reliable information about physical and environmental conditions at the dive site (eg from a reputable local dive operation).
- Be aware of local laws, regulations and etiquette about marine life and the environment.
- Dive only at sites within your realm of experience, and only use the services of professional dive centers with well-trained instructors and dive masters.
- Be aware that underwater conditions vary significantly from one region, or even one site, to another. Seasonal changes can significantly alter any site and dive conditions. These differences influence the way divers dress for a dive and what diving techniques they use.
- Ask about the environmental characteristics that can affect your diving and how local trained divers deal with these considerations.

RESPONSIBLE DIVING

Please consider the following tips when diving and help preserve the ecology and beauty of reefs:

- Never use anchors on the reef, and take care not to ground boats on coral.

- Avoid touching or standing on living marine organisms or dragging equipment across the reef. Polyps can be damaged by even the gentlest contact. Avoid touching the reef; if you must hold on to the reef, only touch exposed rock or dead coral (ie areas of the reef that lack color and have the appearance of rock – often covered with algae or short weed).

- Be conscious of your fins. Even without contact, the surge from fin strokes near the reef can damage delicate organisms. Take care not to kick up clouds of sand, which can smother organisms.

- Practice and maintain proper buoyancy control. Major damage can be done by divers descending too fast and colliding with the reef.

- Take great care in underwater caves. Spend as little time within them as possible, as your air bubbles may be caught within the roof and thereby leave organisms high and dry. Take turns with other divers to inspect the interior of a small cave.

- Resist the temptation to collect or buy corals or shells, or to loot marine archaeological sites.

- Ensure that you take home all your rubbish as well as any litter you may find. Plastics in particular pose a serious threat to marine life.

- Do not feed fish.

- Minimize your disturbance of marine animals, and never ride on the backs of turtles.

Glover's Reef (p185) is the most southerly and isolated of the atolls and earned its name from the notorious pirate John Glover, who once used the islands as a hideout. To dive here use the services of one of several small resorts, each on its own island and all offering an ecofriendly existence. Alternatively, there is day boat diving from Dangriga, Hopkins, Sittee River, Tobacco Caye and South Water Caye, and live-aboard boats occasionally cruise this far south. The spectacular walls and hard-coral formations are just a few minutes from the islands that fringe the eastern side of the atoll. If you get the chance, dive the west side of the atoll as well to explore some wonderful swim-throughs and caves.

C Lavett Smith's *National Audubon Society Field Guide to Tropical Marine Fishes* is the leader in its field.

FISHING

With 160 miles of barrier reef, hundreds of square miles of flats and dozens of jungle-lined rivers and lagoons (all heavily populated by a great variety of fish), Belize is close to an angler's paradise. Spin- and fly-fishing and trolling can all be enjoyed year-round. The best months overall are May through July, with their hot, sunny weather, though every species has its ideal time and place.

Tarpon, snook and jacks inhabit the estuaries, inlets and river mouths, while bonefish, permit and barracuda are found out in the lagoons and flats. The coral reefs support grouper, snapper and jacks, and the deeper waters beyond are home to sailfish, marlin, pompano, tuna and bonito. The flats off the cayes and mainland raise realistic hopes of the angler's 'Grand Slam' of permit, tarpon and bonefish all in one day. Catch-and-release is the norm for these fish and for most snook. Check with your guide or hotel about the regulations for your area and season. Belize's southern waters, from Placencia to Punta Gorda, are gaining almost as good a reputation as the northern cayes for tarpon and bonefish.

Destinations Belize (www.destinationsbelize .com) has heaps of useful information on fishing in Belize.

River fishing for big tarpon, snook, cubera snapper, and 35lb to 100lb jewfish is also practicable year-round. The Sibun and Belize Rivers and Black Creek are the most frequently fished rivers, but the Deep, Monkey, Temash, and Sarstoon Rivers in the south are good too.

It's easy to charter a boat with an experienced guide for a day's fishing for around US$250 (for up to four people) in places including San Pedro (p107), Caye Caulker (p121), Sarteneja (p145), Belize City (p79), Glover's Reef (p185), Hopkins (p186), Placencia (p195) and Punta Gorda (p200).

It's best to bring your own tackle to Belize. Lodges and guides may have equipment to rent but it may not be what you're happy with.

Adult tarpon weigh well over 100lb in summer, and around half that in winter.

KAYAKING & CANOEING

The translucent waters of the Caribbean are as inviting for kayakers as they are for divers and snorkelers. It's amazing how much underwater life is visible from above the surface! And you can enjoy snorkeling and bird-watching as you go. If you fancy some kayaking, consider staying at one of the resorts or hotels on the Placencia peninsula (p197 and p197) or Ambergris Caye (p110 and p110), which provide free kayaks for guests. At San Pedro (p107), Caye Caulker (p119), Hopkins (p188), Placencia village (p195) and Punta Gorda (p200), you can rent a kayak for anywhere between US$13 and US$35 per day. Glover's Atoll Resort (p185) does weekly rentals for US$136.

Inland, on the rivers, canoes are more common. The Mopan and Macal Rivers near San Ignacio (p159) are beautiful canoeing rivers; both have some rapids, so be sure to choose a stretch of river that's right for your level. Many lodge accommodations in the area rent canoes (around US$25 per half-day), and tour outfits in San Ignacio (p156) will also take you out on guided trips. Definitely one of the most unusual canoe trips is the underground river through Barton Creek Cave (p162). Another nice place to use a canoe is the bird paradise Crooked Tree Lagoon (p93).

BELIZE FROM THE SEAT OF A KAYAK

For those who really want to see Belize with a paddle in their hands, a number of Belize- and North America–based firms offer recommended kayaking holidays:

■ **GAP Adventures** (☎ North America 800-465-5600; www.gapadventures.com; 1-week trip around US$1200) Using Placencia as a base, GAP's trip gives you four nights of island-hopping on the cayes.

■ **Island Expeditions** (☎ North America 800-667-1630; www.islandexpeditions.com; 1-week/9-night package US$1588/1800) This ecologically minded, Vancouver-based company has camps of comfortable safari-style tents on Half Moon Caye (Lighthouse Reef) and Southwest Caye (Glover's Reef) for sea kayaking and kayak sailing. Island also does a tasty one-week Cockscomb Whitewater Expedition (US$1699) that includes 1½ days of hiking in the Cockscomb Basin and then three days of kayaking (partly white water) down the Upper Swasey River.

■ **Slickrock Adventures** (☎ US 800-390-5715; www.slickrock.com; 5-/9-night package from US$1395/1895) These top-class water sports holidays are based on Long Caye, Glover's Reef, combining (without experience needed) any of sea kayaking, surf kayaking, windsurfing, snorkeling or diving. Accommodation is in stilt cabanas, and the meals are notably good.

■ **Toadal Adventure** (☎ 523-3207; www.toadaladventure.com; 5-night package US$920) This is a popular Placencia-based outfit (see p195 for more information).

If you prefer to mount your own kayak expedition, Island Expeditions will rent single/double kayaks for US$35/55 per day from a mainland base in Dangriga, and can organize a charter boat to take up to four people and their kayaks and equipment out to the barrier reef for US$175 (one-way).

LIVE-ABOARD BOATS

If you are a truly dedicated diver wanting to maximize the number of dives during your trip, then choosing a live-aboard boat is the only way to go. Your 'hotel' moves with you to the dive site, which gives you the opportunity to dive four or five times a day, including night dives. The boats that operate in Belizean waters are comfortable and well equipped and will even pamper you with hot showers on the dive deck and warm towels to wrap up in. If you do not need dry land and nightlife, then this is definitely the way to see the best that the barrier reef has to offer. All boats depart from Belize City and operators organize all ground transfers for you. Live-aboard boats in Belize include the *Belize Aggressor II* (www.aggressor.com), *Sun Dancer II* (www.peterhughes.com) and *Nekton Pilot* (www.nektoncruises.com).

SAILING

A day's sailing on crystal-clear Caribbean waters, with a spot of snorkeling, wildlife watching and/or an island beach barbecue thrown in, is a nice way to spend a day out of San Pedro (p108), Caye Caulker (p120) or Placencia (p195). Several operators in these places take trips for around US$65 to US$85 per person. Many of these boats do popular boozy sunset and moonlight cruises too. At San Pedro (p107) and Caulker you can rent small craft by the hour or longer for light sailing on your own (during the day).

On longer sailing trips you can reach not only Belize's hundreds of islands but also the attractive Guatemalan ports of Lívingston and Río Dulce, Honduras' Bay Islands and much of the rest of the eastern Caribbean. **Belize Sailing Charters** (☎ 523-3138; www.belize-sailing-charters.com) and **Sailing Belize** (www.sailingbelize.com) offer a variety of crewed, skippered and bare-boat charters on catamarans and monohulls out of Placencia or Belize City. A crewed yacht for up to six people will cost around US$500 to US$700 (plus US$100 per person) per night; seven nights bareboat for four to eight people can run from US$1750 to US$6000.

Learn-to-sail options are also available. Caye Caulker's Raggamuffin Tours (p120) does relatively economical island-hopping sails to Turneffe Atoll, Lighthouse Reef and Placencia.

The Lodge Hopper's Special of Hopkins-based **Under the Sun** (☎ 523-7127, in US 800-285-6967; www.underthesunbelize.com) is an outstanding eight days of Caribbean cruising on an 18ft Hobie Cat, with plenty of stops for snorkeling, fishing, kayaking and hammocking, and instruction provided for novice sailors. Accommodations in lodges on the cayes, food, a guide and support boat are included in the price of US$1985 per person.

The recommended Caribbean charter specialist **TMM Bareboat Charters** (sailtmm.com) has bases in San Pedro and Placencia for its fleet of catamarans and monohulls (from around US$2000 to US$8000 per week), while Placencia is the Belizean base for the luxury catamaran charters of the **Moorings** (www.moorings.com).

RIVER-TUBING

River-tubing – sitting in an inflated inner-tube and floating or paddling along a river – is the latest rage in Belize, blessed as the country is with many fairly gentle and not too cold watercourses working their way through gorgeous scenery. You go downstream most of the time and the only technique that needs to be learnt is to avoid getting beached, eddied or snagged on rocks while continuing to face in roughly the right direction! The Mopan River near San Ignacio (see under Trek Stop, p164; Clarissa Falls Resort, p165; and Mopan River Resort, p167) is a popular

Freya Rauscher's Cruising Guide to Belize and Mexico's Caribbean Coast provides comprehensive information for anyone navigating these complicated waters as well as Guatemala's Río Dulce.

Ian Anderson's Jungle Lodge (p179) pioneered the Caves Branch float and still offers the longest ride (7 miles).

tubing river, but the mother of Belizean tubing adventures is the float in and out of a sequence of caves on the Caves Branch River. People come on day trips from all over Belize for this (it costs around US$65 from San Ignacio), but you can do it for US$20 to US$40 with guides from Xibalba Restaurant (p153) near Jaguar Paw Jungle Resort.

WINDSURFING & KITESURFING

With a light-to-medium warm easterly breeze blowing much of the time and the barrier reef offshore to calm the waters, conditions on Caye Caulker (p120) and Ambergris Caye (p107) are pretty good for windsurfing. Runs of 10 miles are quite possible. You do have to take care with the boat traffic though, especially at San Pedro: try to ride away from the busiest boat areas.

Sailboard rentals run at about US$30 for a couple of hours or US$45 for a half-day, with classes around US$40 per hour. Winds are biggest (typically 10 to 17 knots) from February through April.

Kitesurfers also use sailboards but they catch the wind by a kitelike sail high in the air, to which they're attached by a harness and long cords. You can do introductory courses on Ambergris Caye or Caye Caulker from around US$120.

CAVING

The karstic geology of parts of western Belize has produced many extensive and intricate cave systems, which are fascinating, challenging and often awesome to investigate. The fact that to the ancient Maya caves were entrances to Xibalbá, their underworld and residence of important gods, and that many Belizean caves today still contain relics of Maya ceremonies, offerings or sacrifices, makes cave exploration doubly exciting. One of the few caves in the country that you can enter without a guide is St Herman's Cave (p178), but even there you are required to take a guide if you want to go more than 300yd into the cave.

The most exciting caves in the west of the country include Actun Tunichil Muknal (p161), with its evidence of human sacrifice; Barton Creek Cave (p162), which you explore by canoe; Che Chem Ha (p167), with its vast array of ancient pottery; and the caves through which the Caves Branch River flows near Jaguar Paw Jungle Resort (p152). All of these can be visited with guides, and tours to most of them run from San Ignacio (p156).

When visiting caves, do remember that they and their contents are extremely fragile. Don't disturb artifacts or cave formations, and try to avoid tours with large groups of people. For your own well-being, check the physical demands of a cave trip beforehand, and remember that some caves are subject to flash floods during rainy periods. An extra flashlight

The remote Chiquibul cave system, south of Caracol, is possibly the biggest cave system in the Western Hemisphere. Because of difficult access, it remains largely unexplored.

TOP FIVE ADVENTURES FOR KIDS

- Cave-tubing at Jaguar Paw (p152)
- Canoeing into Barton Creek Cave (p162)
- Snorkeling at the Split, Caye Caulker (p120); Long Caye, Lighthouse Reef (p128); Laughing Bird Caye (p195); or Glover's Reef (p185)
- Horseback riding at Banana Bank (p153) or Crystal Paradise (p163)
- Sailing at Caye Caulker (p120)

and a spare set of batteries is never a bad idea. And finally, if you have claustrophobic tendencies or are terrified of the dark (or bats), it's no shame to admit that caves are not for everyone!

CYCLING

Belize is in the tropics, and mostly at low altitude, so temperatures are high and not terribly conducive to strenuous biking. But the generally flat terrain of most of the country is good for leisurely touring of local areas and short excursions. Cycling tends to be most enjoyable near the coast, where there are refreshing sea breezes and fewer hills. Some coastal accommodations provide free bikes for their guests and you can rent bikes, usually for around US$10 a day, in places such as San Pedro (p115), Caye Caulker (p126), Corozal (p142), Sarteneja (p146), Copper Bank (p144), Hopkins (p189), Sittee River (p190), Placencia (p199) and Punta Gorda (p203).

The Belize Tourism Board website (www.travel belize.org) provides useful overviews of many of Belize's most exciting activities.

HIKING

Most of the hiking you'll do in Belize will be with a guide and for the purposes of nature viewing, not endurance testing. Some lodges have access to trails on their own or nearby properties that you can walk on your own. Among these are Chan Chich Lodge (p139); Black Rock River Lodge (p165); Blancaneaux Lodge (p173); and, especially, Hidden Valley Inn (p173) with its 90 miles of signposted trails. But more often lodge walks are with a guide who'll be showing you the birds, animals and plants along the way. Several places offer night walks, which can be real eye-openers!

Two areas with well-developed and well-maintained jungle trail networks that you can walk with or without guides are Cockscomb Basin Wildlife Sanctuary (p191), with a 12-mile network, and Mayflower Bocawina National Park (p186).

It gets hot and bug infested out in the bush, so carry enough water, a hat and sunscreen, and protect yourself from mosquitoes (with long pants and sleeves as well as bug spray). Compact binoculars are always a plus, as is swimming gear when you reach those welcome swimming holes!

Two seriously demanding expedition-type hikes that the fit and adventurous might contemplate are the three-day Indian Creek Trail (p96) from Monkey Bay Wildlife Sanctuary to Five Blues Lake, and the ascent of Victoria Peak (p192), normally a five-day expedition.

HORSEBACK RIDING

Belize's equestrian tradition is surprisingly strong, and a growing number of lodges offer rides to their guests and, in some cases, nonguests too. Often you'll be riding jungle trails. Preeminent is Banana Bank Lodge (p153) near Belmopan, with a well-tended stable of 150 horses, where you can enjoy anything from a two-hour ride to a multi-day riding package. Windy Hill Resort (p164) near San Ignacio has another large stable.

Also near San Ignacio is Mountain Equestrian Trails (p163), offering rides and riding-based holidays that combine lowland jungles and Mountain Pine Ridge. Other good riding spots include Crystal Paradise Resort (p163); duPlooys' Jungle Lodge (p165); and Black Rock River Lodge (p165), all located around San Ignacio; and Crooked Tree Wildlife Sanctuary (p93). A two-to-three-hour ride can cost anywhere from US$25 to US$65. Full-day outings start at around US$65.

Food & Drink

Being a small, somewhat isolated and relatively poor country, Belize has never developed an elaborate cuisine of its own. Recipes here are mostly borrowed – from the Caribbean, the UK, Mexico and the USA. The typical Belizean diet has a reputation for being bland, but Belizeans adore it and it's certainly filling and nutritious, with plenty of protein and vitamins, if rather a preponderance of carbohydrates. But there's plenty of variety available in most of the country these days: great seafood; Mexican, Chinese and Indian all over the country; and plenty of other international fare – from straightforward travelers' favorites to gourmet haute cuisine – in the main tourist haunts.

You'll find a range of recipes at www.hotelmopan .com/recipebook.htm.

STAPLES & SPECIALTIES

Belizeans love it and most of them would happily eat it every day. Most non-Belizeans think it's filling and inexpensive but not very exciting. It's rice and beans. It comes in two varieties: 'rice and beans,' where the two are cooked together, and 'beans and rice,' or more politely 'stew beans with rice,' where beans in a soupy stew are served separately in a bowl (the idea is to spoon them over the rice). Each variation is usually accompanied by a serving of meat or seafood, plus coleslaw, potato or fried plantain for garnish. Both kinds of rice and beans are flavored with coconut milk.

Recipe Hound (www .recipehound.com) details well over 100 Belizean recipes. Learn to make your own Johnny cakes, fry-jacks and of course cow-foot soup.

Lobster is widely available from mid-June to mid-February and it's always the most expensive item on the menu. Conch (pronounced 'konk') season is October to June: this large snail-like sea creature has a chewy consistency, much like calamari, and is often prepared in ceviche or conch fritters. Belizeans really know how to prepare their fish, be it barbecued, grilled, steamed or stewed. A common preparation is 'Creole-style,' where seafood, peppers, onions and tomatoes are stewed together. Snapper and other fillets are good, reasonably priced fish choices.

Some restaurants serve Belizean wild game such as deer and the guinea pig–like gibnut, which tastes like rabbit.

Maya meals are hard to come by except in the villages of southern Belize. *Caldo* – a stew usually made with chicken (or sometimes beef or pork), corn and root vegetables – is the most common, along with the ubiquitous tortillas. *Ixpa'cha* is steamed fish or shrimp, cooked inside a big leaf.

TRAVEL YOUR TASTEBUDS

Garifuna dishes may appear on restaurant menus, but there are few actual Garifuna restaurants. If you have a chance to try a Garifuna meal you shouldn't pass it up. The most common dish on menus is 'boil-up,' a stew of root vegetables and beef or chicken. Less common is *alabundiga*, a dish of grated green bananas, coconut cream, spices, boiled potato and peppers served with fried fish fillet (often snapper) and rice. *Sere* is fish cooked with coconut milk, spices and maybe some root vegetables. *Hudut* is a stew with similar ingredients including mashed plantain.

We Dare You

Cow-foot soup is a glutinous concoction of pasta, vegetables, spices – and an actual cow's foot. Belizeans seem to like it, particularly in the small hours after a night out. Some say it's 'good for the back' (ie an aphrodisiac).

SHARP ON THE TONGUE

Belizean meals are not usually very spicy, but your table and your meal are always enlivened by the inimitable presence of Marie Sharp's fiery sauces, accurately labeled 'Proud Products of Belize.'

Marie Sharp got into the hot-sauce business in 1981. One season she and her husband found themselves with a surplus of habanero peppers at their family farm near Dangriga. Hating to see them wasted, Marie experimented with sauce recipes in her own kitchen. She felt that other bottled hot sauces were often watery and sometimes too hot to be flavorful. She wanted one that would complement Belizean cuisine, and without artificial ingredients. She tried out some of her blends on her friends and family, and by far the favorite was one that used carrots as a thickener and blended the peppers with onions and garlic.

Once she had her formula, Sharp embarked on a guerrilla marketing campaign, carrying samples of the sauce, along with corn chips and refried beans, door-to-door to shopkeepers all over Belize. When proprietors liked what they tasted, Marie asked them to put the sauce on their shelves and agreed to take back the bottles that didn't sell. The sauce, initially bottled under the name Melinda, caught on and was soon not only in stores but also on restaurant tables all over the country.

Marie bottled the sauces from her kitchen for three years, finally bringing in a couple of workers to help her mix the zealously guarded formula. She eventually hybridized her own red habanero pepper – a mix of Scotch bonnet and Jamaican varieties – which contributes to her sauces' distinctive color. She opened her own factory in 1986 with two three-burner stoves and six women to look after her pots, and moved to her current factory outside Dangriga (see p181) in 1998.

Today, Sharp's hot red-habanero sauces come in six heat levels (Mild, Hot, Fiery Hot, 'No-Wimps-Allowed', 'Belizean Heat' and 'Comatose'), and Sharp also produces a range of mixed sauces (habaneros with prickly pear cactus or citrus fruit), pepper jellies and tropical fruit jams.

The Maya also make Mexican soups-cum-stews such as *chirmole* (chicken with a chili-chocolate sauce) and *escabeche* (chicken with lime and onions) too, though these are not specific to the Maya.

Other Mexican snacks, such as tacos, *salbutes, garnaches, enchalades* and *panades* – all variations on the tortilla, beans and cheese theme (*salbutes* usually add chicken, *panades* generally have fish) – are available in eateries around the country and as snacks from food carts. You'll come across burritos and tamales (wads of corn dough with a filling of meat, beans or chilies), too.

DRINKS
Nonalcoholic Drinks

Delicious and refreshing fruit juices – lime, orange, watermelon, grapefruit, papaya and mango – are available throughout Belize.

'Seaweed shakes' sold by street vendors – a blend of condensed milk, a few spices and extract of *Eucheuma isoforme,* which grows underwater as a tangle of yellow branches – are claimed to have aphrodisiac and many other restorative properties.

Alcoholic Drinks

Belikin is the native beer of Belize (the main temple of Altun Ha is pictured on the label) and you'll be hard-pressed to find any other beer available, except in the resorts. Fear not, as Belikin is always cold and refreshing. Most commonly served is Belikin Regular, a lager, but Belikin also brews a lower-calorie, lower-alcohol beer, called Lighthouse Lager. It's lighter mostly because it comes in a smaller bottle. The stronger Belikin Stout comes in the same sized bottle as Belikin Regular, and there's

The Travellers distillery in Belize City has won several international awards with its thick, spicy One Barrel rum.

Belizious Cuisine, published by the Los Angeles Belizean Educational Network (www.lafn.org/community/laben), features 200 dishes from Belize and instructions for preparing them with easy-to-find spices and ingredients.

also Belikin Premium, in a bigger bottle but the same strength as Belikin Regular. Beer usually costs around US$1.50 to US$2 a bottle, although this can vary from place to place.

In a Caribbean country that produces so much sugarcane, it's not surprising that rum is Belize's number one liquor. The country has four distilleries. Rum-and-coke and piña colada are the most popular ways of diluting your fermented sugarcane juice, but the national drink, according to Belize bartenders (although probably not indigenous to Belize), is a coconut, rum and pineapple-juice concoction known as the 'panty-ripper' or 'brief-ripper,' depending on your gender.

CELEBRATIONS

Belizeans are mad for rice and beans at any time, but on Sunday it is a particularly unmissable ritual. Belize's 10-plus ethnic groups each have their own food preparations for festivals. Before Christmas most folks get baking: rum-flavored, dark fruit cakes are popular. On Christmas Day, many Belizeans consume a more elaborate version of rice and beans – perhaps with turkey or ham instead of chicken. The Maya love their tamales and prepare these at Christmas, while Mestizos might tuck into roast pork and gravy with their corn tortillas.

Cashews can be turned into ice cream, jelly, cake and even a tasty sweet wine.

Several festivals around the country focus chiefly on food. Placencia and Caye Caulker celebrate the opening of the lobster season with their Lobsterfests, on the last weekend of June in Placencia (p196) and usually on the first weekend of July on Caulker (p121). Punta Gorda has a weekend Fish Fest in November (p201), and Crooked Tree celebrates the cashew harvest at its Cashew Festival in May (p93).

WHERE TO EAT & DRINK

Belizean eateries are a wide-ranging lot but you can distinguish between two main types. At the lower end (price-wise) of the scale are the straightforward places aimed mostly at a local clientele, offering mainly Belizean favorites – rice and beans, fried chicken, fried or grilled fish, burgers, Mexican soups and snacks and the occasional Garifuna dish.

Mmmmmm! A Taste of Belizean Cooking brings together about 100 recipes from chefs around the country, some of whose food you'll probably eat while you're in Belize.

At the upper end are the fancier places geared to tourists and middle-class customers, where you can dine on steaks, lobster and shrimp; pasta; Thai, Arabic, Tex-Mex or Indian cuisines; gourmet international salads; wholefoods and vegetarian preparations. The classier places are mostly on Ambergris Caye and Caye Caulker, in and around Belize City and Placencia, and at the better jungle lodges out west. Of course plenty of eateries bridge the gap, serving a selection of Belizean and international fare. In a class of their own are the many Chinese restaurants, some of which are dingy, fly-blown dives while others are sparkling places serving tasty food.

BELIZE'S TOP FIVE

- Habaneros – insanely delicious international fare (Caye Caulker; p124)
- Chef Bob's Bar & Grill – convivial spot serving great Italian, Caribbean and Cajun dishes (Belize City; p85)
- Mare Restaurant – a touch of Italy via northern California (Placencia; p198)
- Cactus Plaza – terrific Mexican food in a fairytale-palace building (Corozal; p142)
- Capricorn Restaurant – best nouvelle cuisine in Belize (Ambergris Caye; p113)

DOS & DON'TS

Belizeans are a pragmatic lot and table etiquette, beyond basic decent table manners, is not a matter of great sophistication. For the sake of preserving stocks of foods and wildlife that would otherwise become depleted, don't eat lobster or conch outside their legal fishing seasons (the legal seasons are June 15 to February 14 for lobster and October 1 to June 30 for conch). Shrimp has a season too (August 15 to April 14). Avoid green iguana ('bamboo chicken') and its eggs at all times: it's a protected species. The hawksbill turtle is also fully protected in Belize. Taking green or loggerhead turtles is legal from November to March, but since these are also endangered species you'll probably want to avoid eating them or their eggs too.

On the whole, service in Belizean restaurants is friendly and fairly prompt and efficient. A tip of around 10% is normal in the fancier places, unless the service charge is already included. In humbler establishments tips are not necessarily expected but they are still appreciated!

Typical restaurant mealtimes are 7am to 9:30am for breakfast, 11:30am to 2pm for lunch and 6pm to 8pm for dinner. Belizeans themselves tend to eat at the early ends of those ranges. In Belize City and tourist haunts, many places don't close between meals and may stay open later at night.

Opening hours of bars are very diverse. Some open from about noon to midnight, others just for a few evening hours, and others from early morning to early evening.

Quick Eats

All around the country you'll encounter street vendors selling a variety of light eats – tacos, tamales, conch fritters, fried chicken, hot dogs, meat pies – and even fuller fare such as rice and beans, or barbecued chicken. Some of this food can be very tasty, and it's always cheap. Pick stands that look clean and are patronized by others – they're likely to provide the tastiest and most hygienic fare.

Toucan Trail (www.toucan trail.com) gives 150 or so Belizean recipes in its Local Flavor section – some of the recipes are helpfully listed by ethnic origin.

VEGETARIANS & VEGANS

Vegetarian items are easily available, but if you're on a camping trip or taking part in a beach barbecue you should make your requirements known beforehand. Be prepared for rice, beans, tortillas and plantains. Potato salad and coleslaw crop up regularly, but fresh greens can be elusive outside of tourist spots. Stew beans are often prepared with ham or bacon, so double-check. Banana bread, coconut bread, pumpkin bread etc make good, filling snacks. Maya and Mestizo foods generally contain meat but *tamales de chaya* (spinach and cheese tamales) and *garnaches* are vegetarian fare.

In tourist areas you'll often find whole menu sections devoted to vegetarian dishes. There's an awareness of wholefood cooking in places like Ambergris Caye and Caye Caulker. Thai and Italian cuisines crop up and these have good vegetarian selections. Lots of vegetarian dishes will use dairy products so vegans will need to check this. Tropical fruit is the natural culinary delight of the region.

EATING WITH KIDS

Children are very much a part of life in Belize and if you're traveling with kids they'll be warmly welcomed. You won't have to work hard to feed your children. Many everyday Belizean foods – sandwiches, rice and beans, fried chicken, hamburgers and fruits – are suitable. In tourist areas bakery goods, pasta and pizzas are additional favorites with kids.

More sophisticated palates will enjoy the manifold ways of fish preparation. Most children will happily quaff a *licuado* (blended fruit juice) or a chocolate milk. They'll also enjoy snacks such as banana bread, which Belizean kids often sell from a basket. If you want to prepare soft foods for infants, you can mash bananas and avocados and other tropical fruits, or, if you're in self-catering accommodations, prepare your own cooked vegetables.

HABITS & CUSTOMS

Belizeans love their food (phobias about weight are rare here) and view the act of sitting down to eat as a deserved pleasure. They love eating with company but there's no shame associated with eating on your own.

Belizeans usually eat their main meal at noon, and many offices, shops and even schools close from noon to 1pm so that people can go home and lunch with their families. Restaurants do stay open after 1pm, but the earlier you eat the fresher and hotter your lunch is likely to be. Dinner for Belizeans is usually a lighter meal, taken early (around sundown, at 6pm to 6:30pm), and outside the bigger towns and tourist resorts you should be sitting down by 7pm. Restaurants with tourist clienteles adapt a bit to foreign eating hours but you'll be hard-pressed to get dinner much later than 8:30pm anywhere in the country.

Belize City

The nation's only sizable city is a place many travelers speed through in no more time than it takes to get from the airport to the bus station or water-taxi terminal. It's true that Belize City lacks beaches, Maya ruins and natural wonders, and does have a security problem, but if you have an interest in Belize the country, this is the best place to get your finger on the nation's pulse. Its ramshackle streets are alive with colorful characters who represent every facet of Belize's ethnic variety, especially the Creoles. The urban scenery encompasses not just odorous old canals and grungy slums, but also handsome colonial houses, seaside parks, bustling shopping areas and sailboats bobbing at the mouth of Haulover Creek. Walking its streets can be extremely hot, and occasionally threatening, but never dull.

Though no longer Belize's political capital, Belize City is still the place where people with ideas and creativity naturally gravitate. Home to a quarter of the nation's population, it boasts Belize's most vibrant arts and entertainment scene, the country's best shops and a broad range of good restaurants and accommodations. For a sense of how Belize's past has given birth to the realities of its present, you can't beat this city.

Belize City is a viable base for visiting many of the country's biggest attractions. Within easy reach are the ruins of Altun Ha, the spectacular bird life and lagoons of Crooked Tree, the howler monkeys of the Community Baboon Sanctuary, and the Belize Zoo, where you'll experience firsthand just how wide a range of wildlife this tiny country shelters.

HIGHLIGHTS

- Soaking up Belize's fascinating history at the **Museum of Belize** (p75) and **Government House** (p75) and on the streets of Belize City

- Enjoying a range of Belize's best food in the city's varied **restaurants** (p83)

- Spotting countless birds you've never seen before at **Crooked Tree Wildlife Sanctuary** (p92)

- Observing Belize's amazing wildlife at the **Belize Zoo** (p95)

- Encountering howler monkeys at close quarters at the **Community Baboon Sanctuary** (p94)

- POPULATION:
  60,000 (BELIZE CITY)

- MONTHLY RAINFALL:
  JAN/JUN 5.5IN/10.2IN

- HIGHEST ELEVATION:
  300FT

HISTORY

Belize City owes its existence to the harbor at the mouth of Haulover Creek, a branch of the Belize River, down which the Baymen (early British woodcutters) floated the lumber from their inland camps. It had little significance until the Spanish briefly captured St George's Caye, the Baymen's first main settlement, in 1779. 'Belize Town' then became and remained the British headquarters in Belize. Popular lore has it that the settlement, at first just a few huts surrounded by mosquito-ridden swamps, grew on a landfill of mahogany chips and rum bottles deposited by the Baymen, who would come to the coast after the rainy season to dispatch their lumber overseas and spend most of the proceeds on rum.

During the 19th century the town grew on both sides of Haulover Creek, with the British merchants' homes and buildings of the ruling elite clustered along and near the southern seafront. African slaves and their descendants lived in cabins inland of here. By the 1880s the town had a population of around 5000, the great majority being Creoles descended from the British and their slaves – though whites still held all the power and wealth. Belize City witnessed most of the significant events on the long road to Belizean independence, including riots in 1894, 1919 and 1950.

The city was devastated by hurricanes in 1931 and 1961. It was 1961's Hurricane Hattie that spurred the government to build a new capital at Belmopan, 52 miles inland. This left Belize City, and the Creole population in general, feeling rather neglected and it was then that people started to emigrate to the USA to seek an escape from overcrowding, unemployment and poor sanitation in Belize City.

Drug-related gangsterism kicked in during the 1980s and 1990s, which helped keep conditions pretty tough for the city's under-employed working class. Middle-class residential areas have developed on the northern and northwestern fringes of the city, while the central areas either side of Haulover Creek remain the country's cultural and commercial hub.

The biggest change to the city's face in the 21st century has been the invasion of cruise-ship tourists: cruise liners anchoring off Belize City brought 850,000 passengers in 2004, up from almost zero five years previously, and most of these tourists came ashore at the city's new Tourism Village, located at the mouth of Haulover Creek. Generally, the passengers wander around the downtown area for a few hours or head off on excursions to inland attractions. Plans for a new cruise terminal (with hotel, casino and shops) to be built at Port Loyola in the south of the city were bogged down in legal challenges at the time of writing.

ORIENTATION

Haulover Creek, running across the middle of the city, separates the downtown commercial area (focused on Albert St) from the slightly more genteel Fort George district to the northeast. Hotels, guesthouses and places to eat are found on both sides of the creek.

The Swing Bridge (the hub of the city) crosses Haulover Creek to link Albert St with Queen St. The Caye Caulker Water Taxi Terminal stands by the north side of the bridge.

North, up the coast from the Fort George district, are the Newtown Barracks and Kings Park neighborhoods, home to some of the city's best restaurants and entertainment venues.

West of Albert St is Southside, the poorest part of the city. The Novelo's bus station and other bus stops are found here, along and near Collet Canal. It's safest to take taxis to and from these bus points.

The Philip Goldson International Airport is some 11 miles northwest of the city center, off the Northern Hwy; the Municipal Airstrip is 2 miles north of the center. Take a taxi to or from either.

INFORMATION

Bookstores

You'll be able to find some Belize-related books at the **National Handicraft Center** (Map pp76-7; ☎ 223-3636; 2 S Park St; ◷ 8am-5pm Mon-Fri, 8am-4pm Sat), **Brodie's** (Map pp76-7; ☎ 227-7070; 2 Albert St; ◷ 8:30am-7pm Mon-Thu, 8:30am-8pm Fri, 8:30am-5pm Sat, 8:30am-1pm Sun) and the better gift shops, but the following three places have more comprehensive selections.

Angelus Press (Map pp76-7; ☎ 223-5777; 10 Queen St; ◷ 7:30am-5:30pm Mon-Fri, 8am-noon Sat) Office-supply store with a reasonable supply of books with Belizean themes.

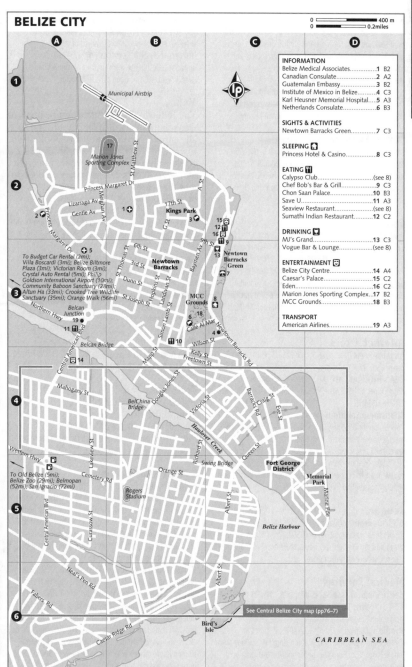

BELIZE CITY

0 — 400 m
0 — 0.2miles

INFORMATION
Belize Medical Associates..............**1** B2
Canadian Consulate....................**2** A2
Guatemalan Embassy...................**3** B2
Institute of Mexico in Belize..........**4** C3
Karl Heusner Memorial Hospital....**5** A3
Netherlands Consulate.................**6** B3

SIGHTS & ACTIVITIES
Newtown Barracks Green.............**7** C3

SLEEPING
Princess Hotel & Casino................**8** C3

EATING
Calypso Club...............................(see 8)
Chef Bob's Bar & Grill...................**9** C3
Chon Saan Palace.......................**10** B3
Save U.......................................**11** A3
Seaview Restaurant....................(see 8)
Sumathi Indian Restaurant.........**12** C2

DRINKING
MJ's Grand................................**13** C3
Vogue Bar & Lounge.................(see 8)

ENTERTAINMENT
Belize City Centre.....................**14** A4
Caesar's Palace.........................**15** C2
Eden.......................................**16** C2
Marion Jones Sporting Complex...**17** B2
MCC Grounds............................**18** B3

TRANSPORT
American Airlines.......................**19** A3

Municipal Airstrip

Marion Jones Sporting Complex

St Matthew St

Princess Margaret Dr

Lizarraga Av

Meighan Av

Gentle Av

Princess Margaret Dr

17th St

Kings Park

A St

G St

9th St

Newtown Barracks Green

To Budget Car Rental (2mi);
Villa Boscardi (3mi); Belize Biltmore
Plaza (3mi); Victorian Room (3mi);
Crystal Auto Rental (5mi); Philip
Goldson International Airport (10mi);
Community Baboon Sanctuary (28mi);
Altun Ha (33mi); Crooked Tree Wildlife
Sanctuary (35mi); Orange Walk (56mi)

Northern Hwy

6th St

Thomas St

3rd St

Dunn St

St Joseph St

Newtown
Barracks

Hopkins St

Landivar St

Simon Lamb St

Baymen Av

MCC
Grounds

Belcan
Junction

Belcan Bridge

Mapp St

Calle Al Mar

Wilson St

Newtown Barracks Rd

Western Hwy

Kelly St

Freetown St

Mahogany St

BelChina
Bridge

Douglas Jones St

Haulover Creek

Victoria St

Barracks Rd

Craig St

Eve St

To Old Belize (5mi);
Belize Zoo (29mi); Belmopan
(52mi); San Ignacio (72mi)

Lakeview St

Cemetery Rd

Orange St

Richard St

Swing Bridge

Queen St

Fort George
District

Memorial
Park

Central American Blvd

Curassow St

Rogers
Stadium

Albert St

Marine Pde

Belize Harbour

Neal's Pen Rd

Albert St

Fabers Rd

Caesar Ridge Rd

Bird's
Isle

See Central Belize City map (pp76–7)

CARIBBEAN SEA

Book Center (Map pp76-7; ☎ 227-7457; 4 Church St; 🕑 8am-noon & 1-5:30pm Mon-Thu, till 9pm Fri, till 6pm Sat) New and second-hand English literature, maps, guidebooks and books on Belizean history, society and natural history.

Image Factory (Map pp76-7; ☎ 203-4151; 91 N Front St; 🕑 9am-5pm Mon-Fri) The country's best range of books, including international literature and titles on Belizean and Caribbean society and history.

Cultural Centers

Institute of Mexico in Belize (Map p73; ☎ 223-0193/4; www.embamexbelize.gob.mx/EduCult/InstMex Ing.htm; cnr Newtown Barracks Rd & Wilson St) Stages an interesting program of mainly Mexican exhibitions, concerts and films.

Emergency

Ambulance (☎ 90, private ambulance ☎ 223-3292)
Crime Stoppers (☎ 922, 224-4646) To report crimes.
Fire Service (☎ 90, 227-2579)
Police (☎ 90, 911, tourist police ☎ 227-6082) Tourist police, who wear a special badge on the left shoulder, patrol central areas of the city. There are police stations located on Queen St (Map pp76-7) and Racoon St (Map pp76-7).

Internet Access

Angelus Press (Map pp76-7; ☎ 223-5777; 10 Queen St; per hr US$3.27; 🕑 7:30am-5:30pm Mon-Fri, 8am-noon Sat)
DEA's Internet Café (Map pp76-7; ☎ 607-9056; 60 King St; per hr US$2.50; 🕑 8am-9pm Mon-Sat) Will burn CDs for US$1.75.
M Business Solutions (Map pp76-7; ☎ 223-6766; 13 Cork St; per hr US$5; 🕑 8am-5pm Mon-Fri) High-speed Internet access, in Great House hotel building.
QuestSoft (Map pp76-7; ☎ 227-1307; Queen St; per hr US$2.50; 🕑 8am-9pm Mon-Sat) Helpful staff; you have to pay in advance, per hour, but can come back for unused time whenever you like.

Laundry

G's Laundromat (Map pp76-7; ☎ 207-4461; 22 Dean St; per load wash US$2.50, dry US$2; 🕑 7:30am-5:30pm) Wash and dry in about 1½ hours. Most hotels can arrange laundry service at similar prices.

Medical Services

Belize Medical Associates (Map p73; ☎ 223-0302/3/4; 5791 St Thomas St; 🕑 24hr emergency services) Private hospital in Kings Park district.
Brodie's (Map pp76-7; ☎ 227-7070; 2 Albert St; 🕑 8:30am-7pm Mon-Thu, 8:30am-8pm Fri, 8:30am-5pm Sat, 8:30am-1pm Sun) This department store has a very well-stocked pharmacy.

Karl Heusner Memorial Hospital (Map p73; ☎ 223-1548/64; Princess Margaret Dr; 🕑 24hr emergency services) Public hospital in the north of town.
Universal Health Services (☎ 223-7870; www.universalhealthbelize.com; cnr Blue Marlin & Chancellor Aves, West Landivar) Good private hospital.

Money

The following banks exchange cash US or Canadian dollars, British pounds and usually euros. The ATMs at Belize Bank downtown and First Caribbean International Bank will accept foreign Visa cards, plus, in Belize Bank's case, MasterCard, Cirrus and Plus cards.

Belize Bank Downtown (Map pp76-7; ☎ 227-7132; 60 Market Sq; 🕑 8am-3pm Mon-Thu, 8am-4:30pm Fri); Philip Goldson International Airport (🕑 8:30am-1pm & 2-4pm Mon-Fri) The downtown branch's ATM is on the east side of the building.
First Caribbean International Bank Downtown (Map pp76-7; ☎ 227-7211; 21 Albert St; 🕑 8am-2:30pm Mon-Thu, 8am-4:30pm Fri)
Scotiabank Downtown (Map pp76-7; ☎ 227-7027; cnr Albert & Bishop Sts; 🕑 8am-2:30pm Mon-Thu, 8:30am-4pm Fri, 9am-noon Sat)

Post

Main post office (Map pp76-7; ☎ 227-2201; N Front St; 🕑 8am-5pm Mon-Thu, 8am-4:30pm Fri)

Telephone

Public card-operated phones can be found around the city.

BTL (Map pp76-7; ☎ 227-7085; 1 Church St; 🕑 8am-6pm Mon-Fri) Has indoor booths where you can make card calls, country-direct calls to Canada and the UK, and collect calls.

Tourist Information

Belize Tourism Board (Map pp76-7; ☎ 223-1913; www.travelbelize.org; Central Bank Bldg, Gabourel Lane; 🕑 8am-5pm Mon-Fri) Has leaflets on Belize City (with maps) and the country's regions, and will do its best to answer questions. The building is directly behind the Museum of Belize, but you must enter from the street via a separate gate, south of the museum.
Belize Tourism Industry Association (BTIA; Map pp76-7; ☎ 227-5717/1144; www.btia.org; 10 N Park St; 🕑 8am-noon & 1-5pm Mon-Fri) The BTIA is an independent association of tourism businesses, actively defending 'sustainable eco-cultural tourism'. The office provides leaflets about the country's regions, copies of its *Destination Belize* annual magazine (free), and information on its members, which include many of Belize's best hotels, restaurants and other tourism businesses.

Travel Agencies

Belize Global Travel Services (Map pp76-7; ☎ 227-7185/7364; www.belizeglobal.com; 41 Albert St; ☼ 8am-noon & 1-5pm Mon-Fri, 8am-noon Sat) American Express representative and full-service travel agency.

Belize International Travel Services (Map pp76-7; ☎ 227-1701; 18 Bishop St; ☼ 8am-noon & 1-5pm Mon-Fri, 8:30am-noon Sat) Agent for American Airlines, Continental, Maya Island Air and Tropic Air.

DANGERS & ANNOYANCES

Yes, Belize City is the scene of most of the shootings and murders that fill the front pages of Belize's newspapers. Most of them happen in the Southside district, south of Haulover Creek and west of Southside Canal. Take a taxi when you're going to or from the Novelo's bus station or other bus stops in this area. Even in the middle of the day these streets can have a threatening atmosphere.

After dark, it's best to take a taxi anywhere you go in the city. If you must walk, even just a couple of blocks, get advice from your hotel about safety in specific neighborhoods. Stay on better-lit major streets and don't go alone if you can help it.

East of Southside Canal you're in the downtown commercial area – Albert St, Regent St and their cross-streets. This is not an area known for shootings, but there are still some dodgy characters around, especially after dark and at other quiet times, such as Sunday afternoon, and tourists are sometimes victims of robberies and (more often) hustlers. Stay alert to everyone around you, and preferably walk with at least one other person, especially around the northern blocks of Albert and Regent Sts. After dark, definitely take a taxi if you go into or through this area.

The Fort George district is generally safer in daylight, but you should still stay alert.

In contrast to the rest of Belize, any stranger who attempts to engage you in conversation – even just by shaking your hand or claiming they have seen you before – is almost certainly after your money. Don't be afraid to shake these people off rapidly. Tricksters may just try to pressure you for a 'gift' or 'tip,' but they may also be aiming to pick your pockets or worse.

Police maintain a fairly visible presence in the main areas frequented by tourists in Belize City, and will intervene to deter hustlers and other shady characters, but you can't rely on them always to be where you need them. Take the commonsense precautions that you would in any major city. Don't flash wads of cash, cameras, jewelry or other signs of wealth. Don't leave valuables lying around your hotel room. Don't use illicit drugs. Avoid deserted streets, even in daylight.

See Dangers & Annoyances (p223) and Women Travelers (p231) in the Directory for general tips on avoiding trouble in Belize.

SIGHTS

The atmosphere and street life, more than anything, are what make Belize City worth exploring, but there are also a few specific sights to focus on.

Museum of Belize

This excellent modern **museum** (Map pp76-7; ☎ 223-4524; Gabourel Lane; admission US$5; ☼ 9am-5pm Mon-Fri) in the Fort George district is a must-see for anyone interested in the story of Belize. Housed in the country's former main jail, built of brick in 1857, the museum preserves one cell in its original state, complete with inmates' graffiti; if you thought your hotel room was cramped, think again! Fascinating historical photos and documents bear testimony to the colonial and independence eras and the destruction wrought by hurricanes.

The Maya Treasures section, upstairs, is rather light on artifacts (most of Belize's finest Maya finds were spirited away to other countries) but makes up for that with informative models and explanations. Other sections of the museum are devoted to Belize's highly colorful postage stamps, and its insect life, with full detail on the disgusting manner in which the human botfly uses living human flesh to nourish its larvae! The museum also has a good little gift shop.

Government House

Fronting the sea down at the end of Regent St, this handsome two-story wooden **colonial mansion** (House of Culture; Map pp76-7; ☎ 227-3050; Regent St; admission US$5; ☼ 9am-4pm Mon-Fri) served as the residence of Britain's superintendents and governors of Belize from its construction in 1814 until 1996. The house, one of the oldest in Belize, is now a cultural center and museum – well worth a visit for its historical exhibits, colorful displays of modern

CENTRAL BELIZE CITY

INFORMATION
Angelus Press.................................1 F3
Belize Bank....................................2 E3
Belize Global Travel Services.........3 E4
Belize International Travel Services.4 E4
Belize Tourism Board.....................5 G2
Belize Tourism Industry Association.6 G3
Book Center...................................7 E4
BTL...8 E3
DEA's Internet Café........................9 E4
First Caribbean International Bank.10 E3
French Consulate...........................11 E1
German Consulate.........................12 F5
G's Laundromat.............................13 E4
M Business Solutions................(see 45)
Main Post Office............................14 F3
Mexican Embassy..........................15 H3
Police Station.................................16 F3
Police Station.................................17 B4
Programme for Belize.....................18 G3
QuestSoft.......................................19 F3
Scotiabank....................................20 E4
US Embassy...................................21 G2

SIGHTS & ACTIVITIES
Baron Bliss Tomb...........................22 H5
Belize Audubon Society.................23 G4
Channel 5 TV.................................24 F4
City Hall...25 F3
Coastal Zone Museum....................26 F3
Discovery Expeditions................(see 45)
Fort George Lighthouse.................27 H5
Government House........................28 F6
Hindu Temple...............................29 E5
Hugh Parkey's Belize Dive
   Connection.................................30 H4
Image Factory................................31 F3
Museum of Belize..........................32 G2
Prime Minister's Office...................33 G2
S&L Travel.....................................34 F3
St John's Cathedral........................35 E6
Sea Sports Belize...........................36 F3
Supreme Court...............................37 F4
Swing Bridge.................................38 F3
Yarborough Cemetery....................39 D6

SLEEPING 🛏
Belcove Hotel................................40 E3
Bellevue Hotel...............................41 F4
Caribbean Palms Inn......................42 F4
Chateau Caribbean Hotel...............43 H3
Coningsby Inn................................44 E5
Great House..................................45 H4
Hotel Mopan..................................46 E5
Radisson Fort George Hotel...........47 H4
Seaside Guest House......................48 F4
Three Sisters Guesthouse..............49 F1

EATING 🍴
Big Daddy's...................................50 F3
Bird's Isle Restaurant.....................51 E6
Dit's Restaurant.............................52 E4
Harbour View Restaurant...............53 G4
Jambel's Jerk Pit............................54 F4
Le Petite Café................................55 H4
Macy's...56 E4
Nerie's II Restaurant......................57 F2
St George's Dining Room..........(see 47)
Smoky Mermaid........................(see 45)
Stonegrill Restaurant................(see 47)
Wet Lizard.....................................58 G4

DRINKING 🍷
Baymen's Tavern......................(see 47)
Radisson Poolside Bar...............(see 47)
Riverside Patio...............................59 F3

ENTERTAINMENT 🎭
Bliss Centre for the Performing
   Arts..60 F4
Rogers Stadium..............................61 C4

SHOPPING 🛍
Belize Photo Lab............................62 E4
Belize Tourist Village.....................63 G4
Brodie's...64 E4
National Handicraft Center............65 G3

TRANSPORT
Caye Caulker Water Taxi
   Association.............................(see 66)
Caye Caulker Water Taxi Terminal.66 F3
Continental Airlines.......................67 E5
Euphrates Auto Rental...................68 D6
Grupo TACA..............................(see 3)
Hertz...69 G4
Jex & Sons Bus Stop......................70 E3
Novelo's Bus Station......................71 C3
Pound Yard Bus Stop.....................72 C3
R-Line Bus Stop.............................73 D3
Sarteneja Bus Line.........................74 F3
Thunderbolt Dock..........................75 E3
Tikal Jets.......................................76 E4
US Airways................................(see 3)

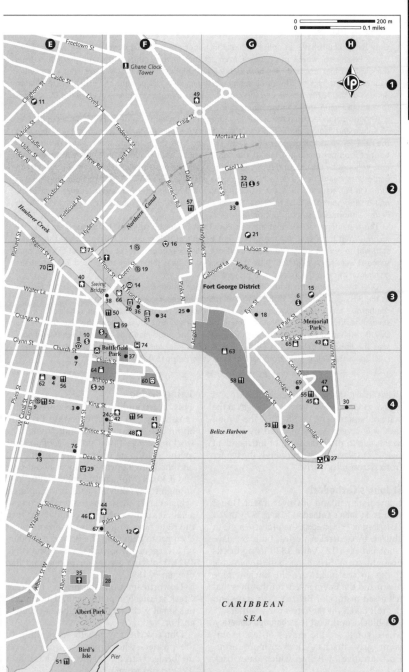

BLISS OF BELIZE

Only Belize could have an annual holiday in honor of a national benefactor with a name like Baron Bliss, who, what's more, never even set foot in the country. The said gentleman, from Buckinghamshire, England, was born Henry Edward Ernest Victor Bliss in 1869, with a family lineage that went back to Edward Bliss, an Englishman who had gained the Portuguese title Baron Barreto in the 1820s. Seemingly, the English Barons Barreto considered that, being Blisses too, they could legitimately use the happy name Baron Bliss.

Though paralyzed from the waist down from 1911 onwards, Baron Henry maintained his love of sailing and fishing, and left his wife and his native land for the Caribbean in 1920, spending the next six years living aboard his yacht *Sea King II* off the Bahamas and Trinidad. After a bad bout of food poisoning in Trinidad, the baron took up an invitation from Belize's Attorney General, Willoughby Bullock, and dropped anchor off Belize on January 14, 1926. After a few weeks, Baron Bliss' health took a decisive turn for the worse, and doctors pronounced that the end was nigh. On February 17, 1926, the baron signed a will aboard the *Sea King II*, leaving most of his one-million-pound fortune to Belize. On March 9 he died. He had, apparently, fallen in love with Belize without ever setting foot on its soil.

The testament decreed that a Baron Bliss Trust be set up to invest his bequest, and that all income from it be used for the permanent benefit of Belize and its citizens, while the capital sum was to remain intact. No churches, dance halls or schools (except agricultural or vocational schools) were to be built with Bliss Trust moneys, nor was the money to be used for any repairs or maintenance to the Trust's own projects!

Over the decades the Baron Bliss Trust has spent more than US$1 million on projects such as the Bliss Centre for the Performing Arts (p86), the Fort George Lighthouse (beside which lies the baron's tomb; see opposite) and the Bliss School of Nursing, which are all in Belize City; and several health centers and libraries around the country. An annual national holiday, Baron Bliss Day, is celebrated on or close to the anniversary of the good man's death, on March 9, and now sees the finish (at Belize City's Belcan Bridge) of La Ruta Maya Belize River Challenge, a canoe race down the Belize River from San Ignacio, Cayo (see p157).

Belizean art, spacious colonial ambience and grassy gardens. It was here at midnight at the start of September 21, 1981 that the Union Jack was ceremonially replaced by the Belizean flag to mark the birth of independent Belize. Displayed in the gardens is the tender from Baron Bliss' yacht.

St John's Cathedral

Immediately inland of Government House stands **St John's Cathedral** (Map pp76-7; ☎ 227-2137; Albert St; ☉ 6am-6pm), the oldest Anglican church in Central America, built by slave labor between 1812 and 1820 using bricks brought from Britain as ballast. Notable things to see inside are the ancient pipe organ and the Baymen-era tombstones that tell a sad history of Belize's early days and the toll taken on the city's early settlers.

A block southwest is **Yarborough Cemetery**, where you'll see the graves of less prominent early citizens – an even more turbulent narrative of Belize, which dates back to 1787.

Swing Bridge

This heart and soul of Belize City life, crossed by just about everyone here just about every day, is the only remaining working **bridge** (Map pp76-7) of its type in the world. Its operators manually rotate the bridge open, usually at about 6am and 5:30pm, Monday to Saturday, just long enough to let tall boats pass, bringing most vehicles and pedestrians in the city center to a halt. It's quite a procedure, and if you're in the right place at the right time, you might even get to help out. The bridge, a product of Liverpool's ironworks, was installed in 1923, replacing an earlier bridge that had opened in 1897.

Downstream from the bridge, Haulover Creek is usually a pretty sight, with numerous small yachts and fishing boats riding at anchor.

Don't waste any breath responding to the hustlers who approach tourists near the bridge with an outstretched hand or a 'Where you from?'

Image Factory

The country's most innovative and exciting **art gallery** (Map pp76-7; www.imagefactory.bz; ☎ 203-4151; 91 N Front St; admission free; ☉ 9am-5pm Mon-Fri), near the Caye Caulker Water Taxi Terminal, stages new exhibitions most months, usually of work by Belizean artists. Opening receptions are usually held early in the month: cocktails are served on the Image Factory's deck, which looks out on Haulover Creek. The adjoining shop sells art, gifts and the country's best range of books.

Baron Bliss Tomb

At the tip of the Fort George peninsula lies the granite **Baron Bliss Tomb** (Map pp76-7), the final resting place of Belize's most famous benefactor (see the boxed text, opposite), who never set foot on Belizean soil while alive. Next to the tomb stands the **Fort George Lighthouse** (not open to the public), one of the many benefits the baron's munificence has yielded the country.

Coastal Zone Museum

Next door to, and entered from, the Caye Caulker Water Taxi Terminal, this small **museum** (Map pp76-7; N Front St; admission adult/student & child US$2/1; ☉ 8:30am-4:30pm) has a limited number of pictures, models and carapaces of Belizean aquatic life, plus summary information on the Belize Barrier Reef World Heritage sites and a few dioramas of marine ecosystems. It merits a peek if you're in the area.

ACTIVITIES

Although most divers and snorkelers base themselves out on the cayes, it is actually quicker to access some of the best sites direct from Belize City. Some hotels in the city offer their guests diving and snorkeling outings; other reputable operators include **Sea Sports Belize** (Map pp76-7; ☎ 223-5505; www .seasportsbelize.com; N Front St) as well as **Hugh Parkey's Belize Dive Connection** (Map pp76-7; ☎ 223-5086; www.belizediving.com; Radisson Fort George Marina, Marine Pde).

The usual destinations are the barrier reef, Turneffe Atoll and Lighthouse Reef. Prices (including equipment) range from around US$120 for a two-tank dive at the barrier reef to US$200 or so for a three-tank dive at Lighthouse Reef (usually in-

cluding the Blue Hole). A day's snorkeling runs from around US$75 to US$145. Sea Sports Belize can also take you sea or river fishing.

WALKING TOUR

The best way to get a feel for Belize City's raffish charms is to walk around it, taking suitable safety precautions such as staying alert to everyone around you (see p75). If you don't have the time or stamina to do all of the route in one go, it divides easily into northern and southern parts. As you go, you'll pass plenty of the city's better shops and places to drop in for a drink or bite to eat.

Beside the north end of the Swing Bridge is the **Caye Caulker Water Taxi Terminal** (**1**; p87), an essential staging post for most travelers heading to or from the northern cayes. Next door is the **Coastal Zone Museum** (**2**; left). A little further along N Front St, don't miss the **Image Factory art gallery** (**3**; left), with its excellent book and gift shop. Continuing eastward along the street you pass the handsome wooden **City Hall** (**4**; 83 N Front St).

If cruise-ship passengers are in town you'll know from the throngs of hawkers, hustlers and hair-braiders that line N Front St. Just past City Hall is the **Belize Tourist Village** (**5**; p87), a waterfront shopping complex where the cruise tourists are disembarked for their forays onto Belizean soil.

Past the Belize Tourist Village you come to the office of the **Belize Audubon Society** (**6**; ☎ 223-5004/4988; www.belizeaudubon.org; 12 Fort St; ☉ 8:30am-4:30pm Mon-Fri), one of the country's most active environmental organizations. Staff in its **gift shop** (☉ 8am-5pm Mon-Fri) can answer some questions, or may pass specific inquiries on to other staff if available.

At the tip of Fort George peninsula are the **Baron Bliss Tomb** (**7**; left) and **Fort George Lighthouse** (**8**; left). Northward, Marine Pde leads past the Radisson Fort George Hotel to the open, grassy **Memorial Park (9)**, surrounded by some of the city's most handsome wooden houses and, on the southern side, the **National Handicraft Center** (**10**; p87). Continue northwards along Marine Pde and then turn left into Hutson St. The area around the corner of Hutson St and Gabourel Lane is dominated by the multiple installations of the **US embassy** (**11**; ☎ 227-7161; 29 Gabourel Lane).

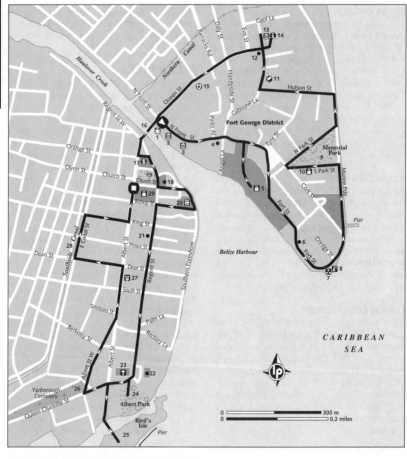

Distance: 3 miles
Duration: 2 hours plus stops

The original structure, on the Gabourel/
Hutson corner, was originally built in New
England in 1866, then dismantled, sent to
Belize on a freighter as ballast, and then
reassembled as a home right here. The US
government bought it for use as a consulate in the 1930s and today it remains as
one of the last wooden embassy structures
in the world. (Read *Our Man in Belize*, by
Richard Timothy Conroy, for a description
of the damage that Hurricane Hattie did to
this building in 1961.) Head north along

Gabourel Lane, passing the **Prime Minister's
Office (12**; cnr Gabourel Lane & Queen St), to the **Museum of Belize (13**; p75), which occupies the
old Belize jail and is not to be missed for its
historical and archaeological exhibits.

The **Belize Tourism Board (14**; p74) is housed
in the Central Bank of Belize, which is located behind the museum. Return to the
Swing Bridge along Queen St, passing the
city's quaint wooden **central police headquarters (15)** en route.

Cross the **Swing Bridge (16**; p78) into the
city's commercial area and walk south
along Regent St, one block from the shore.
The first few blocks of Regent and Albert
Sts, and their side streets, are the most
bustling in the city and are also a favored

haunt of hustlers, would-be con artists, as well as the occasional mugger, so stay alert. Straight ahead as you come off the bridge is the prominent **Belize Bank** (**17**; p74). Heading down Regent St you can't miss the two-story **Supreme Court** (**18**; ☎ 227-4387; Regent St), functioning since 1926 when it replaced an earlier version that burnt down in 1918. The clock tower commemorates Governor William Hart Bennett, who died of injuries after the burning flagpole fell on him in the fire.

Battlefield Park (19) faces the courthouse, offering shade from the midday heat, but you'll probably find the hassle factor from loungers and con artists too high a price to pay. Walk to the waterfront to see the **Bliss Centre for the Performing Arts** (**20**; p86), the city's premier theater, and then return to Regent St and walk south along this relatively broad and airy street that is lined with some fine wooden houses.

Channel 5 TV (**21**; 17 Regent St) occupies one of the oldest buildings in town, dating from the early 19th century. Of similar vintage are the handsome **Government House** (**22**; p75) and **St John's Cathedral** (**23**; p78), hubs of the political and religious life of the British colony, at the south end of Regent St – once the most esteemed address in the city.

Pop into **Albert Park (24)**, which gets nice sea breezes and has a children's playground, and then make for **Bird's Isle** (**25**; south end of Albert St) for a look along the coast that stretches out far to the south, and maybe for a long, refreshing fruit juice at the restaurant here (see p84).

Leaving Bird's Isle, take a look at the **Yarborough Cemetery** (**26**; p78) and then finish your tour with a walk up Albert St. Spot the unlikely little **Hindu temple** (**27**; Albert St btwn Dean & South Sts), which is usually open evenings only, upstairs on the east side of the street.

Head west for a block on any side street to view **Southside Canal (28)**. The city's canals used to carry waste to the sea via Haulover Creek. Enclosed toilets, called 'long drops,' were suspended over the canals. The canals no longer serve quite so blatantly as sewers, but still provide drainage.

The northern blocks of Albert St and its cross-streets comprise the heart of the city's commercial area, with several large banks and the biggest concentration of shops in all of Belize, including **Brodie's** (**29**; p87), the country's largest department store.

TOURS

Popular day-trip activities and destinations from Belize City include cave-tubing at Jaguar Paw, visits to the ruins at Lamanai, Altun Ha, Xunantunich and even Tikal in Guatemala, Crooked Tree Wildlife Sanctuary, the Community Baboon Sanctuary and Belize Zoo. Most such trips cost between US$60 and US$100 per person. Several hotels offer tours to their guests. Tour companies include the following:

Discovery Expeditions (Map pp76-7; ☎ 223-0748; www.discoverybelize.com; 13 Cork St) Has offices at the Great House hotel and international airport.

S&L Travel (Map pp76-7; ☎ 227-7593/5145; sltravel belize.com; 91 N Front St)

Sea Sports Belize (Map pp76-7; ☎ 223-5505; www.sea sportsbelize.com; N Front St) A dive shop that also specializes in manatee-spotting trips to Swallow Caye (three hours, per person US$54.50); also does a popular Wildlife Encounter Tour (US$103.55) that includes a Belize River cruise, barrier-reef snorkeling and manatee- and dolphin-spotting.

For information on diving, snorkeling and fishing trips, see p79.

Many taxi drivers in town are part-time tour guides; they may give you a sales pitch as they drive you around the city. These cabbies/guides can be quite knowledgeable and personable and may suit you if you want a customized tour, probably for about US$100 per day. Hotel staff can often make personal recommendations of cabbies known to them. Make sure your guide has a BTB license.

FESTIVALS & EVENTS

Belize International Film Festival (www.belizefilm festival.com; last week of February) At the Bliss Centre for the Performing Arts.

Baron Bliss Day (March 9) Festivities include a regatta in front of Fort George Lighthouse.

September Celebrations (September 10 to 21) Celebrations all over the city lasting from National Day (September 10) to Independence Day (September 21), including a huge carnival parade, bands, parties, music and dancing, with many of the country's top bands playing on Newtown Barracks Green on September 21.

Wilfrid Peters Brok Dong Competition (December, usually the last Friday before Christmas) Contest of the Creole musical style *brukdown*, at the Bliss Centre for the Performing Arts.

SLEEPING

Accommodations are found both north and south of Haulover Creek. The top-end places are to the north; a trio of good-value midrange establishments sits along Regent St, south of the creek.

Budget

Belcove Hotel (Map pp76-7; ☎ 227-3054; www.bel cove.com; 9 Regent St W; s/d with shared bathroom US$21/27, with private bathroom US$27/32, d/tr with air-con & private bathroom US$48/54; ⊠ ✂) Recently upgraded, this place on the south bank of Haulover Creek has good, clean rooms. Try to get one upstairs or at the river end for maximum throughput of air. All rooms have mosquito-netted windows and fans, and the best are the five air-con rooms, which have TVs. Everyone can enjoy the upstairs terrace that overlooks the river. Management is helpful and in tune with travelers' needs, offering free luggage storage, transportation to the airport for US$20 (book ahead) and diving, snorkeling and tour bookings.

The hotel has good security but the nearby area south of the Swing Bridge attracts hustlers and, potentially, muggers, so stay alert if walking to or from the hotel.

Seaside Guest House (Map pp76-7; ☎ 227-8339; www.seasidebelize.com; 3 Prince St; dm/s/d/tr/q US$13/22/34/43/51, s/d with private bathroom US$31/43; ⊠ ▣) A long-time budget-travelers' favorite, the Seaside is a classic two-story wooden Caribbean house, painted in fetching lilac and white. The six smallish, no-frills, fan-cooled rooms (four-bunk dorms, and private rooms with private or shared hot-water bathrooms) are all upstairs, where you can relax on a breezy verandah facing the sea. There's good security, Internet for US$7.50 per hour, and breakfasts for US$1.50 to US$6. It's worth booking ahead.

Three Sisters Guesthouse (Map pp76-7; ☎ 203-5729; 55 Eve St; r US$25-30) This is a friendly place with large rooms. It's on a quiet residential street, a short distance north of the center of town.

Midrange

Belize Biltmore Plaza (☎ 223-2302; www.belizebilt more.com; Mile 3½ Northern Hwy; r from US$111; ▣ ✂ ▣ ⊕) Located about 4.5 miles northwest of the center on the way to the international airport, the Biltmore is comfortable and spacious. Quality features include the pool (with a popular bar), Victorian Room restaurant (p84) and gift shop. It's convenient for an early getaway from the airport or along the Northern Hwy, but not best-placed for exploring the city. Two children under 12 stay free.

Coningsby Inn (Map pp76-7; ☎ 227-1566; con ingsby_inn@btl.net; 76 Regent St; r without/with air-con US$43/54; ✂ ▣) A friendly and comfortable small hotel in an attractive colonial-style house, the Coningsby is unbeatable for midrange value. Rooms are sparkling clean and decent-sized, all with bathtub, phone, cable TV and fan. Cooked breakfasts (US$5) are served in a pleasant upstairs dining room, the security is impeccable and the welcoming and attentive staff make the Coningsby a home away from home.

Hotel Mopan (Map pp76-7; ☎ 227-7351; www .hotelmopan.com; 55 Regent St; s/d with fan US$37/48, with air-con US$48/59; ⊠ ✂ ▣) Recently refurbished, this big, old, Caribbean-style hotel provides spacious, clean rooms (all non-smoking) with good bathrooms, comfortable beds and cable TV. Broad verandahs provide sitting-out space and there's a large dining room with breakfast available. The best rooms are on the top floor, where you can get a rooftop view of the city. A range of day and half-day trips can be booked at reception.

Villa Boscardi (☎/fax 223-1691; www.villaboscardi .com; 6043 Manatee Dr, Buttonwood Bay; s/d with private bathroom & breakfast US$63/74; ⊠ ✂ ▣) This guesthouse with charming hosts will smooth away any stresses that Belize City's rougher edges might induce. Set in a secure middle-class suburb, Villa Boscardi is just a block from a grassy shoreline strung with residents' private jetties. The six rooms are large and elegant, built with Belizean materials with plenty of comfortable touches, including big beds, cable TV and hair dryers. Two of the rooms have bathtubs. Children under eight stay free.

The Boscardi is off the Northern Hwy, about 4 miles west of the city center and 7 miles from the international airport. The owners provide one courtesy ride to or from the international airport or the city center (Monday to Friday only).

Caribbean Palms Inn (Map pp76-7; ☎ 227-0472; www.thecaribbean-palmsinn.com; 26 Regent St; r US$40-45, with TV US$65; ⊠ ✂) This friendly, homey hotel occupies a rambling two-story house

---

THE AUTHOR'S CHOICE

Great House (Map pp76-7; ☎ 223-3400; www
.greathousebelize.com; 13 Cork St; s/d US$139/150;
P ✗) The Great House occupies a gorgeous, four-story, colonial-style mansion
built in 1927 on a piece of prime Fort George
real estate – and lifted 5.5ft by Mennonite
contractors when it was turned into a hotel
in 1997, to provide extra height on the bottom floor. Most of the charming, individually decorated, hardwood-floored rooms are
spacious, and all are fully equipped with air-
conditioning, phone, safe, big-screen cable
TV, refrigerator, and free coffee, cookies and
fruit! Service is professional and polished
and no rooms in town have as much character. A full range of land and offshore day
trips are available to guests. The hotel usually reduces room rates from May to October,
and in November and December if business
is a bit slow.

---

a few minutes' walk south of the Swing
Bridge. Furnished with attractive wrought
iron and wood, the rooms vary in size and
light: those upstairs at the front are among
the biggest and brightest. All have a private
bathroom. A great rear terrace with bar,
and a comfy indoor sitting area provide
plenty of chill-out and social space. The
owner, Albert, a musician, may provide a
little one-man-band entertainment.

Bellevue Hotel (Map pp76-7; ☎ 227-7051/2;
bellevue@btl.net; 5 Southern Foreshore; r US$54; ✗ ☎)
This rambling seafront hotel has a variety
of plain, fairly worn but clean rooms. Some
(at the back) open along an airy verandah,
all are endowed with air-conditioning, private bathroom and cable TV. The pool and
pool bar at the back are perhaps this hotel's
biggest plus, but keep your room firmly
locked: anyone can wander into the hotel
from the pool bar's street entrance.

Chateau Caribbean Hotel (Map pp76-7; ☎ 223-
0800; www.chateaucaribbean.com; 6 Marine Pde; s/d/tr
US$85/95/106, deluxe d US$117; P ✗) The spacious
lobby, bar and dining room are in what was
once a colonial mansion with brilliant views
of the Caribbean. Unfortunately, the ambience, furnishings and menu are all a let-
down. Standard rooms are no great size and
the two 'deluxe' rooms are under-ventilated.
Seriously ripe for a makeover.

Top End

Radisson Fort George Hotel (Map pp76-7; ☎ 223-
3333; www.radisson.com/belizecitybz; 2 Marine Pde;
s US$127-149, d US$138-159; P ✗ ☐ ☎) The
city's top hotel has 102 conservatively decorated rooms with all the comforts. While
offering top international-class service, the
Radisson avoids the cultural detachment
that often comes with such a package. Local
woods, furnishings and decorations confer
genuine Belizean character.

There are three classes of room here (all
with high-speed Internet connection): Club
Tower (the fanciest option, in a glass tower
where the marble-floored rooms all enjoy
a full sea view); Colonial (in the original
hotel structure, with fine wooden furnishings and partial sea views); and Villa (the
least expensive, across the street from the
main hotel). Besides two swimming pools,
two restaurants (the Stonegrill Restaurant,
p84 and St George's Dining Room, p85)
and bars (p85), the hotel has its own dock,
home to Hugh Parkey's Belize Dive Connection (see p79).

Princess Hotel & Casino (Map p73; ☎ 223-2670/
63; www.princessbelize.com; Newtown Barracks; s/d
US$107/128, s/d ste from US$161/193; P ✗ ☐ ☎)
This six-story, seafront hotel in the north of
the city is also an entertainment and social
center, with plenty of bustle in its lively
lobby and public areas – in fact more of a
place to visit for a bit of diversion than a
place to base yourself. Clocks at reception
show the time in Las Vegas, Miami and
Cancún. The rooms are ample, if unexciting,
with sea views and cable TV, though only
a few have balconies. Prices for all rooms
include breakfast.

The hotel boasts two restaurants (Seaview
Restaurant, p85 and Calypso Club, p85), an
Olympic-size pool, marina, casino, cinema,
bowling alley as well as a lively lounge bar
(p85).

EATING

Belize City's restaurants are a good sam-
pler of Belizean eating options, from plain
but satisfying rice-and-beans-based local
meals to plenty of good seafood and meat
and a few more exotic possibilities from
the Caribbean, Asia or Europe. Most of the
fancier and more upmarket restaurants are
in the Fort George and Newtown Barracks
districts, north of the Swing Bridge, while

you'll find some reliable local restaurants in the commercial area south of the Swing Bridge.

Budget

Dit's Restaurant (Map pp76-7; ☎ 227-3330; 50 King St; snacks US$0.50-1.50, mains US$3-5; ⏰ 7am-8pm Mon-Sat, 8am-4pm Sun & public holidays) Filling portions and friendly service in clean, fan-cooled surroundings – Dit's is a good stop for most food needs, from a solid breakfast or a rice-and-beans lunch to a tasty pastry, Mexican snack, burger or sandwich. The inexpensive coconut and lemon pies, milkshakes, juices and Mexican bites such as *panades* and *salbutes* (variations on the tortilla) are worth a detour at any time!

Big Daddy's (Map pp76-7; ☎ 227-0932; 2nd fl, Commercial Center, Regent St; lunch US$3.25-4.50; ⏰ 7am-4pm) You'll get hearty, low-priced meals and friendly service here. At breakfast, fry-jacks (lightly fried pancake slices), eggs, bacon, sausage and a good juice are under US$4. Lunch is served cafeteria-style from 11am until the food is gone. Rice-and-beans and vegetable-and-rice dishes are the stock in trade, and the view over Haulover Creek from the upper deck is worth a lot.

Macy's (Map pp76-7; ☎ 207-3419; 18 Bishop St; mains US$4-5; ⏰ 9am-8pm Mon-Sat) Macy's provides consistently good Creole cooking, with friendly service and good prices. The menu changes daily, but you're always likely to find chicken, fish fillets and stewed beef or meatballs. Game such as boar, gibnut and deer often makes an appearance. Men visiting the bathroom beware: the entrance has to be one of the narrowest in the world!

Nerie's II Restaurant (Map pp76-7; ☎ 223-4028; cnr Queen & Daly Sts; mains US$3.50-6; ⏰ 7:30am-10pm) Nerie's offers most imaginable accompaniments to rice and beans, including curried lamb, stewed cow foot, lobster, gibnut and deer. You can start things off with a choice of soups, including chicken, *escabeche* (with chicken, lime and onions), *chirmole* (with chicken and a chili-chocolate sauce) or (again!) cow foot, and round it off with cassava pudding. The fare is satisfying without being exactly *cordon bleu*.

Bird's Isle Restaurant (Map pp76-7; ☎ 207-6500; mains US$2.50-12; ⏰ lunch & dinner Mon-Sat; ℗) This open-air restaurant in park-like surroundings serves well-prepared fare, such as burgers, rice and beans, steak, fish and shrimp. You will find it on Bird's Isle at the end of Albert St.

GROCERIES

Brodie's (Map pp76-7; ☎ 227-7070; 2 Albert St; ⏰ 8:30am-7pm Mon-Thu, 8:30am-8pm Fri, 8:30am-5pm Sat, 8:30am-1pm Sun) This department store has the best downtown grocery.

Save U (Map p73; ☎ 223-1291; Sancas Plaza, Belcan Junction; ⏰ 8am-9pm Mon-Sat, 8am-2pm Sun & public holidays; ℗) Large, modern supermarket that is convenient for loading up on supplies if you're driving in or out of town.

Midrange

Jambel's Jerk Pit (Map pp76-7; ☎ 227-6080; 2B King St; mains US$6-13; ⏰ lunch & dinner) A favorite with travelers for its good Belizean and Jamaican food, friendly staff and relaxed atmosphere. Choose between the tiled dining room – perfect for escaping the midday heat – or the leafy patio. Offerings range from spicy jerk chicken or pork with rice, beans and vegetables to a tasty shrimp creole or a lobster-and-fish combo.

Sumathi Indian Restaurant (Map p73; ☎ 223-1172; 190 Newtown Barracks; dishes US$9-13.50; ⏰ 11am-11pm Tue-Sun; ✄) Belize City's best Indian restaurant provides a huge range of flavorsome curries, tandooris and *biryanis* (spicy rice and meat-or-vegetable dishes), with plenty of vegetarian options, all in generous quantities. Bollywood films on the TV intensify the mood. They'll do meals to go if you prefer.

Stonegrill Restaurant (Map pp76-7; ☎ 223-3333; www.radisson.com/belizecitybz; Radisson Fort George Hotel, 2 Marine Pde; mains US$10-15; ⏰ 11am-10pm; ℗) At this thatched poolside restaurant at the Radisson hotel you get to grill your own meal – steak, fajitas, shrimp, chicken satay and the like – on super-hot volcanic stones. It's fun, tasty and free of added fat!

Victorian Room (☎ 223-2302; www.belizebiltmore .com; Belize Biltmore Plaza, Mile 3½ Northern Hwy; mains from US$10, breakfast & lunch buffet US$10; ⏰ breakfast, lunch & dinner; ℗ ✄) The Biltmore's restaurant provides great seafood, steaks and desserts, as well as professional service. A different cuisine is featured daily in the Monday-to-Friday lunch buffet. On Sunday there's a champagne brunch.

Wet Lizard (Map pp76-7; ☎ 223-5973; Fort St; dishes US$6-9; ⏰ 9am-4pm cruise-ship days only) Inside the Belize Tourist Village (p87) but usually also

---

THE AUTHOR'S CHOICE

Chef Bob's Bar & Grill (Map p73; ☎ 223-6908; 164 Newtown Barracks; mains US$14-25; 🕑 11:30am-2pm Mon-Fri & 6-10:30pm Mon-Sat; 🖳) A personal welcome from your host, Chef Bob from Italy, kicks things off to a convivial start at this eclectic eatery in the north of town. Enjoy Bob's tasty Italian, Caribbean or Cajun dishes, or the steak or fish grills, amid colorful Italian-themed murals and a lively atmosphere, and when you leave you'll be thanking him and his staff for their kitchen skills as well as their hospitality. Soups and salads for starters go for US$6 to US$7. Monday, Tuesday and Wednesday are pizza, BBQ and sushi nights, respectively. Happy hour in the small adjoining bar runs from 5pm to 7pm.

---

accessible directly from the street, the Wet Lizard provides solid serves of mainly Belizean and Tex-Mex food amid bright tropical colors, '70s rock and plenty of cruise-ship passengers. Its upper-deck setting is breezy.

Le Petite Café (Map pp76-7; Cork St; pastries US$0.50-2.75, sandwiches US$5.50-6.50; 🕑 6am-8pm) For muffins, croissants, cookies and good coffee, stop in at this excellent little café and bakery run by the Radisson Hotel.

Chon Saan Palace (Map p73; ☎ 223-3008; cnr Kelly & Nurse Seay Sts; dishes US$5-9; 🕑 11:30am-2pm & 5-11:30pm Sat-Thu, till 1am Fri) The sparkling decor is in the best Chinese-restaurant tradition and the tasty food comes in good quantities. Staff will deliver if you don't fancy the taxi ride out to the restaurant, which is north of the center.

Seaview Restaurant (Map p73; ☎ 223-2670/63; www.princessbelize.com; Princess Hotel & Casino, Newtown Barracks; buffet lunch & dinner US$11; 🕑 7-10am, noon-3pm & 6-9pm; 🅿) You can fill up on the self-serve buffet here at the Princess' main restaurant.

Top End

Smoky Mermaid (Map pp76-7; ☎ 223-4759; 13 Cork St; mains US$11-32; 🕑 6:30am-10pm; 🅿 🞩) Attached to the Great House hotel (p83), the Smoky Mermaid serves tasty Caribbean and international food on a lovely patio with tinkling fountains and towering tropical trees. The meals are dependably good and the servings satisfying. Lobster, available eight ways, is a specialty; go for one of the pasta dishes if you want to keep costs down. There's an enclosed air-con section if the heat is just too much.

St George's Dining Room (Map pp76-7; ☎ 223-3333; www.radisson.com/belizecitybz; Radisson Fort George Hotel, 2 Marine Pde; lunch buffet US$13, mains US$13-19; 🕑 breakfast, lunch & dinner; 🅿) The main restaurant at the Radisson serves hearty buffet lunches with a different theme daily (Mexican, Caribbean, Asian etc) and a mainly Mediterranean dinner menu, with plenty of seafood and some vegetarian options. There are also buffets on Friday, Saturday and Sunday nights, and a big Sunday brunch. Dishes are reliably good; the atmosphere is, for Belize, almost staid.

Harbour View Restaurant (Map pp76-7; ☎ 223-6420; Fort St; soups, salads or sandwiches US$7.50-12, mains US$18-29; 🕑 11:30am-2pm & 5-11pm) Perched on a breezy upstairs deck overlooking the bay, the Harbour View provides good service and solid seafood and meat dishes – some with an Asian touch. For something lighter try a spicy grilled-shrimp sandwich or the Thai coconut chicken soup.

Calypso Club (Map p73; ☎ 223-2670/2663; www.princessbelize.com; Princess Hotel & Casino, Newtown Barracks; mains US$12.50-25; 🕑 11am-10pm; 🅿) A waterfront restaurant at the Princess Hotel & Casino, Calypso serves ample portions of Belizean- and Caribbean-style seafood. Burgers, pasta and salads provide lighter and more economical options – but a regular Belikin is US$3.

DRINKING

Top-end hotel bars, especially on Friday evening, are a focus of Belize City social life, and more fun than they might sound, pulling in a range of locals, expats and tourists. Outside the hotels there are only a few dependably respectable places to drink, but plenty of others you might stick your head into. Be judicious: some bars get pretty rowdy and a lot of after-dark activity in Belize City is drug-related.

Vogue Bar & Lounge (Map p73; ☎ 223-2670/2663; www.princessbelize.com; Princess Hotel & Casino, Newtown Barracks; 🕑 noon-midnight Sun-Wed, noon-2am Thu-Sat) This 40-seat lounge at the Princess gets lively later in the week, especially on Friday night when a mixed young crowd launches a new weekend. A DJ helps things get moving from 9pm Thursday to Saturday.

Radisson Poolside Bar (Map pp76-7; ☎ 223-3333; www.radisson.com/belizecitybz; Radisson Fort George Hotel, 2 Marine Pde; ◷ 11am-10pm) The Friday happy hour here (5pm to 9pm) is very popular, and often there is live music and sometimes there's a DJ.

Belize Biltmore Plaza (☎ 223-2302; www.belize biltmore.com; Mile 3½ Northern Hwy; ◷ 11am-10pm) The Friday happy hour (5pm to 8pm) at the Biltmore's poolside bar is a fun session, with a great steel band. There's often live music or cabaret other nights too.

Baymen's Tavern (Map pp76-7; ☎ 223-3333; www .radisson.com/belizecitybz; Radisson Fort George Hotel, 2 Marine Pde; ◷ 10am-10pm) The main bar at the Radisson is friendly and sociable, with a pleasant outdoor deck.

MJ's Grand (Map p73; 170 Newtown Barracks; ◷ 4pm-1am Mon-Fri, 4pm-3am Sat & Sun) You may get to enjoy some funky Belizean rhythms here, but karaoke starts up at 10pm most nights. MJ's is popular with locals both for its indoor pool tables and outdoor terrace tables overlooking Newtown Barracks Green; the atmosphere is relaxed.

Riverside Patio (Map pp76-7; Regent St; ◷ 8am-7pm Mon-Sat) On the riverside, next to the Commercial Center, this is a great place for a beer as the sun goes down. The deck gets just enough breeze to make it comfortable any time of the day.

ENTERTAINMENT

The hub of Belize City nightlife is the Newtown Barracks area in the north of town, where you'll find the Princess Hotel & Casino entertainment complex and the best nightclubs, as well as some of the city's best restaurants.

The local press publicizes up and coming events.

Nightspots

Caesar's Palace (Map p73; ☎ 223-7624; 190 Newtown Barracks; ◷ 10pm-late Thu-Sat) The music and crowd here have a strong Latino element. People start turning up at about 10:30pm and the action on and around the small dance floor can get pretty lively on Friday and Saturday.

Eden (Map p73; ☎ 223-6888; 190 Newtown Barracks; admission US$5; ◷ 10pm-late Thu-Sat) The Eden is a bigger and smarter place than Caesar's Palace, playing classic pop remixes and other commercial dance tracks. It's fairly empty

until about 11:30pm but fills up on Friday and Saturday.

Bellevue Hotel (Map pp76-7; ☎ 227-7051/2; belle vue@btl.net; 5 Southern Foreshore) The karaoke at the pool bar here on Wednesday, Friday and Saturday nights can be fun for participants (including some tourists), but may be less so for the occupants of neighboring rooms! The hotel also stages a Friday night **dance** (hotel guests/nonguests free/US$7.50; ◷ 11pm-3:30am), with live music from reggae and punta rock to *soca* (an up-tempo fusion of calypso and Indian rhythms) and soul.

Casino, Bowling & Cinema

Princess Hotel & Casino (Map p73; ☎ 223-0638; Newtown Barracks; ◷ noon-4am; P) The casino at the Princess Hotel is an informal and fun place to try to boost your budget (set yourself a limit on what you're prepared to lose), with roulette, poker and blackjack tables, plus hundreds of slot machines and a floor show with dancing girls kicking it up at 10pm. You need to show ID such as your passport or driver's license to enter (minimum age is 18). Also here is Belize's only **bowling alley** (per person for 2/4/6/8 games US$7/14.50/20/25; ◷ 11am-11pm; ✗), with eight lanes.

The two-screen **movie theater** (☎ 223-7162; admission US$7.50; screenings usually at 6pm or 7pm & 8pm or 9pm, plus 3pm Sat & Sun) shows mostly second-grade Hollywood films.

Music & Theater

To find out what's on, watch for posters, read the local press or drop by the following venues.

Bliss Centre for the Performing Arts (Map pp76-7; ☎ 227-2458/2110; Southern Foreshore) The revamped Bliss Centre has a fine 600-seat theater that stages a variety of events, including concerts of traditional Belizean music as well as other shows that celebrate Belize and its culture.

Belize City Centre (Map p73; ☎ 227-2051/2092; Central American Blvd; P) The main venue for bigger touring acts.

Government House (House of Culture; Map pp76-7; ☎ 227-3050; Regent St) Some cultural events, including classical concerts, are held here.

Sports

The main venues are the **MCC Grounds** (Map p73; cnr Newtown Barracks Rd & Calle al Mar), for football and cricket, **Rogers Stadium** (Map pp76-7; Dolphin

St) for softball, and the **Marion Jones Sporting Complex** (Map p73; Princess Margaret Dr), which is used for various events.

SHOPPING

Albert St and its side streets are the main shopping streets, with stores dealing in everything from clothes and domestic appliances to spices and music.

National Handicraft Center (Map pp76-7; ☎ 223-3636; 2 S Park St; ☒ 8am-5pm Mon-Fri, 8am-4pm Sat) This store carries the best stock of Belizean crafts, at fair prices. Attractive buys include carvings in the hard, strikingly streaked wood zericote, slate relief carvings of wildlife and Maya deities, and CDs of Belizean music.

Brodie's (Map pp76-7; ☎ 227-7070; 2 Albert St; ☒ 8:30am-7pm Mon-Thu, 8:30am-8pm Fri, 8:30am-5pm Sat, 8:30am-1pm Sun) Brodie's is the biggest department store in the country: some of the 'departments' are pretty small, but it's still a good place to look for many things.

Image Factory (Map pp76-7; ☎ 203-4151; www .imagefactory.bz; 91 N Front St; ☒ 9am-5pm Mon-Fri) Some original Belizean art lurks among the handicrafts and books here.

Belize Photo Lab (Map pp76-7; ☎ 227-4428; photo lab@btl.net; cnr Bishop & E Canal Sts) The best place in town for photographic supplies.

Belize Tourist Village (Map pp76-7; ☎ 223-7789; 8 Fort St; ☒ 8am-4pm, cruise-ship days only) This waterfront complex exists for cruise-ship passengers, who disembark here on their land trips. Non-cruise tourists may enter from the street with a temporary pass that is obtainable on presentation of an identity document such as a passport. Most of the stores are gift shops, liquor stores, jewelers, or pharmacies offering Viagra without prescription. Some items are cheaper than elsewhere in the city; others are more expensive. You'll know when it's open from the crowds of hawkers, hustlers and tour agents thronging the street outside.

You'll also find worthwhile gift shops at the Museum of Belize (see p75), the Radisson (p83), Princess (p83) and Biltmore (p82) hotels, and Old Belize (p95).

GETTING THERE & AWAY
Air

Belize City has two airports: Philip Goldson International Airport (BZE), which is 11 miles northwest of the city center off the Northern Hwy; and the Municipal Airstrip (TZA), around 2 miles north of the center. All international flights (including the short hop to and from Flores, Guatemala) use the international airport. Domestic flights are divided between the two airports, but those using the Municipal Airstrip are always cheaper (sometimes more than 50% cheaper). See p232 and p235 for further information on flights to, from and around Belize. The following airlines fly from Belize City:

American Airlines Sancas Plaza (Map p73; ☎ 223-2522; www.aa.com; Sancas Plaza, Belcan Junction) Direct flights to/from Miami and Dallas/Fort Worth.

Continental Airlines (www.continental.com) Downtown (Map pp76-7; ☎ 227-8309/8223; 80 Regent St); Philip Goldson International Airport (☎ 225-2263) Direct flights to/from Houston.

Delta Air Lines Philip Goldson International Airport (☎ 225-3429; www.delta.com) Direct flights to/from Atlanta.

Grupo TACA (www.taca.com) Downtown (Map pp76-7; ☎ 227-7363/4; Belize Global Travel Services, 41 Albert St); Philip Goldson International Airport (☎ 225-2163) Direct flights to/from Houston and San Salvador (El Salvador).

Maya Island Air (www.mayaairways.com) Philip Goldson International Airport (☎ 225-2219); Municipal Airstrip (Map p73; ☎ 223-1140) Direct flights to Caye Caulker, Dangriga, Placencia, Punta Gorda, San Pedro and Flores (Guatemala).

Tikal Jets Downtown (Map pp76-7; ☎ 227-2583; www .tikaljets.com; Caribbean Holidays, 81 Albert St) Direct flights to Flores.

Tropic Air (www.tropicair.com) Philip Goldson International Airport (☎ 225-2302); Municipal Airstrip (Map p73; ☎ 223-5671) Direct flights to Caye Caulker, Dangriga, Placencia, Punta Gorda, San Pedro and Flores.

US Airways Downtown (Map pp76-7; ☎ 225-3589; www.usairways.com; Belize Global Travel Services, 41 Albert St) Direct flights to Charlotte, North Carolina.

Boat

Caye Caulker Water Taxi Association (Map pp76-7; ☎ 203-1969, 226-0992; www.cayecaulkerwatertaxi.com; Caye Caulker Water Taxi Terminal, 10 N Front St) provides the main service that connects Belize City with Caye Caulker and San Pedro (Ambergris Caye). Departures to Caye Caulker (one-way/return US$10/17.50, one hour) and San Pedro (one-way/return US$15/27.50, 1½ hours) are at 8am, 9am, 10:30am, noon, 1:30pm, 3pm and 4:30pm.

If there are more than enough passengers for one boat, one will go direct to San

Pedro. An extra boat, to Caye Caulker only, goes at 5:30pm. On request from passengers the boats will stop at Long Caye or Caye Chapel (both one-way US$7.50). Boats to St George's Caye (one-way US$12.50) leave at 10:30am and 4:30pm.

The boats are open, have fast twin engines and hold around 40 people each. Captains usually do their best to avoid rainstorms; when they can't, passengers huddle together under large tarps to stay dry.

Thunderbolt (Map pp76-7; ☎ 226-2217/2904), with its triple 250HP outboard motors and interior seating for all passengers, departs for Caye Caulker (US$10) and San Pedro (US$15) from its dock at N Front St, which is located west of the Swing Bridge, at 8am and 1pm.

Bus

NOVELO'S BUS LINE

The most important bus services from Belize City are run by **Novelo's Bus Line** (Map pp76-7; ☎ 227-2025/7146; 19 W Collet Canal St). The terminal is in a run-down area that is not good for walking, especially at night. Take a taxi.

Novelo's express services are a little more expensive than regular services, but they're much quicker because they make limited stops, and are usually more comfortable because they are less crowded.

Schedules are less than reliable, but the overall picture to main destinations from Monday to Saturday is as follows (on Sundays, frequency is reduced by up to half):

Belmopan (express/regular US$3.50/2, 1/1¼ hours, 52 miles) Buses every half-hour or hour, 6am to 8pm, including about eight expresses.

Benque Viejo del Carmen (express/regular US$6/4, 2½/three hours, 80 miles) Buses every half-hour or hour, 6am to 8pm, including about eight expresses.

Chetumal (Mexico; express/regular US$7/5, 3½/4½ hours, 102 miles) Buses every half-hour or hour, from 6am to 6pm, including about six expresses. Quicker buses to Chetumal (US$10) leave from the Caye Caulker Water Taxi Terminal at 10:30am daily, though they are sometimes late, as they come in from Flores, Guatemala. Tickets are sold by the same outlets as for Flores buses (see right).

Corozal (express/regular US$6/4.50, 2½/3¼ hours, 86 miles) Buses about every half-hour or hour, 6am to 7pm, including about six expresses.

Dangriga (express/regular US$7/5, 2½/three hours, 107 miles) About eight buses via Belmopan and the Hummingbird Hwy between 5:30am and 5pm, including two or three expresses; one bus at 5pm (4pm Sunday) via the Coastal Hwy and Gales Point Manatee. See information on James bus line for further options (below).

Maskall (US$1.50, 1½ hours, 42 miles) Buses at 5am, 1pm, 3:30pm and 6pm.

Orange Walk (express/regular US$3.50/2.50, 1½/two hours, 57 miles) Buses about every half-hour or hour, 6am to 7pm, including about six expresses.

Punta Gorda (US$11, six to seven hours, 212 miles) Two to four buses between 6am and 2pm. See information on James bus line for further options.

San Ignacio (express/regular US$5.50/3.50, 2/2½ hours, 72 miles) Buses every half-hour or hour, 6am to 8pm, including about eight expresses.

OTHER SERVICES

James bus line (☎ 702-2049, 722-2625) runs a more reliable service than Novelo's to Punta Gorda, via Belmopan, Dangriga and Independence. Its buses (express/regular US$12/11, six/seven hours) depart daily at 5:30am (express Saturday and Monday, regular other days), 10am (regular), 2:45pm (regular) and 3:30pm (express) from the **Pound Yard bus stop** (Map pp76-7; Cemetery Rd), located just north of Novelo's terminal.

Jex & Sons (☎ 225-7017) runs buses to Crooked Tree (US$1.75, one hour, 36 miles) from the Pound Yard bus stop at 4:30pm and 5pm, Monday to Saturday, and from the corner of Regent St W and W Canal St (Map pp76-7) at 10:45am from Monday to Saturday.

R-Line buses (Map pp76-7; cnr of Euphrates Ave & Cairo St) to Bermudian Landing (US$1.50, one hour, 27 miles) go at 12:15pm, 4pm and 9pm, Monday to Friday, and noon and 5pm Saturday.

Sarteneja Bus Line (Map pp76–7) departs for Sarteneja (US$4.50, 3½ hours, 96 miles) at noon and 4pm, Monday to Saturday from the north side of Supreme Court building, off Regent St.

TO FLORES, GUATEMALA

Buses to Flores (five hours, 145 miles) leave from the **Caye Caulker Water Taxi Terminal** (Map pp76-7; 10 N Front St). The Línea Dorada/Mundo Maya company, which departs at 9:30am daily, has the most reliable reputation: its tickets (US$15) are sold at **Mundo Maya Deli** (☎ 223-0457) in the water taxi terminal. San Juan Travel departs at 9:30am (US$15) and 3:30pm (US$20) daily; you can get tickets from Mundo Maya Deli, **Khan Store** (☎ 223-7611) or **S&L Travel & Tours** (☎ 223-6186), all in the water taxi terminal.

Car & Motorcycle

The main roads in and out of town are the Northern Hwy (to the international airport, Orange Walk and Corozal), which heads northwest from the Belcan Junction, and the Western Hwy (to Belmopan and San Ignacio), which is the westward continuation of Cemetery Rd. Cemetery Rd gets its name from the fantastic, huge, ramshackle Lord's Ridge Cemetery, which it bisects west of Central American Blvd.

Auto rental firms in Belize City include the following:

Avis (☎ 225-2385; www.avis.com) Offices at Philip Goldson International Airport and the Municipal Airstrip (Map p73).

Budget (☎ 223-2435/3986; www.budget-belize.com; Mile 2½ Northern Hwy) There is also an office at Philip Goldson International Airport.

Crystal Auto Rental (☎ 223-1600; www.crystal-belize .com; Mile 5 Northern Hwy) One of the best local firms; allows vehicles to be taken into Guatemala. There's another branch at Philip Goldson International Airport.

Euphrates Auto Rental (Map pp76-7; ☎ 227-5752, 614-6967; www.ears.bz; 143 Euphrates Ave, Southside) Local firm that offers some of the best deals in town.

Hertz (Map pp76-7; ☎ 223-0886/5395; www.hertz .com; 11A Cork St, Fort George District) Hertz also has a branch at Philip Goldson International Airport.

GETTING AROUND

Though many of the spots where travelers go are within walking distance of each other, it's always safest to take a taxi after dark.

To/From the Airports

There is no public transportation to or from either airport. The taxi fare to or from the international airport is US$20. An alternative is to walk the 1.6 miles from the airport to the Northern Hwy, where fairly frequent buses pass heading to or away from Belize City.

Taxis from the Municipal Airstrip to the center of town cost US$4 to US$5.

Car & Motorcycle

Belize City has the heaviest traffic in the country, as intense as that of a medium-sized country town in North America or

Europe. There's a limited one-way system, which is easy to work with. If you need to park on the street, try to do so right outside the place you're staying. Never leave anything that even looks valuable on view inside a parked car.

Taxi

Cabs cost US$3 for rides within the city, usually plus US$0.50 if you call the cab out, and maybe an extra US$0.50 if it's a long trip from one side of town to the other. Confirm the price in advance with your driver. If in doubt, check with your hotel or restaurant staff about what the cost should be before setting out.

AROUND BELIZE CITY

Within an hour's drive of Belize City are the important Maya ruins at Altun Ha, great birding at Crooked Tree Wildlife Sanctuary, howler-monkey observation at the Community Baboon Sanctuary, and close encounters with many of Belize's animal, reptile and bird species at the Belize Zoo. With a vehicle, you can often fit two of these destinations into one day. Most places in this section can be visited in day trips by public transportation too – although some, such as Crooked Tree, really merit an overnight stop.

ALTUN HA

The ruins that have inspired Belikin beer labels and Belizean banknotes, **Altun Ha** (admission US$5; ☼ 8am-5pm), stands 34 miles north of central Belize City, off the Old Northern Hwy.

Altun Ha was a rich and important Maya trading and agricultural town with a population of 8000 to 10,000 at its peak in the Classic Period. The entire site covered some 1500 acres, but what visitors today see is the central ceremonial precinct of two plazas surrounded by temples, excavated in the 1960s and now looking squeaky clean (almost too much so, in some people's view) following a stabilization and conservation program from 2000 to 2004.

Altun Ha existed by at least 200 BC, perhaps even several centuries earlier, and flourished until the mysterious collapse of Classic Maya civilization around AD 900.

BELIZE CITY

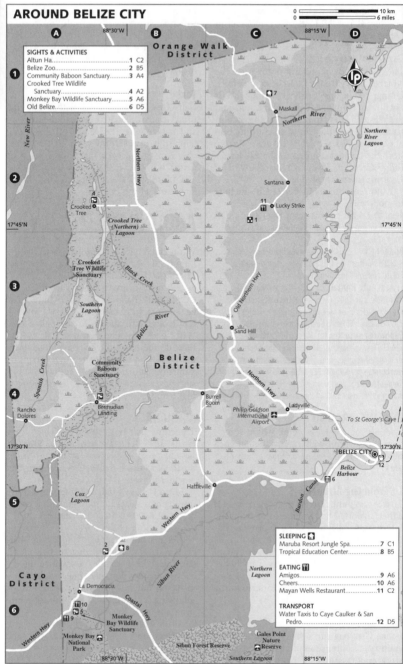

AROUND BELIZE CITY

0 —————— 10 km
0 —————— 6 miles

SIGHTS & ACTIVITIES
Altun Ha...**1** C2
Belize Zoo.......................................**2** B5
Community Baboon Sanctuary..........**3** A4
Crooked Tree Wildlife
   Sanctuary....................................**4** A2
Monkey Bay Wildlife Sanctuary.......**5** A6
Old Belize.......................................**6** D5

SLEEPING 🏠
Maruba Resort Jungle Spa.................**7** C1
Tropical Education Center.................**8** B5

EATING 🍴
Amigos...**9** A6
Cheers..**10** A6
Mayan Wells Restaurant.................**11** C2

TRANSPORT
Water Taxis to Caye Caulker & San
   Pedro..**12** D5

The appearance of most of the temples today date from around AD 550 to 650, though like many Maya temples most of them are composed of several layers, having been built over periodically in a series of renewals.

In Plaza A, Structure A-1 is sometimes called the **Temple of the Green Tomb**. Deep within it was discovered the tomb of a priest-king dating from around AD 600. Tropical humidity had destroyed the garments of the king and the paper of the Maya 'painted book' that was buried with him, but many riches were intact: shell necklaces, pottery, pearls, stingray spines used in bloodletting rites, ceremonial flints and the nearly 300 jade objects (mostly small beads and pendants) that gave rise to the name 'Green Tomb'.

The largest and most important temple is the **Temple of the Masonry Altars** (Structure B-4). The restored structure you see dates from the first half of the 7th century and takes its name from altars on which copal was burned and beautifully carved jade pieces were smashed in sacrifice. This is the Maya temple that's likely to become most familiar during your Belizean travels, since it's the one depicted (in somewhat stylized form) on Belikin beer labels.

Excavation of the structure in 1968 revealed several priestly tombs. Most had been destroyed or desecrated, but one, tomb B-4/7 (inside the stone structure protruding from the upper steps of the broad central staircase), contained the remains of an elderly personage accompanied by numerous jade objects, including a unique 6in-tall carved head of Kinich Ahau, the Maya sun god – the largest well-carved jade object ever recovered from a Maya archaeological site. (Look for the jade head illustration in the top left corner of Belizean banknotes.)

A path heading south from Structure B-6 leads 600yd through the jungle to a broad pond that was the main **Reservoir** of the ancient town.

Modern toilets, and drinks and souvenir stands are near the ticket office, and the site has good wheelchair access.

Sleeping & Eating

Mayan Wells Restaurant (Map p90; ☎ 220-6039; mayanwells@direcway.com; Altun Ha Rd; r US$30, camping per person US$5, lunch US$6; ☷ restaurant 8am-3:30pm

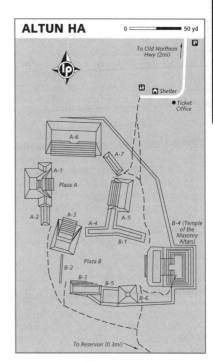

ALTUN HA

0 ▭ 50 yd

To Old Northern Hwy (2mi)

P

Shelter

Ticket Office

A-6

A-7

A-1

Plaza A

A-2

A-3

A-4

A-5

B-4 (Temple of the Masonry Altars)

B-1

Plaza B

B-2

B-3

B-5

B-6

To Reservoir (0.3mi)

Mon-Fri; P ▯) Mayan Wells, 1.4 miles from the ruins on the road in from the Old Northern Hwy, is a fine stop for lunch or refreshments. Traditional Belizean lunches of rice, beans, stewed chicken and a drink are served under a *palapa* (thatched-roof shelter) beside a cenote amid lovely tropical gardens. If you fancy staying, there's a cozy mosquito-netted cabana with private bathroom and hammock-slung verandah, accommodating up to four adults – or you can camp. All meals are available on request for people staying here, as is free Internet. Birders and other nature lovers will particularly enjoy this hospitable place.

Maruba Resort Jungle Spa (Map p90; ☎ 322-2199, in USA ☎ 713-799-2031, 800-627-8227; www.maruba -spa.com; Mile 40½ Old Northern Hwy; s/d US$187.25/214, ste US$289-749, breakfast/lunch/dinner US$12.50/14/35; P ✗ ☰) Maruba, 2 miles north of Maskall village (13 miles from Altun Ha), takes the jungle-lodge and spa concepts to extremes of expensive pampering. There are luxurious amenities and a slew of health and rejuvenation treatments. Lush tropical grounds harbor individually designed rooms in a variety of African, Creole, Maya and even Gaudiesque styles – including honeymoon and 'fertility' suites and a jungle tree house. There are two pools and a tree-house restaurant that serves good seafood, game and salads to nonguests as well as guests. For the active, there are a range of adventures and tours on offer.

Singles/doubles packages for one night start around US$350/510 (adventure) or US$580/830 (health and rejuvenation), but significant discounts on accommodation prices are often offered.

Maruba has come under fire from environmentalists for bottling snakes with rum and serving the concoction as 'viper rum.'

Getting There & Away

Many tours run to Altun Ha from Belize City or San Pedro on Ambergris Caye.

To get here in your own vehicle, turn off the Northern Hwy 20 miles from Belize City at a junction signed 'Altun Ha,' then drive 11.5 miles along the paved but narrow and often potholed Old Northern Hwy to Lucky Strike village, where a better paved road heads off west to Altun Ha (2.4 miles).

Buses to Maskall, four times daily from the Novelo's bus station in Belize City (see p88), will drop you at Lucky Strike. Heading back to the city, buses leave Maskall at 5:30am, 6am, 6:30am and 7am, passing through Lucky Strike 20 to 30 minutes later. Traffic along the jungle-lined Old Northern Hwy is not heavy so hitchhiking is usually difficult.

CROOKED TREE WILDLIFE SANCTUARY

A swift 32 miles up the Northern Hwy from Belize City is the turnoff to the farming village of Crooked Tree (population 900) at the heart of **Crooked Tree Wildlife Sanctuary** (Map p90; admission US$4), one of the best birding areas in Belize and well worth a visit for anyone who loves nature or fancies experiencing a peaceful rural community with an interesting history and a beautiful setting. It's best to stay the night so you can be here at dawn, when the birds are most active. The village has several midrange and budget accommodations. Don't forget your binoculars – though if you don't have any, local guides will probably be able to lend you a pair.

The story goes that Crooked Tree village got its name from early logwood cutters who boated up Belize River and Black Creek to a giant lagoon marked by a tree that seemingly grew in every direction. These 'crooked trees' (cashew trees, in fact) still grow in abundance around the lagoon. Founded in the early 18th century, Crooked Tree may be the oldest village in Belize. Until the 3½-mile causeway from the Northern Hwy was built in 1984, the only way to get here was by boat, so it's no wonder life still maintains the slow rhythm of bygone centuries.

The 25-sq-mile wildlife sanctuary was established in 1984 to protect the large population of resident and migratory birds here. Managed by the Belize Audubon Society (see p54), it comprises a network of waterways, lagoons and logwood swamps. Crooked Tree village itself, on the west bank of Crooked Tree Lagoon (also called Northern Lagoon), is excluded from the sanctuary along with adjacent lands on which its agriculture and livestock mainly rely.

Migrating birds flock to the lagoons, rivers and swamps each year between December and May. The best bird-watching months are usually February to May, when many migrants stop over on their way north, and the low level of the lagoon draws thousands of birds into the open to seek food in the shallows.

Bird-watchers are in for hours of ornithological bliss. Boat-billed, chestnut-bellied and bare-throated tiger herons, Muscovy and black-bellied whistling ducks, snail kites, ospreys, black-collared hawks and all of Belize's five species of kingfisher are among the 286 species recorded here (see a near-complete list at www.belizeaudubon .org/parks/ctws.htm). Jabiru storks, the largest flying bird in the Americas, with wingspans of up to 12ft, congregate here in April and May and a few pairs nest in the sanctuary in the preceding months.

A **visitors center** (☺ 8am-4:30pm), with good displays and a range of books and information materials for sale, stands at the entrance to the village, just off the causeway. Pay your US$4 admission fee here. The helpful, knowledgeable staff will give you a village and trail map and answer questions on anything to do with visiting the sanctuary, including information on expert local bird guides.

The obvious reference point in the village is the 'Welcome to Crooked Tree' sign, at a junction 300yd past the visitors center as you enter the village from the causeway.

A series of reasonably well-signposted walking trails weave along the lakeshores and through and beyond the village. About 3 miles north of the village center are an excellent 700yd boardwalk and an observation tower, allowing access to swampy areas of thick, low vegetation around the lagoon's edge. From December or January to May you can reach the boardwalk by driving and walking; the rest of the year you'll need a boat to reach it.

If you can afford it, take a boat tour as well as walking. A two-to-three-hour boat tour, costing US$70 to US$80 for up to four people, can be arranged at the main accommodations (see Sleeping & Eating below). A boat trip gets you out onto the lagoon and into the surrounding swamps.

You can also explore Spanish and Black Creeks, leading south out of the main lagoon, which, with their thick tree cover, harbor plenty of birds all year. Black Creek is also home to black howler monkeys, Morelet's crocodiles, coatimundi and several species of turtle and iguana; Spanish Creek gives access to Chau Hix, an ancient Maya site with a pyramid 80ft high.

Festivals & Events

Crooked Tree is home to a great number of cashew trees and the village's annual **Cashew Festival** (first weekend in May) celebrates the cashew harvest in a big way, with music and dancing and lots of cracking, shelling, roasting and stewing of cashews, and making of cashew cake, cashew jelly, cashew ice cream, cashew wine (not unlike sweet sherry) and cashew you-name-it. The harvest season continues into July.

Sleeping & Eating

Bird's Eye View Lodge (☎ 205-7027, 203-2040, in USA ☎ 570-588-0844; www.birdseyeviewlodge.com; s/tw/d/tr downstairs US$47/59/71/82, s/d/tr upstairs US$71/94/106, camping per person US$6, meals US$11-13; **P** 🕸) This lodge is right on the lagoonside at the south end of the village, 1 mile from the 'Welcome to Crooked Tree' sign. It's the most comfortable place in town, and it's popular with birders. The ample rooms, with good beds, bathrooms, fans and reading lights,

are clean if old-fashioned, and most look out onto the lagoon. Good meals are served in a bright dining room. For a room with air-conditioning, add US$10.70. Room rates are reduced by up to one-third from May 15 to October 30. The lodge offers lagoon boat tours, nature walks with experienced bird guides (per person per hour US$5), horseback riding (per hour US$10) and canoe rental (per person per hour US$5).

Paradise Inn (☎ 225-7044; fax 203-2579; cabanas for up to 2/4/5/8 US$37/48/55/75, camping per tent US$10, breakfast/lunch/dinner US$4/4/7; **P**) Also enjoying a considerable reputation among birders, the Crawford family offers simple wooden cabanas with bathrooms, hot water, fans, verandahs and mosquito nets and screens, in a beautiful, shaded lagoonside position. Boat trips here are US$70 for up to four people, plus US$15 for each extra person; nature walks are US$25 per group.

One of the family, Glenn Crawford, is a renowned birding guide who leads tours in Belize and several Latin American countries for the US-based company **Wildside Tours** (www.adventurecamera.com).

To get to Paradise Inn, turn right at the 'Welcome to Crooked Tree' sign, veer right after 0.5 miles at the 'Paradise Inn' sign, and stop at the Crawford family house, marked 'Paradise Inn Information,' after 150yd. You'll be shown the lakeside accommodations, 0.5 miles further on.

Sam Tillett's Hotel & Tours (☎ 220-2026; sam hotel@btl.net; s/d/cabanas US$30/41.50/64.75, d with air-con US$53, breakfast/lunch/dinner US$4/6/8; **P** 🕸) Sam Tillett is a celebrated Crooked Tree bird guide, although he's not always around to do the job himself. The nine thatched rooms and cabanas here are clean, and have bird murals and private bathrooms. Sam's is beside the main street, 500yd north of the 'Welcome to Crooked Tree' sign.

Rhaburn's Rooms (☎ 225-7035; s/d US$10/15; **P**) The four wooden rooms here are small but clean and neat, with fans and a shared hot-water bathroom and verandah. Owners Owen and Maggie Rhaburn are friendly and welcoming. Go south at the 'Welcome to Crooked Tree' sign and after 300yd cross the cricket field on the right immediately past the Church of the Nazarene. Follow the track through the trees from the far left corner of the cricket field and you'll see the Rhaburn's sign on the first bend. The house is the cream-colored one on the left side of the broad lawn area.

3-J's Restaurant (snacks US$0.50-1.50, mains US$2.50-4; 🕙 10am-9pm Sun-Thu, 10am-midnight Fri & Sat) The open-to-the-air 3-J's is the hub of Crooked Tree's mellow social life, with a pool table on one side and a restaurant on the other. The menu runs from burgers and *salbutes* to fish and chips or US$4 T-bone steaks (this is cattle-raising country), and plenty of cold Belikins. 3-J's is on the main street, about 300yd north of the 'Welcome to Crooked Tree' sign.

Getting There & Away

Driving to Crooked Tree is easiest. For those without a vehicle, Bird's Eye View Lodge, Paradise Inn and Sam Tillett's Hotel & Tours offer transfers to or from Belize City or the international airport for between US$45 and US$85 per group of up to four people, and **Jex & Sons** (☎ 225-7017) runs buses from Belize City (US$1.75, one hour). See p88 for details of bus departures from Belize City. Departures to Belize City from Crooked Tree are at 5am, 6:30am and 7am, Monday to Saturday. Alternatively, you can get a bus on the Northern Hwy to the Crooked Tree turnoff, then walk the 3.5 miles to the village.

COMMUNITY BABOON SANCTUARY

No real baboons inhabit Belize, but Belizeans use that name for black howler monkeys. Though howler monkeys live throughout Central and South America, the endangered black howler exists only in Belize, northern Guatemala and southern Mexico. The **Community Baboon Sanctuary** (CBS; Map p90; www.howlermonkeys.org), spread over several long-established Creole villages in the Belize River valley, has engineered a big increase in this primate's population and is doubly interesting because it's a completely community-run, grassroots conservation operation. In addition to the near-certainty of seeing some of these fascinating primates, the sanctuary offers river trips (day and night) and horseback riding. There are also nearly 200 bird species here to keep wildlife watchers busy.

The sanctuary came into being in 1985 after American zoologist Robert Horwich discovered that the area's black howler population was shrinking into separate 'islands' due to encroachment of agriculture, logging and hunting. Initially, just a small group of farmers from the village of Bermudian Landing (population 420) signed an agreement to protect the monkeys' habitat. Today, more than 200 landowners not only from Bermudian Landing but also from the exotically named nearby villages of Double Head Cabbage, Flowers Bank, Isabella Bank, Scotland Half Moon, St Pauls Bank and Willows Bank have pledged to conserve the black howler's habitat over approximately 20 sq miles.

The local Women's Conservation Group, led by Jesse Young, took over full management of the sanctuary in the late 1990s. Income to the community from tourism is essential to the sanctuary's success and to the landowners' continued willingness to participate.

Today a growing population of howlers feed, sleep and, at dawn and dusk, howl – or rather, roar – loudly, unmistakably and somewhat eerily in a thriving broadleaf-forest habitat. A howler's call can be heard a mile or more away. Black howlers are vegetarians and spend most of their daylight hours in troops of five to 12, grazing the treetops for fruits, flowers, leaves and other tidbits. They are led by a dominant male (who does most of the 'howling,' to defend his troop's territory). The sanctuary area's black-howler population has risen from around 800 in the 1980s to some 3000 today. In the 1990s, over 60 howlers from here were successfully relocated to the Cockscomb Basin Wildlife Sanctuary in southern Belize, where the species had been destroyed by yellow fever and habitat destruction.

The **visitors center** (☎ 220-2181; admission US$5; 🕙 8am-5pm), in Bermudian Landing, has informative displays on the black howler, the history of the sanctuary, and other Belizean wildlife. Here you can organize activities you'd like to participate in. Included with the admission fee is a one-hour guided nature walk on which you are more or less certain to encounter a resident troop of black howlers. Along the way the trained local guides also impart their knowledge of the many medicinal plants. Other possibilities include a 1½-hour night forest hike (US$10), horseback riding (US$25), a three-hour canoe tour (US$25) on the

Belize River, with its many birds, and a three-hour night canoe tour (US$50) on Mussel Creek, where you're likely to spot crocodiles and other nocturnal wildlife.

Sleeping & Eating

Nature Resort (☎ 223-3668; naturer@btl.net; cabanas US$28-65; P ✖) Right next to the visitor center, this is the most comfortable place to stay, with friendly management and clean, well-maintained cabanas holding up to four people, spread around an attractive lawn area with some trees. Most have private bathrooms (with unheated water); one is air-conditioned.

Bed & Breakfast (d incl 2 meals US$22.50) B&B is available in local homes or specially built visitor cabanas in several Community Baboon Sanctuary villages. Conditions are rustic (not all places have showers or flush toilets), but there's no better way to experience Creole village life. Book at the visitors center.

Howler Monkey Lodge (☎ 220-2158; www.howler monkeylodge.com; s/d/tr cabanas US$15/30/45; P) The cabanas have fans, mosquito screens, solid wooden beds and private bathrooms, but the whole place seems thoroughly uncared for. The only compensations are its setting above a bend above the Belize River, 400yd from the visitors center, and regular visits by howler monkeys.

CBS Restaurant (meals US$3-4; ✖ 7:30am-7:30pm) The restaurant by the visitors center serves plain but adequate local meals – rice and beans, *garnaches*, *panades*, eggs, coffee and soft drinks.

Getting There & Away

Bermudian Landing is 28 miles west of Belize City. In your own vehicle, leave the Northern Hwy at the turnoff for Burrell Boom. Turn right into Burrell Boom village after 3 miles, then carry straight on to Bermudian Landing, 9 miles beyond. If you're heading to western Belize after you visit the sanctuary, save time by taking the direct road 8 miles south from Burrell Boom to Hattieville on the Western Hwy.

R-Line buses run between Belize City and Bermudian Landing (US$1.50, one hour). See p88 for details of departures from Belize City. Departures from Bermudian Landing to Belize City are at 6:20am, 6:30am and 4pm Monday to Friday, and 6:30am and 6:45am Saturday.

OLD BELIZE

Though designed to provide hurried cruise-ship tourists with selected highlights of Belizean history and culture in one handy capsule, this **exhibit** (Map p90; ☎ 222-4129/4286; www.oldbelize.com; Mile 5 Western Hwy; adult/under-13s/under-6s US$7.50/3.75/free; ✖ 8am-4pm Tue-Sat, 10am-4pm Sun & Mon) is kind of fun even if you don't fit into that category.

Guides take roughly 45 minutes to lead you through exhibit sections on rainforest, traditional Maya and Garifuna lifestyles, and the sugarcane, chicle and logging industries, and ends with a reconstruction of an early-20th-century Belize City street. The genuine old machines and artifacts, including a sugarcane press and a steam tractor used for dragging logs, are interesting even if some of the tableaus are a bit kitsch. A good gift shop adds to the appeal. Old Belize's partly open-air restaurant, **Sibun Bite Bar & Grill** (mains US$6-12.50; ✖ 9am-9pm), serves up good burgers and grilled shrimp and chicken dishes. It overlooks the sea.

Any Belmopan-bound bus from the Novelo's terminal will drop you at the Old Belize entrance (US$0.50, 10 minutes).

BELIZE ZOO

Anyone with an interest in Belize's wildlife should visit this very popular and well-cared-for **zoo** (Map p90; ☎ 220-8004; www.belizezoo .org; Mile 29 Western Hwy; adult/child US$8/4; ✖ 8:30am-5pm, closed major public holidays), set in natural forest 31 miles from Belize City along the Western Hwy. You'll see many animals here that you'd otherwise only see in movies or brochures.

When filmmaker Richard Foster shot a wildlife documentary entitled *Path of the Raingods* in Belize in the early 1980s, Sharon Matola – a Baltimore-born biologist, former circus performer and former US Air Force survival instructor – was hired to take care of the animals. By the time filming was over, the animals had become partly tame and Matola was left wondering what to do with her 17 charges. So she founded the Belize Zoo, which displays native Belizean wildlife in natural surroundings on 29-acre grounds.

It takes one to 1½ hours to walk around the zoo. You'll see more than 100 native animals, including jaguars, pumas, ocelots, monkeys, peccaries, crocodiles, tapirs, jabiru storks, scarlet macaws and one magnificent harpy eagle (an effort is underway to reintroduce this largest-of-all-eagles to Belize). All the creatures in the zoo came here orphaned, injured, confiscated from illegal captivity, or were born here or given by other zoos.

One of the Belize Zoo's central goals is to make Belizeans sensitive to the value of preserving native wildlife. To this end, signs throughout the zoo implore visitors not to hunt, skin or eat the wild relatives of the zoo's residents. Matola keeps busy running outreach and educational programs.

Sleeping & Eating

Tropical Education Center (TEC; ☎ 220-8003; tec@belizezoo.org; Mile 29 Western Hwy; camping per person US$6.40, dm per person US$16, d cabanas US$35, d guesthouses US$37.50, meals US$5-6; P) The zoo's environmental education center, situated just over 1 mile away, is an excellent accommodation option for travelers, set on 84 acres of tropical savanna with lush gardens and good birding (with a treetop viewing platform).

Sleeping options run from electricity-free dorms to neat, modern 'tent cabanas' (made of wood, on stilts, with electricity and fan), and two 'VIP guesthouses' with private bathrooms and kitchens overlooking the center's own small lake (home to Morelet's crocodiles). All options have good mosquito screens. If you want meals here, you need to request them in advance.

The TEC also offers nocturnal zoo visits (adult/child US$10/6, with a minimum of five people), and canoe trips on the nearby Sibun River (half/full day per two-person canoe US$30/40). The TEC is 0.9 miles off the Western Hwy, from a signposted turning 0.2 miles east of the zoo. If you're staying, staff can pick you up from the zoo.

A few drinks and snacks are available in the zoo's **gift shop** (8:30am-5pm, closed major public holidays). It's an easy drive a couple of miles along the highway to one of the good restaurants near Monkey Bay Wildlife Sanctuary (see opposite).

Getting There & Away

Any nonexpress bus heading along the Western Hwy will drop you at the zoo entrance (US$1.50, 45 minutes from Belize City).

MONKEY BAY WILDLIFE SANCTUARY & AROUND

Monkey Bay Wildlife Sanctuary (Map p90; ☎ 820-3032; www.monkeybaybelize.org; Mile 31½ Western Hwy; camping per person US$7.50, bunkhouses per person US$10, tr cabanas US$17.50; P) is a wildlife refuge and environmental education center that also offers lodging and activities for travelers. Established in the 1980s by conservationists Matthew and Marga Miller, the 1.7-sq-mile sanctuary stretches from the Western Hwy to the Sibun River, encompassing areas of tropical forest and savannah.

Across the river is the remote, 3.5-sq-mile **Monkey Bay National Park**, which together with the sanctuary creates a sizable forest corridor in the Sibun River Valley. Monkey Bay itself is a riverbend once noted for its resident black howler monkeys. Black howlers have recently returned to the national park thanks to a rehabilitation project (not open to visitors) based at Monkey Bay Wildlife Sanctuary.

Accommodations at the sanctuary range from camping out on offground decks to mosquito-screened bunkhouses or cabanas for three with fans. The amenities demonstrate ecological principles in action, with bio-gas latrines producing methane for cooking, rainwater catchment and partial solar energy. Independent visitors can partake of group meals if a group is present: otherwise you can make your own meals. By the time you read this the sanctuary should have further accommodations and possibly a restaurant (located at the former JB's Watering Hole some 400yd along the Western Hwy).

Around 230 bird species have been identified at the sanctuary. Larger wildlife such as pumas and coatimundi have been spotted on the 2-mile track running down beside the sanctuary to the river. A well-stocked library provides plenty of reference and reading matter on natural history and Belize. Also at the site is a splendid green iguana enclosure – these monarchs of the lizard world can grow 6ft long.

It's advisable to contact the sanctuary in advance to find out what activities will be available when you visit. Possibilities include canoe and caving trips and dry-season trips to Cox Lagoon, about 12 miles north, which is home to jabiru storks, deer, tapir, black howlers and lots of crocodiles. For the hardy and adventurous, the Indian Creek Trail is a demanding 21-mile, three-day, guided jungle trek south to Five Blues Lake National Park, which costs around US$300 for a group of four. You must supply your own food and tent or hammock (or rent a tent or jungle hammock with mosquito net for US$7.50 per day).

Eating

Within a few hundred yards along the Western Hwy, either side of Monkey Bay Wildlife Sanctuary, are two fun eateries that are often filled with just-off-the-plane travelers happily adjusting to the fact that they're on holiday. Each serves Belizean, Mexican and American dishes and ice-cold Belikins, all at moderate prices.

Cheers (Map p90; ☎ 614-9311; Mile 31¼ Western Hwy; mains US$5-10; ☯ breakfast, lunch & dinner) This large, airy and friendly place serves hearty meals, from all-day breakfasts to rice and beans, burritos and steaks. It's about 500yd east of the Monkey Bay turnoff.

Amigos (Map p90; ☎ 822-3031; Mile 31⅔ Western Hwy; mains US$4-8.50; ☯ 8am-10pm) Mosquito-screened windows and the views to distant southern mountains make a great backdrop to the satisfying fare here, 200yd west of the sanctuary turnoff.

Getting There & Away

Any nonexpress bus on the Western Hwy will drop you at the sanctuary turnoff (around 220yd from the main entrance) or at Cheers or Amigos (US$1.50, 50 minutes from Belize City).

Northern Cayes

This beautiful part of the world has over a hundred islands or cayes, two captivating atolls and 80 miles of virtually uninterrupted barrier reef. Accommodations from camping to fancy resorts are available. The beauty that you see above water level – waters of all hues of blue, white sands, swaying coconut palms, fluffy clouds, soaring birds – is equaled underwater with coral gardens, canyons, shark and ray alleys and schools of colorful fish that never fail to delight.

The two most visited islands are Ambergris Caye and Caye Caulker. Ambergris is expensive and resorty, while relaxed and popular Caulker is consciously shifting its image upmarket. Both islands have an appealing, laid-back Belizean atmosphere. It's normal to slip into a hammock and sip a tropical fruit juice, maybe spiked with rum. Nature envelops you even on these two more populous islands: glistening turquoise waters lap the sandy shores, white-tipped waves crash onto the reef in the distance and lush tropical foliage abounds. Attractive palm-thatched huts function as bars and eateries, serving up the freshest of seafood. Traditional wooden Caribbean houses, colorfully decorated or on stilts, add character. Wooden piers or docks make quaint additions to the landscape. You'll also find a party atmosphere if you want it, spectacular sunrises and sunsets, gentle breezes and a background of hypnotic reggae.

Residents include Creoles, Mestizos and a growing number of North American and European expats. Costs are high compared with other Central American destinations, but not outrageously expensive when compared with other Caribbean destinations.

HIGHLIGHTS

- Snorkeling the exciting **Hol Chan Marine Reserve** and **Shark Ray Alley** (p105)
- Diving among the pristine coral on the **atolls** (p126) and adventuring down the **Blue Hole** (p127)
- Enjoying the carefree, Caribbean lifestyle of **San Pedro** (p100)
- Chilling out on **Caye Caulker** (p116)
- **Kayaking** (p107 and p119) in translucent ocean waters

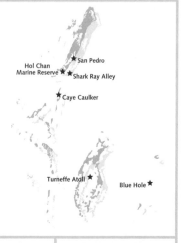

- POPULATION: 10,000
- MONTHLY RAINFALL: JAN/JUN 4IN/8IN (SAN PEDRO)
- HIGHEST ELEVATION: 50FT

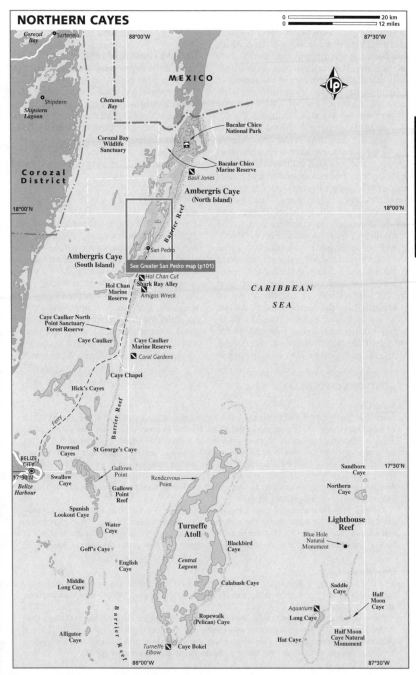

NORTHERN CAYES

NORTHERN CAYES

0 ────────── 20 km
0 ────────── 12 miles

88°00'W
87°30'W

Corozal Bay ○ Sarteneja

MEXICO

● Shipstern
Shipstern Lagoon

Chetumal Bay

Bacalar Chico National Park

Corozal Bay Wildlife Sanctuary

Corozal District

Bacalar Chico Marine Reserve

🔲 Basil Jones

18°00'N

Ambergris Caye (North Island)

18°00'N

Ambergris Caye (South Island)

○ San Pedro

See Greater San Pedro map (p101)

🔲 Hol Chan Cut
Shark Ray Alley

Hol Chan Marine Reserve

🔲 Amigos Wreck

CARIBBEAN SEA

Caye Caulker North Point Sanctuary Forest Reserve

Caye Caulker

Caye Caulker Marine Reserve

🔲 Coral Gardens

Caye Chapel

Hick's Cayes

Ferry

Barrier Reef

Drowned Cayes

St George's Caye

BELIZE CITY ◉

17°30'N

Gallows Point

Rendezvous Point

Sandbore Caye

17°30'N

Belize Harbour

Swallow Caye

Gallows Point Reef

Northern Caye

Spanish Lookout Caye

Lighthouse Reef

Water Caye

Turneffe Atoll

Blue Hole Natural Monument ●

Goff's Caye

Blackbird Caye

English Caye

Central Lagoon

Middle Long Caye

Calabash Caye

Saddle Caye

Half Moon Caye

Aquarium 🔲
Long Caye

Alligator Caye

Turneffe Elbow 🔲 Caye Bokel

Ropewalk (Pelican) Caye

Hat Caye

Half Moon Caye Natural Monument

88°00'W
87°30'W

History

The history of the northern cayes is essentially the history of Ambergris Caye, which has been the main population center since Maya times. The northern part of the island, with its strategic position at the mouth of Chetumal Bay, was a hub in the Maya trade network, a port of call for traders coming down from the Yucatán Peninsula.

The Maya evaporated during the era of the whalers and the British buccaneers. Small treasure troves have been discovered on the island, and gold coins and old bottles have been washed ashore, evidence of pirates using the island for its fresh water, abundant resources and hidden coves. These swashbucklers turned into mainland loggers who partly depended on manatees and turtles from the northern cayes for their survival.

Following on from the buccaneers came the ancestors of today's residents, who were fisherfolk and worked on the coconut plantations. The 20th century was dominated by the lobster industry and the arrival of tourism. Today the northern cayes are fast catching up on technology. Tourism, high-speed Internet and satellite telephones have increased contact with the outside world. While life goes slow on the cayes, the population is acquiring the accoutrements of the Western world in the 21st century.

Getting There & Around

Scheduled flights and regular passenger boats go from Belize City to San Pedro (on Ambergris Caye) and Caye Caulker, and from Corozal to San Pedro. Caye Chapel and Northern Caye (Lighthouse Reef) also have airstrips. No scheduled boats run to/from the outer islands. To reach them, take a tour or charter your own boat. If you're staying at resorts on the outer islands, transportation may well be provided.

AMBERGRIS CAYE

pop 7600

The largest of Belize's cayes, palm-fringed Ambergris ('am-*ber*-griss', sometimes 'am-*ber*-jis') is the country's top getaway destination. It's 36 miles north of Belize City and is long and thin, measuring about 25 miles long and 5 miles wide at its widest point, though much of it is less than half a mile wide. Its unpopulated northern extremity abuts Mexican territory, so most locals speak a form of Spanish as well as English and Creole, and some Mexican customs, foods and fiestas continue. Sun-drenched

---

NORTHERN CAYES IN...

Four Days

Starting at San Pedro, breakfast on day one at a choice spot like **Celi's Deli & Restaurant** (p112) or **Sandbucks** (see p112). Snorkel at **Hol Chan Marine Reserve** and **Shark Ray Alley** (p105). Enjoy a leisurely lunch south of town at **Admiral Nelson's Barefoot Beachfront Bar** (p113), hang out on the beach then stroll back to town with the sunset. Head to **Fido's Courtyard Bar** (p114) for the rest of the evening. Start day two with a take-out breakfast from **Ruby's Cafe** (p112) then cycle north, stopping for a drink and a swim wherever you fancy. Lunch at **Capricorn Restaurant** (p113). Cycle on as far as you wish then dine at **Mambo Restaurant** (p114). Finally, put your bicycle on a boat back to town.

On day three take a boat to Caye Caulker. Swim at the Split. Lunch at **Rasta Pasta Rainforest Cafe** (p124). Rent a bicycle for the afternoon and cruise around. Dine and then nightcap at **Habaneros** restaurant (p124). Day four begins early with a snorkel tour to **Lighthouse Reef** (p127). Dine at **Don Corleone** (p124). Wind down with reggae and rum at the **I&I Reggae Bar** (p125).

One Week

Add one day extra on Ambergris and two further days on Caulker. On Ambergris, kayak the lagoon side of San Pedro, then take a **sunset sail** (p107). Afterward, sample **Caramba Restaurant's** savory flavors (p112).

For your extra two days on Caulker, first **bird-watch** at dawn (p121). Breakfast at **Cindy's Café** (p125) and relax in a hammock before **snorkeling** the local reef in the afternoon (p121). Dine at **Coco Plum Gardens** (p125). On your last day take a **manatee tour** (p119) and choose a restaurant for dinner before Rasta Ripper nightcaps at **Rasta Pasta Rainforest Cafe** (p124).

GREATER SAN PEDRO

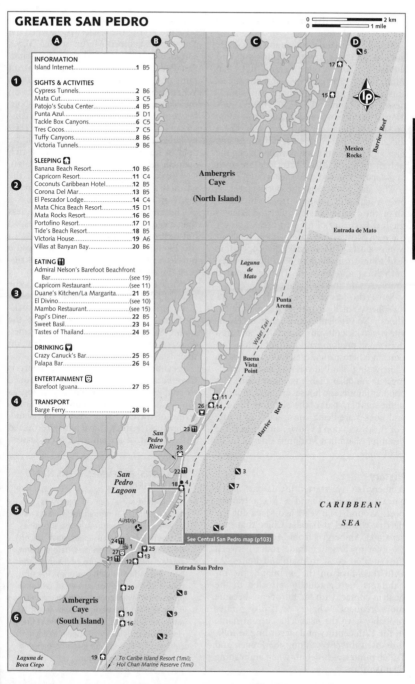

NORTHERN CAYES

0   2 km
0   1 mile

Ambergris
Caye

(North Island)

Mexico
Rocks

Barrier Reef

Entrada de Mato

Laguna
de
Mato

Punta
Arena

Water Taxi

Buena
Vista
Point

Barrier Reef

San
Pedro
River

San
Pedro
Lagoon

CARIBBEAN

SEA

Airstrip

See Central San Pedro map (p103)

Entrada San Pedro

Ambergris
Caye

(South Island)

Laguna de
Boca Ciego

To Caribe Island Resort (1mi);
Hol Chan Marine Reserve (1mi)

and activity-filled days by turquoise seas are the drawcard here.

Most of the island's population lives in the town of San Pedro, near the southern tip, and the entire island is often referred to as San Pedro. San Pedro's colorful and sandy streets are lined with resorts, gift shops, banks, businesses and homes. There are many traditional Caribbean wooden houses – some on stilts, some are brightly painted, others dilapidated – but concrete is fast appearing. Bars and restaurants, many strung along the waterfront on the island's reef side, are often in *palapas* (thatched-roof shelters).

The star attraction, the barrier reef, is only a half-mile offshore from San Pedro. Sit on the docks when it's quiet and listen to the low bass roar of the surf breaking over the reef. Most visitors are passionate about water sports. The island's dive operators lead tours to more than 35 different sites, both local and beyond. The reef-related tours are safe and well managed.

San Pedro has an engaging, laid-back atmosphere. You'll see plenty of 'No Shirt, No Shoes – No Problem!' signs. Sandy streets invite you to kick off your shoes. Golf carts are a quirky and predominant form of transportation, and there are few cars, though car traffic is increasing. San Pedro is no Cancún (buildings are no taller than a coconut palm), but condominiums and houses are mushrooming in the southern part of the island, and resorts and houses are being constructed up north. For those who don't know, Ambergris is the beautiful island that Madonna sings of in 'La Isla Bonita.'

History

Ambergris Caye started life as part of the Yucatán Peninsula and a Maya trading post. Around 1500 years ago Maya dug the narrow channel at Bacalar Chico that now separates Ambergris from Mexico in order to open up a better trade route between the Yucatán coast to mainland Belize. As with the Maya on the mainland, the inhabitants here gradually retreated to the bush as contact with the Europeans became more frequent. Whalers or British pirates probably gave the island its current name in the 17th century and, according to folklore, used the coves, alongside French and Dutch pirates, as hideouts when ambushing Spanish ships.

Ambergris wasn't significantly populated until the War of the Castes (p29), when the Yucatán first forced Mestizos, then Maya, across Bacalar Chico and onto the island. San Pedro (named for Peter, the patron saint of fishermen) was founded in 1848. While fisherfolk lived in relative peace on the island, its ownership was bandied about between a group of wealthy British mainlanders. The land was purchased in 1869 by James Hume Blake for US$625 with the gold of his wife, Antonia Andrade, a rich Spanish refugee widow from the Yucatán. The Blake family converted much of the island to a coconut plantation, conscripting many of the islanders to work the land.

The coconut business thrived for less than a century. By the 1950s it had been all but destroyed by a series of hurricanes. In the 1960s, the Belize government forced a purchase of Ambergris Caye and redistributed the land to the islanders.

While the coconut industry declined, the island's lobster industry began to develop. The market for these crustaceans skyrocketed once refrigerated ships came to the island. San Pedro lobster catchers formed cooperatives and built a freezer plant on their island.

Inevitably, the waters close to Ambergris Caye became fished out. Fisherfolk looked to supplement their income by acting as tour, fishing and dive guides for the smattering of travelers who visited the island. Today lobster stocks have partly recovered with the aid of an annual closed season,

DRAGONS, PERFUMES & THE NAME 'AMBERGRIS'

The commonly accepted theory is that Ambergris Caye is named for a waxy gray substance manufactured in the intestines of sperm whales. It used to wash up on the island in great quantities, before sperm whales were hunted into oblivion in the late 19th and early 20th centuries. The substance was valued for its use in perfume production. When combined with civet and musk, it fixed the perfume, allowing it to retain its fragrance for a longer time. Precious ambergris was well known to ancient cultures: the Chinese, for instance, believed it was produced by dragons.

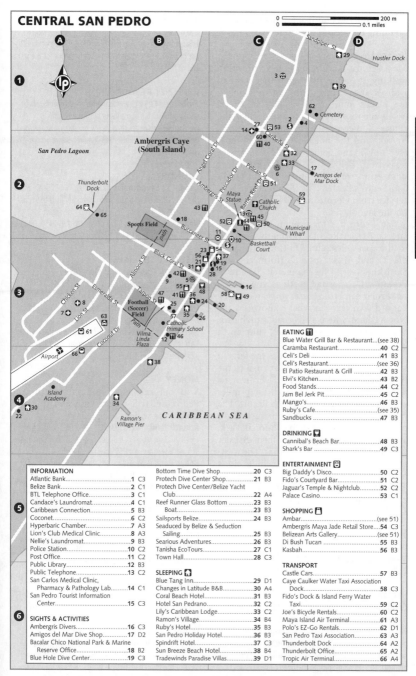

CENTRAL SAN PEDRO

NORTHERN CAYES

and it's tourism and real estate that are the booming businesses on Ambergris.

Orientation

Most services and many hotels are within walking distance of each other in San Pedro's town center. The airstrip is only a few blocks south of the center. Numerous hotels and resorts are south and north of the center. You can reach the southern resorts by taxi and the northern resorts by boat (see p115), and some by golf cart. Water taxis from Belize City and Caye Caulker dock on the reef side of the island right in San Pedro's center. The Thunderbolt boat service from Corozal and Belize City docks on the lagoon side.

San Pedro has three main north–south streets: Barrier Reef Dr (formerly Front St, to the east); Pescador Dr (formerly Middle St); and Angel Coral Dr (formerly Back St, to the west). The channel at the end of Pescador Dr is as far north as you can go by regular car. From there, you can cross by hand-drawn ferry to what's known as the North Island, where a dirt road, suitable for 4WDs, golf carts and bicycles, runs north for at least 8.5 miles.

About half a mile north from the ferry, a side track branches off the dirt road to the beach and Palapa Bar (see p114). From here, a path hugs the narrow beach for 6 miles north to the Mata Chica Beach Resort. The northernmost section of Ambergris Caye constitutes Bacalar Chico National Park, and the surrounding waters form Bacalar Chico Marine Reserve (see p108). The western shore has mangroves and wildlife along much of its length.

There may soon be a bridge across the channel and a 13-mile paved road to the southern edge of the national park.

Information

EMERGENCY
Medical, fire & police (☎ 911)
Police (Map p103; ☎ 226-2022; Barrier Reef Dr)

INTERNET ACCESS
Caribbean Connection (Map p103; ☎ 226-4664; cnr Barrier Reef Dr & Black Coral St; per hr US$8; ☼ 7am-10pm) High-speed connections, CD burning, international phone calls, excellent coffee, unique jewelry.
Coconet (Map p103; ☎ 226-2834; Barrier Reef Dr; per hr US$9; ☼ 8am-9pm) High-speed connections, CD burning, international phone calls, and (after 15 minutes) free drinks.
Island Internet (Map p101; ☎ 226-3777; Coconut Dr; per hr US$10; ☼ 7:30am-10pm) Convenient for the south end of the island.

INTERNET RESOURCES
Ambergris Caye (www.ambergriscaye.com) Excellent island information and a lively message board.
Go Ambergriscaye.com (www.goambergriscaye.com) Detailed information including comprehensive accommodations listings.

LAUNDRY
Candace's Laundromat (Map p103; ☎ 226-2052; Barrier Reef Dr; do-it-yourself wash & dry per load US$7, full service US$8; ☼ 8am-9pm Mon-Fri, 10am-6pm Sun)
Nellie's Laundromat (Map p103; ☎ 226-2454; Pescador Dr; full service per lb US$1; ☼ 7am-9pm Mon-Sat)

MEDICAL SERVICES
Hyperbaric Chamber (Map p103; ☎ 226-2851; Lion St) Center for diving accidents, next door to the Lions Club.
Lions Club Medical Clinic (Map p103; ☎ 226-4052, 603-1755; Lion St) Across the street from the Maya Island Air terminal at the airport.
San Carlos Medical Clinic, Pharmacy & Pathology Lab (Map p103; ☎ 226-2918, emergencies ☎ 614-9251; Pescador Dr) Treats ailments and does blood tests.

MONEY
You can exchange money easily in San Pedro, and US dollars cash and traveler's checks are widely accepted.
Atlantic Bank (Map p103; ☎ 226-2195; Barrier Reef Dr; ☼ 8am-2pm Mon-Fri, 8:30am-noon Sat) Near Buccaneer St; cash advances cost US$5 per transaction.
Belize Bank (Map p103; ☎ 226-2450; Barrier Reef Dr; ☼ 8am-3pm Mon-Thu, 8am-4:30pm Fri) At the north end of San Pedro; has the only ATM in town for international Visa, MasterCard and American Express cards; cash advances are US$8.

POST
Post office (Map p103; ☎ 226-2250; Alijua Bldg, Barrier Reef Dr; ☼ 8am-noon & 1-4pm Mon-Fri)

TOURIST INFORMATION
The weekly *San Pedro Sun* is full of news and helpful information. It comes out on Friday. The rival *Ambergris Today*, also published weekly, is useful.
San Pedro Tourist Information Center (Map p103; ☎ 226-2903; Barrier Reef Dr; ☼ 10am-1pm Mon-Sat) Next to the town hall; has plentiful giveaway information.

DIVING & SNORKELING AROUND AMBERGRIS CAYE

Dive masters usually choose a site based on weather conditions. On stormy or windy days you're likely to stay within the reef where the water is calmer and the visibility better. High gas prices may keep the sites chosen closer to San Pedro too.

Sites are usually named for a nearby landmark. So, for example, you have Victoria Tunnels (Map p101) across from Victoria House. The popular Tackle Box Canyons (Map p101) site is named after the former Tackle Box Bar (where Shark's Bar is now). Local dives include cuts, canyons, tunnels and caverns. Apart from the otherworldly coral and sponge formations, you'll see grouper, shark and barracuda, schools of colorful smaller fish darting about, and a variety of worms, shrimp and other creatures living in the coral crevices.

Most Popular Sites

Hol Chan Cut, Tackle Box Canyons, Tres Cocos, Tuffy Canyons, Cypress Tunnels and nearby Victoria Tunnels, as well as *Amigos Wreck,* have the widest variety of coral formations and marine life around Ambergris Caye.

Best to See Large Animals

Sites near cuts are usually good for seeing large, hungry fish, which are attracted by the currents and the variety of tasty marine life that comes into the cuts. These include Mata Cut and Punta Azul.

Best for Coral-Viewing

Tuffy Canyon maintains a terrific variety of coral, including staghorn, elkhorn, brain, lettuce and gorgonian fans.

Best to See Turtles

You'll have a good chance of seeing turtles around Tackle Box Canyons and Coral Gardens during March and April.

Best & Only Wreck

Amigos Wreck, the only one on the reef, is in Hol Chan Marine Reserve. It's a 60ft barge intentionally sunk to provide a marine habitat. Living in and around it are several nurse sharks and large green moray eels.

Hol Chan & Shark Ray Alley

The Hol Chan Marine Reserve lies close to Ambergris Caye and so is perhaps the best known as well as the longest-established marine reserve in Belize. It encompasses 5 sq miles, and is dotted with coral formations, at depths to 30ft. Visiting divers will make first for the Hol Chan Cut (Hol Chan is Mayan for a 'small channel' in the reef), where there are many steep-sided swim-throughs and caves, and the steady current supports abundant coral growth and numerous varieties of fish.

Inshore from the cut is a lagoon area with sea-grass beds and coral outcrops, which are home to a multitude of juvenile fish species. Not far from the cut and also in the reserve is the famous Shark Ray Alley – a marine experience not to be missed (see p107).

Rangers patrol the marine park, enforcing the regulations and collecting the entrance fee (US$10). On busy days the water around the area becomes a boat parking lot. The earlier you get there the better, as the marine life is more active in the morning. The best guides will show you around, find animals and keep an eye on you. For more information check out the excellent www.holchanbelize.org or visit the **Hol Chan Marine Reserve Office & Visitors Center** (Buccaneer St; 9am-5pm).

Do your part for reef conservation by not touching any coral, especially with your flippers.

Activities

Ambergris is good for all water sports, including scuba diving, snorkeling, windsurfing, sailing, swimming and deep-sea fishing. The town is awash with tour companies and individuals who organize water sports and other trips.

DIVING

Many hotels have their own dive shops that rent equipment, provide instruction and organize diving excursions. Numerous dive sites are within a 10- to 15-minute boat trip from town. Most popular is undoubtedly Hol Chan Marine Reserve, south of the island.

Following is a list of reputable independent dive operators; some also run a full range of nondiving tours:

Ambergris Divers (Map p103; ☎ 226-2634; www .ambergrisdivers.com) Runs a variety of diving, snorkeling, fishing and mainland trips. Offers all levels of diving instruction.

Amigos del Mar Dive Shop (Map p103; ☎ 226-2706; www.amigosdive.com) Rents scuba and snorkeling gear, offers all levels of diving instruction and leads diving, snorkeling and fishing trips. Has a large boat for comfy and quick rides back from outer sites.

Blue Hole Dive Center (Map p103; ☎ 226-2982; www.bluedive.com; Barrier Reef Dr) Offers a variety of snorkeling and diving trips, including overnight excursions once or twice a month. Known for the competence and professionalism of its staff. Large modern boat for outer atoll trips. Rents dive cameras, dive computers and prescription masks. Runs snorkel trips to the Blue Hole.

Patojo's Scuba Center (Map p103; ☎ 226-2283; www.ambergriscaye.com/tides) Connected with Tides Beach Resort, a small, family-run operation offering knowledgeable and personal service. Has dive packages.

Protech Dive Center (Map p103; ☎ 226-3367; www .protechbelize.com; Barrier Reef Dr) Only technical dive outfit in Belize, located opposite the tourist office. Offers courses in recreational and technical diving at all levels. Has a live-aboard boat for up to six people. There's also an outlet at the Belize Yacht Club (Coconut Dr).

To the prices that follow, add marine park fees of US$10 for Hol Chan and US$30 for the Blue Hole.

A one-tank local dive, without equipment, costs US$35 to US$50; with two tanks it's US$55 to US$70. Night dives to Hol Chan cost US$53 and include a lamp. Buoyancy-control device (BCD), mask and fins rent for around US$15, while full diving equipment is US$25. Four-day full-certification courses cost US$350, including equipment. A one-day Discover Scuba Diving course costs US$125.

Day trips further afield to the Blue Hole and Lighthouse Reef (three dives) cost US$185, and overnights (offered at least by the Blue Hole and Protech Dive Centers) include five dives for US$275 to US$350. Multinight trips can also be arranged. Day trips to Turneffe Atoll (three dives) cost around US$165.

SNORKELING

There are plenty of snorkeling excursions around the island (US$25 to US$45, depending on how many stops you make; a night snorkel costs US$45). Hol Chan Marine Reserve (for which a US$10 park fee is charged) is tops for this activity too.

Popular stops north of San Pedro include Basil Jones and Mexico Rocks. Snorkel, mask and fins rent for US$6.

All-day snorkel trips also run to the outer island. A trip to the Blue Hole and Lighthouse Reef costs US$125 (overnight US$175 to US$225), plus the US$30 marine-park fee; to Turneffe Atoll costs US$125. See p126 for details on these sites. Most dive outfits offer snorkel trips, including morning, afternoon and night trips to Hol Chan.

MANATEE-WATCHING

The best offshore manatee-watching (day trip US$90) is off Swallow Caye near Belize City. Trips to this site usually include a few snorkel stops as well. If you're planning to spend time on Caye Caulker as well as San Pedro, this trip might be better done from Caye Caulker, since travel time and costs are less. Folk on Caye Caulker are working on manatee conservation (see p120).

SWIMMING

While sandy beaches are plentiful, sea grass at the water line makes entry from the shore unpleasant, so you'll mostly be swimming from piers in waters protected by the reef. When you do this, watch carefully for boats: while there's plenty to see down under if you snorkel, you can't see or hear if a boat is coming your way. Have someone look out for you! Ramon's Village pier (Map p103), distinguished by its four *palapas*, is good for swimming and snorkeling.

SHARKS & RAYS – TO TOUCH OR NOT TO TOUCH?

A visit to one of the shark and southern stingray habitats off Ambergris Caye or Caye Caulker (Ambergris' is called Shark Ray Alley, Caulker's Shark Ray Village) is exhilarating, especially if you're new to snorkeling. Visitors come here for the raved-about close contact with these animals. However, the format of the outings, firstly feeding the sharks and rays and, secondly, handling them, is controversial. For most tour companies, 'feeding' is not an issue. They argue that the shark and ray habitats occur where generations of fishers have cleaned their fish, thus attracting the creatures. If they're not fed, animals won't congregate at these sites. However, it can be counterargued that if the animals are not disturbed, they will probably still be around most of the time, though they may not be so numerous.

There is some danger associated with these wild animals, as they can get aggressive around feeding time. The local website www.holchanbelize.org recommends not handling them. Nurse sharks have rows of small, sharp teeth, usually used for crushing shellfish, but they could be harmful if your hand or fingers were to find their way into a mouth. The rays have stingers at the end of their tails, which they won't use unless they're trodden on. So, watch your fins in these habitats to avoid an agonizing sting.

On most of the tours, nurse sharks and stingrays will swim up to boats and around the legs of snorkelers, encouraged by chum (bait) from tour operators. As you arrive the animals will rush your boat, anxious to see what snacks are on offer. Adventurous visitors jump into the water and dive with the animals. Some of the sharks and rays are tame enough to be held, so many visitors pet them (the rays feel like velvet, the sharks like sandpaper) and even cradle them in their arms for a photo op. Some guides are overenthusiastic about handling the animals as they think every visitor wants interaction, whereas other guides take a more distant approach.

If you stand still, the rays and sharks will brush up against you like friendly cats. Nurse sharks look intimidating when you first see them, especially underwater where everything looks bigger. They eat by suction (hence the name) and will make a huge slurp when they get close to the surface.

If you're unsure about all this, you can stay in the boat, hang around the perimeter of the action or go view these awesome creatures with an outfit that simply observes them.

All beaches are public and most waterside hotels are generous with their deck chairs, but a proprietorial air is developing about the piers, which are also supposed to be public. The beach in front of the Banana Beach Resort is clear of sea grass but the water is very shallow. The pier next to it is a good bet. And, of course, the farther north or south you go on the island, the fewer people there are on the piers.

FISHING

San Pedro draws anglers and fly-fishing enthusiasts who are anxious to take a crack at Belize's classic tarpon flats, which cover over 200 sq miles. Anglers come to attempt a Grand Slam: catching bonefish, permit (best from March to May) and tarpon (best from May to September) all in one day. In addition, wahoo, sailfish, snook, snapper, barracuda and grouper also bite. The fishing here is mostly on a catch-and-release basis.

Deep-sea fishing isn't the greatest draw in Belize – people come here for the reef. There are, however, stories of giant marlin caught out in the deep beyond. In December there is a Deep Sea Fishing Tournament hosted by Belikin, Belize's native beer.

A half-day's local fishing for one or two people costs from US$160 to US$185. A full day is US$220 to US$250.

OTHER WATER SPORTS

Sailsports Belize (☎ 226-4488; www.sailsportsbelize .com) has an office on the beach in front of San Pedro Holiday Hotel. You can rent sailboards (from US$20 per hour) and sailboats (from US$30 to US$60 per hour); windsurfing lessons cost US$45 per hour. An introduction to kitesurfing costs US$150.

Kayaks can be rented from the dock at **Fido's** (Map p103; ☎ 226-3513). Waters between the shore and the reef can be treacherous with traffic, so it's best to kayak on the lagoon side of the island.

NORTHERN CAYES

Tours

BOAT TOURS

Any hotel, travel agency or dive shop can fill you in on tours. Most operators have offices in the town. In addition to the following, there are independent operators who can arrange smaller, lower-priced tours for you. Most operators offer everything from snorkeling on the reef to lagoon, manatee and Caye Caulker tours.

Bottom Time Dive Shop (Map p103; ☎ 226-2348) On dock in front of San Pedro Holiday Hotel.

Lady Sharon (☎ 226-2292; adult/child US$25/15; 🕙 4:30pm Wed & Sat) Party sunset cruise with champagne and live music; boat docks in the center.

Reef Runner Glass Bottom Boat (Map p103; ☎ 226-2172, Barrier Reef Dr) Another option, especially if you can't or don't want to get wet; short trips to reef US$25.

Rum Punch II & Wm Stella (☎ 226-2340; sunset sail US$25, day sail US$30-75) Sunset sail to south Ambergris Caye; snorkel trips to Caulker and north Ambergris Caye.

Seaduced by Belize & Seaduction Sailing (Map p103; ☎ 226-2254; Vilma Linda Plaza, Tarpon St; sailing tours US$45-85) Offers family discounts, a range of sailing trips, including a sunset and full-moon cruise, and manatee tours; child-friendly.

Searious Adventures (Map p103; ☎ 226-4202) On the beach in front of Ruby's Hotel.

Tanisha EcoTours (Map p103; ☎ 226-2314; www.tanishatours.com; Barrier Reef Dr)

The **Rocky Point Snorkel Trip and Barbecue** (incl lunch & soft drinks US$60-80) is unmissable. Boats leave early in the morning and head north to snorkel stops including Blue Point, Basil Jones and Mexico Rocks. You'll go ashore at a beach near Mexico Rocks (different tour operators have different spots), and on some tours, while you relax, your tour leader catches lunch, which is then barbecued on the beach. Operators running this trip include **Amigos del Mar** (Map p103; ☎ 226-2634; www.ambergrisdivers.com); **Bottom Time Dive Shop** (Map p103; ☎ 226-2348), on the dock in front of the San Pedro Holiday Hotel; and **Seaduction Sailing** (☎ 226-2254; Vilma Linda Plaza, Tarpon St).

Bacalar Chico National Park & Marine Reserve, at the northern tip of Ambergris Caye, is part of the Belize Barrier-Reef Reserve System World Heritage site, declared in 1996. Tours visit the channel dug 1500 years ago by sea-trading Maya to separate Ambergris Caye from the mainland to its north. There's a nature trail and some small Maya ruins to explore on land, and pristine coral and plentiful marine life in the sea, not to mention plenty of birds and the chance of seeing manatees, turtles and crocodiles. Green and loggerhead turtles nest here. The trip makes a stop at Rocky Point, notable as one of the only places in the world where land meets reef. If you want to spend more time on land than diving or snorkeling, it may be better to charter a boat than take a tour, but you'll have to pay a small park-entrance fee.

Tour operators don't go daily to Bacalar Chico (the 90-minute boat ride keeps the number of visitors down), so you'll need to plan ahead for this trip. When seas are rough, tour boats travel up the west side of the island to reach the sites. The following run day trips to Bacalar Chico:

Ambergris Divers (Map p103; ☎ 226-2634; www.ambergrisdivers.com; diver US$125, snorkeler US$85)

Bottom Time Dive Shop (Map p103; ☎ 226-2348; US$85)

Searious Adventures (Map p103; ☎ 226-4202; US$75)

MAINLAND TOURS

Many visitors to Belize use San Pedro as their base and make excursions by plane or boat to other parts of the country. Mainland trips are operated by many of the dive and boat-tour firms.

Altun Ha (p89), the closest Maya ruin to the cayes, is one of the most popular day trips. If you have just one day and wish to see a sample of mainland attractions, you can pair Altun Ha with one or two other stops (US$75 to US$125).

Trips go by boat across the San Pedro Lagoon and up the Northern River to Bomba village and then by bus to Altun Ha. One trip pairs Altun Ha with a stop at the exotic **Maruba Resort Jungle Spa** (p91). The pause at Maruba can be filled with lunch (US$14) then swimming, horseback riding or a spa (at extra cost).

If you're interested in seeing more wildlife, you might combine Altun Ha with a trip to the **Community Baboon Sanctuary** (p94); **Crooked Tree Wildlife Sanctuary** (p92); or **Belize Zoo** (p95). Zoo trips from San Pedro are also often combined with **cave-tubing** (see opposite).

Altun Ha is lovely, but it doesn't have the importance or architectural variety of **Lamanai** (p135). If you want a closer look at Maya history and ruins, consider the Lamanai River Trip (US$135), which takes you up the Lamanai River (lots of bird and croc spotting) to the spectacular ruins. This is a great tour, but it makes for a long day trip in a variety of vehicles – ocean boat, van, river boat and then back again.

Another option is a **cave-tubing** adventure (US$150 to US$155). Tours combine a river-tube float and a tour of a cave, where you'll see stalagmites and stalactites and possibly pottery shards and other evidence of the ancient Maya. At some point during the tour, the group spends a few spooky moments in total darkness. For those craving more adrenaline, try the Black Hole Drop offered by **Ian Anderson's Caves Branch Adventure Company** (see p178) for US$155.

Tours all the way west to San Ignacio, Xunantunich and Mountain Pine Ridge are available from San Pedro, but you'll spend most of the day getting to/from these sites. It's better to spend a few days in the west instead of trying to visit from the cayes.

Sleeping

Most places are near the water, convenient for the beach. It's best to make reservations for the winter season, between December and May. All but the cheapest hotels accept major credit cards, though you may pay a steep surcharge. For more apartments, suites and condominiums with kitchens, check www.ambergriscaye.com.

SAN PEDRO
Budget

Ruby's Hotel (Map p103; ☎ 226-2063; www.ambergris caye.com/rubys; Barrier Reef Dr; r from US$18, tw with bathroom US$38, oceanfront d with bathroom & balcony US$54; ✸) Ruby's attracts return visitors keen to rent the rooms with fine vistas in this central, white-with-red-trim hotel. This despite the fact that many rooms have thin walls, tired mattresses and shabby decor. A new block houses better rooms with a balcony, but for these you need to book well ahead. Ruby's has large terraces where guests gather for breakfast, with goods from the attached bakery. Street-side rooms are noisy.

Hotel San Pedrano (Map p103; ☎ 226-2054; san pedrano@btl.net; cnr Barrier Reef Dr & Caribeña St; r with fan US$32, with air-con US$43, additional person US$11; ✸) Off the beach, but close enough to allow plenty of breeze, this freshly painted, white-and-green, wooden hotel has spacious rooms, all with private bathroom. All

rooms have at least a double and single bed, and there are two rooms that can take four to five people. Most rooms don't catch an ocean view, but you can always sit out on the wraparound porch. It's best to book in advance.

Midrange

Changes in Latitude B&B (Map p103; ☎ 226-2986; www .ambergriscaye.com/latitudes; Coconut Dr; s/d with private bathroom US$97/102; ✸) Painted in distinctive blues, this neat two-story guesthouse with friendly owners has attractive but small rooms with tiled floors and bathrooms arranged along the periphery of the ground floor. It's just a short block inland from the beach in a large garden with a flower-covered pagoda. The price includes breakfast and there's a common kitchen area and little library. Guests can use the pool and dock of the Belize Yacht Club next door.

Corona Del Mar (Map p101; ☎ 226-2055; www.amber griscaye.com/coronadelmar; Coconut Dr; r with/without balcony US$99/76, r with sea view US$146-158, 1-bedroom ste US$170, additional person US$23; ✸) Friendly, casual service is offered at this tall, white hotel on a small seafront plot. All rooms are well ventilated, spacious and comfortable, and breakfast is included in the price. There is an elevator, possibly the only one on the island. Out front, the dock is good for swimming and there are plenty of sun beds and hammocks on the white sandy beach.

Coconuts Caribbean Hotel (Map p101; ☎ 226-3500; www.coconutshotel.com; Coconut Dr; s/d/tr incl breakfast US$107/130/145, children under 10 free; P ✸ ▯ ▣) This smallish, concrete hotel features some attractive wooden trimmings and a pool with a swim-up bar. It gets high marks for friendly, attentive service and a down-to-earth atmosphere. The remodeled rooms, most with sea views, are spacious and comfy, with lots of polished wood. Outside are wide porches and tidy, sandy grounds with deck chairs and hammocks. It's a mile south of the town.

Coral Beach Hotel (Map p103; ☎ 226-2013; www .coralbeachhotel.com; cnr Barrier Reef Dr & Black Coral St; s/d with fan US$46/57, with air-con US$57/69; ✸) Previously a simple, weatherboard hotel offering good-value dive packages, the Coral Beach has been completely rebuilt in concrete and is now painted a vivid green with white trim. Rooms are cheerful and comfortable and all come with TV and telephone. There are balconies that front the street and from the top level there are sea views. Dive packages are also available.

Lily's Caribbean Lodge (Map p103; ☎ 226-2059; www.ambergriscaye.com/lilys; cnr Barrier Reef Dr & Caribeña St; s/d seaside US$56/70, beachfront US$70/80, extra person US$10; ⚡) Decking and clever trellising have fancied up this family-run, old wooden hotel right on the beach facing the sea. It has clean, prettily decorated rooms, all with two double beds, en suite, refrigerator and cable TV; many have good views. The 84-year-old owner wants to sell and retire.

Spindrift Hotel (Map p103; ☎ 226-2018, 226-2174; spinhotel@btl.net; cnr Barrier Reef Dr & Buccaneer St; d with fan US$53.20, r with patio/sea view US$74/92, beachfront apt US$123; ⚡) This modern, concrete hotel is well sited in the center of town on the beach. Some rooms front the beach, while others are set around a central patio with a few pot plants. Decor is homely Belizean and staff are welcoming. All but the cheapest rooms have air-con. There's also a Mexican restaurant.

Top End

Blue Tang Inn (Map p103; ☎ 226-2326, in US ☎ 866-337-8203; www.bluetanginn.com; Sandpiper St; ste US$145-187, additional person US$11; ⓟ ⚡) A very enticing beachside retreat on the quietish north side of town, the Blue Tang (named for a gentle, bright blue reef fish) has roomy, thoughtfully decorated, semiluxurious units. All units have kitchen facilities, dining furniture and sofas; the deluxe rooms have polished-wood vaulted ceilings and spa tubs. A third-floor sun deck offers splendid views, while the leafy garden and pool area are private and inviting.

San Pedro Holiday Hotel (Map p103; ☎ 226-2014; www.ambergriscaye.com/holidayhotel; Barrier Reef Dr; r US$130, tr US$155; ⚡) The Holiday Hotel has rooms and an apartment in three cheery, candy pink-and-white wooden buildings, all facing the sea. The sandy grounds are defined by pretty white trellis work. Right in the thick of things, it's a fun place to spend a few days. Rooms are well equipped and decorated in relaxed tones. There's a good beachfront restaurant and a terrific deli (p112) opposite the entrance on Barrier Reef Dr.

Ramon's Village (Map p103; ☎ 226-2071; www.ramons.com; Coconut Dr; d US$139-396, extra person US$14; ⓟ ⚡ ⚡) With its jungle-beach setting and

two-story thatched-roof cabanas, you could think you were in Southeast Asia at Ramon's. This place has everything. There are abundant lounge chairs on the good beach facing the pretty dock, a huge *palapa* restaurant, a swimming pool that curves through the grounds, a dive shop, excursion boats, sailboards etc. Rooms come in a variety of styles – those back from the beach have the lowest rates. The higher-priced rooms have views, kitchenettes and sitting rooms.

Tradewinds Paradise Villas (Map p103; ☎ 226-2087; www.belizeparadisevillas.com; Barrier Reef Dr; d/q villa US$144/187; ⚡ ⚡) This is just the ticket if you want to stay a while. One- and two-bedroom apartments, with fully equipped kitchens and CD players, occupy a large block, planted with tropical trees and shrubs, on the beach just north of town. You can feel secluded here while only minutes from all services. There's a large sparkling pool and an excellent dock out front for swimming.

Tide's Beach Resort (Map p101; ☎ 226-2283; www.ambergriscaye.com/tides; s/d incl breakfast US$115/134; ⚡ ⚡) Just 10 minutes' walk from the center and built by the owners of Patojo's Scuba Center, this colonial-style hotel has a friendly, family atmosphere. The front terrace has a swimming pool, bar and extensive decking, complete with totem poles. Spacious, comfortable rooms all have ocean views. Parquet floors and headboards hand-painted with the Blue Hole give an individual stamp. There are also apartments available.

Sun Breeze Beach Hotel (Map p103; ☎ 226-2191; sunbreeze@btl.net; Coconut Dr; s/d US$134/146, deluxe with better view US$146/157, premier with Jacuzzi & oceanfront view US$168/179; ⚡ ⚡ ⚡) Across Coconut Dr from the airport, this large, U-shaped, two-level concrete complex is set in substantial grounds dotted with coconut palms. Balconies with Spanish-style arches provide some architectural interest. The comfy rooms have tiled floors, colorful bedcovers and all mod-cons. A large, curved swimming pool with decking faces the beach. To one side is a dive shop and to the other, a popular open-air, oceanfront bar/restaurant (see p113).

SOUTH OF TOWN

The following places include resorts over a mile south of town. Down here you get seclusion without isolation, and a number of services and restaurants have cropped up so you don't have to head all the way into town.

Victoria House (Map p101; ☎ 226-2067, in US ☎ 800-247-5159; www.victoria-house.com; Coconut Dr; d US$198-315, ste US$415, 2-/3-bedroom villa US$790/1024, additional person US$41; ✂ ☎) Two miles south of the airport, this elegant beach resort is one of the oldest on the island, though constantly updated. Rooms are in thatched-roof casitas or colonial-style 'plantation' houses and have a white-on-white color scheme. By contrast, the individual Rainforest Casita has bright Caribbean colors. Three 'plantation' villas ooze luxury. The beach and grassy grounds are beautifully kept, shaded by a healthy stand of palm trees. The food is superb, and there's a dive shop, too.

Banana Beach Resort (Map p101; ☎ 226-3890; www.bananabeach.com; d poolside/oceanfront US$130/216, oceanfront apt US$245-375; ✂ ☐ ☎) Banana Beach is popular for its terrific-value rates, which include breakfast. It has two swimming pools and a sea grass–free beach. All but the standard rooms have a kitchenette. Bright, one-bedroom apartments, good for families, have a well-appointed kitchen, rattan furniture, cable TV, and a foldout couch in the living room. Rooms are arranged on two levels around two courtyards, and oceanfront apartments have private terraces. The restaurant gets upbeat reviews.

Mata Rocks Resort (Map p101; ☎ 226-2336; www.matarocks.com; d/ste US$157/165; ✂ ☎) This intimate, minimalist-style resort is neatly tucked into a small block next to Banana Beach Resort and shares the same pretty setting. The place is cleverly angled for rooms to catch an ocean view and through breeze. The fresh rooms have wooden or tiled floors and a fridge. Suites also have kitchens and cable TV. Outside is a small swimming pool and a beachside *palapa* bar, with sun beds and hammocks.

Villas at Banyan Bay (Map p101; ☎ 226-3739; www.banyanbay.com; d oceanfront apt incl breakfast US$294; ✂ ☐ ☎) Just a touch north of Banana Beach Resort, the Banyan Bay luxury resort caters for the 'discriminating beachcomber.' It has well-appointed two-bedroom, two-bathroom (one with Jacuzzi) apartments with tiled floors and hardwood interiors. The extensive grounds have a large swimming pool. Active guests can choose from a complete array of water sports (kayaks, glass-bottom dinghies, hobbie cats and sailboards are available); dive packages are also available.

Caribe Island Resort (Map p101; ☎ 226-3233; www.caribeisland.net; d ste US$129-195, ste for 1-6 people US$266; ✂ ☐ ☎) Quite a hike (3 miles) south of town, this bright pink place has a reputation for good service, although it seems more laid-back than other places in its price range. The multibedroom suites, some on two levels, are popular with families. All of the rooms have kitchens, tiled floors, Maya-inspired interiors as well as wide, breezy verandahs. Guests have the use of bicycles, kayaks and sailboats.

NORTH ISLAND

North Island is where you want to go if you really want to get away from it all. These resorts are all top end and mainly accessible by boat, though the hand ferry does run after dark and you can travel in and out by golf cart from at least as far north as the Portofino Resort (see p104). North of Portofino, where the reef meets the coast, are a few more resorts.

Mata Chica Beach Resort (Map p101; ☎ 220-5010; www.ambergriscaye.com/matachica; sea-view bungalow/ste/casita US$269/345/380, luxury villa for 4 US$760, beach mansion for 8 US$1111, incl breakfast; ✂ ☐) Extravagantly decorated and managed by an Italian-French couple who set out to bring *la dolce vita* to Ambergris Caye, this place is the island's most chic. The exotic communal areas, heavily influenced by India and southeast Asia, are gorgeous. The luxurious thatched-roof casitas are decorated in a unique tropical-fruit theme. If you're not staying, you can still visit for dinner at Mambo (p114), the resort's equally high-end restaurant.

Capricorn Resort (Map p101; ☎ 226-2809; www.capricornresort.net, s/d US$181/216; closed mid-Sep–mid-Oct; ✂) Owned by a young chef and his wife, this wonderful place has received a shot of youthful vigor. There are only a few cabins. Though they seem rustic they have all the comforts: spacious bathrooms, wide porches and funky decor (bold fuchsias, greens and yellows, Guatemalan and oriental fabrics and giant palm fronds). Capricorn heats up for a few hours during dinner when people from town boat up to enjoy the outstanding restaurant.

El Pescador Lodge & Villas (Map p101; ☎ 226-2398; www.elpescador.com; standard r US$214, 1-/2-/3-bedroom villa US$375/535/696; ⚓ 🖳 🛎) This charming old-time fishing lodge has had a face-lift, including the addition of swimming pools and luxury villas to the 21-acre property. Tours have been amplified to include all of those offered by San Pedro operators. The standard rooms, in a white, colonial-style building with a wraparound porch, are more than adequate. However, the self-catering villas, featuring polished wood, colorful Guatemalan fabrics, Mexican tiles, high, wooden ceilings and French doors, are really quite something.

Eating

SAN PEDRO

It's easier to get fed at irregular hours here than in other parts of Belize, but your best bets for freshness and good selection will still be at traditional mealtimes.

Several small cafés and restaurants in the town center serve cheap, simple meals. Try the food stands in front of the park, where a plate of chicken with rice and beans, barbecue meat or fish and other delicacies is under US$4.

Caramba Restaurant (Map p103; ☎ 226-4321; www.ambergriscaye.com/caramba; Pescador Dr; mains US$5-25; ☽ lunch & dinner Thu-Tue) Caramba is the busiest place in town due to its excellent food, good prices and attentive service. It offers local, Mexican and Caribbean cuisine, specializing in fresh fish and seafood cooked in at least 10 tasty ways. Your host, Rene, has thought of everything: marimbas on the street, a brightly lit entrance, dim interior lighting and attractive decor. Before dinner you receive a complimentary spicy snapper ceviche, and a rum punch. The good-sized main meals are delicious, and vegetarians are well catered for.

El Patio Restaurant & Grill (Map p103; ☎ 226-3693; Black Coral St; lunch mains US$4-8, dinner mains US$8-25; ☽ lunch & dinner Wed-Mon) This sand-floored *palapa* set back from the beach is prettiest at night when it's candlelit. Comfy chairs, potted plants and a fountain contribute to the smart decor. The grilled fish, seafoods and meats on offer are very good – don't miss the fish-finger starter with a spicy dipping sauce. They do great coconut rice and a thirst-quenching watermelon juice.

Celi's Deli & Restaurant (Map p103; ☎ 226-2014; Barrier Reef Dr; café dishes US$1-5, restaurant US$8-16; ☽ café 6am-6pm, restaurant lunch & dinner) Celi's Deli, opposite the San Pedro Holiday Hotel, serves food to go – fried chicken, small sandwiches, meat pies, tacos, tamales and homemade cakes. Service is fairly quick and you have the right to eat your food on the deck at Celi's Restaurant, on the beach side. The restaurant, known for its ceviche, specializes in seafood and attracts a good-sized crowd. You can eat in the 'greenhouse' or out on the expansive deck.

Mango's (Map p103; ☎ 226-2859; Barrier Reef Dr; mains US$6-15; ☽ 11am-11pm Thu-Tue) Right on the beach, and just south of Ruby's Cafe, this place is consistently good. Mango's cuisine combines Caribbean and Louisiana creole, reflecting the owners' background. Most items on the menu – po' boys, tropical grilled chicken breasts and fresh green salads – are in the US$5 to US$9 range. The more elaborate jambalaya is slow-cooked meat with cajun spices. Don't miss the fruit smoothies.

Elvi's Kitchen (Map p103; ☎ 226-2176; Pescador Dr; lunch mains US$4-14, dinner mains US$13-27; ☽ lunch & dinner) Elvi's, specializing in seafood and traditional Belizean dishes, is a San Pedro institution. The food is very good and service is quick. Lots of wood, splashes of tropical color and whirring fans make for a pleasant setting. Marimba music is belted out on Saturday night at least, so it's not the place for serious conversation. You can get everything from chicken, rice and beans to a snapper with a jacket potato and vegetables.

Sandbucks (Map p103; Vilma Linda Plaza, Tarpon St; dishes US$2.50-9; ☽ 7am-9pm) This simple, deli-style café is great for breakfast, light lunches and snacks. Coffee freaks should definitely head here for their fix, even if it's a little expensive at US$4 for a café latte. The fruit platter is a good way to start the day. You can also have cakes, buns, pastries, sandwiches, rolls, burritos and salads, all served with a smile from the chatty owner.

Ruby's Cafe (Map p103; ☎ 226-2063; Barrier Reef Dr; dishes US$2-4; ☽ 6am-7:30pm Mon, Tue, Thu & Fri, 6am-2pm Wed, 6am-noon Sun) This tiny place, next to Ruby's Hotel, has good cakes, pastries and brewed coffee and does a roaring trade, especially from 7am to 9am. Options include cinnamon buns, chicken-filled Johnny cakes, banana cake, tortillas filled with ham, cheese and beans, and more. There's only one table but most folk buy to take away. The patient staff wear a different color every day of the week.

Jam Bel Jerk Pit (Map p103; ☎ 226-3303; Ambergris St; mains US$11-13; lunch & dinner) Located next to Big Daddy's Disco, Jam Bel serves spicy, hot Jamaican dishes at reasonable prices. Dine under the stars on the only rooftop patio on the island. Food can be spiced according to your tolerance. 'Jamaican Crazy Shrimp' is a favorite dish and there are vegetarian choices.

Blue Water Grill Bar & Restaurant (Map p103; ☎ 226-3347; Sun Breeze Beach Hotel, Coconut Dr; starters, snacks & salads US$4-15, mains US$10-24; 7am-9:30pm) This huge open-air restaurant has a prime beachfront spot. The food inspires mixed opinions but the place is always busy. You can play it safe with pasta dishes, lasagne and wood-fired pizzas or be adventurous and go for Thai-style food. On Tuesday and Thursday sushi rolls are on offer. Coffee fans note that there is a complete espresso bar.

Papi's Diner (Map p101; ☎ 226-2047; Pescador Dr; breakfast dishes US$1-4, lunch & dinner dishes US$2-19; breakfast, lunch & dinner) At the far north end of town, this small, friendly place is an excellent budget option. For breakfast, choose from burritos, huevos rancheros, omelets or bacon with hash browns. For lunch and dinner, it offers elaborate main courses but the bargains are in the burgers, chicken, pork chops and fish fillets.

SOUTH OF TOWN

El Divino (Map p101; ☎ 226-2444; www.bananabeach .com; Banana Beach Resort, Coconut Dr; breakfast items US$4-11, mains US$5-29; breakfast, lunch & dinner) This street-side eatery gets heaps of praise, especially for its filling breakfasts, steaks and wood-fired pizzas with gourmet ingredients. For breakfast you might have tropical fruits and banana pancakes with cream, or a muffin, fry-jack, or slice of banana bread direct from their bakery. Fish fillet served with garlic mashed potatoes and grapefruit butter makes an unusual dinner choice.

Admiral Nelson's Barefoot Beachfront Bar (Map p101; ☎ 226-2067; www.victoria-house.com; Coconut Dr; lunch with drink US$26; breakfast, lunch & dinner) Victoria House's Palmilla Restaurant has excellent food but day-trippers might like to try

its more casual thatched-roof, plantation-style café-restaurant, set only a few yards from the water. Both restaurants are overseen by a New York–trained chef. Reggae plays in the background, the view is real pretty, service is prompt and the very good light meals are not excessively priced.

Tastes of Thailand (Map p101; ☎ 226-2601; Sea Grape Dr; mains US$9-25; 6-10pm Mon-Sat) This restaurant is in an appealing traditional-style house opposite the Island Mini Golf. There are only six tables and the bar-restaurant is a bit enclosed but there's air-con. Owned by an English-Thai couple, the food is largely prepared to authentic recipes, although experimentation happens too. Thai favorites, including tofu or cashew dishes, satays, *tom yum* (spicy soup with lemongrass, prawns etc), prawn, steak and vegetarian dishes, are all available.

Duane's Kitchen/La Margarita (Map p101; ☎ 226-2222; Coconut Dr; mains US$6-14; breakfast, lunch & dinner) South of the airport and convenient to hotels south of town, this place has tables on an upstairs verandah with treetop views. The owner-chef offers appealing breakfasts of pancakes or French toast with banana and cream cheese (both US$6) and eclectic lunches and dinners with Tex-Mex and Caribbean options.

NORTH ISLAND

Some visitors take the dirt road only as far as the Sweet Basil restaurant for lunch, or the Palapa Bar for drinks, before heading back to San Pedro. Others travel up the coast by launch for an exotic starlit evening at one of the north island's excellent restaurants. You can expect unusual menus featuring excellent seafood dishes. Reservations are necessary.

With the Island Ferry Water Taxi service, a launch costs US$10 per person round-trip as far as Journey's End Resort; beyond that, for example to the Mata Chica, it costs US$20 roundtrip. For the schedule of the Island Ferry, see p115.

Capricorn Restaurant (Map p101; ☎ 226-2809; Capricorn Resort; taster & lunch items US$6-15, dinner mains US$15-31; Thu-Tue) This restaurant's nouvelle cuisine has long been considered among the best in Belize, and new owner-chef, Meritt, is ensuring that reputation continues. At night the place is lit by festive twinkling lights. The most requested item is a sensational sun-dried tomato pesto drizzled over cream cheese and basil leaves, served with home-made bread. Dinners include stone-crab claws with a garlic and herb dip, filet mignon with portobello mushroom sauce, and seafood crepes.

Mambo Restaurant (Map p101; ☎ 220-5011; Mata Chica Beach Resort; mains US$15-38; ⏲ breakfast, lunch & dinner) Mata Chica's famed and stylish restaurant serves food with a Mediterranean flourish. The elaborate dinners here include bruschetta, filet mignon with blue cheese, and blackened fish done with exotic sauces containing papaya. Don't pass up the unique pasta fillings concocted by the Italian owner and be sure to stroll around the grounds to thoroughly appreciate this tropical fantasy.

Sweet Basil (Map p101; ☎ 226-3870; mains US$6-17, wine bottle US$19-25; ⏲ 11am-6pm Tue-Sun) A quarter mile north of the river, this high-end gourmet deli is only open for lunch. It prepares light meals of sandwiches made with home-baked bread, pâtés, platters of imported cheeses and meats, and pasta dishes. International wines are available. The open-air restaurant is set in a wooden, Victorian-style home amid a flower-filled tropical garden.

Drinking

Sipping, sitting, talking and dancing are part of everyday life on Ambergris. Most hotels have comfortable bars, often with sand floors, thatched roofs and reggae. The following bars open from late morning till late at night.

Crazy Canuck's Bar (Map p101; San Pedro south) Open to cooling sea breezes, this beach bar near Corona del Mar is a good drinking spot. Staff are friendly and regular patrons welcoming. Monday is the big night, as there's live music – often local punta rock.

Cannibal's Beach Bar (Map p103; ☎ 226-3706; cnr Barrier Reef Dr & Black Coral St) Tropical drinks, including Brazilian *caipirinhas*, are served up at this central and popular palm-thatched beach bar.

Shark's Bar (Map p103; ☎ 226-3235) This place was being completely refitted at press time. It's located on the same pier as the Caye Caulker Water Taxi Association Dock. You can count on reggae throbbing for most of the day and evening from this hangout. Food is available.

Palapa Bar (Map p101; ☎ 226-3111) This over-the-water *palapa* is about a half-mile north of the San Pedro River. It's a special spot for a drink at any time. Happy hour is from 4pm to 6pm daily; on Sunday afternoon there's a jam session.

Entertainment

Fido's Courtyard Bar (Map p103; ☎ 226-3176; cnr Barrier Reef Dr & Pelican St; ⏲ 11am-midnight) This enormous *palapa* decorated with seafaring memorabilia is fun. Crowds gather around the bar drinking, but there's plenty of seating and an ample-sized dance floor. Live music happens most nights – generally a full rock/reggae band plays old and current favorites, and all ages get down and boogie.

Big Daddy's Disco (Map p103; ⏲ 9pm-3:30am Wed-Sun) Near San Pedro's church and the Jam Bel Jerk Pit, this hot nightspot on the beach has a regular DJ, but you may hear live reggae, especially in winter.

Jaguar's Temple & Nightclub (Map p103; ☎ 226-4077; Barrier Reef Dr; ⏲ 9pm-3am Thu-Sat) Across from the central beachside park, this jungle-themed bar has papier-mâché dioramas for decor. Want to dance? This place rocks.

Barefoot Iguana (Map p101; ⏲ from 10pm Wed & Sat, Sun afternoon street-side bar only) Like Jaguar's and Big Daddy's, this two-story high-energy place with special-effects lighting gets going late. The music is good and loud, the decor fanciful, with an indoor waterfall and other rainforesty touches. Sometimes only its street-side bar is open.

Palace Casino (Map p103; ☎ 226-3570; cnr Pescador Dr & Caribeña St; ⏲ from 3pm Thu-Tue) With low ceilings, slots, blackjack tables and a seedy ambience, this small gambling hall should satisfy those who need a little flutter on their vacation.

Shopping

Plenty of gift shops in the hotels and on and around Barrier Reef Dr sell T-shirts, beachwear, hammocks, jewelry and ceramics. Fancy boutiques, fancier gift shops and even art galleries and woodwork shops are appearing. Prices are high for unusual items imported from afar. Street vendors appear on the weekends.

Belizean Arts Gallery (Map p103; ☎ 226-3019; www.belizeanarts.com; Fido's Courtyard; ⏲ 9am-9pm Mon-Sat) This is one of the best shops, selling ceramics, woodcarvings, Garifuna drums, antiques and paintings alongside affordable and tasteful knickknacks. Rainforest-flora beauty products, including soaps, are on sale. There are also products from beyond Belize.

Ambar (Map p103; ☎ 226-3101; Fido's Courtyard; ☺ 9am-9pm Mon-Sat) Sells appealing hand-made jewelry produced on the island.

Di Bush Tucan (Map p103; Barrier Reef Dr) A large shop with a good selection of beach gear, T-shirts, cheap jewelry and local crafts, this place also sells maps, guidebooks and some books by Belizean writers.

Kasbah (Map p103; Barrier Reef Dr) This shop has a fantastic selection of Mexican glassware, exotic fabrics and more.

Ambergris Maya Jade Retail Store (Map p103; ☎ 226-3311; 45 Barrier Reef Dr) Come here for at-tractive jade jewelry and information on the Maya of Ambergris.

Getting There & Away

Travel between Belize City and San Pedro is quick and easy, though you'll certainly get windswept on the 90-minute water-taxi journey.

Both **Maya Island Air** (☎ 226-2435; www.mayaair ways.com) and **Tropic Air** (☎ 226-2012; www.tropicair .com) offer several flights daily to/from San Pedro and Belize City's International Air-port (US$51, 15 to 20 minutes) and munici-pal airstrip 12 miles from the international airport (US$29, 15 to 20 minutes); Caye Caulker (US$27, 10 minutes); and Corozal (US$39, 25 minutes).

Maya Island Air flies from San Pedro to Belize City hourly from 7am to 4pm, with half the flights stopping at Caye Caulker (US$27). Four flights go daily to/from Coro-zal. Tropic Air goes to Belize City hourly from 6am to 5pm, stopping at Caye Caulker on request. From San Pedro to Corozal there are five daily flights.

Caye Caulker Water Taxi Association (☎ 226-0992; www.cayecaulkerwatertaxi.com; Shark's Dock) runs boats between San Pedro, Caye Caulker and Belize City. Boats to Belize City (one-way/roundtrip US$15/$28, one to 1½ hours) via Caye Caulker (one-way/ roundtrip US$10/17, 35 minutes) leave San Pedro at 7am, 8am, 9:30am, 11:30am, 1pm, 2:30pm and 3:30pm (also 4:30pm Friday through Sunday and holidays).

The **Thunderbolt** (☎ 226-2904) departs San Pedro's lagoon-side dock at 3:30pm for Corozal (one-way/roundtrip US$23/40, two hours) stopping at Sarteneja. It also goes twice daily (except Sunday) to Belize City (one-way/roundtrip US$15/25) via Caulker (one-way/roundtrip US$10/15), leaving San Pedro at 7am and 10am.

Getting Around

You can walk into town from the airport in 10 minutes or less, and the walk from the boat docks is even shorter. San Pedro **Air-strip Taxi Association** (☎ 206-2076) drives mini-vans. From the airport one or two people pay US$3 to any place in town, US$6 to the hotels south of town as far as Victoria House and US$10 further south.

San Pedranos get around on foot, bicycle or golf cart, although the truck and minivan population is increasing. There are at least six golf-cart rental places, some with gas-powered carts, some with battery. The gas ones can go further. Try **Polo's EZ-Go Rentals** (☎ 226-2467; Barrier Reef Dr), at the north end of the street, or **Castle Cars** (☎ 226-2421; Barrier Reef Dr). With Polo's EZ-Go Rentals, four-seaters cost US$25/45/61 for one/eight/24 hours and US$245 per week (five days). Castle Cars is more expensive but its carts run on gas. Golf-cart users need to check how far they can go along the dirt road on the north of the island.

You can rent bikes at **Joe's Bicycle Rent-als** (Map p103; ☎ 226-5371; cnr Pescador Dr & Caribeña St; 3hr/24hr/week US$6/9/40; ☺ 8am-6pm). It takes an hour or so to cycle up the north island from the hand ferry to Mata Chica Resort via the dirt road and the beach track from the Palapa Bar.

The **Island Ferry** (☎ 226-3231) operates an Ambergris-only water-taxi service north and south from Fido's dock. In high season, boats depart every two hours from 7am to 5pm and hourly from 6pm to 10pm, stop-ping at the north-end resorts. There are mid-night and 2am runs on Wednesday, Friday and Saturday nights. For return runs you need to check at the resort. Cost is US$5 per person one-way to Journey's End, US$10 per person one-way to resorts north of Jour-ney's End. Special runs out of hours cost US$20 from Fido's dock to Journey's End for one to three people and US$30 to resorts beyond Journey's End. North island resorts also frequently run their own shuttle service for guests to/from San Pedro.

To cross on the hand ferry to the North Island costs only US$0.50. It operates at least from 8am to 8pm but you may have to pay considerably more after hours.

CAYE CAULKER

pop 1300

Caye Caulker has had a reputation for being a budget-travelers' mecca, part of a classic backpacker route from Tulum in Mexico to Tikal and Antigua in Guatemala. However, times are a-changing and, though Caulker retains some shacky, low-rent charms, better accommodations and fancy restaurants are springing up. People of varied ages and incomes are becoming aware of Caulker's unique attributes – no cars, no fumes, beautiful white sandy beaches, balmy breezes, good food, laid-back inhabitants, azure waters and a fantastic barrier reef on its doorstep. You feel close to nature here: it's a perfect place to chill out, aided by the reggae beat.

You can rev up the pace with a variety of activities, from diving or snorkeling the local reef to chasing photos at the south end of the island (the place is unbelievably photogenic). Caye Caulker lies some 20 miles north of Belize City and 15 miles south of San Pedro. The island is about 4 miles long and only about 0.7 miles wide at its widest point. Mangrove covers much of the shore and coconut palms provide shade. Actually Caulker is two islands. In 1961,

Hurricane Hattie carved 'the Split' through the island just north of the village. North of the Split is mostly undeveloped, although not for much longer, as the land has been subdivided for housing and a road is going through; there's no electricity yet. A few folk live on the north island just over the Split. The most northerly part of Caulker is the Caye Caulker North Point Sanctuary Forest Reserve.

The town council is responsible for colorful 'Go Slow' and 'Stop' signs, even though golf carts, bicycles, pedestrians and the odd iguana are the only traffic on the sandy streets. Many gardens and paths have pretty borders of conch shells. But, even paradise has negatives. When the mostly constant sea breezes drop, the heat immediately becomes noticeable and sand flies and mosquitoes can become unbearable. Also, an acrid smell may arise from your bathroom or your freshly laundered clothes. This is from desalinated seawater or ground water, which is used for everything other than bathing, drinking and cooking.

History

Caye Caulker was a fishing settlement and popular with 17th-century British buccaneers as a place to stop for water and work on their boats. Like Ambergris Caye, it grew in population with the War of the Castes (p29), and is known mainly as a Mestizo island. It was purchased in 1870 by Luciano Reyes, whose descendants live on the island. Reyes parceled the land out to a handful of families and to this day, descendants of those first landowners still live in the general vicinities of those original parcels. These islanders were self-sufficient and exported turtle meat until the turtle population was decimated.

During much of the 20th century, coconut processing, fishing, lobster trapping and boat building formed the backbone of the island's economy. Caulker was one of the first islands to establish a fisherfolks' cooperative in the 1960s, allowing members to receive fair prices for the lobster and other sea life pulled from their waters.

Caye Caulker remains a fishing village, and boat design and construction continue, but tourism is taking over the economy. Tourism began in the late 1960s and 1970s when small numbers of hippies found their

---

LA ISLA CARINOSA

You'll see signs referring to Caye Caulker as La Isla Carinosa (the 'affectionate' island). Most say this was manufactured in response to Ambergris' nickname La Isla Bonita (beautiful island).

Caye Caulker's name probably morphed from its Spanish name, Hicaco (referring to the coco plum trees that were once prevalent on the islands), with encouragement from the explorers, pirates and buccaneers who stopped here to work on their boats (corking, or caulking, their hulls). You'll see it labeled Caye Corker on some maps. Another theory has it that the seafarers bottled water from the plentiful supply of fresh water from the spring at La Aguada on the island and then 'corked' the bottles.

CAYE CAULKER

0 ━━━━━━━━ 200 m
0 ━━━━━━━━ 0.1 miles

NORTHERN CAYES

INFORMATION
Atlantic Bank...........................**1** A4
BTL Office **2** A4
Caye Caulker Coin Laundromat.**3** B4
Caye Caulker Cyber Café........**4** B3
Caye Caulker Health Center....**5** B4
Caye Caulker Mini Reserve
    Information Center..........(see 12)
Cayeboard Connection...........**6** B3
Police Station.........................**7** B3
Post Office.........................(see 5)
Ruby's Laundry.......................**8** B4

SIGHTS & ACTIVITIES
Anwar Snorkel & Tours...........**9** B3
Belize Diving Service.............**10** A3
Carlos Tours...........................**11** B4
Caye Caulker Mini Reserve....**12** B6
Chocolate's...........................**13** B2
Dorothy Beveridge................(see 5)
E-Z Boy **14** B3
Ellen McCrae (Tours)...........(see 16)
Kitexplorer..........................(see 28)
Michael's Windsurf &
    Watersports.....................**15** B3

Orlando's Windsurfing/Galeria
    Hicaco...............................**16** B5
Public Beach.........................**17** B1
Ragamuffin Tours..................**18** B2
SayLking................................**19** B3
Seagull Adventures...............**20** B4
Treasured Travels..................**21** B4
Tsunami Adventures............(see 28)

SLEEPING
Amanda's Place **22** B4
Auxillou Suites......................**23** B4
Barefoot Beach Belize/
    Seaview Hotel...................**24** B5
Barefoot Caribe....................**25** B2
Blue Wave.............................**26** B2
Caye Caulker Condos............**27** B1
Chocolate's........................(see 13)
Costa Maya Beach Cabanas...**28** B2
De Real Macaw Guest House.**29** B2
Iguana Reef Inn.....................**30** A2
Jaguar Morning Star..............**31** A5
Lazy Iguana...........................**32** A5
Mara's Place **33** B1
Rainbow Hotel.......................**34** B2
Seaside Cabanas **35** B4
Shirley's Guest House............**36** B6
Tina's Backpacker Hostel.......**37** B4
Tree Tops Hotel.....................**38** B5
Trends Beachfront Hotel........**39** B4
Tropical Paradise Hotel..........**40** B5
Tropics Hotel **41** B3

EATING
Albert's Mini-Mart.................**42** B3
Caye Caulker Bakery.............**43** A3
Chan's Mini-Mart..................**44** B4
Cindy's Café..........................**45** B4
Coco Plum Gardens...............**46** A6
Don Corleone.......................**47** B2
Glenda's Cafe.......................**48** A4
Habaneros.............................**49** B4
Happy Lobster.......................**50** B3
Marin's Restaurant................**51** B5
Marla's Kitchen **52** B3
Mirin's Fruit & Juices.............**53** B3
Rainbow Grill & Bar...............**54** B2
Rasta Pasta Rainforest Cafe...**55** B3
Syd's....................................**56** A4
Tropical Paradise Hotel
    Restaurant.......................(see 40)
Wish Willy's Bar & Grill.........**57** A2

DRINKING
Herbal Tribe.........................(see 25)
I&I Reggae Bar......................**58** B5
Lazy Lizard...........................**59** B1
Sand Box............................(see 11)

ENTERTAINMENT
Oceanside..............................**60** B3

SHOPPING
Caribbean Colors **61** B3
Chocolate's Gift Shop.........(see 13)
Coco Plum Giftshop.............(see 46)

TRANSPORT
Caye Caulker Golf Cart
    Rentals.............................**62** A4
Caye Caulker Water Taxi
    Association Dock...............**63** B4
Maya Island Air.....................**64** A6
Rainbow Taxi Service..........(see 34)
Tropic Air..............................**65** A6

way to the island. Today, international visitors come in steady numbers and, although many islanders operate tourism-related businesses, there are no plans for large-scale development. Caulker residents enjoy the slow rhythm of life as much as visitors do.

Orientation

Approaching Caye Caulker by launch, you glide along the eastern shore, past dozens of wooden docks and stilted houses painted in bright colors. Off to the east, about a mile away, the barrier reef is marked by a thin white line of surf. When you disembark and wander ashore, you'll find a place of unpaved 'streets.' Caulker village has three main north–south streets: from east to west these are Front, Middle and Back Sts, now officially called Avenidas Hicaco, Langosta and Mangle, though you're unlikely to hear the new names used. The main dock street runs east–west through the center of the village. There are another 15 or so east–west streets, all nameless.

From the dock street north to the Split is around half a mile. The village stretches another half mile or so south from the dock street to the airstrip and there are a few houses south of the airstrip. Most of the tour operators are clustered on either side of Front St, north of the dock street. North of the dock is where most of the action and 'nightlife' is. The south side is quieter, with a mixture of accommodations that range from shacky places to secluded beachside hotels, mostly accessed by a beach path. There are also a few restaurants, shops and businesses south-side.

Though most of the tourist facilities are on the east side of the village, there are a couple of places to stay and a restaurant or two 'to the back.' Here you get lovely sunsets and seclusion, but you pay with a longer walk into civilization and extra bugs.

Information

At present there is no tourist office, though one is planned. Opposite the main dock, Seaside Tourism Travel in Seaside Cabanas (p123) happily gives out info. Websites with useful information include www.gocaye caulker.com, which is the official site of the Caye Caulker branch of the Belize Tourism Industry Association (BTIA); www.caye caulker.org (with extensive coverage), www .cayecaulkerbelize.net (the village council's site, which has news of upcoming events); www.cybercayecaulker.com (shopping and art specialist) and www.belizecayecaulker .net (a private site, free for businesses, which is very good on accommodations).

Atlantic Bank (☎ 226-0201; Middle St; ☽ 8am-2pm Mon-Fri, 8:30am-noon Sat) Cost for a cash advance is US$5; there are no ATMs on Caye Caulker.

Caye Caulker Coin Laundromat (dock st; wash, dry & soap per load US$9; ☽ 7am-9pm)

Caye Caulker Cyber Cafe (Front St; per hr US$4.50; ☽ 7am-10pm) Air-conditioned; has a bar with happy hour from 3pm to 6pm.

Caye Caulker Health Center (☎ 226-0166) Just off Front St, two blocks south of the dock street. Free.

Caye Caulker Mini Reserve Information Center (☎ 226-2251; ☽ 9am-noon) South of the village, run by the Caye Caulker branch of the BTIA; visitors center with information on the island's flora and fauna and short interpretative trail (always open) through the littoral forest.

Cayeboard Connection (Front St; per hr US$6; ☽ 8am-9pm) In an air-conditioned prefab building; also has a book exchange.

Post office (Caye Caulker Health Center building; ☽ 8:30am-4:30pm Mon-Fri)

Ruby's Laundry (dock st; wash, dry & soap per load US$9; ☽ 8am-9pm)

Sights
CAYE CAULKER MARINE RESERVE

Caye Caulker's sector of the Belize barrier reef was declared a 61-sq-mile marine reserve in 1998. The reef is regenerating from patchy hurricane damage. A local marine biologist recently identified 49 fish in a few hours here. Divers and snorkelers will see colorful sponges, blue and yellow queen angel fish, Christmas tree worms, star coral, redband parrotfish, yellow gorgonians and

---

CAYE CAULKER NORTH POINT SANCTUARY FOREST RESERVE

The protected northern tip of Caye Caulker, also declared a reserve in 1998, consists of mangrove forest and lagoons and is only accessible by boat. There is a visitors center/research center and picnic area, and a platform trail through the mangrove forest. You'll see lots of birds and maybe nesting crocs, turtles, iguanas and lizards. To visit, you can rent a kayak or charter a boat; see p121.

more. You may even spot a turtle, or a manatee from April to September. For tour operators, see below.

Activities

Activity on the island focuses on water sports and spotting sea life. Several places in town rent water-sports equipment. You can get snorkeling gear (all day US$5) or sea kayaks (singles per hour/half-day US$8/13). Single/triple sailboats cost US$15/20 per hour. For windsurfing and kitesurfing rentals see the boxed text, p120. You can also walk nature trails, bird-watch or cycle.

DIVING

Common dives made from Caye Caulker include two-tank dives to the local reef (US$65); two-tank dives in the Hol Chan Marine Reserve area (US$82 plus US$10 marine park fee); three dives off Turneffe Atoll (US$120 to US$150) and three-dive trips to the Blue Hole Natural Monument and Half Moon Caye (US$160 to US$190 including equipment, plus US$40 for park fees). Though prices are roughly the same with each dive operator, there may be differences in level of service, quality of equipment, and quantity and quality of meals. Talk with other divers, and inspect boats and equipment very carefully before choosing your dive operator. For more information about Turneffe Atoll, Blue Hole and Half Moon Caye, see p126.

There are four or five dive companies on Caulker and many of the dive masters have grown up on the reef. **Belize Diving Service** (☎ 226-0143; www.belizedivingservices.com) is professional and highly recommended, but they don't go to the Blue Hole. They do run PADI certification courses – Advanced Open Water costs US$272 for two days, including five dives.

If you want to dive the Blue Hole, it's best to go with one of the companies based at San Pedro on Ambergris Caye (p106).

SNORKELING

The local stretch of the barrier reef is only a five- to 10-minute boat ride away, and Hol Chan Marine Reserve is 30 minutes away. The best guides will get in the water with you to point out interesting coral formations. They also know many of the animals' territories and favorite spots.

Half-/full-day snorkeling trips to Hol Chan Marine Reserve and Shark Ray Alley (see p105) cost US$30/45, including a US$10 marine park fee. Half-day trips leave at 9:30am or 10:30am and 2pm. Full-day tours include a stop in San Pedro for lunch (not included in the price).

Other half-day snorkeling trips visit the Caye Caulker Marine Reserve, leaving at 10:30am and 2pm. Destinations include Coral Gardens, the Swoosh (a stand of coral near an opening in the reef where the current and swells attract a good variety of marine life) and Shark Ray Village, Caulker's own shark and ray habitat. Cost is US$25. If you prefer to reach these snorkel spots by a leisurely sail, try **Raggamuffin Tours** (☎ 226-0348; www.raggamuffintours.com; Front St). Prices are the same as with the launches. For more about Raggamuffin Tours, see p120. For other tour operators, see p121.

Snorkeling trips also go further afield to the Blue Hole and Half Moon Caye, as well as Turneffe Atoll. **Seagull Adventures** (☎ 226-0384; seagulladventures@hotmail.com; dock st), run by capable Luciana Essenziale, specializes in snorkelers-only trips. You snorkel the inside perimeter of the Blue Hole (depth 9ft) then lunch and visit the red-footed boobies at Half Moon Caye before a second snorkel stop on the west side of Half Moon Caye. You'll see fantastic coral and sponges – a completely alive reef. **Tsunami Adventures** (☎ 226-0462; www.tsunamiadventures .com; Front St), fronted by a very helpful Canadian, Heather Martin, also runs snorkel trips to the Blue Hole and Half Moon Caye, and to Turneffe. Cost to the Blue Hole (two hours) is US$90 to US$95 (plus park fees of US$40) and to the northern section of Turneffe Atoll (one hour) US$72.

MANATEE-WATCHING

The best bet for manatee-spotting is in a habitat off Swallow Caye, just 4 miles east of Belize City. This is either the first or last stop of three on a day trip from Caulker. Other stops are made for snorkeling and for a lunch break on either Sergeant's Caye or tiny, picture-postcard Goff's Caye. Be sure to bring a sun hat, as this trip involves a lot of waiting, chatting with other travelers and bubble-watching. Tours (US$60) can be arranged through most of Caulker's boat-tour operators (p121). However, the specialist is

---

MANATEE CONSERVATION – HELP AT LAST!

Over the past 15 years, manatee-watching off Swallow Caye, 4 miles off Belize City, has become a popular tour from Caye Caulker, San Pedro and Belize City. As traffic to the area increased, so too did the stress and strain on the manatee population. Lionel 'Chocolate' Heredia, one of the first Caulker fishermen to begin ferrying backpackers on his fishing boat from Belize City to the island, took notice of the impact of increased traffic on the manatees and decided to take action. He devoted himself tirelessly to manatee conservation, especially the protection of the manatee habitat around Swallow Caye.

Eventually, guidelines were put in place to protect the gentle creatures, while encouraging them to stay in the area and be on view for visitors. Swimming with manatees is now forbidden by the Belizean authorities and signs have been posted to dissuade boat operators from using their motors near the manatees and from speeding through the area. (Propeller injuries are one of the chief causes of death to manatees.)

Though these guidelines are in place, not all boaters and tour operators who visit the island respect them. Chocolate and other conservationists have worked to install a permanent caretaker in these waters. They have also worked to protect the sea grass around Swallow Caye – essential for these vegetarian animals – and to lobby for a ban on spearfishing in the area. To these ends the 14-sq-mile Swallow Caye Wildlife Sanctuary was established in 2002. Funded by the UN and by private donations, it is administered by the Friends of Swallow Caye (a nongovernment organisation) and the Belizean government.

For more about manatees, see p49.

Lionel Heredia, or 'Chocolate', found at his premises of the same name on Front St. For more information about the manatees and Chocolate's work to protect them, see the boxed text, above.

SAILING

A handful of sailboats takes travelers out to various sites. Boats usually leave around 11:30am and return before 5pm. Guests need to bring their own refreshments. Boats typically carry a big ice chest and a good sound system. For availability, check by the main dock before 10am or the evening before.

Raggamuffin Tours (☎ 226-0348; www.raggamuffin tours.com; Front St) offers a full range of nondiving sailboat tours, both local and to the outer islands. Their sunset and moonlight sailing trips cost US$25 and US$35 per person, respectively. Island-hopping trips include Lighthouse Reef, stopping at Turneffe Atoll and the Blue Hole, with a camp base at Half Moon Caye (US$273 for three days). Other trips go south to Placencia.

For sailboat rentals try **SayLKing** (☎ 226-0489) on the beach north of the main dock.

SWIMMING

Hurricanes Mitch and Keith in 1998 and 2000 left strips of sand on Caye Caulker where there once were sea shrubs, but the authorities have also built up sandy beaches. Sea grass is under the water along much of the shore, which doesn't make for pleasant wading or swimming. The best swimming is at the end of docks at the southern end of the island and at the Split, Caulker's public beach, north of the village. The Split is small, popular and a fun place to get to know the locals. It looks a bit postapocalyptic with beach-goers lounging on bits of a broken bridge. The water is cool and clean, kept that way by a strong current that runs through it. There's good snorkeling here but you need to keep well out of the path of boats passing through the deeper water on the north side. Accidents have happened.

The surf breaks off the shore on the barrier reef and is easily visible from the eastern shore of Caye Caulker. Don't attempt to swim out to it as powerful boats speed through these waters. Crocodiles live in the waters on the west side of the island.

The docks are supposed to be public, but hotel owners are becoming proprietorial and putting up gates to give privacy to their guests who use the sun lounges and deck chairs provided.

WINDSURFING & KITESURFING

With an easterly wind blowing much of the time, and shallow waters protected by the barrier reef, Caulker has superb conditions for these sports. Sailboard rental is available south of town at **Orlando's Windsurfing** (Morgan's Inn; ☎ 226-0178; 2hr session US$30). Newer **Michael's Windsurf & Watersports** (☎ 226-0452; www.wind surfbelize.com; 1hr beginner's lesson US$40, board rental per 1hr/half-day US$20/45) is based on the beach just north of the dock and is child friendly. Kite-board rental is a recent addition.

Kitesurfing is new to Caulker. French kitesurfers have established a base toward the Split and show off their skills, performing acrobatics on and off through the day. They give classes and rent equipment from their office situated beside Tsunami Adventures. Contact **Kitexplorer** (☎ 602-9297; www .kitexplorer.com; Front St; 3/8hr course US$120/330).

FISHING

Just about any skipper will take you fishing, and it's cheaper than from Ambergris Caye. Try **Tsunami Adventures** (☎ 226-0462) or **Raggamuffin Tours** (☎ 226-0348). Half-/full-day deep-sea fishing trips for two to three people run at US$200/300.

Tours
BOAT TOURS

Tour operators generally have their own specialty, but prices are much the same. Most tour operators work closely together, consolidating tours on slow days and juggling overflow at busier times. If you want to go with a particular tour operator, reserve as far ahead as possible. If you prefer a smaller group, gather a group and arrange for a charter instead of a general tour. Snorkel gear, water and fruit are included in the price of most boat trips.

When booking boat tours, check numbers, duration, areas to be visited and the seaworthiness of the boat. The boat and motor should be in good condition. Even sailboats should have motors in case of emergency, as the weather can change quickly. For sailboat tours, see Sailing (opposite).

The following are among Caye Caulker's tour operators.

Anwar Snorkel & Tours (☎ 226-0327; liznovelo@ hotmail.com; Front St) Well recommended.
Carlos Tours (☎ 226-0458; carlosayala10@hotmail; Front St) Well recommended and has reference books on reef life. Groups of 10 maximum.
Chocolate's (☎ 226-0151; chocolate@btl.net; Front St) Chocolate is the pioneer of manatee tours; also rents kayaks.

Ellen McRae (☎ 226-0178; sbf@btl.net; Galeria Hicaco; full day US$33) Reef-ecology trips led by marine biologists.
E-Z Boy (☎ 226-0349; e-zboytours@yahoo.ca) Offers a few unusual tours: kayaking, night snorkeling, herbal walks, stargazing.
Seagull Adventures (☎ 226-0384, 608-3920; seagull adventures@hotmail.com) Best known for Blue Hole snorkel tours.
Tsunami Adventures (☎ 226-0462; www.tsunami adventures; Front St) Connected with large seafaring family.

LAND TOURS

Nature and bird-watching tours can be arranged through marine biologist **Ellen McRae** (☎ 226-0178; sbf@btl.net; Galleria Hicaco, Front St; 3½hr bird-watching tour US$35) and **Dorothy Beveridge** (☎ 220-4079; nature tour per person US$30).

Mainland tours can be arranged from Caulker, but they don't run as frequently as those from Ambergris. The most popular is the Altun Ha River trip (US$80), which stops at Maruba Resort for lunch, swimming and, at further expense, horseback riding.

Festivals & Events

A weekend of music, fun and lots of lobster makes up Caye Caulker's **Lobsterfest**, held to mark the new lobster-fishing season in the first weekend in July.

Sleeping

There are telephones on Front St near the dock and by the airstrip if you want to phone around on arrival. Golf-cart taxis meet boats and flights and will take you around to look at a few places to stay. It's best to book in advance if you're coming at Christmas and Easter.

For families or those staying longer than three days, consider cutting costs by renting a house, but you'll need to plan ahead. Try www.cayecaulkerrentals.com.

NORTH OF THE DOCK STREET
Budget

Mara's Place (☎ 206-0056; 27 Front St; r US$25-38, additional person US$7) This friendly establishment is in a good location near the Split. It has two-story wooden cabins, painted beige with yellow and brown trim. Rooms have hot water, fans and cable TV. The sandy beach and dock with hammocks across the street are attractive extras.

Tina's Backpacker Hostel (☎ 226-0351; dolphin bay@btl.net; Front St; dm/d US$8/20) Just north of the main dock, this green two-story place has a striking mermaid mural, leafy front yard and hammocks strung out by the water's edge. Enjoy unlimited kitchen privileges, TV and the local artwork hung on the walls. There is space for 16 people in the three dorms and two double rooms. You might have to queue for a shower.

Midrange

Chocolate's (☎ 226-0151; chocolate@btl.net; Front St; r US$75) Built over a gift shop near the Split is this lovingly crafted room with vaulted-mahogany ceiling, green-tiled bathroom and wraparound porch. The front part of the porch overlooks Front St – great for people-watching. Book well in advance.

Caye Caulker Condos (☎ 226-0072; www.cayecaulker condos.com; Front St; apt US$107-128; 🌊) These fantastic apartments near the Split have full kitchens and fancy bathrooms featuring unique stonework, and showers with two sets of faucets. Each unit has its own balcony with private entrance. The rooftop terrace with hammocks has stunning 360-degree views taking in part of the north island.

Blue Wave (☎ 206-0114; bluewave@btl.net; Front St; r US$30-75; 🌊) Toward the Split, Blue Wave is run by a friendly local couple who rent various parts of their property. They live on the top floor of their clapboard house, which is set in a shady garden. To the side, facing south, is an attractive series of two-story wooden buildings with excellent rooms, all with little balcony, TV, cheerful bathroom and views. Beneath the owners' house are three cheaper rooms with shared bathroom.

De Real Macaw Guest House (☎ 226-0459; www .derealmacaw.com; Front St; r US$43-64, apt for 1-6 people US$128; 🌊 🖳) This super-value place has a variety of jungle-inspired lodgings on a sandy block across the street from beachside public land. All rooms have fans, TV, fridge and coffeemaker. A holiday mood is created by thatched-roof verandahs with hammocks and, inside, funky fabrics and colors. The well-appointed apartment has polished wooden floors, cathedral ceiling and Internet connection.

Costa Maya Beach Cabanas (☎ 226-0432; www .tsunamiadventures.com; Front St; r US$48, q US$64-80; 🌊) Connected with Tsunami Adventures

out front, this place has cabanas in a number of two-story wooden buildings, most with hexagonal roofs and all with porches. The sandy property is just minutes from the Split, the cabanas are well kitted out (fridge, coffeemaker, cable TV, fan) and you get complimentary bicycles, beach chairs and kayaks, and tour discounts.

Tropics Hotel (☎ 226-0374; www.startours.bz; Front St; r with private bathroom US$30-66, extra person US$10; 🌊) Belizean vacationers love this hotel for its good prices and position between the dock street and the Split. Set on a large block, it has an upstairs porch with ocean views. It's affiliated with the Tropical Paradise Hotel at the south end of town. Rooms are clean but bland: the more expensive ones have TV, fridge, tiled floors and two double beds.

Rainbow Hotel (☎ 226-0123; rainbowhotel@btl.net; Front St; s/d US$59/70, with air-con US$91/102, extra person US$11, 1-4 person apt US$107; 🌊) Bright blue paint, a couple of rainbows for decoration, and upgraded rooms make this bunker-like concrete building relatively appealing, but the rooms are cell-sized. Bottom-floor rooms open right onto the street: some folks sit on a chair out front and enjoy the street life. For privacy, choose a room on the top floor.

Barefoot Caribe (☎ 226-0161; Front St; r US$43-70, ste US$86; 🌊) Toward the Split, this blue building with wooden trimmings is a large (by Caye Caulker standards) new hotel right in front of the beach. It has its own restaurant with an open-air top deck.

Top End

Iguana Reef Inn (☎ 226-0213; www.iguanareefinn.com; junior/deluxe seaside ste incl breakfast US$120/141; 🌊) Guests will welcome the amenities offered at this upscale but good-value hotel on the west side. Solidly built and decorated with bright Mexican colors. Rooms are spacious and comfortable and beds are big. Junior suites have a sitting area, foldout bed, refrigerator, minibar and tiled bathroom. Service is friendly and efficient, and there's a *palapa* sunset bar.

Wanting a luxury apartment? Clustered on the beach by the main dock and all owned by members of the Auxillou family, **Auxillou Suites** (☎ 226-0083; www.staycayecaulker.com; 1-/2-bed ste US$138/159), Sailwind's Beach Suites and Diane's Beach House have 10 quality suites between them. All three places are painted in unmissable hectic colors. Check for availability at the Treasured Travels office on the beach to the north of the main dock.

SOUTH OF THE DOCK STREET
Budget

Jaguar Morning Star (☎ 226-0347; www.jaguarmorningstar.com; r US$35-38; ✷) Run by a gracious Belizean-Canadian couple, this is an attractive and well-priced option. There are only three rooms in total, two on the top floor of the three-story house, painted with a jaguar mural, and one cabana in the quiet garden. Amenities are comfortable, and the position, a few blocks back from the beach and a few blocks south of the dock street, is improved by renting a bicycle.

Tropical Paradise Hotel (☎ 226-0124; www.startours.bz; Front St; r US$35-47, cabin US$53-82; ✷) Plenty of guests quickly find this densely packed property that's next to the cemetery and a short walk from the dock. Most of the buildings are white with crimson trim. Rooms are modern enough, neat and comfortable, and there's a big dock out front. The restaurant is dependable and a good meeting place.

Trends Beachfront Hotel (☎ 226-0094; www.trendsbze.com; d/cabana US$40/50) On the beach just west of the water-taxi dock, this happy, turquoise hotel with pink trim beckons. It has gracious porches with sea views, large grounds and the best view of the dock area. Rooms are clean and freshly decorated.

Midrange

Lazy Iguana (☎ 226-0350; www.lazyiguana.net; d US$102; ✷ 💻) On the island's southwest side, this place is off the beaten track but tall enough to provide a good view of the island and the sea. Four prettily decorated rooms are for rent and a rooftop patio with thatched roof offers 360-degree views. A sumptuous breakfast is served in the owners' kitchen. The leafy garden hides a water-fountain feature, orchids and a perfume laboratory. Be sure to reserve.

Tree Tops Hotel (☎ 226-0240; www.treetopsbelize.com; r without/with bathroom from US$44/47, ste US$91; ✷ 💻) This friendly hotel is among the best on the island, so reserve well in advance. The hospitable owners run a tight ship. Each of the four well-appointed rooms, two with sea views, has fridge, TV and unique

decor. Upstairs are two new semiluxurious suites. You'll notice flamboyant artistic touches around the place as both owners enjoy crafts and painting. The buildings are set back from the beach in a small, palm-shaded garden. A roof terrace with panoramic vistas towers over the treetops.

Barefoot Beach Belize/Seaview Hotel (☎ 226-0205; www.barefootbeachbelize.com; r US$53, cottage for 2-4 per day/week US$70/455, cottage for 2 per week US$535) This low-key place on a delicious stretch of quiet beach offers attractive rooms with fan and private hot-water bathroom, and two fully fitted cottages with porch. Guests can enjoy the sea from a hammock under a *palapa* at the end of the dock. The hotel is small and in demand so it's best to reserve in advance.

Amanda's Place (☎ 226-0029; Front St; www.cayecaulkerrentals.com; r from US$82; ✗ ✷ 💻) The owner is the energy behind www.cayecaulkerrentals.com and, as well as renting out other people's houses, she offers two well-fitted apartments with kitchenettes beneath her own house. Only a block back from the beach, the grounds are leafy and the attractive apartments each have a little porch from where you can watch street life and see the ocean.

Shirley's Guest House (☎ 226-0145; www.shirleysguesthouse.com; r without/with bathroom US$54/70, cabin with private bathroom US$86) On the south beachside near the airstrip, this secluded place (adults only) has pretty cabins and duplexes with striking interior decoration in a beautiful garden setting. Window grills have a unique sun design. All accommodations have fan, hot water and fridge, and there's a dock out front.

Top End

Seaside Cabanas (☎ 226-0498; www.seasidecabanas.com; r/cabana US$110/128; ✷ 🏊) On the beach in view of the main dock, this attractive hotel has been completely rebuilt after a fire. Its thatched-palm roofs give it a typical Caribbean look, but the interior decor, with desert colors and Arabic-style accessories, owes more to Morocco. Rooms and a suite occupy the main building facing the ocean. Closer to the sea, concrete cabanas hold further high-quality lodgings with big comfy beds and cable TV. The English-owned hotel has the island's only swimming pool.

Eating

With three superb restaurants (Habaneros, Rasta Pasta Rainforest Cafe and Don Corleone), there's feasting to be had on Caulker. Seafood is wonderful here: locals really know how to complement its flavors. Caulker's hippy heritage is seen in widely available wholewheat and vegetarian cuisines.

If you like these seafoods, the lobster season is from mid-June to mid-February, and conch season is from July to October, so these are good times to visit.

NORTH OF THE DOCK

Rasta Pasta Rainforest Cafe (☎ 206-0356; mains US$8-12; ✆ breakfast, lunch & dinner Thu-Tue) On the beach just north of the dock, this relaxed *palapa* restaurant – famous for its unique savory flavors, good pasta and seafood dishes, home-baked goods and wonderful mixed drinks – is run by a red-headed mother-and-daughter combo. Prices are reasonable, and vegetarians are well catered for. You can buy their spice mixtures to take home or even order them online. Their home-brew ginger beer is a recipe they're not giving away.

Don Corleone (☎ 226-0025; Front St; breakfast dishes US$7, lunch mains US$8, dinner mains US$9-20; ✆ breakfast, lunch & dinner) Caulker's fabulous Italian restaurant is Dutch owned and has a fun-loving Italian chef who's had his own restaurants around the world. Decor is sophisticated and the service impeccable. Whatever you order lives up to management's promise to make you a meal you can't refuse, be it one of the gorgeous salads, a pasta with an aromatic sauce or a more substantial fish or meat main. The espresso is excellent.

Wish Willy's Bar & Grill (breakfast US$3-4, mains US$7-12, mixed drinks US$1.50; ✆ breakfast, lunch & dinner Dec-Aug) Head to this funky place (named for a scaly-tailed iguana) at the bottom of the little street running east–west opposite Frenchie's Dock. The 'dining room' consists of a deck outside a shack, transformed by night with white tablecloths, candlelight and cool background music. Maurice, a Belizean who's spent time stateside, cooks up delicious seafood and internationally inspired dishes including Thai and Indian curries.

Rainbow Grill & Bar (☎ 226-0281; lunch mains US$4-8, dinner mains US9-22; ✆ lunch & dinner Tue-Sun) Opposite the Rainbow Hotel with a deck over the water, this local favorite is evidence of Caulker's agreeable temperatures. Light lunches of vegetarian plates, burgers, quesadillas, burritos and sandwiches are available. At night fancier fare is prepared. You can have your fish, shrimp, conch and lobster cooked in a number of ways, from simple lemon with butter to Jamaican jerk or oriental style.

Marla's Kitchen (btwn Front & Middle Sts; mains US$3-16; ✆ breakfast & dinner Tue-Sun) This open-air haunt, inland from Rasta Pasta, was once a Front St barbecue. Visitors love the hearty servings here and you'll probably hear some Garifuna drumming. For breakfast take your pick of waffles, pancakes, fry-jacks, omelets or tortillas. For dinner, how about a Creole fish fillet, or a snapper with a spicy tomato sauce, served with two of creamed potatoes, coleslaw, rice and beans, and garlic bread?

Glenda's Cafe (☎ 226-0148; Back St; mains US$2-4; ✆ breakfast & lunch Mon-Fri) Glenda's serves traditional Belizean food in a clapboard house on the island's west side. It has the best cheap breakfasts in town from cinnamon rolls and orange juice to full breakfasts of eggs, bacon or ham, bread and coffee. Burritos, tacos, sandwiches and chicken with rice and beans are offered for lunch. Get there early for breakfast.

Happy Lobster (☎ 226-0064; Front St; mains US$7-16; ✆ breakfast, lunch & dinner Fri-Wed) Sit on the porch and catch the sea view and breeze. This is more functional than gourmet, but the food's fine and the service is brisker than at a lot of Caulker restaurants, especially at lunchtime. The menu offers fish and seafood choices spiced up or sweetened with coconut, and plenty of vegetarian dishes. Breakfast is popular.

SOUTH OF THE DOCK

Habaneros (☎ 226-0487; www.gocayecaulker.net; cnr Front St & dock st; mains US$13-27; ✆ dinner Wed-Sun) Caulker's 'hottest' restaurant, named for the habanero chili, is in a brightly painted clapboard. Here chefs prepare gourmet international food, combining fresh seafood, meat and vegetables with insanely delicious sauces and flavors. They also dish up housemade pastas and baked goods. Enjoy the buzz and eat by candlelight at the tables on the verandah, or sit in the funky bar. You'll be wowed if you choose one of their specials. Fine wines and jugs of margarita or sangria are available. Reservations are recommended.

Cindy's Café (☎ 226-0093; www.cybercayecaulker .com; Front St; breakfast US$3-7; ☺ 7:30am-noon Tue-Sun) This buzzing breakfast spot serves organic Guatemalan coffee, espresso drinks, homemade fresh bagels and breads, granola, fruit, yogurt and eggs done every which way. It's very small with a few tables inside and out on the verandah. Early birds get a table. Check the notice board for info on the 'alternative' scene.

Coco Plum Gardens (☎ 226-0226; US$7-14; ☺ 8am-noon & 4-8pm Wed-Sun) Dutch-Belizean owned, this unusual restaurant has peaceful one-acre garden surroundings and a conservationist vibe. (Spot the ceiba tree at the entrance.) Off Back St near the airstrip, Coco Plum is off the beaten track but worth the walk for home-baked breads and wholesome breakfasts, gourmet pizzas for dinner or one of the best cappuccinos in Belize. A courtesy taxi service runs from Footprints Gallery, next to Cindy's Café on Front St.

Syd's (☎ 206-0294; Middle St; mains US$7-14; ☺ lunch & dinner Mon-Sat) Syd's is an expat favorite for its hearty, good-value Belizean and Mexican-style dishes and convivial atmosphere. You can eat out in the pretty, flowery patio, inside in the not-so-pretty dining room, or out front and watch the world go by. This is a good place to try steamed conch (US$8) or grilled lobster (US$14), which arrive with a couple of side dishes.

Marin's Restaurant (☎ 226-0104; Middle St; mains US$5-13; ☺ breakfast & dinner, bar open all day) Dine in the open air at treetop level on hearty Belizean fare, seafood dishes and more at Marin's, one of the oldest restaurants on the island. Grilled lobster tops the price list. The breakfast menu includes pancakes and fruit, yoghurt and honey, and fry-jacks.

Tropical Paradise Hotel Restaurant (☎ 226-0124; Front St; breakfast US$2-4, lunch US$2-10, dinner mains US$4-15; ☺ breakfast, lunch & dinner Mon-Sat) The service and cuisine are a bit tired, but it's a popular gathering place. You can eat in air-con comfort or in the breezy open-air section. Perhaps try curried shrimp or lobster (US$10 to US$15), fish and chips (US$4.50) or a daily special.

GROCERIES & BAKERIES

Caye Caulker Bakery (Middle St; ☺ 7:30am-noon & 2-7pm Mon-Sat) This is the place to pick up fresh bread, rolls and buns (baked goods cost under US$1).

Other picnic supplies are available at **Chan's Mini-Mart** (☎ 226-0165; cnr Middle St & dock st) and **Albert's Mini-Mart** (☎ 226-0277; Front St). **Mirin's Fruits & Juices** (Front St; fruit salad small/large US$1.25/2.50) operates from a stall set up in front of Albert's Mini-Mart – the best food to go!

Drinking & Entertainment

I&I Reggae Bar (☺ from 6pm) Off Front St and south of dock street, this happening reggae bar is in a three-level tree house, with swings for chairs, and a good sound system. Its construction resembles an adult jungle gym. A great place for a sunset drink!

Herbal Tribe (Front St; ☺ happy hr 6-8pm) A large open-air restaurant and hip reggae joint with great pizzas. Happy hour fills the place with merry folks drinking and chatting.

Rasta Pasta Rainforest Cafe (☎ 206-0356; ☺ 7am-midnight Tue-Thu, happy hour 4-7pm) Located on the beach just north of main dock, this is a good place to hang out and drink terrific mixed drinks – anything with rum, or the Rasta Ripper, a concoction of home-brewed ginger beer and coconut rum.

Oceanside (☎ 226-0233; Front St; happy hour 4-7pm) This central place is good for drinking and making new friends, and often hosts live bands. Friday night is country and western night, while karaoke or punta rock happens on Saturday night.

Lazy Lizard (☎ 226-0368; the Split; ☺ 11am-11pm) The Lazy Lizard is described as a 'sunny place for shady people' – see what you think. It mainly serves beer to swimmers and other hangers-about, but has some menu items as well.

Sand Box (☎ 226-0200; Front St; ☺ happy hr 3-6pm) Sharing the same owner as Trends Beachfront Hotel, this place has outdoor seating facing the dock. It's a local favorite for socializing and catching up on gossip.

Shopping

Caulker has many shops selling T-shirts, beach gear and souvenirs. There are also a few pricier shops and art galleries.

Caribbean Colors (☎ 206-0206; Front St) This shop stocks a collection of silk-screened fabrics, jewelry and paintings by the owner, Lee Vanderwalker, and the artist Nelson Young.

Chocolate's Gift Shop (☎ 226-0151; Front St) Chocolate's wife, Annie, sells lovely Indonesian sarongs and clothing and Guatemalan textiles that she gathers on yearly shopping trips.

Coco Plum Giftshop (☎ 226-0226) Off Back St, this is another place for out-of-the-ordinary souvenirs.

Getting There & Away

AIR

Half the flights with **Maya Island Air** (☎ 226-0012; www.mayaairways.com) between the Belize City airports and Ambergris Caye stop at Caye Caulker, and half of those with **Tropic Air** (☎ 226-0040; www.tropicair.com) will do so on request. Caye Caulker to Belize City International Airport costs US$51, and to the municipal airstrip it's US$29. For flight frequencies, see p115. The airline offices are at Caye Caulker's newly renovated airstrip. **Tsunami Adventures** (☎ 226-0462; www.tsunami adventures.com; Front St) can also book tickets.

BOAT

Caye Caulker Water Taxi Association (☎ 226-0992; www.cayecaulkerwatertaxi.com) runs boats from the main dock on Caulker to Belize City (one-way/roundtrip US$10/18, one hour) at 6:30am, 7:30am, 8:30am, 10am, noon, 1:30pm, 3pm and 4pm (and 5pm Saturday, Sunday and holidays). Boats to San Pedro (one way/roundtrip US$10/18, 20 to 30 minutes) go at 7am, 8am, 10am, 11:30am, 1pm, 2:30pm, 4pm and 5pm.

Water taxis also run to St George's Caye and Caye Chapel, but you must request these stops and arrange pick-up in advance.

Getting Around

Caulker is so small that most people walk everywhere. If need be, you can rent a bicycle or golf cart at **Caye Caulker Golf Cart Rentals** (☎ 226-0237; dock st; bicycles per hr/day/week US$2/10/35, golf carts per hr/day US$13/50). The golf-cart **Rainbow Taxi Service** (☎ 226-0123; Front St) costs US$5 for a one-way trip anywhere on the island.

OTHER NORTHERN CAYES

Most visits to the other northern cayes are made by day trip from Caye Caulker or San Pedro, usually as part of a snorkel or dive trip. But you can stay on a number of the smaller and outlying islands. Serious divers, nature lovers and honeymooners are the most usual customers at the camps and resorts on these cayes. Often a boat charter is necessary to reach them. Inquire when you book lodgings.

Caye Chapel

Caye Chapel Island Resort (☎ 226-8250; www.caye chapel.com; casita from US$229, villa from US$1000; ❷ ❑) Just south of Caye Caulker, this private 265-acre island holds an 18-hole golf course and a super-deluxe corporate retreat center. Room rates include all meals and unlimited golfing. The golf course (☎ 226-8250) is open to the public by reservation. Cost is US$200 for the day, which includes unlimited golf, golf carts, clubs, poolside Caribbean lunch and use of the resort's swimming-pool complex, hot tub and private beach. Arrange boat transportation in advance with boats going to/from San Pedro or Caye Caulker with the Caye Caulker Water Taxi Association, left.

Turneffe Atoll

The Turneffe Islands together comprise Turneffe Atoll, one of the three atoll reefs in Belize's waters. The atoll is 30 miles long and 10 miles wide. Turneffe Atoll is usually visited by day trip, as it's within easy reach of Caulker, Ambergris and Belize City to the north, and Glover's Reef and Hopkins village to the south. Even Placencia dive boats occasionally make the trip to Turneffe Elbow, the southern tip of the islands.

The atoll is alive with coral, fish and large rays, and the terrain is quite varied: you can enjoy wall- and current-diving, as well as protected shallow areas abundant with coral (perfect for novice divers and snorkelers). On rough days it's favored by San Pedro dive operators because much of the trip can be made behind the barrier reef, protecting passengers from choppy open seas. The most popular sites are around the Elbow, where the current attracts big hungry fish in large numbers and affords one of the only drift dives in Belize. Other sites include Rendezvous, Hollywood and Cabbage Patch (with an impressive stand of brain coral). Fishing enthusiasts are attracted by the flats, which are ideal for saltwater fly-fishing.

Incredibly, the Turneffe Islands have as yet no environmental protection. However

Belize University's Institute of Marine Studies monitors environmental impact from a field station on Calabash Caye.

On Turneffe Atoll you'll find quite a few acccommodations:

Turneffe Flats Lodge (☎ 220-2046; www.tflats.com; Blackbird Caye; weekly package diving/fishing US$1607/2947; ✺) Although its principal fame is as a fishing retreat with expert guides, this lodge on Blackbird Caye, a 90-minute boat ride from Belize City, also offers dive trips that are often far less crowded than those from other resorts (because most of the other guests are out fishing). Accommodation is in spacious terracotta-tiled duplex apartments, each with balcony and dramatic views of the waves crashing on the nearby reef.

Blackbird Caye Resort (☎ 223-2772; www.blackbird resort.com; Blackbird Caye; weekly package diving/snorkeling US$1695/1495; ✺) Blackbird offers fishing and diving as well, but is popular with snorkelers, as they have two dedicated snorkeling boat trips per day. Enthusiasts can kayak out to the reef for even more snorkeling. Accommodation is in separate, roomy cabanas with stereo systems, and meals are eaten in a huge *palapa* restaurant near the main dock.

Oceanic Society (☎ 220-4256; www.oceanic-society .org; Blackbird Caye; weekly snorkel package US$1450) The society has a field station about five minutes' walk from Blackbird Caye Resort. Accommodations here are in basic but comfortable white wooden beachfront cabanas. The society also accepts volunteers on a paying basis to help with natural history research, documenting the incredibly diverse wildlife (manatees, crocodiles, bottlenosed dolphins and hawksbill sea turtles among others) that lives in the Turneffe Islands. Special family-education programs are worthwhile.

Amigos Dive Camp (in San Ignacio ☎ 603-3984; www.amigosbelize.com; Ropewalk Caye; 3-/5-day diving, fishing & snorkel package US$350/700, 3-day fishing & snorkeling US$250) This more affordable place is on Ropewalk Caye (Pelican Caye) in the southeast of the atoll. From here you can walk out to the reef. Guests sleep in simple upstairs rooms with shared bathrooms.

Turneffe Island Lodge (☎ 220-4011; www.belize travelcentral.com; Caye Bokel; weekly nondiving/diving package r US$1760/1995, cabana US$2100/2335; ✺ ▣) Definitely the fanciest of the Turneffe Atoll resorts, this place at the southern tip of the atoll, offers gorgeous cabanas with screened porches (where your morning coffee will be delivered), wooden floorboards, and indoor and outdoor showers, all set amid coconut palms just yards from the beach. Proximity to the famous Elbow dive site means trips go there frequently, and some of the best tarpon fishing is a three-minute boat ride away.

Lighthouse Reef

Lighthouse Reef, with six cayes, is the furthest atoll from the Belize shore and offers transparent waters. The famous Blue Hole is the most unique dive site in the region. There is spectacular wall-diving in the area, as well as opportunities for on-land exploring.

In addition to what follows, other top sites in Lighthouse Reef include the Aquarium, North Long Wall, Gorgonian Wall, Manta Wall and the Zoo. Half Moon Caye Wall is probably the best of the lot for its variety of coral formations along the wall, and within canyons and swim-throughs. Of particular interest is a field of garden eels found on the sand flats near the wall. Snorkelers don't despair: the shallows around these sites are interesting as well.

BLUE HOLE

In the center of Lighthouse Reef is the Blue Hole, one of Belize's natural wonders and its most popular dive site. Its unusual appearance – a deep blue pupil with an aquamarine border surrounded by the lighter shades of the reef – has become a logo for tourist publicity. This sinkhole is around 400ft deep and 1000ft across, and to dive it is to take a journey back into geological history. For millions of years the Blue Hole was a dry cave where huge stalactites and stalagmites slowly formed. When the last ice age ended, sea levels rose about 350ft, flooding the cave. At the same time, its ceiling collapsed, leaving the hole you see today.

You drop quickly to 130ft where you swim beneath an overhang, observing stalactites above you and, usually, a school of reef sharks below you. You might see four or five varieties of shark. Although the water is clear, light levels are low as you wend your way through the formations. A good dive light will enable you to appreciate the sponge and invertebrate life. Because of the depth, ascent begins after eight minutes; the brevity of the dive does disappoint some divers.

This trip is usually combined with other dives at Lighthouse Reef. Experienced divers will tell you that those other dives are the real highlight of the trip. But judging from its popularity – most dive shops make twice-weekly runs to the Blue Hole – plenty want to make the deep descent.

On day trips the Blue Hole will be your first dive, which can be nerve-racking if you're unfamiliar with the dive master and the other divers, or if you haven't been underwater lately. Do some local dives with your dive masters before setting out cold on a Blue Hole trip. An alternative is to take an overnight trip to Lighthouse Reef. For dive outfits and tour details see p106 and p119.

Snorkelers can enjoy a trip to the Blue Hole, too, as there's plenty to see around the shallow inner perimeter of the circular reef. For tour operators, see p119.

Note: this trip involves two hours each way by boat in possibly rough, open waters, and there's a US$30 marine-park fee for diving or snorkeling at the Blue Hole.

HALF MOON CAYE

A bird sanctuary that's home to the rare red-footed booby, Half Moon Caye is the most visited of Lighthouse Reef's cayes. Underwater visibility can extend more than 200ft here. The caye has a lighthouse, excellent beaches and spectacular submerged walls teeming with marine flora and fauna. Rising less than 10ft above sea level, the caye's 45 acres hold two distinct ecosystems. To the west is lush vegetation fertilized by the droppings of thousands of sea birds, including some 4000 red-footed boobies, the wonderfully named magnificent frigate bird and 98 other bird species. The east side has less vegetation but more palms. Loggerhead and hawksbill sea turtles, both endangered, lay their eggs on the southern beaches.

A nature trail weaves through the southern part of the island to an observation platform that brings viewers to eye level with nesting boobies and frigate birds. Along the path you'll see thousands of seashells, many inhabited by hermit crabs (unnerving when you first notice them moving!).

Organized boat trips, mainly from San Pedro and Caye Caulker, stop at Half Moon Caye and the nearby Blue Hole. Camping is permitted and there is a picnic area and toilets, but you need to bring all your water. The Belize Audubon Society has a visitors center where you must register and pay a US$10 park fee on arrival. This part of the island is also used as a base camp for kayaking, snorkeling and diving holidays by adventure-tour company, Island Expeditions (see p62).

OTHER LIGHTHOUSE REEF CAYES

Northern Caye, another small but lovely caye, is home to the **Lighthouse Reef Resort** (☎ 223-1205; in US ☎ 800-423-3114; www.scubabelize .com; 7-day diving/nondiving packages from US$1850/1502; ✕). This luxurious resort attracts divers who wish to roll out of bed and into the sea. You fly in and out of the caye's airstrip as part of the package.

Of the remaining four cayes, Sandbore, Saddle Caye and Hat Caye, are popular with mosquitoes and crocodiles, and mostly admired from afar by humans. **Long Caye** is another story. This idyllic private island, 2.5 miles long and 3.25 miles wide with white sandy beaches and plentiful coconut palms, has been earmarked for an ecovillage and ecoresorts. Some construction is finished and includes a couple of places to stay, a medical center with a decompression chamber, some houses and a couple of docks.

The rest of the island is divided into housing lots and public areas. Boardwalks, many already built, are to be used around the island to protect the wildlife. The government is overseeing environmental concerns. A boat charter from Belize City (see p87) costs US$700 roundtrip and takes around 2½ hours.

Calypso Beach Retreat (☎ in US 303-523-8165; www.calypsobeachretreat.com; Long Caye; weekly beachcomber/snorkel package US$795/995) is an attractive B&B on the northeast corner of the caye. It has four double rooms with bamboo four-poster beds in a two-story wooden island retreat, all with beachfront views. The price includes all meals, boat transfers from Belize City, snorkel gear and kayaks. Diving and fishing packages are available.

Long Caye Island Resort & Dive Shop (☎ 227-1220; http://longcayeislandresort.com; Long Caye), also at the north end of the island, may take over the name Blue Hole Resort from another planned development. Long Caye Island Resort was not receiving guests at the time of research. Lucky Dog Bunkhouse has bunk beds but also was not open for guests at the time of research.

Northern Belize

The northern Belize most commonly seen by visitors is farmland. Vast sugarcane fields grow alongside the paved, swift Northern Hwy, and off on the side roads Mennonites, Maya and Mestizos tend efficient multipurpose farms. Deeper into the back country you'll hit vast expanses of jungle in the hilly west, and mangrove swamps and saline lagoons along the Caribbean shoreline. The biggest draw here is the beautiful Maya site of Lamanai. Lamanai was continuously occupied for at least 3200 years – the longest known unbroken span in the Maya world. The journey to Lamanai up the New River, rich in bird life, makes the visit doubly exciting.

The far west of the region is covered in some of the largest swaths of tropical rainforest in Central America – over 600 sq miles of well-protected jungle in the Rio Bravo Conservation & Management Area and the Gallon Jug Parcel. Chan Chich Lodge and the Hill Bank and La Milpa Field Stations provide comfortable accommodations and a range of trails and activities for visitors to explore this special environment.

Corozal is Belize's northernmost town of appreciable size and a gateway for travelers going to and from Mexico's Yucatán Peninsula – a relaxed seaside town with a combination of Maya, Mexican, Caribbean, North American and Chinese cultures. Orange Walk is the commercial center for farming and the starting point for trips along the New River to Lamanai. Near the northeast tip of mainland Belize, the remote fishing village of Sarteneja has a relaxed charm and is a base for visiting Shipstern Nature Reserve.

NORTHERN BELIZE

HIGHLIGHTS

- Taking a boat tour up the jungle-clad New River to the magnificent ruins at **Lamanai** (p135)
- Experiencing the true delights of rainforest at **Chan Chich Lodge** (p139)
- Enjoying exceptional birding and wildlife-viewing at the Rio Bravo Conservation & Management Area's **La Milpa Field Station** (p138)
- Cooling off in the saltwater breezes and enjoying good meals at relaxed **Corozal** (p140)
- Escaping to the sleepy fishing village of **Sarteneja** (p145)

POPULATION: 79,000	MONTHLY RAINFALL: JAN/JUN 4IN/5IN (COROZAL)	HIGHEST ELEVATION: 777FT

History

Northern Belize was on the eastern fringe of the ancient Maya heartland, and though it supported many settlements it didn't give rise to any cities of the size or grandeur of Caracol, further south in Belize, or Tikal in Guatemala. But important river trade routes linking the interior with the coast and thus the Yucatán Peninsula ran through here: the north's major Maya site, Lamanai, commanded one of these routes and grew to a city of up to 35,000 people.

A Spanish expedition into northern Belize from the Yucatán in 1544 conquered many Maya settlements, and afterwards a series of Spanish missions was set up in the region, distantly controlled by a priest at Bacalar in the southeastern Yucatán. But the Maya here rebelled repeatedly against Spanish attempts to control them and drove them out for good in 1640.

British loggers began moving into the region in search of mahogany in the 18th century, encountering sporadic resistance from the depleted Maya, who had been ravaged by European-introduced diseases.

In 1847 the Maya in the Yucatán rose up against their Spanish-descended overlords in the War of the Castes ('Guerra de Castas' in Spanish), a vicious conflict that continued in diminishing form into the 20th century. Refugees from both sides of the conflict took shelter in northern British Honduras (as Belize was then called), with

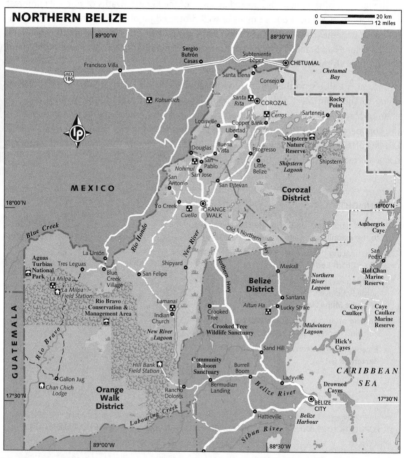

NORTHERN BELIZE IN...

One Day
Take the trip up the bird-rich New River to the jungle-clad Maya ruins at **Lamanai** (p135).

Three Days
Make the Lamanai trip and treat yourself to a couple of days at **Chan Chich Lodge** (p139).

Five or Six Days
Do the three-day agenda and deepen your knowledge of the northwestern jungles with a visit to **La Milpa** or **Hill Bank Field Stations** (p138).

Ten Days
To the five- or six-day itinerary, add a couple of chill-out days at **Corozal** (p140), a trip to the ruins at **Cerros** (p144), followed by a couple of days at **Sarteneja** (p145), and a visit to the **Shipstern Nature Reserve** (p145).

---

people of Spanish descent founding the towns of Orange Walk and Corozal, and the Maya moving into the forests and countryside. It wasn't surprising that intermittent hostilities took place in British Honduras. One group of Maya, the Icaiché, were repulsed from Orange Walk after fierce fighting in 1872. The border between Mexico and British Honduras was not agreed between the two states until 1893.

Caste War migrants from the Yucatán laid the foundations of modern northern Belize by starting the area's first sugarcane plantations. Despite the sugar industry's many vicissitudes, it is now the backbone of the northern Belize economy, with some 900 cane farms around the region.

Language

Because of its proximity to Mexico and Guatemala's Petén, and the Mexican or Guatemalan origins of many of the people living here, Spanish is the first language of many northerners, be they Maya, Mestizo of Mexican origin or more recent immigrant workers from El Salvador and Guatemala. However, nearly everybody speaks English as well.

Getting There & Around

The Northern Hwy runs through the region linking Belize City with the Mexican border via the region's two main towns: Orange Walk and Corozal. Frequent buses travel up and down this artery and continue on to Chetumal, 7 miles into Mexico. Daily boat services and flights connect Corozal with Sarteneja near the northeast tip of the mainland, and San Pedro (Ambergris Caye). At San Pedro you can connect with flights to/from Belize City.

ORANGE WALK
pop 15,000

The agricultural and economic hub of northern Belize, 57 miles from Belize City, Orange Walk is not a tourist town, but is the starting point for a superlative trip to the ruins of Lamanai (p135). Orange Walk has a fine location beside the New River, which meanders lazily along the east side of town, but the town itself is a down-to-earth, workaday place. An adequate number of reasonable hotels and restaurants serve the needs of visitors who aren't whizzing in and out on day trips from other parts of Belize.

Orange Walk is a commercial center for the region's farmers, including many Mennonites (see p36). Citrus fruits and papaya are among the crops, but the real name of the game is sugarcane and its byproducts – sugar, molasses (the thick syrup that drains off during sugar refining), bagasse (refuse from the sugar-refining process) and rum. Two brands of rum are distilled in Orange Walk: Caribbean and Rum Master, which are both cheap and readily available throughout the country. Don't be surprised if you see the occasional local looking a little worse for wear here in Orange Walk!

The Tower Hill sugar refinery, 4 miles south of Orange Walk, processes all of the sugarcane in Belize – over a million tons per year. Tower Hill employs about 600 workers, and most of Orange Walk's inhabitants work in jobs related to cane production. Altogether some 40,000 Belizeans rely one way or another on the sugarcane industry, which makes its recurring instability a headache not just for Orange Walk but for the government of Belize, and economic planners as far away as the US and Europe (see the boxed text on p134).

Orientation & Information

It's easy to find your way around Orange Walk. The Northern Hwy, called Queen Victoria Ave in town, is the main thoroughfare. A recently built bypass now keeps the lumbering sugarcane trucks out of the town center. The center of town is shady Central Park, on the east side of Queen Victoria Ave. Orange Walk lacks an official tourism information center, though hotels can provide local information.

Belize Bank (☎ 322-2019; 34 Main St; ☒ 8am-3pm Mon-Thu, 8am-4:30pm Fri) The ATMs here and at the Shell fuel station (Queen Victoria Ave) accept international Visa, MasterCard, Plus and Cirrus cards.

K&N Print Shop (☎ 322-0294; Queen Victoria Ave; Internet per hr US$2; ☒ 8am-noon, 2-5pm & 7-9pm Mon-Sat, 8am-5pm Sun) Downtown Internet access.

Northern Regional Hospital (☎ 322-2072; ☒ 24hr emergency services) At the north end of town, beside the Northern Hwy.

Post office (☎ 322-2345; cnr Queen Victoria Ave & Arthur St; ☒ 8am-noon & 1-4:30pm Mon-Thu, till 4pm Fri)

Sights

BANQUITAS HOUSE OF CULTURE

The modern **House of Culture** (☎ 322-0517; admission free; ☒ 10am-6pm Tue-Fri, 8am-noon Sat) has an attractively displayed exhibit on Orange Walk's history. It's especially good on the local Maya sites and has artifacts, maps and illustrations, as well as exhibits that change monthly. It's set in a pleasant, small, riverside park with an amphitheater.

CUELLO

Close by to Orange Walk, **Cuello** (*kway*-yo) is one of the earliest-known settled communities in the Maya world, probably dating back to around 2400 BC, although there's not very much left to show for it. The Maya of Cuello, a small farming community, were excellent potters and prolific farmers, and though archaeologists have found plenty here, only Structure 350, a nine-tiered pyramid, is of much interest to the non-expert. The pyramid was constructed around AD 200–300 but its lower levels date from before 2000 BC.

The site is on private property owned by **Cuello Distillery** (☎ 320-9085; Yo Creek Rd), 2.5 miles west of Orange Walk (take San Antonio Rd out of town). The rum distillery, on the south side of the road, is unmarked except for a gate; the site is through and beyond it. The distillery is free to explore, but ask permission at the gate. A taxi to Cuello from Orange Walk costs about US$12, roundtrip.

THE WAR OF THE CASTES COMES TO ORANGE WALK

Orange Walk was born as a logging camp in the 18th century, from where mahogany was floated down the New River to Corozal Bay. It began to develop as a town around 1850, when Mexican refugees from the War of the Castes arrived. These migrants, whose agricultural experience was welcomed by the British colonial authorities, started northern Belize's first sugar boom (which lasted from the 1850s to the 1870s).

The complex War of the Castes itself reached Orange Walk in 1872, when a force of some 150 Icaiché Maya attacked the town's British garrison. After several hours of fierce fighting the Icaiché were repelled, and their leader Marcos Canul was fatally wounded in the attack, which has gone down in history as the last significant armed Maya resistance in Belize. The Icaiché had been at odds with the British for several reasons, including encroachments by British loggers into lands that the Icaiché considered their own around the Rio Hondo (which today forms Belize's border with Mexico), and arms supplies from British Honduras to the Cruzob Maya (bitter enemies of the Icaiché).

The scant remains of two British forts in Orange Walk, Fort Mundy and Fort Cairnes, serve as reminders of the conflict. A flagpole behind Orange Walk's town hall is the only remnant of Fort Cairnes, while Independence Plaza marks the site of Fort Mundy.

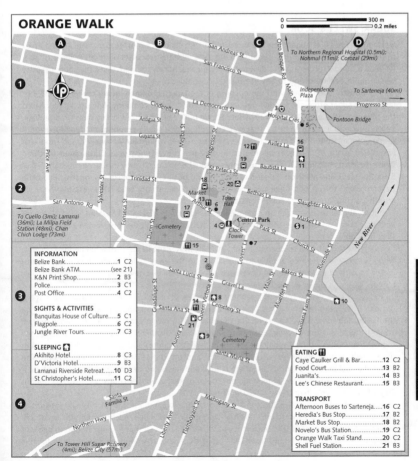

ORANGE WALK

INFORMATION
Belize Bank.....................................1 C2
Belize Bank ATM.....................(see 21)
K&N Print Shop.............................2 B3
Police..3 C1
Post Office.....................................4 C2

SIGHTS & ACTIVITIES
Banquitas House of Culture......5 C1
Flagpole..6 C2
Jungle River Tours........................7 C3

SLEEPING
Akihito Hotel.................................8 C3
D'Victoria Hotel............................9 B3
Lamanai Riverside Retreat......10 D3
St Christopher's Hotel.............11 C2

EATING
Caye Caulker Grill & Bar.........12 C2
Food Court....................................13 B2
Juanita's..14 B3
Lee's Chinese Restaurant........15 B3

TRANSPORT
Afternoon Buses to Sarteneja.....16 C2
Heredia's Bus Stop.....................17 B2
Market Bus Stop..........................18 B2
Novelo's Bus Station...................19 C2
Orange Walk Taxi Stand...........20 C2
Shell Fuel Station........................21 B3

NOHMUL

'Great Mound' in Mayan, **Nohmul** (noh-*mool*) was, in its day, a much more important site than Cuello. In the late Classic Period this was a town of some 3000 people. The vast site covers more than 7 sq miles, though most of it is overgrown with grass and sugarcane. Although the ruins themselves aren't exactly spectacular, the view from the tallest of them, Structure 2, a lofty acropolis, is. You can see clear across the Orange Walk District, over endless fields of cane.

From the northern edge of Orange Walk, drive 9.6 miles north on the Northern Hwy to the village of San Jose. At the north end of the village look for the sign directing you 1.3 miles west to Nohmul. The dirt road slightly forks twice – keep your eyes on the odometer and stay right; the actual site is not well marked. If you don't have a car, you can take a bus to San Jose, and walk the dirt road. A taxi from Orange Walk is about US$15, roundtrip.

Sleeping

St Christopher's Hotel (☎ 322-2420; rowbze@btl.net; 10 Main St; r with fan/air-con US$29/45, garden or riverview with fan/air-con US$35/51; ℗ ✕) This yellow-painted, well-run hotel offers the best value in Orange Walk. The large, quiet rooms are clean and have private bathroom, tiled floors and cable TV. The newer, off-street, garden rooms are the nicest. You can embark right here for the boat trip to Lamanai.

SUGAR: SWEET & SOUR

Northern Belize's first 'sugar cycle' occurred in the 19th century, when Mestizo Caste War refugees from the Yucatán brought their sugar-planting skills with them and set up modest sugar estates. By 1868 around 2700 acres were devoted to sugarcane, but by the mid-1880s the sugar industry was in rapid decline owing to adverse market conditions.

The industry was revived with the opening of the Libertad refinery near Corozal in 1935, but large-scale sugar production didn't get underway until a British company, Tate & Lyle, purchased the refinery in the early 1960s. In 1974 Tate & Lyle built a second big refinery near Orange Walk. Belize now had a major industry that was controlled by a single corporation, dependent on a mono-crop agriculture and intensely vulnerable to market whims. But no-one worried too much about this as the 1970s sugar boom put dollar signs in everyone's eyes. Throughout northern Belize, peasants became pillars of prosperity and the boom significantly increased the standard of living for Maya and Mestizos. Sugar had become big business and, unlike mahogany, sugarcane never seemed to run out. Cane grows easily in hot climates; the crop is harvestable every six months, giving farmers two solid crops a year.

But an almost total reliance on cane meant a reduction in diversified farming. More and more land was taken up by cane, and where farmers had grown food for their families and villages, they now grew cane.

When the sugar boom reached its height in 1980, most cane farmers were full-fledged *cañeros*, whose crops were devoted entirely to cane. Then, in the early 1980s, world sugar prices plummeted as widespread recession in developed countries reduced demand for sugar. The Libertad refinery was shut down in 1985.

Today, Orange Walk's Tower Hill refinery processes all of Belize's cane. The industry is still a big one in Belizean terms – it has provided around 37% of the country's export earnings since the 1980s, and some 65,000 acres on 900 farms are still growing cane. But farmers today receive around US$20 per ton of cane, against US$30 to US$35 in the 1970s. The chief challenge for the Belizean sugar industry today is that the preferential quotas and subsidies it has enjoyed in the EU (which buys about half of Belize's sugar) and the US (15%) are coming to an end. The prices that Belize receives for its sugar are falling, and Belizeans are going to have to fight even harder to sell it. The Tower Hill refinery, now belonging to a worker-controlled trust, BSI (Belize Sugar Industries Ltd), had to lay off 90 workers in 2004.

Belize needs both to raise the yields from its sugar plantations and to diversify into other cane products. A step forward was taken in December 2004 when Belcogen, an affiliate of BSI, signed a deal to supply BEL (Belize Electricity Ltd) with 13.5MW of power generated from bagasse (the wastes from sugar refining) from 2007 onwards. A special new plant is being built for this purpose beside the Tower Hill refinery.

Lamanai Riverside Retreat (☎ 302-3955; Lamanai Alley; r US$30; P ✷) The plain but decent wooden rooms, which have private bathrooms and TVs, face the river. Adjoining the retreat is one of Orange Walk's best places to eat and drink (see opposite). The owner has a quaint hobby of capturing, measuring and generally keeping an eye on the 60 or so crocodiles that reside in the area. Boats to Lamanai will pick you up here, too.

D'Victoria Hotel (☎ 322-2518; www.dvictoria.com; 40 Queen Victoria Ave; s/d/t US$24/32/45, with air-con US$40/46/57; P ✷ ✷) The rooms at this medium-size hotel are clean and reasonably cheery, with colorful bedspreads, cable

TV and tiled private bathrooms with good showers. The best rooms are those at the side and back (with exterior windows). The bonuses here are the outdoor swimming pool, friendly staff and the hammocks out the back.

Akihito Hotel (☎ 302-0185; www.akihitobelize.com; 22 Queen Victoria Ave; dm/d/tr with shared bathroom US$8/13/18, d/tr with private bathroom US$23/28, d/tr with private bathroom & air-con US$30/33; ✷ ▢) The Akihito's drab concrete exterior is an accurate indicator of the style of the interior, but the super-friendly owners and the cleanliness of their hotel make this the best budget bet in town. Nearly all rooms here have cable TV.

Eating & Drinking

Caye Caulker Grill & Bar (☎ 322-0355; Queen Victoria Ave; mains US$4-8; ☺ 11:30am-10pm Tue-Thu, 11:30am-11pm Fri-Sun) Eat under an awning with colorful fish murals along the wall and sand-colored dirt on the floor – not quite enough to make you think you're on Caulker, but come anyway for the tasty seafood, meat, burgers and side orders of coconut rice.

Lamanai Riverside Retreat (☎ 302-3955; Lamanai Alley; mains US$5-10; ☺ 8am-10pm) This is the best place in town to be when the sun goes down, with its breezy deck and tables right by the river. Good shrimp, lobster and meat dishes are served here, as well as ceviches, burgers and salads if you fancy something lighter.

Lee's Chinese Restaurant (☎ 322-2174; 11 San Antonio Rd; dishes US$4-8; ☺ 11am-midnight) Easily the best of Orange Walk's many Chinese eateries, Lee's serves up a full range of Chinese options in sparkling clean surroundings, with a stylish dragon-theme decor, kept cool by whirring ceiling fans.

Juanita's (☎ 322-2677; 8 Santa Ana St; dishes US$2-3; ☺ 6am-2pm & 6-9pm) You can tell by the dedicated locals who flock here that the food is satisfying. A simple, clean, very well-priced place, Juanita's serves eggs and bacon for breakfast, rice and beans and other local favorites, such as cow-foot soup, during the rest of the day.

Food Court (Arthur St; breakfast US$2-2.50, snacks US$0.50-1; ☺ 6am-6pm) This line of cafés and snack stalls beside the market offers some of the best-value eats in town, including good-size breakfasts, lots of Mexican snacks and great sponge cakes.

Getting There & Away

Novelo's Bus Line (☎ 302-2858; cnr Queen Victoria Ave & St Peter's St) runs once or twice an hour to Belize City (one-way express/regular US$3.50/2.50, 1½/two hours, from 6am to 8:30pm), Corozal (express/regular US$2.50/2, 45 minutes/one hour, from 7:30am to 9pm) and Chetumal (express/regular US$3.50/2.75, 1½/two hours, from 7:30am to 6:30pm).

Buses to less-popular destinations depart from various points mostly near the market, and schedules are subject to change:

Copper Bank (US$2, one hour) Heredia's buses depart at 11:30am and 5pm Monday to Saturday, half a block south of the market.

Lamanai (US$2.50, 1½ hour) Tillett's buses depart at 3:30pm Monday, Wednesday and Friday from the market bus stop.

Sarteneja (US$2.50, 1½ hour) Buses depart at 11:30am and noon Monday to Saturday from the market bus stop; they also depart hourly from 1pm to 5pm Monday to Saturday, and 3pm Sunday, from the north end of Main St.

LAMANAI

Easily the most spectacular and fascinating Maya site in northern Belize, **Lamanai** (admission US$5; ☺ 8am-5pm) is 24 miles south of Orange Walk up the New River, or 36 miles if you take the road. Lamanai's impressive architecture has a marvelous setting amid the jungle overlooking the New River Lagoon, and the way most visitors approach it – by guided river trip from Orange Walk – makes this two trips in one because the New River is home to countless colorful and unusual birds and most of the guides are expert at spotting them.

History

Lamanai not only spans all phases of ancient Maya civilization but also tells a tale of ongoing Maya occupation and resistance for centuries after the Europeans arrived. This adds up to the longest known unbroken occupation in the Maya world. Lamanai was inhabited at least as early as 1500 BC and was already a major ceremonial center, with large temples, in late-Preclassic times.

It seems to have surged in importance (perhaps thanks to its location on trade routes between the Caribbean and the interior) around 200 or 100 BC, and its major buildings were mostly constructed between then and AD 700, although additions and changes went on up to at least the 15th century. At its peak it is estimated to have had a population of around 35,000.

When the Spanish invaded northern Belize from the Yucatán in 1544, one of the most important of the missions they set up was Lamanai, where they had found a thriving Maya community. But the Maya never readily accepted Spanish overlordship, and a rebellion in 1640 left the Lamanai mission burned and deserted. Maya continued to live here until the late 17th or 18th century when they were decimated by an epidemic, probably smallpox.

Archaeological excavations commenced as early as 1917, but large-scale digging, by

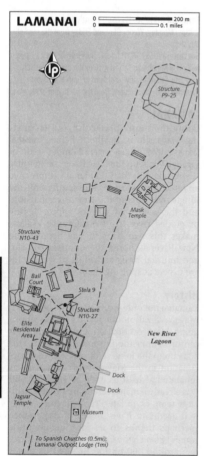

LAMANAI

0   200 m
0   0.1 miles

Structure
P9-25

Mask
Temple

Structure
N10-43

Ball
Court

Stela 9

Structure
N10-27

Elite
Residential
Area

New River
Lagoon

Dock

Dock

Jaguar
Temple

Museum

To Spanish Churches (0.5mi);
Lamanai Outpost Lodge (1mi)

David Pendergast of Canada's Royal Ontario Museum, began in 1974. The painstaking work of uncovering more than 700 structures found here will take several lifetimes, not to mention huge amounts of funding.

New River Voyage

Most visitors opt to reach Lamanai on a spectacular boat ride up the New River from Orange Walk. On this trip, available only as part of an organized tour (see opposite), you motor 1½ hours upriver, between riverbanks crowded with dense jungle vegetation. En route, your skipper/guide points out the many local birds and you will almost certainly spot a crocodile or two. You also pass the austere Mennonite community at Shipyard. Eventually the river broadens out into the New River Lagoon and you soon land at Lamanai on the west bank.

The Site

Arriving at Lamanai by boat, you'll probably first visit the small **museum**, which exhibits some beautiful examples of pottery and obsidian and jade jewelry. Then you'll head into the jungle, passing gigantic guanacaste (tubroos), ceiba and ramón (breadnut) trees, strangler figs, allspice, epiphytes and examples of Belize's national flower, the black orchid. In the canopy overhead you might see (or hear) one of the groups of resident howler monkeys. A tour of the ruins takes a minimum of 90 minutes, but can be done more comfortably in two or three hours.

JAGUAR TEMPLE

This temple (Structure N10-9), fronting a 100yd-wide plaza, was built in the 6th century AD and modified several times up to at least the 15th century – a fine example of the longevity of the Lamanai settlement. It was still in use when the Spanish arrived. The stone patterning on the lowest level turns depict two cleverly designed jaguar faces, dating from the initial 6th-century construction. On the opposite (north) side of the plaza is a set of buildings that was used as residences for Lamanai's royal elite.

STELA 9

North of the elite residential complex, this intricately carved standing stone in front of Structure N10-27 was erected in AD 625 to commemorate the accession of Lord Smoking Shell in 608. He is shown in ceremonial regalia, wearing a rattlesnake headdress with quetzal feathers at the back, and holding a double-headed serpent bar diagonally across his body, with a deity emerging from the serpent's jaw at the top. The remains of five children – ranging in age from newborn to eight – were buried beneath the stela. Archaeologists believe the burial must have been highly significant, since offerings are not usually associated with the dedication of monuments.

BALL COURT

Not far west of Stela 9 is Lamanai's ball court, one of the smallest in the Maya world – but with the largest ball-court marker yet found! A ceremonial vessel containing liquid mercury, probably from Guatemala, was found beneath the marker.

STRUCTURE N10-43

North of the ball court, across a plaza shaded by trees, is Structure N10-43, the highest at Lamanai, which rises 125ft above the jungle canopy. Few large buildings in the Maya world were built as early as this one, which was initially constructed around 100 BC. This grand ceremonial temple was built from nothing on a site that had previously been residential, which indicated a dramatic surge in Lamanai's importance at the time. You can climb to its summit for fabulous panoramas over the rest of Lamanai, the New River Lagoon and plains and forests stretching out on all sides.

MASK TEMPLE

To the northeast along a jungle path, the Mask Temple (Structure N9-56) was begun around 200 BC and was modified several times up to AD 1300. It has a 13ft stylized mask of a man in a crocodile headdress emblazoned on the southern part of its west face. The name Lamanai meant Submerged Crocodile in the language of its ancient inhabitants, and this animal clearly had great significance for them.

Dating from about AD 400, this is one of the finest big masks in the Maya world and unusual in that it is made of limestone blocks rather than plaster. A similar mask is hidden beneath the façade on the northern side. Deep within this building archaeologists found the tombs of a man adorned with shell and jade jewelry, and a woman from almost the same date. The pair are thought to be a succession of leaders – perhaps a husband and wife, or brother and sister.

STRUCTURE P9-25

At the far north end of the site, and often missed out on tours, this large platform, 120yd by 100yd in area, supports several large buildings up to 92ft high. Next to it is a river inlet that formed an ancient harbor.

COLONIAL STRUCTURES

Some 400yd south of Jaguar Temple are the remains of the thick stone walls of two Spanish churches, which were built from the remains of a temple by Maya forced labor.

The southern church was built in 1544, and the northern one in the 1560s. Both were destroyed by the Maya, the second one in the 1640 rebellion. Unknown to the Spanish, the Maya placed sacred objects such as crocodile figurines inside the churches while building them.

A 300yd path opposite the churches leads to the partly overgrown remains of a 19th-century sugar mill.

Tours

Two firms in Orange Walk will take you on the six- to seven-hour river trip to Lamanai and back. Both have guides who know their birds as well as their archaeology. They usually require a minimum of four people to make the trip, and you should reserve your place the day before, although you may still be lucky on the morning you want to go. It's also feasible to take this tour in a long day trip from as far away as Belize City or Corozal, even by bus.

Jungle River Tours (Map p133; ☎ 302-2293; lamanai mayatour@btl.net; 20 Lovers' Lane, Orange Walk) The tour costs US$45 per person and includes lunch, refreshments and site admission. Be at its office by 9am or you can be picked up at St Christopher's Hotel or Lamanai Riverside Retreat.

Reyes & Sons (☎ /fax 322-3327, 610-1548; riverman reyes@hotmail.com) The tour costs US$38 per person and includes lunch, refreshments and site admission. It costs US$25 without lunch or refreshments. The tour departs from the Northern Hwy bridge over the New River, 5 miles south of Orange Walk. Be there by 9am. The company can usually give you a ride from Orange Walk.

Sleeping

Lamanai Outpost Lodge (☎ 223-3578, in US ☎ 888-733-7864; www.lamanai.com; 2-/3-/4-night package for 2 US$1452/1980/2540; Ⓟ 🖳) About 1 mile south of the ruins, this classy lodge is perched on a hillside just above the lagoon, and boasts panoramic views from its bar and gorgeous open-air dining room. The 20 thatched-roof bungalows, each with fan, private bathroom and verandah, are cozy and perfectly suited to the casual jungle atmosphere. Packages include meals, most drinks, transfers to/from Belize City and three guided, small-group activities per day. The list of activities ranges from visiting the ruins or observing howler monkeys to starlight canoeing or nocturnal crocodile encounters. Birding is big here: almost 400 species have been documented within 3 miles of the lodge. The lodge sometimes offers guests generous discounts on reservations made within five days of your visit.

Getting There & Away

Though the river voyage is part of the fun of visiting Lamanai, it can also be reached by road (36 miles) from Orange Walk via Yo Creek and San Felipe. Allow at least an hour to drive the bumpy roads. Buses run to and from Orange Walk (US$2.50, 1½ hours) on Monday, Wednesday and Friday, leaving Indian Church at 4am and returning in the afternoon, so they're no use for a day trip to Lamanai (the service is primarily for villagers going into town for marketing).

RIO BRAVO CONSERVATION & MANAGEMENT AREA

Protecting 406 sq miles of tropical forest in northwest Belize, the **Rio Bravo Conservation & Management Area** (RBCMA) occupies 4% of Belize's total land area. Owned and managed by the Belizean nonprofit organization Programme for Belize (PFB), the RBCMA harbors astonishing biological diversity – 392 bird species (more than two-thirds of Belize's total), 200 tree species, 70 mammal species, including all five of Belize's cats (jaguar, puma, ocelot, jaguarundi and margay).

Rio Bravo is said to have the largest concentration of jaguars in Central America. If you're looking for true, wild tropical rainforest, this is it – and visitors are welcomed by the PFB in an ecotourism program that offers comfortable accommodations at two field stations: La Milpa and Hill Bank.

Parts of the territory of the RBCMA were logged for mahogany and other woods from the 18th century until the 1980s, but since the logging was selective the forest has survived. At least 60 Maya sites have been located in the area. Preeminent is **La Milpa**, the third largest Maya site in Belize and believed to have had a population of 50,000 at its peak between AD 750 and 850. Its 5-acre Great Plaza, one of the biggest of all Maya plazas, is surrounded by four pyramids up to 80ft high. Archaeologists from Boston University are conducting long-term investigations at the site.

At the RBCMA the PFB seeks to link conservation with the development of sustainable land uses. Programs include tree nurseries, extraction of nontimber products such as chicle, thatch and palm, experimental operations in sustainable timber extraction, and ecotourism. The thousands of visitors annually include many Belizean and international students.

History

Maya lived in this area as early as 800 BC. When Spanish expeditions first journeyed here the Maya were still using the same river trade routes, though by then their population was seriously depleted. Mahogany loggers moved into the area by the mid-18th century but were subject to intermittent attacks by the Maya for at least a century. By the late 19th century the Belize Estate and Produce Company (BEC) owned almost all of the land in northwestern Belize. The company carried out major timber extractions, floating mahogany and Mexican cedar out through the river system to the coast. With the advent of rail systems and logging trucks, operations flourished until over-cutting and a moody market finally prompted the BEC to stop cutting trees in the early 1980s.

Intensive chicle tapping also took place throughout the 20th century, and you can still see slash scars from this on sapodilla trees throughout the RBCMA.

The Belizean businessman Barry Bowen, owner of the Belikin brewery and the country's Coca-Cola distribution rights, bought the BEC and its nearly 1100 sq miles of land in 1982. He quickly sold off massive chunks to Yalbac Ranch (owned by a Texan cattle farmer) and Coca-Cola Foods. Meanwhile the Massachusetts Audubon Society was looking for a reserve for migrating birds. Coca-Cola donated 66 sq miles to support the initiative (a further 86 sq miles followed in 1992), and Programme for Belize was created to manage the land. Bowen also donated some land and PFB, helped by more than US$2 million raised by the UK-based World Land Trust, bought the rest, bringing its total up to today's 406 sq miles.

Sleeping & Eating

It's a long trek out here, so most visitors stay overnight at one of the two **field stations** (dm/cabana per person incl meals US$100/115; **P**). Hill Bank Field Station is in the southeastern part of the RBCMA beside the New River

---

CHICLE & CHEWING GUM

Chicle, a pinkish to reddish-brown gum, is actually the coagulated milky sap, or latex, of the sapodilla tree (Achras zapota), a tropical evergreen native to Central America. Chicleros (chicle workers) enter the forest and cut large gashes in the sapodillas' trunks, making a pattern of V-shaped cuts on the trunk of the tree. The sap runs from the wounds down the trunk, where it's collected in a cloth container at the base. After being boiled, it is shaped into blocks, called marquetas, for shipping. Repeated cutting can kill the tree, so chicle harvesting tends to result in serious depletion of sapodilla forests. A typical tree used for harvesting chicle has a life span of just 10 years.

First used as a substitute for natural rubber (to which the sapodilla is related), by about 1890 chicle was best known as the main ingredient in chewing gum (including the ever-popular Chiclets). Belizean chicle exports, chiefly to the USA, jumped from 3561lb in 1893 to more than 3 million lb after 1912. The chicleros, mainly Maya, harvested in the forests of west and northwest Belize and across the Guatemalan and Mexican borders.

As a result of war research for a rubber substitute during the 1940s, synthetic substitutes were developed for chicle. Now chewing gum is made mostly from these synthetic solutions. The Programme for Belize organization is, however, investigating possibilities of reviving the chicle industry in a sustainable way in the Rio Bravo Conservation & Management Area.

Lagoon (upstream from Lamanai), on the site of an abandoned logging station where old wooden buildings and antique steam engines remain. La Milpa Field Station is in the northwest of the RBCMA, 3 miles from La Milpa Maya site. The birding at La Milpa is exceptional, and spider and howler monkeys, coatimundi, peccaries and agoutis (as well as jaguar and ocelot tracks) are all commonly seen in the area.

Visiting arrangements for either place must be made in advance through **Programme for Belize** (Map pp76-7; ☎ 227-5616/1020; www.pfbelize .org; 1 Eyre St, Belize City; ☽ 8am-5pm Mon-Fri).

The stations' lovely thatched cabanas come complete with private bathroom, hot water, fresh linens, verandah and mosquito nets. The four-person dorm rooms incorporate eco-technology such as solar power and gray-water recycling. There are plenty of hammocks in which to lie back and listen to birdsong.

The prices include all meals and two guided tours of your choice from the selection on offer: trail hikes, early morning bird walks, a visit to La Milpa archaeological site (from La Milpa Field Station), canoeing or nighttime crocodile-spotlighting at Hill Bank. At an extra cost you can visit nearby communities or Lamanai (from La Milpa Field Station) or take a lagoon boat tour (from Hill Bank Field Station). There are also opportunities to meet visiting researchers and archaeologists.

Getting There & Away

Most visitors rent a vehicle to get to either field station: it's about a three-hour drive from Belize City to La Milpa (via Orange Walk, Yo Creek, San Felipe, Blue Creek and Tres Leguas), or two hours to Hill Bank (via Burrell Boom, Bermudian Landing and Rancho Dolores). The PFB can advise on road conditions and give you detailed directions. The later stages of both trips involve sections on unpaved roads. The PFB can also arrange transfers, at a price: US$175 one-way for up to three people from Belize City to La Milpa or Hill Bank, and US$75 from Orange Walk to La Milpa.

CHAN CHICH LODGE

Located in the remote far west of the Orange Walk District, **Chan Chich Lodge** (☎ /fax 223-4419, in US ☎ 800-343-8009; www.chanchich.com; s cabanas US$191-262, d cabanas US$223-305, with meals & activities s US$325-380, d US$485-550; P ⬛ ☒) is truly a destination unto itself; in fact, many of its visitors take a charter flight from Belize City and spend their entire trip here. Its setting is incredible: thatched cabanas – each with bathroom, fan, two queen-size beds and a wrap-around verandah – share space with partly excavated ruins in an ancient Maya plaza. The limited number of cabanas keeps it uncrowded and helps maintain the feeling that you're really in the middle of nowhere.

One of Belize's original eco-lodges, Chan Chich remains among the very best, but keeps its casual, shorts-and-T-shirt atmosphere. The remote jungle setting and prolific wildlife are very hard to beat. While you may not see jaguars during your visit, you'll definitely feel their presence, and you are likely to see coatimundis, kinkajous, deer, howler and spider monkeys and an enormous array of bird life. Ornithologists have identified more than 350 bird species here.

Chan Chich lies within a private reserve of over 200 sq miles known as the Gallon Jug Parcel, maintained by Belizean businessman Barry Bowen after his purchase of the BEC's lands in the 1980s (see p138). Intensive agriculture is practiced in a small part of the reserve, but the rest is subject to strict conservation. The lodge offers guided walks, vehicle tours and other activities throughout the day (and some at night), and 9 miles of trails invite independent exploration. One tour goes to Gallon Jug, the center of the reserve's very orderly agricultural operations. Crops grown here include corn, soybeans, cacao and organic coffee beans, and another program aims to raise the quality of local beef using embryo transfer technology from English Herefords.

The lodge is about 25 miles south of La Milpa Field Station (see p138) and 4 miles from the Guatemalan border. It's most easily reached by chartered plane from Belize City (about US$250 per person roundtrip), though you can also drive (130 miles, four hours from Belize City). The 73 miles from Orange Walk are mostly unpaved but all-weather. A car with driver from Belize City costs around US$200.

COROZAL
pop 8600

Corozal is a prosperous (by Belizean standards) commercial and farming center 29 miles north of Orange Walk. It's a relaxed place and a popular stop for travelers heading to or from Mexico – an easy place to acclimatize to Belize if you've just arrived. Two Maya sites vie for your attention, as do some good midrange and budget hotels and eateries. Parkland runs along the waterfront on Corozal Bay and there are many places to jump in the water and cool off.

In recent years, Corozal's unassuming charms have lured a growing number of North Americans, who have made this area their home.

History

The ruins of the Postclassic Maya trading center, now called Santa Rita (probably the original Chetumal), lie beneath parts of modern Corozal. Across the bay, Cerros was a substantial coastal trade center in the Preclassic Period.

Modern Corozal dates from 1849, when it was founded by Mexicans fleeing the War of the Castes. The refugees built Fort Barlee for protection from attacks by hostile Maya and named their town Corozal after the Spanish word for cohune palm, a strong symbol of fertility. Remains of brick corner turrets are still visible on the fort site.

For years Corozal had the look of a typical Mexican town, with thatched-roof homes. Then Hurricane Janet roared through in 1955 and blew away many of the buildings. Much of Corozal's wood and concrete architecture dates from the late 1950s.

Like Orange Walk, the Corozal economy is based on sugarcane farming. A large sugar refinery operated at Libertad, a few miles south of Corozal, from 1935 to 1985, but today all of Belize's cane is processed at Tower Hill near Orange Walk.

Orientation & Information

Corozal is arranged around a town square. The main highway passes through town as Santa Rita Rd and 7th Ave, briefly skirting the sea at the south end of town.

Belize Bank (☎ 422-2087; cnr 5th Ave & 1st St N; ☒ 8am-1pm Mon-Thu, 8am-4:30pm Fri) Situated on the plaza, it does currency exchange, and the ATM accepts international Visa, MasterCard, Plus and Cirrus cards.

Belize Tourism Board office (BTB; ☎ 422-3176; 1st Ave) Housed in the museum building by the *Thunderbolt* dock; closed at the time of research but expected to reopen by late 2005.

Charlotte's Web (☎ 422-0135; 78 5th Ave; Internet per hr US$3; ☒ 8:30am-6pm Mon-Thu, 8:30am-4pm Fri & Sat) Internet, CD burning and a big selection of second-hand books to swap or sell.

Cyber Zone (☎ 602-6255; N Park St; Internet per hr US$2; ☒ 9am-9pm)

Hospital (☎ 422-2076) Northwest of the center, off the Chetumal road.

Post office (☎ 422-2462; 5th Ave; ☒ 8:30am-noon & 1-4:30pm Mon-Thu, 8am-noon & 1-4pm Fri) On the site of Fort Barlee, facing the plaza.

Scotiabank (☎ 422-2046; 4th Ave; ☒ 8:30am-2:30pm Mon-Thu, 8:30am-4pm Fri, 9am-noon Sat) Currency exchange and cash advances.

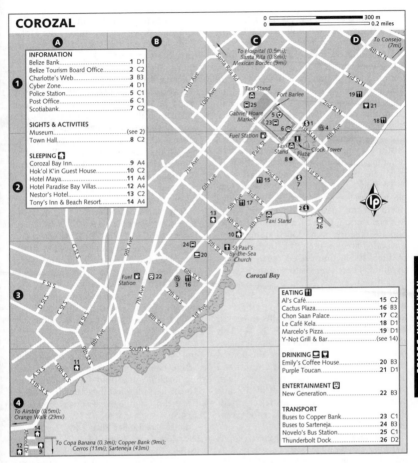

COROZAL

0   300 m
0   0.2 miles

INFORMATION	
Belize Bank	1 D1
Belize Tourism Board Office	2 C2
Charlotte's Web	3 B3
Cyber Zone	4 D1
Police Station	5 C1
Post Office	6 C1
Scotiabank	7 C2

SIGHTS & ACTIVITIES	
Museum	(see 2)
Town Hall	8 C2

SLEEPING	
Corozal Bay Inn	9 A4
Hok'ol K'in Guest House	10 C2
Hotel Maya	11 A4
Hotel Paradise Bay Villas	12 A4
Nestor's Hotel	13 C2
Tony's Inn & Beach Resort	14 A4

EATING	
Al's Café	15 C2
Cactus Plaza	16 B3
Chon Saan Palace	17 C2
Le Café Kela	18 D1
Marcelo's Pizza	19 D1
Y-Not Grill & Bar	(see 14)

DRINKING	
Emily's Coffee House	20 B3
Purple Toucan	21 D1

ENTERTAINMENT	
New Generation	22 B3

TRANSPORT	
Buses to Copper Bank	23 C1
Buses to Sarteneja	24 B3
Novelo's Bus Station	25 C1
Thunderbolt Dock	26 D2

To Consejo (7mi)
To Hospital (0.5mi); Santa Rita (0.8mi); Mexican Border (9mi)
To Airstrip (0.5mi); Orange Walk (29mi)
To Copa Banana (0.3mi); Copper Bank (9mi); Cerros (11mi); Sarteneja (43mi)

Corozal Bay

St Paul's By-the-Sea Church

Sights

TOWN HALL

A colorful and graphic mural that depicts Corozal's history by the Belizean-Mexican artist Manual Villamor Reyes enlivens the lobby of the **town hall** (☎ 422-2072; 1st St S; admission free; ☉ 9am-noon & 1-5pm Mon-Sat), which faces the plaza. Episodes depicted in the murals include the War of the Castes, with the talking cross and the fall of Bacalar, the flight of refugees into British Honduras, the founding of Corozal and Hurricane Janet.

MUSEUM

Corozal's old market and customs house, built in 1886 and one of only 11 buildings spared by Hurricane Janet, houses a tourist office and a small town **museum** (☎ 422-3176; 1st Ave), both of which are expected to reopen in late 2005.

SANTA RITA

This ancient coastal town occupied a strategic position between two major river trade routes – the Rio Hondo (now the Belize–Mexico border) and the New River, which enters Corozal Bay south of Corozal. These rivers were a vital link between the coast and areas as far inland as the Petén in Guatemala. Trade items included honey, vanilla and cacao. Though established by 1000 BC, Santa Rita didn't reach its heyday until the Postclassic Period, when it was probably the capital of the late Maya state of Chetumal.

NORTHERN BELIZE

It's estimated to have had 7000 people in the 15th century and was still occupied when Spanish explorers arrived.

Unfortunately, little of the ancient town is left. Excavations in the early 20th century found jade and pottery artifacts, most of which were dispersed to museums, and the site's important frescoes – in a style similar to that of the Mixtec people of Oaxaca, Mexico – have long been destroyed. When Corozal expanded from a tiny village into a bustling town, many of the ancient mounds became road fill and the stones of the temples were used for house foundations.

To find Santa Rita's restored **Maya temple** (admission free; ☻ during daylight), go 1200yd north on the main highway from Novelo's bus station, then turn left at the Super Santa Rita store. Some 350yd along here is a wooded area on the right. In the middle of this is the medium-sized, partly restored pyramid. There's no visitors center.

Sleeping
BUDGET

Nestor's Hotel (☎ 422-0196, 602-5186; www.nestors hotel.com; 123 5th Ave S; r US$30-50; P ⊠ 🖳) This old traveler's haunt has had a complete makeover and now offers sparkling tile-floored rooms of varied sizes, with hot showers and air-conditioning. A restaurant, guests' bar, lounge and pool should be ready by the time you get here, continuing the Nestor's tradition as a sociable gathering place for travelers. There's secure parking.

Hotel Maya (☎ 422-2082; www.hotelmaya.net; 7th Ave; d/tr/q with fan US$30/33/38, d/q with fan & TV US$33/43, d/q with air-con & TV US$43/50; ⊠ 🐾) This friendly place is a longtime budget favorite, where the aged but clean and mostly breezy rooms come with private bathroom and good showers. Some are enlivened by colorful bedspreads and pictures. Breakfast is available and guests can rent bicycles for US$10 per day.

MIDRANGE

Hok'ol K'in Guest House (☎ 422-3329; www.corozal .net; 89 4th Ave; s/d/q without air-con US$36/49/51, with air-con US$54/60/64; 🐾) With a Maya name meaning 'rising sun,' this modern, well-run, small hotel overlooking the bay is the best value in town. The large, impeccably clean rooms are designed to catch sea breezes, and each has two double beds, a bathroom

and a balcony with hammock. Owned by a former peace corps worker, the Hok'ol K'in also serves meals at reasonable prices (breakfasts are particularly good) in a pleasant dining room.

Corozal Bay Inn (☎ 422-2691; www.corozalbayinn .com; Almond Dr; s/d/tr/q US$70/80/90/100, dishes US$4-15; P ⊠ 🖳 🏊) Fronting the sea at the far south end of town, this relaxed, family-run place has cozy, tiled, mosquito-netted, air-conditioned cabanas set around a broad sandy area. Each has a fridge, coffee maker, cable TV and hot shower. Hospitable staff, a good restaurant (see opposite), a sociable outdoor bar, good pool and informal atmosphere make this a hugely enjoyable place to stay.

Tony's Inn & Beach Resort (☎ 422-2055; www .tonysinn.com; Almond Dr; s/d/tr/q US$49/60/71/82, with TV & air-con US$71/82/93/104; P ⊠ 🖳) Next door to the Corozal Bay Inn, Tony's has similar standards but a more formal atmosphere. The rooms are on two floors in pretty gardens. Lawn chairs are set to enjoy the view of the bay next to the breezy waterside restaurant (Y-Not Grill & Bar, opposite).

Copa Banana (☎ 422-0284; www.copabanana.bz; 409 Corozal Bay Rd; r US$55; P ⊠ 🐾) This is a cozy and spotless place at the far south end of town, with themed rooms (palms, beach, nautical etc), shared kitchen, washing machine, and dining and sitting areas. The owners offer free bicycles, car rental and free pickup from Novelo's bus station or the airstrip.

Hotel Paradise Bay Villas (☎ 422-0209; shanny belize@hotmail.com; 7 Almond Dr; 2-/3-room apt for 2 US$50/75) Slightly dingy but good-sized apartments with kitchen, bathroom, sitting area and terrace or balcony. Friendly owners. Add US$13 per extra person.

Eating

Cactus Plaza (☎ 422-0394; 6 6th St S; snacks US$0.50-2.50, ceviches US$5-10; ☻ 6pm-1am Wed-Sun) Cactus Plaza serves terrific light Mexican meals in an extraordinary piece of fairy-palace fantasy architecture. Two or three items make a filling and tasty meal. There are tacos, *salbutes* and *panuchos* (fried corn tortillas with fillings), *caldos* (broths), as well as shrimp, sea-snail or mixed-seafood ceviches. There are also plenty of good drinks including *licuados con leche* (milk shakes) and fresh fruit juices. This place also has a disco from Friday to Sunday (see opposite).

Le Café Kela (☎ 422-2833; 37 1st Ave; crepes US$4, meat & seafood dishes US$6-8; ☻ breakfast & dinner) Set in a *palapa* (thatch-roofed shelter) surrounded by colorful blooms and ocean breezes, with the sea just across the street, Kela blends Belizean dishes with French cuisine. Here you'll find the best crepes in Belize, along with pasta, steaks and seafood. Everything is made to order, so service may be slow, but it's worth the wait. There are only five tables so come early or make a reservation.

Corozal Bay Inn (☎ 422-2691; Almond Dr; dishes US$4-15; ☻ breakfast, lunch & dinner) This friendly seafront place at the south end of town serves Mexican, Japanese and Belizean food, surrounded by a lovely water feature. There's a pool here, too.

Y-Not Grill & Bar (☎ 422-2055; Tony's Inn & Beach Resort, Almond Dr; dishes US$4-16; ☻ 11am-11pm or midnight) This hotel restaurant serves well-prepared grills, shrimp and fajitas under a huge, breezy, waterfront *palapa*.

Chon Saan Palace (☎ 422-0169; 5th Ave; dishes US$5-15; ☻ 10:30am-11:30pm; ✿) The best and most expensive Chinese eatery in town, the Chon Saan welcomes you with a laughing Buddha statue at the door, attractive Chinese prints and a spotlessly clean, air-conditioned ambience. The food comes in generous portions but could be a touch more flavorful.

Al's Café (☎ 422-3654; 5th Ave; snacks US$0.50-0.75, mains US$2.50-3; ☻ 8am-2pm Mon-Sat & 6-10pm Mon, Wed, Fri & Sat) A popular small sidewalk café, Al's does tasty Mexican snacks. Try the burritos with beans, chicken, cheese and very hot green sauce! No alcohol is served.

Marcelo's Pizza (☎ 422-3275; 25 4th Ave; pizzas US$3.50-8; ☻ 8am-midnight; ✿) This friendly spot serves good cheesy pizzas (to match the decor?).

Drinking & Entertainment

Emily's Coffee House (5th Ave; coffees US$0.50-2; ☻ 7:30am-1pm & 2:30-5pm Mon-Fri, 7:30am-1pm Sat) Head here for real coffee, banana bread and lovely wall maps.

Cactus Plaza (☎ 422-0394; 6 6th St S; ☻ 9pm-3am or 4am Fri-Sun) The neat disco at this restaurant features a DJ on Saturday and karaoke on Friday and Sunday. Colorful low-relief murals demonstrate the same amusing taste as the building itself.

Purple Toucan (☎ 422-2727; 52 4th Ave; ☻ 6pm-midnight) One of the more salubrious bars in

town, with a busy pool table and small beer garden out the back.

New Generation (☎ 605-7773; 7th Ave; ☻ 8pm-2am) Come to this Chinese restaurant on Saturday or Sunday night for dancing to local bands that play punta rock, Mexican hits, reggae and other styles.

Getting There & Around

AIR

Tropic Air (☎ 422-0356; www.tropicair.com) and **Maya Island Air** (☎ 422-2333; www.mayaairways.com) both fly to San Pedro (US$39, 25 minutes) four or five times daily. Some flights stop at Sarteneja (US$35, 10 minutes) en route. Corozal's airstrip (CZH) is about 1 mile south of the town center. Taxis (US$5) meet incoming flights. Hotel Maya (opposite) sells tickets for both airlines.

BOAT

Thunderbolt (☎ 422-0026, 226-2904), with triple 250HP outboard motors and interior seating for all passengers, departs for Sarteneja (US$15, 30 minutes) and San Pedro (US$23, two hours) at 7am daily from its dock on 1st Ave.

BUS

Novelo's Bus Line (☎ 402-2132, 402-3030; cnr 7th Ave & 1st St S) runs once or twice an hour to Orange Walk (express/regular US$2.50/2, 45 minutes/one hour) and Belize City (express/regular US$6/4.50, 2½/3¼ hours) from 5am to 7:30pm, and across the Mexican border to Chetumal (express/regular US$2/1, one/1¼ hours), once or twice hourly from 7:30am to 7:30pm. Services are reduced by about half on Sundays.

In Chetumal, buses from Corozal stop at the Nuevo Mercado (New Market), about 0.75 miles north of the town center. A few continue to Chetumal's inter-city bus station, a further 0.6 miles north, where buses leave for Mexico. A taxi from the Nuevo Mercado to the bus station or town center is US$1. From Chetumal to Corozal, buses leave the north side of the Nuevo Mercado from about 4:30am to 6pm.

If you're shooting straight through to Flores in Guatemala (eight to nine hours), the Línea Dorada (one-way US$20) and San Juan Travel (US$25) buses from Chetumal both stop at Corozal's Hotel Maya (opposite) at 7am – the hotel sells tickets.

THE BELIZE–MEXICO BORDER

The border point at Santa Elena (Belize) and Subteniente López (Mexico) is 9 miles north of Corozal and 7 miles west of Chetumal. If you are crossing from Mexico to Belize you will normally have to hand in your Mexican tourist card to Mexican immigration as you leave. If you plan to return to Mexico within the card's period of validity you are entitled to keep it and reuse it for your return visit. Officials at this border have a habit of demanding US$10 to allow you to keep the card; this is still cheaper than the US$20 you would have to pay for a new card on your return.

Travelers departing Belize by land have to pay a US$15 exit fee plus a US$3.75 conservation fee.

Bus travelers, in either direction, have to get off the bus and carry their luggage through customs.

Buses to Copper Bank (US$0.75, 30 minutes) depart from behind the post office at 11am and 4pm Monday to Friday and 10:30am Saturday. Buses to Sarteneja (US$4, three hours) via Orange Walk depart at 2pm daily from 5th Ave, almost opposite Emily's Coffee House.

AROUND COROZAL
Cerros

This **Maya site** (Cerro Maya; admission US$5; ☼ 8am-5pm), 3.5 miles across the bay from Corozal, flourished as a coastal trade center in late Preclassic times. Cerros' proximity to the mouth of the New River gave it a key position on the trade route between the Yucatán coast and the Petén region.

A series of temples built from about 50 BC surpassed anything previously known here, in size and grandeur, and archaeologists believe Cerros may have been taken over then by an outside power, quite possibly Lamanai. Cerros flourished until about AD 150, after which it reverted rapidly to small, unimportant village status.

Though the site is still mostly a mass of grass-covered mounds, the center has been cleared and consolidated. Climb Structure 4, a funerary temple more than 65ft high, for stunning panoramic views. Northwest of this, Structure 5 stands with its back to the sea. This was the first temple to be built and may have been the most important. Large stucco masks flanking its central staircase have been covered over by stone walls for their protection. Southwest of Structure 5, Structure 6 exhibits a 'triadic' arrangement (one main temple flanked by two lesser ones, all atop the same mound) that is also found in Preclassic buildings at Lamanai and El Mirador in the Petén.

Cerros is 2.5 miles north of the village of Copper Bank, which is 8.5 miles from Corozal. All-weather roads run from Corozal to Copper Bank (crossing the New River by hand-cranked ferry) and on to Cerros. Bus schedules to Copper Bank don't permit day trips to Cerros. Most people opt to visit Cerros on a guided tour from Corozal, typically costing US$40/50/75/100 for one/two/three/four people. If you come in the rainy season, cover up and bring bug spray! Accommodations in Corozal will put you in touch with recommended guides: one excellent, highly experienced guide is **Francisco Puck** (☎ 423-0054, 602-7634; franz_puck@yahoo.com).

Copper Bank

This small fishing village (called San Fernando on some maps) of 500 people on the Laguna Seca, a brackish (part fresh, part salt water) lagoon just inland from Corozal Bay, is a place you might stay if you want to hole up somewhere tranquil and away-from-it-all for a spell. Curiously, the lagoon's water level sinks dramatically when there's a cold front from the north.

The friendly **Last Resort** (☎ 606-1585; donna flores25@yahoo.com; campsites US$5, cabins US$20-35, restaurant mains US$4-6; ℗ ▯) has rustic *palapa* cabins dotted around a spacious grassy site right by the lagoon. It also has a large restaurant, a reading room and book exchange, and canoes (per hour US$3) and bikes (per hour/day US$1/5) for rent. The cabanas have fans, toilets, washbasins, sleeping and sitting areas and hammocks. Most have shared showers but a couple have their own. Fishers can try to catch tarpon at the lagoon mouth.

See p143 for information on buses from Corozal to Copper Bank, and p135 for buses from Orange Walk. Departures from Copper Bank to both places are at 6:30am (Monday to Saturday) and 1:30pm (Monday to Friday).

Consejo

A small North American and European expatriate community resides in a couple of retirement developments near tiny Consejo village, on the coast 7 miles northeast of Corozal by unpaved road. There's not much to do here except walk along the beach, swing in a hammock or look at real estate. But there are two good places to stay.

Smuggler's Den (☎ 614-8146; smugglersdenbelize .tripod.com; bungalows US$30-50, houses US$75; P 🗷 ▣) There's a bit of sandy beach here and the thatched bungalows are available with or without a kitchenette, while the house has a full kitchen, air-conditioning and two bedrooms. A vaguely nautical-theme restaurant and bar serves mainly seafood and Belizean favorites, but the Sunday roast beef and potatoes are particularly popular. Canoes, a pool table and a library help you while away the time. Turn left just after the Consejo Shores development and go 1 mile.

CasaBlanca by the Sea (☎ 423-1018, in US ☎ 781-235-1024; www.casablancabelize.com; s US$76-99, d US$88-111, ste US$164-175; P 🗷) On the breezy shore in Consejo village, the rooms have beautiful wooden doors carved with Maya-style reliefs, but they could do with a little modernization. The restaurant serves up good seafood and meat.

A taxi from Corozal to Consejo will cost you US$10.

SARTENEJA & AROUND

pop 2000

Sarteneja (sar-ten-*eh*-ha) is a fishing village near the northeast tip of the Belizean mainland – pretty quiet most of the time as many of the village's 500 fishers base their boats at Belize City, returning home only in their time off. The village spreads just a few blocks back from its long, grassy seafront. You can cruise around on a rented bike, head out to the Shipstern Nature Reserve, and take birding, snorkeling, fishing or manatee-watching trips. Sarteneja is still a great option for travelers who want to get off the beaten track, though ecotourism is set to expand under the wing of the Sarteneja Wildlife, Environmental & Ecotourism Team (SWEET), which plans to set up a visitors center at the east end of North Front St and retrain local fishers as tourist guides.

Shipstern Nature Reserve

This large **nature reserve** (for information contact Fernando's Seaside Guesthouse; ☎ 423-2085; N Front St), whose headquarters is 3.5 miles southwest of Sarteneja on the road to Orange Walk, protects 43 sq miles of semi-deciduous hardwood forests, wetlands and lagoons and coastal mangrove belts. Lying in a transition zone between Central America's tropical forests and a drier Yucatán-type ecosystem, its mosaic of habitats is rare in Belize.

All five of Belize's wild cats and a score of other mammals are found here, and its 250 bird species include ospreys, roseate spoonbills, white ibis and a colony of 300 pairs of American wood storks, one of this bird's few breeding colonies in Belize. The reserve is owned by a Belizean nonprofit organization, Shipstern Nature Reserve Belize, and is funded by the Swiss- and Dutch-based **International Tropical Conservation Foundation** (www.papiliorama.ch).

The most basic visit (US$5 per person, about 1½ hours) covers a small museum and butterfly house at the headquarters and a botanical trail from there. More exciting are tours using the reserve's safari-type vehicles. Charges for these are reasonable compared with many other 'ecotourism' operations in Belize, and can be split between up to eight people.

The Xo-Pol area, 40 minutes from the headquarters, has a treetop hide overlooking a large forest-surrounded pond where you can hope to see crocodiles, waterfowl, peccaries, deer and, if you're lucky, a tapir. As always, you'll see most in the early morning. Xo-Pol tours cost US$5 per hour plus US$15 for fuel. A day lagoon tour with a visit to the wood stork colony is US$75. It's also possible to stay overnight at Xo-Pol, or at Iguana Camp, where park staff watch over the wood storks.

The reserve staff will transport up to eight people from Sarteneja for US$5 roundtrip. Don't forget your long sleeves, pants and bug spray!

Sleeping & Eating

Fernando's Seaside Guesthouse (☎ 423-2085; www.cybercayecaulker.com/sarteneja.html; N Front St; s/d US$27/33, dinner US$6) This immaculate, friendly and sea-breezy guesthouse facing the waterfront was the Belize Tourism Board's 'Best Small Hotel in Belize' in 2004. It has just four rooms, each with a sparkling private bathroom. Good meals are served on the broad upstairs balcony. Owner Fernando Alamilla is well up on things to do around Sarteneja and can arrange snorkeling or fishing day trips to Bacalar Chico Marine Reserve off Ambergris Caye (US$250 plus equipment rental for up to four), bird-watching or manatee-watching.

Krisami's Bayview Lodge (☎ 423-2283; www .krisamis.com; N Front St; r US$60, meals US$5-10; P ⊠ ▣) At the west end of the waterfront street, Krisami's has comfortable, good-sized rooms with big bathrooms, cable TV and large wooden beds. Meals are available on request and Krisami's offers many of the same outings as Fernando's.

Getting There & Around

Tropic Air (☎ 422-0356; www.tropicair.com) flies at least twice daily to/from San Pedro (US$39, 15 minutes) and Corozal (US$35, 10 minutes). Other flights between San Pedro and Corozal may stop here on request.

The **Thunderbolt** (☎ 422-0026, 610-4475), a fast water taxi that has covered seating, heads daily to Corozal (US$15, 30 minutes) at 4:15pm and to San Pedro (US$23, 1½ hours) at 7:30am.

Sarteneja is 40 miles northeast of Orange Walk by a mostly unpaved all-weather road passing through the village of San Estevan and the scattered Mennonite community of Little Belize. See p135 for information on buses from Orange Walk and p88 for buses from Belize City. Departures from Sarteneja to Orange Walk (US$2.50, 1½ hours) are early in the morning, roughly every half-hour from 4am to 6am Monday to Saturday, and at 6am only on Sunday, and to Belize City (US$4.50, 3½ hours) at 5am and 5:30am Monday to Saturday.

Drivers from Corozal can reach Sarteneja (43 miles) by taking the road toward Copper Bank but turning right 6 miles from Corozal at a junction signposted to Progresso and Sarteneja. This road meets the road from Orange Walk shortly before Little Belize.

You can rent good bicycles at **Fernando's Seaside Guesthouse** (☎ 423-2085; www.cybercaye caulker.com/sarteneja.html; N Front St) for US$2/10 per hour/day.

Western Belize

As you travel west from Belize City, the landscape takes a dramatic and refreshing turn. Pine savannah gives way to rainforest and the flat plains become ever more crinkled, rising in the south to the purple-hued hills of the Mountain Pine Ridge. This is the Cayo District – a lush land peppered with waterfalls, rivers, caves and ruins and teeming with orchids, parrots, keel-billed toucans and other exotic flora and fauna. It is prime territory for nature lovers and a burgeoning ecotourism industry is in place to enable everyone to make the most of it.

Though it is home to the biggest of Belize's ancient cities, Caracol, more recently Cayo District was considered a last frontier, a patch of impenetrable jungle way out west. Though the Western Hwy was built in the 1930s, paving wasn't completed until the 1980s, when the first lodge owners bought land and started their endless tussle with the jungle. A dose of British, Canadian and American expats now spices the district's eclectic cultural brew of Maya, Mestizos, Creoles, Garifuna, Chinese and Lebanese. Soon after entering Cayo District from the east you encounter Belmopan, the nation's miniature capital, perhaps most helpfully regarded as a transportation hub.

San Ignacio is the beating heart of Cayo District for visitors and locals alike. You can base yourself here, taking day trips out to the area's ruins, waterfalls, rivers, caves, forest trails, gardens, birding spots and butterfly farms. Or you can stay out in the forests, valleys or hills in one of the area's many marvelous lodges and enjoy much the same range of excitements.

WESTERN BELIZE

HIGHLIGHTS

- Rediscovering the amazing remnants of ancient Maya cave rituals inside **Actun Tunichil Muknal** (p161)

- Exploring Belize's biggest ancient city, **Caracol** (p171), at the end of a two-hour forest drive

- Enjoying comfort and wild nature simultaneously at superb lodges such as **duPlooys' Jungle Lodge** (p165), the **Lodge at Chaa Creek** (p166), **Blancaneaux Lodge** (p173) or **Hidden Valley Inn** (p173)

- **Cave-tubing** (p152) at Jaguar Paw Jungle Resort

- Dipping in the mountain streams and admiring the waterfalls of the **Mountain Pine Ridge area** (p170)

POPULATION: 62,000	MONTHLY RAINFALL: JAN/JUN 4.7IN/9.1IN (SAN IGNACIO)	HIGHEST ELEVATION: 3640FT

History

In ancient Maya times, the Belize River valley was a key trade route between the Caribbean coast and cities such as Tikal and Naranjo. Cahal Pech on the outskirts of San Ignacio is the oldest site in the valley, settled between 1500 and 1000 BC. Both Cahal Pech and nearby Xunantunich reached their peak in the 7th and 8th centuries AD, in late-Classic times. The more splendid Xunantunich probably controlled the valley during these final centuries of Classic Maya civilization. But the most important ancient city of western Belize – indeed of all Belize – lay 23 miles south of Xunantunich, up on the Vaca Plateau: this was Caracol, which conquered the mighty Tikal in AD 562 and grew to a city of perhaps 150,000 people (far bigger than modern-day Belize City) in the succeeding century or so.

Classic Maya civilization ended abruptly in western Belize, as elsewhere, around AD 850–900, although Xunantunich remained occupied a little longer. When the Spanish arrived in the 16th century, the town of Tipu, now on the site of Negroman Farm south of San Ignacio (not open to visitors), was capital of the Postclassic Maya province of Dzuluinicob. A Spanish expedition from the Yucatán in 1544 conquered Maya settlements as far inland as Tipu. But the Tipuans never really accepted Spanish political or religious control, rebelling several times and burning down their Catholic church in 1618. Tipu was the epicenter of a major rebellion beginning in 1638 that drove the Spanish out of most of Belize for good. The Spanish had the last laugh over Tipu itself, however, returning to rebaptize more than 600 people in 1680, and eventually resettling the Tipuans on Lago Petén-Itzá (near Flores, Guatemala) in 1707.

Mahogany cutters moved up the Belize River into western Belize in the late 18th century, suffering attacks from Maya who were scattered in the forests until well into the 19th century. The town of San Ignacio (p154), near the confluence of the Macal and Mopan Rivers, began life as a collecting point for mahogany and, later, chicle, which were floated downriver to the coast. Work in the mahogany camps was one reason people began to move into the area from Guatemala in the 19th century. River and mule remained Cayo's only means of contact with the outside world until the

---

WESTERN BELIZE IN...

Two Days

Stay in the best lodge or hotel you can afford and take your pick of the activities and tours on offer – birding, night jungle walks, canoeing and river-tubing – with a one-day trip to a highlight attraction such as **Actun Tunichil Muknal** (p161) or **Caracol** (p171).

Four Days

Add further highlights to the two-day itinerary, such as the **Belize Botanic Gardens** (p165), the ruins of **Xunantunich** (p163) and **cave-tubing** (p152) the Caves Branch River at Jaguar Paw.

One Week

Spend two days in **San Ignacio** (p154) and the rest of your week at one or two **lodges** (ideally one near the Macal River and one in the Mountain Pine Ridge area), indulging in the best of the area's attractions. Visit ruins at **Caracol** (p171) and **Xunantunich** (p163), check out the **Belize Botanic Gardens** (p165) and the **Mountain Pine Ridge** (p169), explore the amazing ritual cave of **Actun Tunichil Muknal** (p161) and tube through the caves of **Jaguar Paw** (p152).

Ten to 12 Days

Add further activities and attractions to the one-week itinerary, such as horseback riding at **Banana Bank Lodge & Jungle Equestrian Adventure** (p153), canoeing through **Barton Creek Cave** (p162) and a visit to one of the butterfly farms, such as **Green Hills Butterfly Ranch** (p162), **Tropical Wings Nature Center** (p165) or **Chaa Creek Natural History Center & Butterfly Farm** (p167).

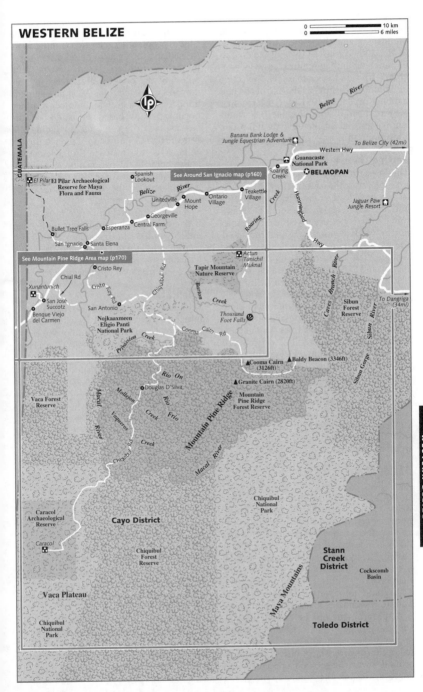

WESTERN BELIZE

Western Hwy was built in the 1930s. As the logging and chicle industries declined in the 20th century, Cayo turned to cattle ranching and agriculture, growing sorghum, fruit and vegetables. The selection of Belmopan (below) as the site of the new national capital in 1971 gave the region a big push forward, and since the 1980s tourism has proved an increasingly important addition to the local economy.

Getting There & Around

The Western Hwy is the region's artery, running across the country from Belize City to San Ignacio, Benque Viejo del Carmen and the Guatemalan border. The Hummingbird Hwy diverges southward 2 miles northwest of Belmopan. Buses run along the Western Hwy between Belize City and Benque Viejo del Carmen, stopping in Belmopan and San Ignacio. Bus travelers going between western and southern Belize need to change in Belmopan.

Unpaved roads head off the main highway to villages, farms and remote lodges and attractions, the most important of these routes being Chiquibul Rd, which heads up and over the Mountain Pine Ridge, and Cristo Rey Rd, which links Chiquibul Rd directly with San Ignacio.

There are few bus services off the main highway. To access isolated lodges and attractions, if you don't have your own vehicle, you need to take tours from San Ignacio (or from the lodges themselves) or use taxis, or transfers, organized by the lodges.

BELMOPAN

pop 12,300

In 1961, Hurricane Hattie all but destroyed Belize City. Certain that Belize City could never be secure from further terrible hurricanes, the government decided to move. Many people were skeptical when in 1971 it declared its intention to build a new capital in the center of the country, with the name Belmopan.

A grand new National Assembly was built to resemble a Maya temple and plaza, with government offices around it. Unsurprisingly, government needs have outgrown these core buildings and a variety of less-uniform government offices are spread around town. The capital has been slow to come to life but the gradually increasing population is friendly and content. Though a lot of people still prefer to commute from Belize City, San Ignacio or even Dangriga, increasing numbers are seeing the plus points of the broad, leafy streets of Belmopan's quiet suburbia. Most government ministries and a growing number of other organizations are based here, and a few embassies liven the place up (including the British High Commission, although the US embassy is still in Belize City). Belmopan is also home to the national police training center, and if you strike a match in Belize, it'll probably be the Toucan brand, made right here in Belmopan.

A Belmopan branch of the Museum of Belize may one day open, but until then, unless you have business here or find it a convenient place to break a journey, you'll probably stay only long enough to change buses and maybe have something to eat.

Orientation

Belmopan is located 1 mile east of the Hummingbird Hwy, reached by either of two turnings, 1 and 2 miles south of the Hummingbird's junction with the Western Hwy, 50 miles from Belize City. Belmopan is a small place that is easily negotiated on foot. A ring road encircles the central area of town. The Novelo's bus station, James bus stop and the main commercial area are just within the west side of this central ring, with many government buildings just to their northeast.

Information

Belize Bank (☎ 822-2303; Constitution Dr; ◷ 8am-3pm Mon-Thu, 8am-4pm Fri) Exchanges currency and the ATM accepts international Visa, MasterCard, Plus and Cirrus cards.

Belmopan Hospital (☎ 822-2264; off N Ring Rd) The only emergency facility between Belize City and San Ignacio, it's just north of the center.

Ministry of Natural Resources (☎ 822-2226; lincenbze @btl.net; ◷ 8am-noon, 1-5pm Mon-Thu, to 4:30pm Fri) The Land Information Centre here sells the best topographic maps of Belize available, including 1:50,000 sheets at US$20 each.

Post office (☎ 822-2122; ◷ 8am-noon & 1-5pm Mon-Thu, to 4:30pm Fri) Just southeast of the Ministry of Natural Resources.

Pross Computers (Constitution Dr; Internet per hr US$2.50; ◷ 9am-7pm Mon-Fri, 9am-6pm Sat) Fast Internet.

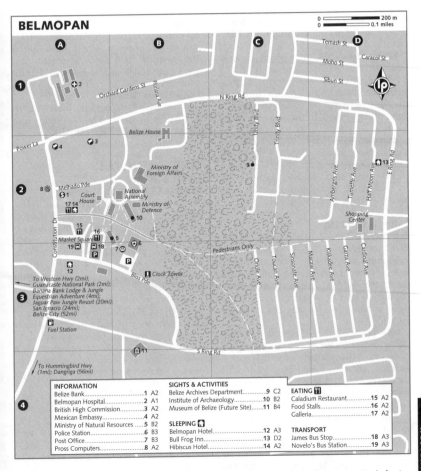

BELMOPAN

INFORMATION		SIGHTS & ACTIVITIES		EATING	
Belize Bank...............................1 A2		Belize Archives Department.............9 C2		Caladium Restaurant..............15 A2	
Belmopan Hospital....................2 A1		Institute of Archaeology...............10 B2		Food Stalls...........................16 A2	
British High Commission............3 A2		Museum of Belize (Future Site).....11 B4		Galleria...............................17 A2	
Mexican Embassy......................4 A2					
Ministry of Natural Resources 5 B2		SLEEPING		TRANSPORT	
Police Station...........................6 B3		Belmopan Hotel.........................12 A3		James Bus Stop....................18 A3	
Post Office...............................7 B3		Bull Frog Inn.............................13 D2		Novelo's Bus Station............19 A3	
Pross Computers.......................8 A2		Hibiscus Hotel...........................14 A2			

Sights

The government buildings at the heart of town are surrounded by grassy lawns and are vehicle-free, but look like a drab college campus of concrete bunkers. The square National Assembly building occupies the highest point of the area, surrounded by various ministry buildings.

The **Institute of Archaeology** (☎ 822-2106; fax 822-3345; ☽ 8am-noon & 1-5pm Mon-Thu, to 4:30pm Fri) contains a vault full of artifacts gathered from archaeological sites throughout Belize. The vault's contents will one day be displayed in the Museum of Belize but until then there's nothing on view except a meager display in the office hallway. If you have specific questions about archaeological work (eg which

sites are currently under excavation) the institute may be able to help you.

The **Belize Archives Department** (☎ 822-2097; www.belizearchives.org; 26-28 Unity Blvd; ☽ 8am-5:30pm Mon-Thu, to 5pm Fri) has rotating displays on hurricanes, the Garifuna, Belmopan, Baron Bliss and other subjects, and search rooms where the public can consult the quite extensive collections of photographs, newspapers, books, maps, documents and sound and video archives.

Sleeping

Bull Frog Inn (☎ 822-2111; www.bullfroginn.com; 25 Half Moon Ave; s US$49-65, d US$54-82; P ☼) With 25 cheerful rooms, a bar and good restaurant, the Bull Frog is Belmopan's nicest place to stay. The rooms have one or two double beds, phone, fan and air-con, private bathroom and cable TV.

Hibiscus Hotel (☎ 822-1418; hibiscus@btl.net; off Constitution Dr; s/d/t US$33/45/58, s/d with TV US$43/55; ☒ ☒) This almost new little hotel provides clean, neat and spacious rooms with tiled floors and nice bathrooms (with tub) – good value, especially in such a central location.

Belmopan Hotel (☎ 822-2130; www.belmopan hotel.com; Market Sq; s/d/tr US$50/54/60; ℗ ☒ ☒) Though central and equipped with a restaurant, pool and spacious rooms (with bathrooms), this hotel is much more tired and worn than the previous two.

Eating & Drinking

Bull Frog Inn (☎ 822-2111; www.bullfroginn.com; 25 Half Moon Ave; mains US$8-13; ☺ restaurant 7am-9:30pm, bar till midnight) This popular and breezy hotel-restaurant serves up particularly good steaks and seafood. The adjoining bar is a popular Belmopan watering hole, livened up by karaoke on Thursday and mariachis on Friday.

Galleria (☎ 802-0263; off Constitution Dr; dishes US$2-6; ☺ 8am-5pm Mon-Sat; ☒) Come to the neat, almost twee Galleria for well-prepared burritos, fajitas, rice and beans, Mennonite ice cream and probably the best coffee in town. Owned by the Carrs of Banana Bank Lodge (see opposite) it's adjoined by a gallery that displays the art of Carolyn Carr and others.

Caladium Restaurant (☎ 822-2754; Market Sq; mains US$4-10; ☺ 7:15am-8pm Mon-Fri, 8am-7pm Sat; ☒ ☒) Just across the street from the bus station, the Caladium offers a good variety of dependable Belizean specials, burgers and seafood.

Food Stalls (Market Sq; rice & beans US$2.50; ☺ 7am-6pm) For a cheap meal, you can't go wrong at the market stalls just east of the bus station. They serve Mexican snacks such as burritos and *salbutes* amid the sounds of rhythm and blues.

Getting There & Away

Novelo's bus station (☎ 802-2799; Market Sq) is a stop for all Novelo's buses operating along the Western and Hummingbird Hwys. Buses head east to Belize City (express/regular US$3.50/2, 1/1¼ hours) and west to San Ignacio (express/regular US$2.50/1.50, 45 minutes/1¼ hours) as well as Benque Viejo del Carmen (express/regular US$3/2, 1/1½ hours) once or twice an hour from 6am to 7pm or 8pm. Eight buses depart for Dangriga (US$3, 1¾ hours) between 8:30am and 5:30pm, half of them continuing to Punta Gorda (US$9, 5½ hours).

A few daily **James bus line** (☎ 702-2049, 722-2625) buses to Belize City, Dangriga and Punta Gorda stop in the car park just east of the Novelo's station.

AROUND BELMOPAN
Sights & Activities
GUANACASTE NATIONAL PARK

At the junction of the Western and Hummingbird Hwys – and an excellent place to break a drive – **Guanacaste National Park** (admission US$2.50; ☺ 8am-4:30pm) is Belize's smallest national park. This 250,000 sq yd area around the confluence of Roaring Creek and the Belize River is named for a giant guanacaste tree on its southwestern edge. Somehow, possibly thanks to the odd shape of its trunk, the tree survived the axes of canoe-makers and still rises majestically in its jungle habitat. Festooned with bromeliads, epiphytes, ferns and dozens of other varieties of plants, the great tree supports a whole ecosystem of its own.

The guanacaste (tubroos) tree is one of Central America's largest trees. Its light wood was used by the Maya to make dugout canoes. The tree is identifiable by its wide, straight trunk and broad, flat seed pods that coil up into what looks like a giant, shriveled ear (you'll see fallen 'ears' on trails throughout Belize).

A hike along the park's 2 miles of trails will introduce you to the abundant local trees and colorful birds. Birding is best here in winter, when migrants arrive from North America. After your hike, you can head down to the river for a dip in the park's good, deep swimming hole.

CAVE-TUBING

River-tubing – sitting inside an inflated inner-tube and floating or paddling down a river – is all the rage in Belize, and the most exciting variety of river-tubing is cave-tubing, where a river flows through caves. The country's most popular cave-tubing site is a series of five caverns (officially termed the **Nohoch Che'en Caves Branch Archaeological**

Reserve) on the Caves Branch River east of Belmopan. A ride through the **Caves Branch** caves is both exhilarating and relaxing as you float in and out between the open air and the dark caverns, with their stalactites, stalagmites, crystalline formations and artifacts from ancient Maya rituals. Some caves have side passages to explore, and some side passages lead to other caves, such as the spectacular **Crystal Cave**.

Tubing on the Caves Branch is a popular day trip for tourists from as far away as San Pedro and Placencia, and even from cruise ships, so if avoiding groups of other tourists is important to you, do your cave-tubing elsewhere. At the busiest peaks of the tourist season several hundred people per day are enjoying this run. The starting point is near the Jaguar Paw Jungle Resort (right), 6 unpaved miles south off the Western Hwy from a turning-point 11 miles east of Guanacaste National Park.

Guides gather round the **Xibalba Restaurant** (chicken lunch US$5; 🕐 8am-4pm), just past the Jaguar Paw entrance gate. You can choose between the full five-cave float (about two hours, US$30 to US$40 for independent participants) or a shorter two- or three-cave venture (US$20). Both involve a jungle walk to your starting point (about half an hour for the shorter trip and one hour for the longer one). Come with swimming costume, T-shirt, shorts and tennis shoes, and preferably a second set of clothes to change into afterwards!

HORSEBACK RIDING

Banana Bank Lodge & Jungle Equestrian Adventure (☎ 820-2020; www.bananabank.com; Mile 47 Western Hwy) is Belize's largest equestrian center, set on a jungle-and-pastures property of more than 6 sq miles, and is 4 miles from Belmopan. Banana Bank has 150 well-tended horses enjoying modern facilities. Experienced equestrians and novices alike can take two-to-three-hour (US$65) or longer riding trips through the jungle, and a variety of multiday riding packages are offered. Owner John Carr has lived and worked with horses all his life, having grown up on a Montana ranch and worked as a rodeo rider and cattleman before coming to Belize in the 1970s. After half a century, he says he's still learning ways to communicate with horses. See right for directions to Banana Bank.

ZIP-LINING

Another exhilarating adventure at Jaguar Paw Jungle Resort (below) is the **Aerialtrek** zip-line trip (US$55) where you zoom through the treetops from platform to platform on six linked cable runs up to 200ft long. Trained guides give you a safety briefing and help you into your harness.

Sleeping & Eating

Banana Bank Lodge & Jungle Equestrian Adventure (☎ 820-2020; www.bananabank.com; Mile 47 Western Hwy; s/d/tr US$128/142/158, s/d/tr/q cabana US$120/158/185/213, all incl breakfast; lunch/dinner US$11/16; Ⓟ 🐾 🐕) This wonderful lodge and equestrian center (see left) sits on the banks of the Belize River, 4 miles from Belmopan. With a fascinating history as an old logging-company headquarters and the scene of colonial-era horse races, Banana Bank is very much an expression of the personalities and interests of its owners, horseman John Carr and his artist wife Carolyn. For those with non-equestrian interests, a wide range of activities and tours to western Belize's many attractions are available.

Each of the mahogany-and-thatch cabanas has a unique two-bedroom design, with sitting room, bathtub, mosquito nets and ceiling fans. The lodge rooms are large and air-conditioned, with beautiful bathrooms and wrought-iron or carved-mahogany bedsteads. Good meals are served family-style in the high thatched-roof restaurant. Lodge inhabitants include two spider monkeys and Tika, the Carrs' pet jaguar who appears in most of Belize's tourist brochures.

The turnoff to Banana Bank is 1 mile east along the Western Hwy from Guanacaste National Park. Just over 1 mile north of the highway you reach a metal gong hanging beside a path leading down to the river. Bang the gong and someone will come from the lodge (on the opposite bank) to get you in a hand-operated ferry. It's also possible to drive to the lodge via a vehicle ferry over the Belize River just west of Roaring Creek village.

Jaguar Paw Jungle Resort (☎ 820-2023, US 888-77-jungle; www.jaguarpaw.com; s/d US$179/202, breakfast US$5-8, lunch dishes US$8-10, dinner mains US$15-28; Ⓟ 🐾 🐕) Set amid jungle, Jaguar Paw is 6 miles south of the Western Hwy and just 200yd from where the Caves Branch River issues from one of its caves.

You're right on the spot for cave-tubing, zip-lining and further jungle, cave and river activities offered by the lodge. Nine miles of trails wind around the property, which also includes the Crystal Cave, a spectacular side chamber of the Caves Branch system. There's a strong Maya theme to the design, and the rooms, four each in four separate all-air-con units among the forest, are decorated with unique assortments of artifacts and curios. The restaurant serves creative Belizean and international dishes.

SAN IGNACIO & SANTA ELENA
pop 16,000 (combined)

San Ignacio is located on the west bank of the Macal River a couple of miles upstream from its confluence with the Mopan River – a meeting of waters that gives birth to the Belize River, flowing northeast to enter the sea near Belize City. This once-remote location between two rivers gives San Ignacio its alternative name of Cayo – a Spanish word meaning 'island.'

Together with neighboring Santa Elena, on the east bank of the river, San Ignacio forms the chief population center of Cayo District. It's a busy, moderately prosperous place, with a constant stream of traffic passing through en route to or from Guatemala and an equally steady stream of tourists and travelers making San Ignacio their base for explorations and adventures in western Cayo and the Mountain Pine Ridge area.

The town has a good range of mostly inexpensive accommodations, some good places to eat and any number of guides and agencies waiting to show you the region's attractions. It also makes a good staging post before or after you cross the Guatemalan border, just 9 miles southwest.

Orientation

Two bridges cross the Macal: the Hawkesworth Bridge (a suspension bridge) and the lower, wooden New Bridge to the north. Traffic is normally westbound-only over the wooden bridge and eastbound over the Hawkesworth. Thus if you're coming into San Ignacio along the Western Hwy from Belmopan or Belize City you'll pass through Santa Elena first and then cross the northern bridge and hit San Ignacio at the north end of its football ground. Sometimes during the rainy season the northern bridge floods and traffic goes both ways across the Hawkesworth Bridge. Burns Ave, running north–south, is San Ignacio's main street.

Information

BOOKSTORES
Green Dragon (☎ 824-4782; 8 Hudson St; ⊙ 8am-8pm) Reasonable selection of books on Belize and the Maya.

EMERGENCY
Police station (☎ 824-2022; cnr Missiah & Buena Vista Sts)

INTERNET ACCESS
Cayo Community Computer Center (☎ 824-3736; Hudson St; Internet per hr US$1.50; ⊙ 8am-9pm Mon-Sat, 10am-6pm Sun) Cheap but slow.
Green Dragon (☎ 824-4782; 8 Hudson St; Internet per hr US$3; ⊙ 8am-8pm) There's a bookstore and a café with good coffee and smoothies.
Tradewinds (☎ 824-2396; Hudson St; Internet per hr US$2.50; ⊙ 7am-11pm Mon-Sat, 10am-10pm Sun) High-speed Internet access.

LAUNDRY
Martha's Guest House (☎ 804-3647; 10 West St) Washing costs US$3 per load.

MEDICAL SERVICES
La Loma Luz Hospital (☎ 804-2985, 824-2087; Western Hwy; ⊙ 24hr emergency services) This Adventist hospital in Santa Elena is one of the best in the country.

MONEY
Belize Bank (☎ 824-2031; 16 Burns Ave; ⊙ 8am-1pm Mon-Thu, 8am-4:30pm Fri, 9am-noon Sat) The ATM here accepts international Visa, MasterCard, Plus and Cirrus cards.
Scotiabank (☎ 824-4190; cnr Burns Ave & King St; ⊙ 8am-2:30pm Mon-Thu, 8am-4pm Fri, 9am-noon Sat)

POST
Post office (☎ 824-2049; Hudson St; ⊙ 8am-noon & 1-5pm Mon-Thu, to 4pm Fri)

TOURIST INFORMATION
Eva's Restaurant (☎ 804-2267; www.evasonline.com; 22 Burns Ave; ⊙ 6:30am-10:30pm) has quite a lot of information posted up and staff are happy enough to answer customers' questions. Also, most places to stay are pretty well informed about attractions and transportation in the area.

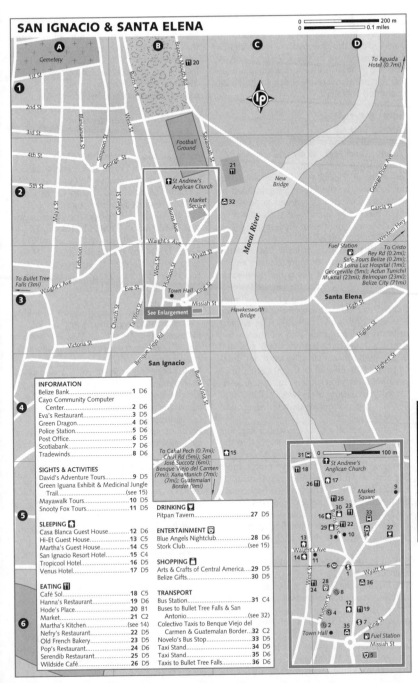

SAN IGNACIO & SANTA ELENA

INFORMATION

Belize Bank	1 D6
Cayo Community Computer Center	2 D6
Eva's Restaurant	3 D5
Green Dragon	4 D6
Police Station	5 D6
Post Office	6 D5
Scotiabank	7 D6
Tradewinds	8 D6

SIGHTS & ACTIVITIES

David's Adventure Tours	9 D5
Green Iguana Exhibit & Medicinal Jungle Trail	(see 15)
Mayawalk Tours	10 D5
Snooty Fox Tours	11 D5

SLEEPING 🛏

Casa Blanca Guest House	12 D6
Hi-Et Guest House	13 C5
Martha's Guest House	14 C5
San Ignacio Resort Hotel	15 C4
Tropicool Hotel	16 D5
Venus Hotel	17 D5

EATING 🍴

Café Sol	18 C5
Hanna's Restaurant	19 D6
Hode's Place	20 B1
Market	21 C2
Martha's Kitchen	(see 14)
Nefry's Restaurant	22 D5
Old French Bakery	23 D5
Pop's Restaurant	24 D6
Serendib Restaurant	25 D5
Wildside Café	26 D5

DRINKING 🍷

Pitpan Tavern	27 D5

ENTERTAINMENT 🎭

Blue Angels Nightclub	28 D6
Stork Club	(see 15)

SHOPPING 🛍

Arts & Crafts of Central America	29 D5
Belize Gifts	30 D5

TRANSPORT

Bus Station	31 C4
Buses to Bullet Tree Falls & San Antonio	(see 32)
Colectivo Taxis to Benque Viejo del Carmen & Guatemalan Border	32 C2
Novelo's Bus Stop	33 D5
Taxi Stand	34 C5
Taxi Stand	35 D6
Taxis to Bullet Tree Falls	36 D6

WESTERN BELIZE

Dangers & Annoyances

Travelers should exercise extra caution on Burns Ave in the area north of the Waight's Ave intersection in the evening. Lonely Planet has heard of an attack on a female traveler in this vicinity, which included an attempted robbery.

Sights & Activities

CAHAL PECH

Atop a hill on the southern outskirts of San Ignacio, **Cahal Pech** (☎ 824-4236; admission US$5; ⏰ 6am-6pm) is Mopan and Yucatec Mayan for 'Place of Ticks,' a nickname earned in the 1950s when the site was surrounded by pastures grazed by tick-infested cattle. Today it's a pleasantly shady site with plenty of trees. Though architecturally less impressive than Xunantunich (p163), Cahal Pech (kah-*hahl* pech) was a significant Maya settlement for 2000 years or more. Its core area of seven interconnected plazas has been excavated and restored since the late 1980s.

This is the oldest known Maya site in the Belize River valley, having been first settled between 1500 and 1000 BC. The earliest monumental religious architecture in Belize was built here between 600 and 400 BC, though most of what we see today dates from AD 600–800, when Cahal Pech and its peripheral farming settlements had an estimated population of between 10,000 and 20,000. The place was abandoned around AD 850.

From the visitors center, which explains some of the history, it's about 150yd to the area of excavated and restored plazas and temples. Plaza B is the largest and most impressive, while Structure A1, off plaza A, is the site's tallest temple. Two ball courts lie at either end of the restored area.

Cahal Pech is 1 mile from central San Ignacio. Head up Buena Vista St and turn left immediately before the Texaco station.

GREEN IGUANA EXHIBIT & MEDICINAL JUNGLE TRAIL

The **Green Iguana Exhibit** (admission US$5; ⏰ 7am-5pm) and **medicinal jungle trail** (admission US$5; ⏰ 7am-5pm) are in the lush Macal Valley grounds of the **San Ignacio Resort Hotel** (☎ 824-2034; www.sanignaciobelize.com; 18 Buena Vista). The green iguana can grow a very impressive 6ft long but is threatened chiefly because people have killed the females for their eggs (a practice that's now illegal). This exhibit breeds iguanas with the aim of releasing them into the wild, and provides visitors with plenty of up-close iguana contact and lessons on their ecological value. The medicinal trail winds through the neighboring forests: information from your guide about medicinal uses of Belizean plants is complemented by on-site material.

Tours

Many of the most exciting sights and activities in Cayo District are easiest reached on a guided trip and some (such as Actun Tunichil Muknal and Barton Creek Cave) cannot be visited without a guide.

Typical day-trip prices per person are US$80 for Actun Tunichil Muknal, US$30 to US$45 for a half-day trip to Barton Creek Cave; US$60 to US$65 to Caracol, US$65 for a cave-tubing trip to Jaguar Paw, US$30 to US$45 for Mountain Pine Ridge and US$65 to US$75 (plus border fees) for Tikal in Guatemala.

Leading tour companies or booking agencies based in or near San Ignacio:

Belizean Sun (☎ 824-4841, 601-2630; www.belizeansun.com) Good range of the best destinations and activities available.

David's Adventure Tours (☎ 804-3674; www.davidsadventuretours.com; Savannah St) Rastafarian Afro-Maya David Simpson leads river and Barton Creek canoe trips, morning bird-watching and overnight camping at his El Guacamallo camp on the Macal River.

Eva's Restaurant (☎ 804-2267; 22 Burns Ave; www.evasonline.com) You can book tours to Caracol, Tikal, Barton Creek Cave and other places, and contact many guides.

Everald's Caracol Shuttle (☎ 804-0090, 604-5097; caracolshuttle@hotmail.com; Crystal Paradise Resort, p163) Day trips to Caracol with knowledgeable guide Everald Tut. The company is also contactable through Snooty Fox Tours (cnr West St & Waight's Ave, San Ignacio).

Green Dragon (☎ 824-4782; 8 Hudson St) Books tours with some of the better guides and operators.

Mayawalk Tours (☎ 824-3070; www.mayawalk.com; 19 Burns Ave) Good range of canoeing, caving and archaeological trips.

Pacz Tours (☎ 824-2477; pacztours@btl.net) Excellent Actun Tunichil Muknal trips; you can book at Eva's Restaurant or Green Dragon.

Paradise Expeditions (☎ 820-4014, 610-5593; www.birdinginbelize.com; Crystal Paradise Resort) Run by the accomplished local bird guide Jeronie Tut, offering trips for both the 'casual and serious birder.' Operates from Crystal Paradise Resort (p163).

THE BIG PADDLE

One morning in March the waters of the Macal River beneath San Ignacio's Hawkesworth Bridge are the gathering place for a colorful flotilla of, in recent years, over 80 three-person canoes. They are assembled for the start of La Ruta Maya Belize River Challenge, a grueling four-day race down the Belize River to Belize City, where they arrive on Baron Bliss Day, a national holiday in memory of a great Belizean benefactor (see p78). From relatively humble beginnings in 1998, the race has grown rapidly into Central America's biggest canoe event, attracting international as well as Belizean canoeists.

Even though it's all downstream, this is no gentle paddle. The fastest teams cover the river's 170 or so winding and beautiful miles from San Ignacio to Belize City in around 19 hours, while the slowest take around 36 hours. The race is divided into four one-day stages: Hawkesworth Bridge to Banana Bank Lodge near Belmopan (around 50 miles); Banana Bank to Bermudian Landing (60 miles including Big Falls Rapids); Bermudian Landing to Burrell Boom (35 miles); and Burrell Boom to Belcan Bridge, Belize City (25 miles). Entrants are grouped into seven classes: male, female, mixed, masters (over-40s), intramural (school students), dory (traditional-style canoes carved from one piece of timber) and pleasure craft. The entrance fee is US$125. If the idea tempts you, check out **Belize River Challenge** (www.larutamayabelize.com)!

River Rat Expeditions (☎ 824-2166, 605-4480; www .riverratbelize.com) Specialist in kayaking and cave trips; you can book at Eva's Restaurant or Green Dragon.

Some agencies can pick you up from hotels and lodges for an extra fee – for example US$8 from the Trek Stop, US$20 from the Lodge at Chaa Creek or duPlooys' Jungle Lodge, US$60 from Blancaneaux or Five Sisters Lodge (all for up to four people).

Sleeping

San Ignacio accommodations are mostly in the budget bracket but there are also some excellent-value establishments here. Luxurious options can be found at lodges out of town (see p159).

BUDGET

Casa Blanca Guest House (☎ 824-2080; www.casablan caguesthouse.com; 10 Burns Ave; s/d/tr US$24/29/35, s/d with air-con US$40/49; ✗ ✗) Friendly and immaculately kept, the Casa Blanca fully deserves the BTB 'Best Small Hotel in Belize' award that it received in 2003. Guests have a comfy sitting area and good, clean kitchenette with free instant coffee; the rooms are good-sized, with private bathroom and cable TV.

Aguada Hotel (☎ 804-3609; www.aguadahotel.com; Aguada St, Santa Elena; r downstairs/upstairs US$30/38; ℗ ✗ ▣ ▣) On a quiet street tucked away in Santa Elena, the tranquil Aguada has neat rooms with private bathroom. Those upstairs, surrounded by a wooden verandah, are the better choice. There's a garden

with a pond and swimming pool and a good ground-floor restaurant that serves steaks, snapper, pasta and rice and beans (mains US$4 to US$8).

Venus Hotel (☎ 824-3203; emorfing@btl.net; s/d with shared bathroom US$14/16, with private bathroom US$22/24, d with private bathroom & air-con US$32-38; ✗) The recently revamped Venus provides pretty good value, with 32 unspectacular but well-kept rooms on two floors. Rooms with private bathroom also sport cable TV.

Hi-Et Guest House (☎ 824-2828; thehiet@btl.net; 12 West St; s/d with shared bathroom US$10/13, with private bathroom US$15/20) The friendly Hi-Et occupies two adjacent and connected houses. One has rooms with private bathroom, hot showers and free morning coffee; the other has rooms that share a bathroom, are small and thinly partitioned but clean; each has its own little verandah.

Tropicool Hotel (☎ 824-3052; 30 Burns Ave; s/d/tw/ tr with shared bathroom US$12/15/17/20, d/tr with shared bathroom & TV US$17/23, cabins with private bathroom & TV US$30; ✗) The rooms in the main building are bare and basic but clean and equipped with fans and mosquito screens; the cabins in the back garden are more appealing. The clothes sink, washing line and card phone in the lobby are good touches for budget travelers. Checkout is at 10am.

MIDRANGE

Martha's Guest House (☎ 804-3647; www.marthas belize.com; 10 West St; s/d US$38/49, ste US$54-70, all incl breakfast; ✗) This family-run guesthouse has bright, sparkling clean and attractively decorated rooms, all accented by mahogany floors and private balconies. Hotel amenities include a laundromat and an excellent ground-floor restaurant. Add US$11 each for third and fourth occupants of any room.

San Ignacio Resort Hotel (☎ 824-2034; www.sanignacio belize.com; 18 Buena Vista St; economy s/d/tr US$45/50/56, s/d US$94/123; P ✖ ⛱) About 400yd uphill from the town center, this is the most up-market hotel in town and is popular with tour groups. The rooms are not in the first flush of youth but are air-conditioned and brightly decorated, with comfy beds and bathtubs. With grounds running down to the lushly vegetated Macal River, the hotel boasts good birding from its own terrace, plus a pool, restaurant and bar, the Stork Club (opposite).

Cahal Pech Village (☎ 824-3740; www.cahalpech .com; Cahal Pech Hill; s/d with air-con US$77/79, s/d/q cabin US$66/68/84; P ✖ 🖵 ⛱) Atop Cahal Pech hill 1¼ miles up from the town center, you can enjoy splendid views from most of the bright, tile-floored, air-con rooms in the large main building and from the comfortable thatched cabins. All have TV and a balcony or verandah. Cahal Pech Village also has a bar, a restaurant serving good international food (mains US$6 to US$10) and an inviting swimming pool. In summer the place is very popular with groups of archaeology students, who spend their days doing field work.

Eating

Hanna's Restaurant (☎ 824-3014; 5 Burns Ave; breakfast US$4-6, Belizean dishes US$3-6, Indian dishes US$6-11; ✲ 6am-9pm) You can't beat this sidewalk restaurant for good, solid Belizean and Indian meals and international breakfasts, which are well prepared and served with efficiency and a smile. Vegetarians will find lots of choices, while carnivores should sample the tasty beef curry or chicken *tikka*.

Martha's Kitchen (☎ 804-3647; 10 West St; breakfast & light meals US$3-6, mains US$9-10; ✲ 6:30am-3pm & 4-11pm) Martha's serves San Ignacio's most varied menu, with freshly prepared food. Sit inside or out on the terrace that is separated from the street by foliage and enjoy anything from steaks or burritos to pizzas or vegetarian kebabs.

Wildside Café (34 Burns Ave; breakfast US$2-3, lunch & dinner mains US$2.50-5; ✲ 7am-9pm) Good vegetar-

ian food is served at equally good prices on the pleasant little patio here. Breakfasts include oatmeal, granola and eggs scrambled with the local green vegetable *chaya*. Later in the day you can choose from spinach pesto, hummus, falafel burritos or tofu baguettes. Sip a herbal tea to the reggae music and soak up the positive vibrations!

Serendib Restaurant (☎ 824-2302; 27 Burns Ave; mains US$3-10; ✲ 10am-3pm & 6-10pm Mon-Sat; ✖) Exchange rice and beans for rice and curry at possibly the only Sri Lankan restaurant in Belize. The owners came here with the British army and stayed. As well as rather mild curries, there's steaks, seafood, burgers and Belizean dishes. There's a pleasant garden patio as well as the fan-cooled dining room.

Hode's Place (☎ 804-2522; Branch Mouth Rd; rice & beans US$2.50-5, steaks & seafood US$6-12; ✲ 10am-midnight) In the north of town, Hode's is a large terrace restaurant that opens onto a citrus orchard and kids' playground. It attracts a mainly local crowd including lots of families at weekends. A jukebox and games room help keep the kids happy. Friendly service and satisfying food – from burritos and fajitas to steaks, seafood and rice and beans – complete the successful recipe.

Café Sol (West St; mains US$6-9; ✲ lunch & dinner) With just four tables inside and a couple more on the terrace, spacious Café Sol has plenty of room for sofas and easy chairs. You can enjoy a meal from the eclectic menu (eg Greek salad wraps, pineapple ginger chicken, Thai noodle shrimp salad) or just sit back and read or chat with a key lime pie and a coffee or fruit-yoghurt smoothie.

Nefry's Restaurant (☎ 604-5826; 19 Burns Ave; mains US$6-10; ✲ 6am-10pm Mon-Sat, 6-10am Sun) A spacious, relaxed spot with interesting old B&W photos, Nefry's serves very tasty if not huge Arabic and vegetarian dishes. Arabic items come with mint tea and a choice of ginger rice, baked potato or rice and beans.

Pop's Restaurant (☎ 824-3366; West St; breakfast US$4-5; ✲ 6:30am-2pm & 6:30-10pm, closed Wed night; ✖) This small, friendly diner is a good choice for a filling, slightly greasy breakfast at a good price, served all day.

Old French Bakery (☎ 824-2532; Market Sq; baked goods around US$0.75; ✲ 7am-8pm Mon-Sat) Load up here with cinnamon rolls, apple strudels and ham-and-cheese croissants.

Market (Savannah St; ☻ 6am-noon Fri & Sat) Come early for San Ignacio's best fruit, vegetables, jams and dairy products. Farmers sell from all over the Cayo District – you can't get fresher than this.

Drinking & Entertainment

Pitpan Tavern (10 Savannah St; ☻ 10am-midnight Sun-Thu, 10am-2am Fri & Sat) Lively garden-bar frequented by travelers and the local twenties set.

Blue Angels Nightclub (Hudson St; cover charge for bands usually US$2.50-5; ☻ 9pm-2am or 3am Thu-Sat) No-frills establishment that often has a punta rock and/or reggae band to dance to at weekends. If big-name artists are in town, this is where they're likely to play.

Stork Club (☎ 824-2034; San Ignacio Resort Hotel, 18 Buena Vista St; ☻ bands & DJs 9:30pm-2am Fri & Sat) This hotel is a bit of a social hub and sometimes has a band on the first or last Saturday of the month. Otherwise there's a DJ on Friday and Saturday.

Shopping

Belize Gifts (JNC Mall, Burns Ave) This place has the widest range of Belizean souvenirs in town.

Arts & Crafts of Central America (☎ 824-2253; 24 Burns Ave) There are Guatemalan crafts available here.

Getting There & Around

TO/FROM THE AIRPORT

The **Tropicool Hotel** (☎ 824-3052; 30 Burns Ave) will transport up to three people to or from Belize City international airport for US$63. **Mayawalk Tours** (☎ 824-3070; 19 Burns Ave) offers the same service at US$100 for up to four, and US$25 per extra person.

BUS

Novelo's Bus Line (☎ 824-3360; Market Sq) runs east to Belmopan (express/regular US$2.50/1.50, 45 minutes/1¼ hours) and Belize City (express/regular US$6/3.50, two/2½ hours) about every half-hour from 4am to 6pm, and west to Benque Viejo del Carmen (express/regular US$1/0.75, 20/30 minutes) around every half-hour from 7am to 9pm. Services are reduced by about half on Sundays. A bus to Dangriga (US$5, three hours) goes at 2pm Friday to Monday only. At the time of writing, Novelo's buses were stopping at Market Sq; the bus station on Burns Ave was out of use.

From a vacant lot on Savannah St, buses leave for Bullet Tree Falls (US$0.50, 15 minutes) at 10:30am, 11am, 11:30am, 12:30pm, 3:30pm, 4pm and 5pm, Monday to Saturday, and for San Antonio (US$1.50, 45 minutes) at 10:45am, 1:15pm, 3:15pm and 5:15pm, Monday to Saturday.

CAR

Safe Tours Belize (☎ 824-4262, 614-4476; www.safe toursbelize.com; 278 Western Hwy, Santa Elena; ☻ 7am-9pm) rents reliable vehicles from US$82 per day including mileage, tax and insurance.

TAXI

Several taxi stands are dotted around the town center. Sample fares are US$8 to US$10 to the Guatemalan border (9 miles) or Crystal Paradise Resort (5 miles), US$30 roundtrip to Xunantunich, and US$45 to US$50 one-way to the Mountain Pine Ridge lodges. Colectivo taxis (charging per person and leaving when they have a car full) head from a vacant lot on Savannah St almost opposite the Novelo's bus stop to Benque Viejo del Carmen (US$1.50) and the Guatemalan border (US$2). Taxis to Bullet Tree Falls (colectivo/private US$1/5) go from Wyatt St, just off Burns Ave.

AROUND SAN IGNACIO

The lush environs of San Ignacio are peppered with Maya ruins; jungle-clad rivers where you can swim, canoe, kayak or river-tube; butterfly farms; a botanic garden; spectacular caves through which you can canoe, tube, climb, walk, crawl or scramble to find amazing evidence of ancient Maya rituals; and wonderful jungle lodges where you can stay in the midst of the tropical forest and explore its secrets on your own or with expert guides. The birding is pretty good at almost any lodge.

Having your own vehicle, while not essential, helps make the most of this region. You will still probably want to take some guided trips, but a vehicle allows you to come and go when you please without having to depend on taxis or pay for transfers to/from the lodges. The lodges and attractions mostly lie along back-country roads that are unpaved but normally quite drivable for any car with reasonably high clearance. If you plan to stay several days, look into the packages offered by most lodges

WESTERN BELIZE

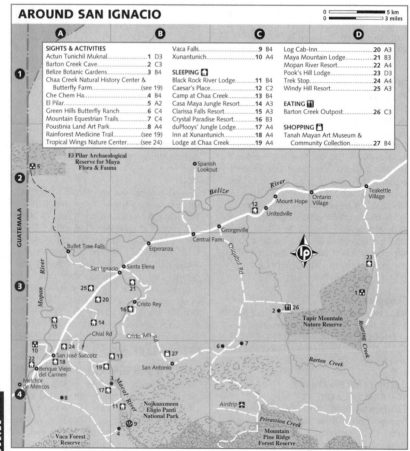

AROUND SAN IGNACIO

0 —————— 5 km
0 —————— 3 miles

that include accommodation, meals, tours, activities and transfers if needed. For those staying in San Ignacio – generally the more economical option – plenty of tour firms and guides are waiting to take you out to enjoy the attractions and activities of the surrounding area (see p156).

This section covers the area's array of activities and sights in a clockwise order.

Dangers & Annoyances

There have been a few incidents of robbery (including armed robbery) against tourists in remote but regularly frequented spots in Cayo. Keep your ear to the ground, ask around and if you are venturing anywhere at all that is isolated without a licensed guide, inquire beforehand about safety. The black spot at the time of writing was the Macal River, and the victims were people canoeing the river with guides (a popular and normally highly enjoyable activity organized from lodges on the river or through tour firms in San Ignacio). With luck this particular spate of incidents will prove short-lived.

Western Hwy Eastward

The 22 miles of the Western Hwy between San Ignacio and the Belmopan turnoff wind through well-treed, pretty country, with a number of villages strung along the road. Chiquibul Rd (see opposite), heading to Barton Creek, Green Hills Butterfly Ranch and the Mountain Pine Ridge, heads south off the highway at Georgeville, 6 miles from San Ignacio. The road to Actun Tunichil Muknal (below) heads off south at Teakettle Village, a further 10 miles east.

Right on the highway, east of Georgeville, **Caesar's Place** (☎ 824-2341; www.blackrocklodge.com; Mile 60 Western Hwy; s/d US$40/50, with air-con US$55/65, camping per person US$4; **P** **⊠**) is a combined guesthouse, restaurant, bar and one of the best gift shops in the country. The shop has a wide selection of Belizean and some Guatemalan souvenirs and handicrafts at good prices, including fine hardwood furniture, kitchen equipment and sculptures made right here in the family's own workshop. The rooms are good and clean if not luxurious, and there's a lovely swimming hole in Barton Creek at the bottom of its grounds. Owner Caesar Sherrard is, among other things, a drummer and his jazz band plays here on the first Saturday of each month.

Actun Tunichil Muknal

One of the most unforgettable and adventurous tours you can make in Belize, the trip into 'ATM' takes you deep into the underworld that the ancient Maya knew as Xibalbá. The entrance to the 3-mile-long cave lies in the northern foothills of the Maya Mountains, approximately 8 miles south of Teakettle Village on the Western Hwy. The trip is a moderately strenuous one for which you need to be able to swim. You start with an easy 45-minute hike along trails and across creeks (your feet will be wet all day) to the cave's wide, hourglass-shaped entrance, surrounded by lush jungle. You'll then don your helmet, complete with headlamp, follow your guide into the cave (starting with a frosty swim across a 20ft-deep pool), and then walk, climb, twist and turn your way through the cave.

Giant shimmering flowstone rock formations compete for your attention with thick calcium-carbonate stalactites dripping from the ceiling. Phallic stalagmites grow up from the cave floor. Eventually you'll follow your guide up into a massive opening, where you'll see hundreds of pottery vessels and shards, along with human remains. One of the most shocking displays is the calcite-encrusted remains of the woman who Actun Tunichil Muknal (Cave of the Stone Sepulcher) is named for.

ATM was discovered in 1989 and investigated in detail in the 1990s by Belizean and North American archaeologists who revealed it to be one of the most spectacular of all Maya cave sites. The researchers found some 200 ceramic vessels and the skeletal remains of 14 humans (seven of them children), all almost certainly sacrificial victims. The people and the pottery are all believed to have been offerings to the rain god Chac (who dwelt in caves) in supplication for rain at a time of drought in the second half of the 9th century.

In view of the unique value and the fragility of the cave's contents, visits are fairly strictly controlled. At the time of writing, visits are permitted only with trained guides from two San Ignacio–based companies, in groups of six to eight at a time: **Pacz Tours** (☎ 824-2477; pacztours@btl.net), the original ATM company, still doing excellent trips, and **Mayawalk Tours** (☎ 824-3070; www.mayawalk .com; 19 Burns Ave, San Ignacio). A day trip, lasting about 10 hours (including a one-hour drive each way), costs US$80 and includes lunch and equipment. Most hotels and lodges can book these trips for you. Bring shoes (not sandals) and a change of clothes.

Off the dirt road that leads to ATM is **Pook's Hill Lodge** (☎ 820-2017; www.pookshilllodge .com; s/d/tr cabana US$122/173/201, breakfast/lunch/dinner US$8/10/20; **P**), a beautiful lodge on the site of a small Classic Period Maya residential complex within a 300-acre private reserve. The round, thatch-and-stucco cabanas, set on lawn areas, sport wrap-around windows and immaculate natural-stone bathrooms. The birding is superb here, from the lodge verandah or along the forest trails or the river frontage on Roaring Creek. Swimming and river-tubing and guided walks are free; horseback riding is US$40 and a variety of tours and activities further afield in Cayo are available, too.

Chiquibul Rd

Chiquibul Rd (sometimes called Pine Ridge Rd) turns south off the Western Hwy at Georgeville, heading for the Mountain Pine Ridge and the Vaca Plateau far to the south. If you are heading to the Mountain Pine Ridge from the Belize City and Belmopan direction, this is the route you'll take. After 9 miles, the Cristo Rey Rd from San Ignacio and Santa Elena enters from the west.

WESTERN BELIZE

RAIN, RAIN, COME AGAIN

The limestone outcrops of the northern foothills of the Maya Mountains have been eroded over millennia by the action of water running off the older crystalline rocks of the range's central core. Absorbing carbon dioxide from the atmosphere when it falls as rain, and more carbon dioxide from the decaying plant material on the ground, the water becomes a weak acid that dissolves into limestone, eventually producing what is known as a karst landscape, characterized by caves, sinkholes and underground rivers.

To the ancient – and many modern – Maya, caves were entrances to the underworld, Xibalbá, and the homes of all-important deities such as the agricultural fertility god and Chac, the rain god. The Maya entered caves to present the ritual offerings considered necessary to keep the gods happy: pottery, tools, food such as corn, chili peppers, pine needles and cacao seeds. Very few known caves in Belize do not contain some evidence of ancient Maya ritual activity more than a millennium ago. The most important offerings were human blood and human lives. Caves in western Belize such as Barton Creek Cave (below) and Actun Tunichil Muknal (p161) contain the remains of many children and adults, the majority almost certainly sacrificial victims, although some may have been interred in a form of ancestor worship.

Ritual activity in caves seems to have increased in the last century of Classic Maya civilization, from about AD 750. This was a time of growing stress and discord in the Maya world, leading to the Classic Maya collapse of 850–900. If, as recent research suggests, it was a series of devastating droughts that put paid to Classic Maya civilization, then it would be no more than logical for the Maya to have been redoubling their efforts to propitiate their rain god at this time.

Visiting caves is a relatively new and exciting tourist activity in Belize. In addition to the fascinating Maya history, you'll be awed by the geomorphological structures where undulating flowstone decorates the walls, stalactites and stalagmites grow like ancient trees, bats flit in and out of ceiling nooks and darkness prevails. When visiting, do remember that the caves themselves and their contents are very fragile. You can help by making sure you don't disturb artifacts and cave formations, and by not going on tours with large groups of people.

BARTON CREEK CAVE

Barton Creek rises high in the Mountain Pine Ridge and flows north to join the Belize River near Georgeville. Along the way it dips underground for a spell to form the Barton Creek Cave, where during the Classic Period the ancient Maya interred at least 28 people and left thousands of pottery jars and fragments and other artifacts on 10 ledges. A visit to the cave by canoe and/or cave-tube is one of the more popular day trips offered from San Ignacio. You'll canoe or ride an inner-tube about a mile into the cave, looking at the formations and the spooky skulls, bones and pottery shards.

You're not allowed to go in without a guide, and guides cannot take more than six people with them. Quite a few San Ignacio firms (see p156) run trips here – around 4½ hours all up for US$30 to US$45 per person. One of the most knowledgeable and experienced is **David's Adventure Tours** (☎ 804-3674; www.davidsadventuretours.com; Savannah St).

The narrow and very rough 4-mile track to Barton Creek Cave heads east off the Chiquibul Rd, 5 miles from the Western Hwy. Along the way you pass through the scattered traditional Mennonite farming community of Upper Barton Creek and ford both Barton Creek itself then one of its tributaries. Between the two fords a turning to the right leads to the friendly **Barton Creek Outpost** (☎ 607-1813; dishes US$5-8; ⊗ 10am-5pm), which serves drinks and home-prepared food on a deck by an inviting river swimming hole.

GREEN HILLS BUTTERFLY RANCH

Biologists Jan Meerman and Tineke Boomsma breed around 35 exotic and colorful butterfly species at **Green Hills Butterfly Ranch** (☎ /fax 820-4017; biological-diversity.info/greenhills .htm; Mile 8 Chiquibul Rd; adult/child US$5/2.50; ⊗ 8am-4pm), 8 miles off the Western Hwy. On the guided tours (minimum two people; the last one starts at 3:30pm), knowledgeable guides will walk you around the largest live butterfly display in Belize and explain the insects' life cycle from egg to caterpillar to pupa to butterfly. The gorgeous iridescent colors of many of the butterflies here will captivate you. They're bred mainly for export to butterfly houses in the USA.

HORSEBACK RIDING

Mountain Equestrian Trails (☎ 820-4041, in US ☎ 800-838-3918; www.metbelize.com; Mile 8 Chiquibul Rd; cabanas US$65-120, tents US$20, breakfast/lunch/dinner US$7/10/18; **P**), along a 0.75-mile driveway immediately opposite Green Hills Butterfly Ranch, provides spacious cabanas that have private bathrooms, mosquito nets and kerosene lamps (no electricity) in a beautiful forested valley setting, along with good home-style meals. Host Arran Bevis has lived hereabouts all his life and knows the country like the back of his hand. Full-day rides to Barton Creek Cave (including canoeing into the cave) or to Big Rock Falls on the Mountain Pine Ridge are about US$75 to US$80 per person. Packages and transfers are available.

Cristo Rey Rd

The Cristo Rey Rd turns south off the Western Hwy in Santa Elena and winds up through the forests and the villages of Cristo Rey and San Antonio to meet the Chiquibul Rd after 12.5 miles. You'll come this way if you're heading to the Mountain Pine Ridge from San Ignacio.

Buses from San Ignacio to San Antonio (p159) run along the Cristo Rey Rd. Return buses leave San Antonio at 6am, 7am, 1:15pm and 4:15pm.

Half a mile before San Antonio, the **Tanah Mayan Art Museum & Community Collection** (admission US$3; ⏰ 7am-7pm) displays a rather dusty assortment of everyday and traditional artifacts from Maya village life. Adjoining is a shop that sells the excellent black-slate carvings of San Antonio's five García sisters, the originators of a craft now widely imitated around Belize. Their carvings, selling for between US$5 and US$100, depict a variety of subjects including local wildlife and Maya deities. The sisters see their art as one way of keeping alive their people's knowledge and traditions.

SLEEPING

Two friendly lodges lie just off the Cristo Rey Rd.

Crystal Paradise Resort (☎ 820-4014; www.crystal paradise.com; s US$60-104, d US$82-136, tr US$104-169,

all incl breakfast & dinner; **P**) Crystal Paradise is one of the few Cayo lodges owned by a local family. It sits in well-tended gardens just above the Macal River, with cabanas and rooms of various designs, all with private hot-water bathrooms, verandah, hammocks, tiled floors and fans. The best ones sport palm-thatch roofs that the owners, the Tut family, are well known in these parts for making. The women of the family cook up good Belizean meals and a large range of tours and activities are available. Son Jeronie Tut is a top-class bird guide who runs Paradise Expeditions (p156). Other possibilities here include horseback riding (per person US$35), canoeing on the Macal (guided/unguided US$40/28), excursions to Caracol (US$75) and the region's best cave trips.

Maya Mountain Lodge (☎ 824-2164; www.maya mountain.com; 9 Cristo Rey Rd; r without/with air-con US$57/81, cottages without/with air-con US$116/139, breakfast US$8, 4-course dinners US$18; **P** 🖥 🍽) Only 0.7 miles out of Santa Elena, this lodge has beautiful grounds with a refreshing swimming pool and a trail to a small ancient Maya ceremonial site. The eight thatched cottages and six smaller, less-attractive rooms all have fan and private bathrooms with hot water. Hearty home-style meals are served on the verandah restaurant. Bart and Suzi Mickler, the owners, pioneered many of the tours that are now widely offered throughout the region, including right here from their own lodge. Add US$12 per person for more than double occupancy.

Western Hwy Southwestward

Southwest from San Ignacio, the Western Hwy runs across rolling countryside toward Benque Viejo del Carmen and the Guatemalan border. A variety of places to stay along and near the highway can make good bases for exploring the region. Buses between San Ignacio and Benque Viejo del Carmen will drop you anywhere along the highway.

XUNANTUNICH

Belize's most accessible Maya site of significance, **Xunantunich** (admission US$5; ⏰ 7:30am-4pm), pronounced shoo-nahn-too-*neech*, is reached via a free hand-cranked ferry across the Mopan River at San José Succotz, 6.5 miles from San Ignacio. From the ferry, which comes and goes on demand, it's 0.9 miles uphill to the parking lot and ticket office.

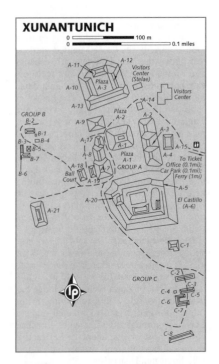

XUNANTUNICH

Set on a leveled hilltop, Xunantunich may have been occupied as early as 1000 BC but was little more than a village until the 7th century AD, when the large architecture we now see began to be built. From about 700 to 850 Xunantunich was possibly politically aligned with Naranjo, 9 miles west in Guatemala, and controlled the western part of the Belize River valley, although its population probably never exceeded 10,000. Xunantunich partially survived the initial Classic Maya collapse of about 850–900 (when nearby Cahal Pech was abandoned), but was abandoned by about 1000.

A good visitors center, between the ticket office and the hilltop ruins, explains Xunantunich's history. The site centers on Plazas A-2 and A-1, separated by Structure A-1. Just north of Plaza A-2, Structure A-11 and Plaza A-3 formed a residential 'palace' area for the ruling family. The dominant El Castillo (Structure A-6) rises 130ft high at the south end of Plaza A-1. El Castillo may have been the ruling family's ancestral shrine, where they were buried and/or represented in sculpted friezes. Structures A-1 and A-13, at either end of Plaza A-2, were not built until the 9th century and would have had the effect of separating the ruling family from the rest of the population, possibly a response to the pressures that came with the decline of Classic Maya civilization at that time.

You can climb to the top of El Castillo to enjoy a spectacular 360-degree view. Its upper levels were constructed in two distinct phases. The first, around 800, included an elaborate plaster frieze encircling the building; the second, around 900, covered over most of the first and its frieze. The frieze on the east end of the building and part of the western one have been uncovered by archaeologists and depict a series of Maya deities, with Chac, the rain god, probably being the central figure at the east end.

The friezes you see today are actually replicas, with the originals underneath for safe keeping. South of El Castillo is a partly overgrown area of lesser structures that were abandoned as the city shrank after 900, leaving El Castillo (formerly at the center of the ancient city) on the southern edge of the occupied area.

SLEEPING & EATING

Windy Hill Resort (☎ 824-2017; www.windyhillresort .com; Graceland Ranch; 3-night/4-day package s/d/tr/q from US$1017/1252/1471/1615; P ⊠ ☒) Windy Hill, set on (yes) a breezy hillside located 1 mile west of the edge of San Ignacio, is a family-run resort for the interested and active, offering two- to six-night packages covering all of the major sights and activities of western Belize – Maya ruins (including Tikal in Guatemala), caves, canoeing, horseback riding in its own stable of 60 mounts – combined with lodging, meals and airport transfers. Accommodations are in well-built wooden cottages spread across manicured gardens, all with private bathroom, well-made furnishings, cable TV and ceiling fans or air-con. Plentiful meals are served in a large *palapa* (thatched-roof shelter) restaurant, and the swimming pool, bar, games room and well-equipped fitness center will help you while away any spare moments.

Trek Stop (☎ 823-2265; www.thetrekstop.com; Mile 71½ Western Hwy; camping per person US$5, s cabins US$12, d cabins US$20-24, q cabins US$40, d cabins with private bathroom US$35, breakfast US$2-4, main dishes US$3.50-5; ☺ restaurant 7am-8pm; P ⊑) Six miles from San Ignacio, just before San José Succotz, this is an ideal spot for backpackers. The clean and comfortable hand-hewn cabins come with their own little verandahs. The toilets are composting and some of the power is solar. As well as a restaurant with traveler's-style food there's also a kitchen for guests.

You'll never be bored here: there's a jungle Frisbee golf course (you attempt to float the disc through the trees into baskets), inner-tubes and kayaks to rent on the nearby Mopan River, and the **Tropical Wings Nature Center** (admission for guests free, half-hour guided tours for nonguests US$2.50; ☺ 9am-5pm), which has a butterfly house, interactive tropical ecology exhibits, medicinal gardens and the opportunity to hold a tarantula in your hand!

Log Cab-Inn (☎ 824-3367; www.logcabinns-belize .com; Mile 68 Western Hwy; s/d US$60/71, with air-con US$82/93, mains US$5-10; ☺ breakfast, lunch & dinner; **P** ☒ ☒) Almost opposite Windy Hill, the welcoming Log Cab-Inn offers clean, spacious, tile-floored log cabins with hot-water bathrooms, and a good open-air restaurant and pool set at the top of its grassy grounds. Also recommended:

Clarissa Falls Resort (☎/fax 824-3916; www.clarissa falls.com; Mile 70 Western Hwy; camping/bunkhouses per person US$8/15, s/d/q cabins US$33/65/88, mains US$3-9; ☺ restaurant 7am-7pm; **P**) The cabins are fairly basic; what's special is the peaceful setting right by the Mopan River, 1 mile off the highway, with horseback riding, river rafting and river-tubing all available.

Casa Maya Jungle Resort (☎ 820-4020; www.casa mayaresort.com; Mile 68½ Western Hwy; r US$38, s/d cabanas US$109/120, breakfast & dinner US$26, all meals US$39; **P** ☒) Secluded resort 1.4 miles off the highway with extensive lawn and jungle grounds, a pool, nature and medicinal trails, mountain bikes and a beautiful two-story hilltop bird-watching *palapa*. A full range of tours and activities is offered, including multiday wilderness treks.

Inn at Xunantunich (☎ 803-2115; xunantunichinn @yahoo.com; Mile 72 Western Hwy, San José Succotz; r US$50-100, dishes from US$4; ☺ breakfast, lunch & dinner; ☒ ☒ **P**) Right opposite the ferry to Xunantunich, this hotel provides brightly colored rooms set around a patio with bar and pool. The dining terrace overlooking the river is a lovely place to eat.

Chial Rd

Chial Rd, heading southeast off the Western Hwy, 5 miles from San Ignacio, gives access to three beautiful lodges on the west bank of the Macal River.

duPlooys' Jungle Lodge (☎ 824-3101; www.du plooys.com; r & bungalows US$165-222, ste or 2-story casitas for 3 or 4 US$313, extra person US$17, dinner & breakfast US$29, 3 meals US$38; **P** ☒ ☒) This relaxed but very well-managed, family-run lodge sits in large and lovely well-treed grounds above the Macal, which is overlooked by a walkway from the bar. Founded in 1989 it's one of the longest-running Cayo lodges. All rooms are spacious and comfortable, with bathrooms, fans and patios. Guests can enjoy swimming in the river, sunbathing on the white, sandy beach, and coffee and bird observation from the bar in the morning, all for free. You can also ride horses, take a massage, paddle canoes and take any number of excursions to caves, Maya sites, waterfalls or birding spots. To reach duPlooys', turn right off Chial Rd after 2.5 miles and go on for 1.7 miles.

Also here – and well worth visiting even if you're not staying at the lodge – is the **Belize Botanic Gardens** (www.belizebotanic.org; per person unguided/guided tour US$2.50/5, per 2 people with self-guiding booklet US$8; ☺ 7am-4pm), a bountiful 45-acre zone with 2 miles of trails, an orchid house, many fruit trees and four different Belizean habitats: wetlands, rainforest, Mountain Pine Ridge (with a lookout tower) and plants of the Maya. Two ponds attract a variety of waterfowl. The gardens were cleared farmland when bought by founders Ken and Judy duPlooy in 1993. Their now lushly-vegetated state is testament both to the tropical climate and to the duPlooys' dedication to planting!

Black Rock River Lodge (☎ 824-2341; www.black rocklodge.com; s US$87-142, d US$104-158, tr US$120-174, q US$131-185, all incl private bathroom; breakfast US$10, lunch items US$4-6, dinner US$37; **P**) High up the Macal in beautiful Black Rock Canyon, this is a place where you can go beyond the usual lodge experience. Comfortable slate-and-wood cabins and a dining area under a great big *palapa* look down on the river, where there are sandy beaches for swimming. From here you can hike a signed trail up the mountain behind the lodge, or hike or ride a horse to Vaca Falls up the Macal or to the little-visited Flour Camp Cave, with its abundant ancient Maya pottery, stalactites and stalagmites. The birding is great and you'll probably see black howler monkeys and otters, too. The electricity here is solar and hydro. Black Rock River Lodge is at the end of a good, well signposted, 6-mile unpaved road that leaves the Chial Rd 0.8 miles off the Western Hwy.

Lodge at Chaa Creek (☎ 824-2037, 820-4010; www .chaacreek.com; s/d/tr US$190/220/257, ste from US$256, breakfast/packed lunch/dinner US$12/10/31; P □) Consistently rated among the best lodges in Belize, Chaa Creek's tropical gardens and beautifully kept thatched cottages spread across a gentle slope above the Macal, 3 miles from the highway. Owned and operated by Lucy and Mick Fleming, who stumbled upon it in 1977, Chaa Creek blossomed from an overgrown farm into Belize's original jungle lodge. The cottages, richly decorated with Maya textiles and local crafts, all have good decks, fans and private bathrooms. An array of tours and activities is offered and Chaa Creek is proud of its state-of-the-art spa on a hilltop overlooking the river.

The **Camp at Chaa Creek** (Macal River Camp; per person incl dinner & breakfast US$65) is Chaa Creek's more economical alternative, half a mile away, and has screened wooden stilt cabins near the river. A campfire is lit nightly and the shared bathrooms have excellent hot showers. Room rates at both the Lodge and the Camp include canoeing, guided bird walks and visits to the on-site rainforest medicine trail, natural history center and butterfly farm.

The following Chaa Creek attractions, as well as its restaurant, are open to nonguests as well:

Rainforest Medicine Trail (guided tour US$5; ☺ hourly 8am-5pm) This trail through the jungle just above the river was established by Dr Rosita Arvigo (see the boxed text, below) and originally named for her Maya mentor, Don Eligio Panti, as one of a series of projects to spread knowledge of traditional healing methods and to preserve the rainforest

---

ROSITA ARVIGO & DON ELIGIO PANTI

In 1969 Rosita Arvigo left Chicago in search of something more meaningful in life. After a spell in southern Mexico and time back in Chicago learning naprapathy, an offshoot of chiropractic medicine, Arvigo moved to western Belize in 1981 with her two children and husband, Greg Shropshire. They bought 35 acres of untamed land, at the time only accessible by canoe, on the Macal River. Nearby, Arvigo's friends Mick and Lucy Fleming were also wrestling with the challenges of their own jungle plot, which later became Chaa Creek (above).

In 1982 Arvigo met 86-year-old Don Eligio Panti, a Maya natural healer from San Antonio village. In decades of healing, Don Eligio had treated thousands of patients who traveled from all over Belize to seek his help with physical, emotional and spiritual ailments. To Arvigo, it seemed that the illiterate Don Eligio had an almost magical power to heal. But she knew from what she'd witnessed in Mexico that this healing power didn't come out of thin air; rather, it came from plants, flowers and the Maya spirits that lived high on tree branches, under bushes and in the ground. She studied and worked with Eligio, gathering plants from the forests and knowledge from the old man's wisdom, until his death in 1996, at age 103. Before Don Eligio's death, Arvigo also began working with Dr Michael Balick, director of the Institute of Economic Botany at the New York Botanical Garden. Together, under the Belize Ethnobotany Project, they identified, cataloged and collected 3560 plants, some of which are being investigated in the US for potential use in the fights against cancer and AIDS.

Arvigo set up the Ix Chel Tropical Research Foundation (named for the Maya goddess of healing and medicine), with a mandate to preserve traditional healing methods and conserve the rainforest through research and education. At her farm she established the Rainforest Medicine Trail (above), now operated by Chaa Creek, which demonstrates the medicinal values of Belize's plant life. Arvigo was also involved in starting Rainforest Remedies, a San Ignacio enterprise whose herbal remedies are on sale throughout Belize. These remedies, with names such as 'Belly Be Good,' help everything from backaches and colds to traveler's diarrhea and frayed nerves.

More recently Dr Arvigo has focused on abdominal massage centered on ancient Maya techniques that reposition organs that have dropped, seeking to restore the body's balance (see www.arvigomassage.com). Arvigo's story is told in her fascinating book *Sastun: My Apprenticeship with a Maya Healer*, coauthored by Nadine Epstein. She has also co-authored *Rainforest Remedies: 100 Healing Herbs of Belize* and *Rainforest Remedies: The Maya Way to Heal Your Body & Replenish Your Soul*.

habitats from which many healing plants come. It identifies about 100 medicinal plants used in traditional Maya and/or modern medicine. A gift shop near the start of the trail sells a guide to the trail's plants and some of Dr Arvigo's books.

Chaa Creek Natural History Center & Butterfly Farm (guided tours US$5-8; ☺ hourly 8am-4pm) The butterfly farm breeds only the dazzlingly iridescent blue morpho *(Morpho peleides)*, whose pupae are exported for about US$3 each. The tour will show you the creature's full cycle. The small natural history center has informative displays on Belize's natural history and the early Maya.

Benque Viejo del Carmen & Around

Benque Viejo del Carmen (population 6700) is 7 miles down the Western Hwy from San Ignacio. It's home to a classy all-inclusive resort, and two interesting attractions lie a few miles south, but otherwise Benque is mainly a place to pass through, and maybe change transport, on the way to or from the Guatemalan border. Benque does break out of its tropical somnolence in mid-July, when the **Benque Viejo del Carmen Fiesta** celebrates the town's patron saint with several days of music and fun.

The highway turns left as you enter Benque and then curves right as George Price Blvd, a dual carriageway. The Novelo's bus station is 100m along George St, straight ahead where the highway turns left on entering Benque.

POUSTINIA

Hydro Rd, turning south off George Price Blvd, beside the Long Lucky Super Store, leads 2.5 miles to **Poustinia Land Art Park** (☎ 822-3532; www.poustiniaonline.org; Mile 2½ Hydro Rd; admission by appointment only US$5), a highly unexpected avant-garde sculpture park in 60 acres of rainforest. Created by Benque brothers Luis and David Ruiz, it displays some 30 works by Belizean and international artists. Poustinia is conceived as an environmental art project, where, once in place, the exhibits – including a car, a greenhouse and a strip of parquet flooring – become subject to the action of nature, which may rot, corrode or otherwise transmute them.

One piece, *Stone Labyrinth*, is set on top of an unexcavated Maya mound with views to Xunantunich (p163). Poustinia is best enjoyed if you have time to contemplate the art and the nature it's set in. Allow at least two hours, preferably more. Arrangements to visit can be made at **Benque Viejo House of Cul-** **ture** (☎ 823-2697; 64 St Joseph St; ☺ 9am-4pm Mon-Fri), just off Campo Santo Memorial Park. Equip yourself to deter mosquitoes, and bring water and maybe something to eat.

CHE CHEM HA

William Morales' dog was busy chasing down a gibnut on his lush property one day in 1989 when it seemingly disappeared into a rock wall. Morales pressed into the 'wall' and found it was actually a cave mouth, and inside he came upon probably the largest collection of Maya pottery ever discovered. The cave is **Che Chem Ha** (☎ 820-4063; Mile 8 Hydro Rd; tour per person US$20; ☺ 9:30am & 1:30pm), entered from Hydro Rd 5.5 miles beyond Poustinia.

Morales' family has been farming this land since the 1940s, and today they also conduct tours through the cave, offering lunches and simple lodgings to visitors. The cave, about 800ft long, was used by the Maya for many centuries for food storage and rituals.

Narrow passages wind past ceremonial pots, many of them intact, to a stela at the end of the tunnel. Short ladders enable you to climb up rock ledges. Bring strong shoes, water and a flashlight. The tour lasts about 90 minutes, following an uphill jungle walk of about 30 minutes to the cave mouth. After the cave, you can visit a lovely waterfall on the property and/or hike about 30 minutes down to **Vaca Falls** for a swim in the Macal River.

It's a good idea to ring ahead – and, if you like, order a good home-cooked lunch (US$7 including soft drinks). The Morales can arrange to pick you up in San Ignacio if you wish. They also have a few rustic but tidy thatched-roof **cabanas** (s/d incl 3 meals US$41/80) with shared bathroom.

SLEEPING

Mopan River Resort (☎ 823-2047; www.mopanriver resort.com; Riverside North; s/d 6-night package in cabanas US$1088/2096, ste US$1298/2516; ☺ closed Jul-Oct; ☒ ☒) Set in beautifully manicured gardens on the north bank of the Mopan River (you'll be ferried across from Benque on arrival), this resort specializes in worry-free adventure vacations with camaraderie. Guests get to know each other remarkably easily with the assistance of the banana velvet cocktail during pre-dinner drinks! The packages (from three nights upward) include meals, drinks, airport transfers and a daily tour and activity program (to archaeological sites including Tikal and Caracol, caves, river-tubing, bird-watching and kayaking). The accommodations have lovely hardwood floors, walls and furniture, nice modern bathrooms with tub, and verandahs. The food is first class, with a different international buffet each night.

GETTING THERE & AWAY

Benque Viejo del Carmen is the end of the line for Western Hwy buses from Belize City. **Novelo's Bus Line** (☎ 823-2054; 119 George St) departs for San Ignacio (express/regular US$1/0.75, 20/30 minutes), Belmopan (express/regular US$3/2, one/1½ hours) and Belize City (express/regular US$6/4, 2½/ three hours) about every half-hour from 3:30am to 5:30pm (and about every hour on Sundays). An express to Chetumal, Mexico (US$13, 6½ hours) leaves at 4am, Friday to Monday only.

The Guatemalan Border

The border is 1 mile beyond Benque Viejo del Carmen (2 miles from the Novelo's bus station). It's advisable to cross in the morning as onward transportation dwindles with the approach of nightfall. Travelers leaving Belize must pay the normal land-exit fee of US$15 and conservation fee of US$3.75. See p210 for information on Guatemalan visa requirements. Money changers on the Belizean side buy and sell Guatemalan, Mexican, Belizean and US currencies at rates not much worse than you would get at banks.

Taxis run between San Ignacio and Benque bus stations and the border. On a colectivo basis you pay US$2 to/from San Ignacio and US$1 to/from Benque. A private taxi costs US$8 to/from San Ignacio and US$4 to US$5 for Benque.

On the Guatemalan side of the border you can often charter a taxi or minibus to Flores or Tikal (both US$40 to US$50 for up to four people, two hours): chances of this are best in the morning. Otherwise, walk (about half a mile) or take colectivo transportation (around US$0.50) to the market at the border town of Melchor de Mencos. From the market there are minibuses (US$3) to Flores about every half-hour from around 5am to 6pm, and occasional buses (US$1.50). If you're heading for El Remate, these vehicles can drop you at Puente Ixlú (El Cruce).

Northwest of San Ignacio

The pretty village of Bullet Tree Falls, straddling the Mopan River 3 miles northwest of San Ignacio, is home to several budget and midrange places to stay that make easy-going bases in the area at affordable prices. Beyond Bullet Tree Falls is the isolated Maya site of El Pilar.

BULLET TREE FALLS

As you come into the village you'll see the bus stop at the junction of a road to the right (which leads to Iguana Junction and Cohune Palms). Straight ahead, the main road continues 200yd to the bridge over the Mopan.

Buses run six times daily (except Sunday) from San Ignacio to Bullet Tree Falls (US$0.50, 15 minutes) and back. See p159 for details on departures from San Ignacio and taxi services between the two places.

Eighty yards past the bus stop, **Be Pukte Cultural Center** (☉ varies) has a display on El Pilar, with a model of the site and booklets for sale. It also sells tickets for El Pilar and can arrange a taxi there (US$25 roundtrip with one hour at the site).

Iguana Junction (☎ 820-4021; www.iguanajunction .com; r with shared bathroom US$33, cabins with private bathroom US$44, breakfast/dinner US$4/8; ☉ breakfast, lunch & dinner, closed to nonguests Sun) In grassy grounds right on the riverbank, 350yd from the bus stop, Iguana Junction is a friendly place with clean, wooden rooms and cabins. The restaurant serves good Belizean home cooking: you will need to book for dinner.

Cohune Palms (☎ 600-7508, 609-3728; www.cohune palms.com; cabins US$33-50; P) A mellow spot, Cohune Palms is set in riverbank gardens and offers a guest kitchen. Bicycles and river-tubes are available. Staff can usually pick you up in San Ignacio.

Hummingbird Hills (☎ 614-4699; www.humming birdhills.com; cabanas US$30-80, breakfast US$5, dinner US$5-10; P) Here you'll find half a dozen good cabanas with private or shared bathroom, and one cute tree house, on verdant 12-acre grounds. The gardens contain hammock and lounge *palapas* and the owners can book you on Cayo excursions. They'll give you one free pickup from San Ignacio and charge US$5 for other transfers. It's 500yd along the road to the left between Be Pukte Cultural Center and the bridge.

Riverside Lodge (☎ 820-4007; www.riversidelodge belize.com; cabanas US$65; P ✖) Sitting by the north side of the bridge, Riverside Lodge has cabanas with hot showers, two double beds, bright decor and terraces overlooking the river. Canoes are available for around US$13/25 per half/full day. The *palapa* restaurant hosts live bands or DJs every second Saturday or so and can pull in quite a crowd. When there's something on, you'll hear it all over the village.

EL PILAR

The road to **El Pilar** (admission US$5; ☻ 8am-4pm) heads off to the left 400yd past the bridge in Bullet Tree Falls. It's 7 miles to the site. El Pilar was occupied for at least 15 centuries, from the middle Preclassic (around 500 BC) to the late Classic (about AD 1000) Period. Long before present-day political borders, El Pilar stretched to modern-day Pilar Poniente in Guatemala, and the two countries are now working as partners to preserve the area. **El Pilar Archaeological Reserve for Maya Flora & Fauna** straddles the international boundary.

With 25 plazas and 70 major structures, El Pilar was more than three times the size of Xunantunich (p163). Despite excavations since 1993, not much of El Pilar is cleared, to avoid the decay that often follows clearing of ancient buildings. While appreciating El Pilar's greatness requires some imagination, this may actually help to give you the feeling that you're discovering the place rather than following a well-worn tourist trail.

Six archaeological and nature trails meander among the mounds. The most impressive area is Plaza Copal, which has four pyramids 45ft to 60ft high. A partly visible Maya causeway runs 500yd west from here to Pilar Poniente. The site attracts archaeology enthusiasts and is also a favorite with birders. Toucans, orioles, toucanets, hummingbirds, woodpeckers and even the occasional scarlet macaw can be seen here. You can explore El Pilar on your own, but you'll need a car, tour guide or taxi to get here.

MOUNTAIN PINE RIDGE AREA

South of San Ignacio and the Western Hwy, the land begins to climb toward the heights of the Maya Mountains, whose arcing ridge forms the border separating Cayo District from Stann Creek District to the east and Toledo District to the south.

In the heart of this highland area, 200 sq miles of submontane (ie on the foothills or lower slopes of mountains) pine forest is protected as the **Mountain Pine Ridge Forest Reserve**. Unlike the tropical broadleaf forests so prevalent in Belize, whose shallow soils sit on limestone, much of the Mountain Pine Ridge's soil sits on a superficial level of red clay, beneath which lies solid granite. This infertile ground makes agriculture almost impossible.

The sudden switch from tropical rainforest to pine trees as you ascend to the Mountain Pine Ridge – a broad upland area of multiple ridges and valleys – is truly bizarre; you'll hear much exclaiming from visitors about this. Also eliciting exclamations these days is the number of dead pines, the result of an infestation by the southern pine beetle in 2000. Fortunately the forest is growing back, thanks in part to a reforestation program, and initial fears that the beetle would kill the entire forest have proved groundless. With luck it will be back to something like its former glory in 20 or 30 years.

The reserve is full of rivers, pools, waterfalls and caves, and the higher elevation means relief from both heat and mosquitoes. Beyond the Pine Ridge, to the southwest, are the ruins of Caracol (p171), Belize's largest and most important Maya site.

When visiting this remote region keep in mind that except for a small presence of forestry and dam-construction workers in the village of Douglas D'Silva (also called Augustine), staff at the area lodges, a few archaeologists, occasional troops on training exercises and a smattering of illegal squatters from Guatemala, this massive area is mostly uninhabited.

The main road into the Mountain Pine Ridge area is the Chiquibul Rd (also called the Pine Ridge Rd), which heads south off the Western Hwy at Georgeville. The Cristo Rey Rd from Santa Elena (near San Ignacio) meets up with the Chiquibul Rd after 9 miles. Both of these roads and all others in the area (except for the final 12 miles to Caracol) are unpaved and are drivable in an ordinary car with reasonably high clearance, except in some cases after a lot of rain. Give priority to any large trucks you meet. Without a car, you can take one of the Mountain Pine Ridge or Caracol tours from San Ignacio (p156).

At the entrance to the protected area, 1.4 miles up the Chiquibul Rd from the Cristo

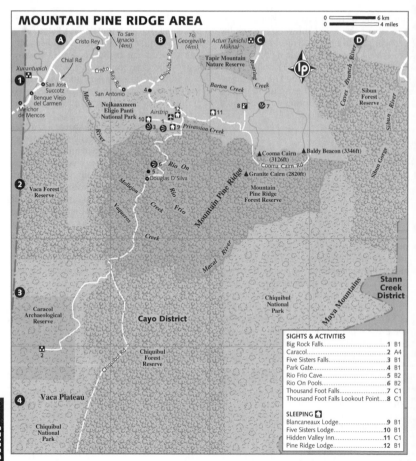

MOUNTAIN PINE RIDGE AREA

Rey Rd junction, a warden stops all vehicles and registers names and license plates. This is to control illegal activity and to keep track of who is in the area in case of accidents or bad weather. You can check here about road conditions further on.

Waterfalls & Caves
Thousand Foot Falls, 10 miles off the Chiquibul Rd, are reckoned the highest falls in Central America. Access them by turning onto Cooma Cairn Rd, then turning left at the '1000 Ft Falls' sign after 7 miles. What you actually reach is a **lookout point** (admission US$1; 8am-5pm) with a view of the falls plunging over the edge of the pine-covered plateau into the tropical broadleaf valley far below.

The falls are in fact around 1600ft high but the thin long stream of falling water is unlikely to hold your interest for a very long time. Birders should keep their eyes peeled for the rare orange-breasted falcon around here. The highest point of the Mountain Pine Ridge, a further 8 miles of driving (signposted) from the Thousand Foot Falls turnoff, is **Baldy Beacon** (3346ft), topped by a cluster of transmitter masts.

The shorter (150ft) and wider **Big Rock Falls** on Privassion Creek are more powerful and, for many people, more beautiful and impressive than Thousand Foot Falls. Take the road toward Five Sisters Lodge and, 1.5 miles past Blancaneaux Lodge (p173), turn along a track to the left where a 'Five Sisters Lodge' sign points straight ahead. The track ends after about 175yd, and a foot trail continues 400yd down to the river. You can swim in the river and the falls are 100yd upstream. There's also a trail to the falls from Blancaneaux Lodge. **Five Sisters Falls**, a set of smaller cascades with swimming pools and shelter pavilions at their foot, are on the property of Five Sisters Lodge (p173) and can be reached from the lodge by a walking trail of about 45 minutes, or a hydro-powered **mini-tram** (lodge guests/nonguests free/US$2.50; ✆ 8am-5pm). It's a nice idea to walk down and take the tram up!

Rio On Pools, just off Chiquibul Rd 2.5 miles north of Douglas D'Silva, are a series of small waterfalls connecting pools that the river has carved out of granite boulders. It's a beautiful spot: the pools are refreshing for a dip and the smooth slabs of granite are perfect for stretching out to dry off. A picnic area and outhouse are the only amenities here. In Douglas D'Silva itself is the signed turnoff to the large, easily accessed **Rio Frio Cave**, less than 1 mile away. The river gurgles through the sizeable cave, keeping it cool while you explore. Rio Frio Cave and Rio On Pools are usually included on Caracol and Mountain Pine Ridge tours.

Caracol

Once one of the most powerful cities in the entire Maya world, **Caracol** (admission US$8; ✆ 8am-5pm) now lies enshrouded by thick jungles near the Guatemalan border, a 52-mile, two-hour drive from San Ignacio.

Sitting high on the Vaca Plateau, 1650ft above sea level, this is the largest Maya site in Belize, having stretched over possibly 70 sq miles at its peak around AD 650. Nearly 40 miles of internal causeways radiate from the center to large outlying plazas and residential areas, and connect parts of the city. At its height, the city's population may have approached 150,000, more than twice as many people as Belize City has today. Though they had no natural water source, the people of Caracol dug artificial reservoirs to catch rainwater and grew food on extensive agricultural terraces. Its central area was a bustling place of temples, palaces, busy thoroughfares, craft workshops and markets.

Caracol is not only the preeminent archaeological site in Belize but also exciting for its jungle setting and the chance of seeing some bird life. Most people come on a guided tour but it's possible to drive on your own. The paving of the final 12 miles to the site from the bridge over the Macal River has made the drive relatively easy. At the ticket office is a small visitors center that outlines Caracol's history, and has a helpful scale model. A museum under construction will house much of the sculpture found at Caracol. There are toilets and picnic tables, but no other services, so be sure to have food, water and, if you're driving, a spare tire. Overnight stays are not permitted.

MAYA HISTORY

Caracol was settled by 600 BC but remained a modest place until the Classic Period. What sparked a sudden explosive growth in the 6th century AD was a confrontation with mighty Tikal, some 50 miles northwest. Caracol appears to have been allied with Calakmul (in Campeche state, Mexico), Tikal's major rival in the ancient Maya world. Caracol's Altar 21 (actually a ball court marker) records an 'axe event' in AD 556 that is thought to have been the sacrifice at Tikal of someone from Caracol, triggering hostilities between the two cities.

Altar 21 further records a successful war against Tikal by Caracol's ruler Lord Water in 562. Tikal's ruler Double Bird may have been sacrificed by Caracol at this time. The decades following these events saw a surge of construction and population at Caracol and a halt in the erection of monuments at Tikal. Tikal may have been forced to hand over much of its wealth to Caracol in the form of tribute for a century or more. Caracol's Lord Kan II conquered Naranjo, 25 miles north (in Guatemala), in 631, but Naranjo later turned the tables, defeating Caracol in 680. Thereafter Caracol declined in importance, although a prosperous elite continued to occupy the central area until around 895.

EXCAVATION HISTORY

The ruins were first stumbled upon in 1937 by a logger named Rosa Mai. In 1938 commissioner of archaeology AH Anderson named the site Caracol (Spanish for snail), perhaps because of all the snail shells found in the soil. In 1950 Linton Satterthwaite from the University of Pennsylvania recorded the visible stone monuments, mapped the site core and excavated several tombs, buildings and monuments. Many stelae were

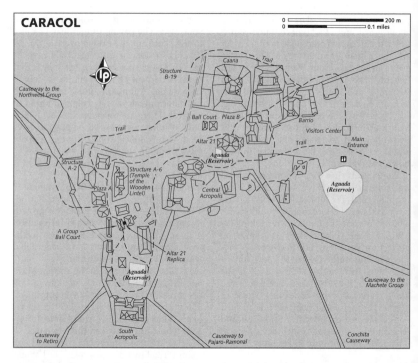

CARACOL

removed and sent to Pennsylvania. Since 1985, Drs Diane and Arlen Chase have led the **Caracol Archaeological Project** (www.caracol.org), with annual field seasons conducting surveys and excavations that have revealed Caracol's massive central core and complex urban development. From 2000 to 2004 the Tourism Development Project carried out an excavation and conservation program led by Belizean archaeologist Jaime Awe, and improved the road access to Caracol.

TOURING THE SITE

A system of trails meanders through Caracol, but Plazas A and B are the most excavated. The highlight is **Caana** (Sky-Place), which rises from Plaza B, and at 141ft is still the tallest building in Belize! Caana underwent many construction phases until its completion in about 800. It supports four palace compounds and three temples. High steps narrowing up to the top probably led to the royal family's compound, where Structure B-19 housed Caracol's largest and most elaborate tomb, containing the remains of a woman, possibly Lady Batz' Ek

from Calakmul, who married into Caracol's ruling dynasty in 584. Climb to the top of Caana to feast upon one of the most magnificent views in all of Belize. Other than the occasional patch-farm fire, it's jungle as far as the eye can see.

South of Plaza B, the **Central Acropolis** was an elite residential group with palaces and shrines. To its west, Plaza A contained many stelae, some of which are still in place. Atop **Structure A-2** is a replica of a stela found here in 2003 that is engraved with the longest Maya inscription found in Belize. Structure A-6, the **Temple of the Wooden Lintel**, is one of the oldest buildings at Caracol. One of its lintels (the one to the left as you enter the top chamber) is original.

South of the Temple of the Wooden Lintel is the **A Group Ball Court** where the all-important Altar 21, telling us so much about Caracol's history, was found. A replica of the 'altar,' actually a ball court marker, sits in the middle. Further south is one of Caracol's many **reservoirs**, and beyond that the **South Acropolis**, a Classic Period elite residential complex where you can enter two tombs.

Tours

Most tour companies and lodges in and around San Ignacio run tours to the Mountain Pine Ridge (p169) and Caracol. On a typical day tour you'll visit the Rio On Pools, Rio Frio Cave and one of the waterfalls. This usually costs between US$30 and US$45 per person. Caracol trips usually include Rio On Pools and Rio Frio Cave too, for around US$60 to US$65.

Everald's Caracol Shuttle (☎ 804-0090, 604-5097; caracolshuttle@hotmail.com), run by knowledgeable Everald Tut, does Caracol trips for US$58 that include lunch, admission, and stops at Rio On Pools and Rio Frio Cave. Everald operates from Crystal Paradise Resort (p163), but does pickups in San Ignacio. You can also contact him through **Snooty Fox Tours** (☎ 804-0050; cnr West St & Waight's Ave, San Ignacio). The trip runs from about 8am to 5pm.

Sleeping & Eating

The Mountain Pine Ridge has a handful of lodges that offer accommodations, meals and tours and activities (some of them free, others at a price). Two (Blancaneaux Lodge and Hidden Valley Inn) are among the most luxurious in the country. Although you can sometimes show up unannounced and find a room, it's best to book ahead.

If you don't have your own transport, you'll need a taxi or lodge transfer to get to/from these places. A taxi from San Ignacio should cost US$45 to US$50; lodge transfers are US$65 to US$75 for up to four people.

Blancaneaux Lodge (☎ 824-3878, 824-4912, in US 800-746-3743; www.blancaneaux.com; s cabanas US$214-250, d cabanas US$250-333, tr/q cabanas US$303/339, d/tr/q villas US$506/565/625, all incl breakfast; lunch & dinner mains US$12-24; P 🕹) This indulgent lodge was formerly a private retreat for its owner, movie director Francis Ford Coppola. Blancaneaux offers 17 thatched cabins and luxury villas, spread around beautifully manicured gardens and some looking right over the picturesque Privassion Creek. The lodgings feature beautiful tiled bathrooms, with open-air living rooms in the villas, and handicrafts from Belize, Guatemala, Mexico and Thailand. Blancaneaux has its own stables, walking trails and riverside spa with a large hot pool, and its restaurant serves mainly Italian cuisine (Coppola's own recipes) and wines from the Niebaum-Coppola Estate Winery in California's Napa Valley.

Much of the produce comes from the lodge's own organic garden. A bottle of Coppola's famed Rubicon goes for US$153.

Hidden Valley Inn (☎ 822-3320; www.hiddenvalley inn.com; s/d/tr US$179/202/226, breakfast/lunch/dinner US$12/14/31; P 🖳 🕹) This inn has 11 beautiful sq miles of Mountain Pine Ridge for the exclusive use of its guests, straddling pine and tropical forest ecosystems and including 90 miles of signposted trails, eight sets of waterfalls and some inviting swimming spots and spectacular lookouts. Set out on foot, on a free mountain bike, or get a vehicle drop-off and make your own way back – whichever you choose, you get a map and a two-way radio and, if you like, they'll ensure that no-one else is walking your trails at the same time! You can even rent a waterfall for the day, complete with champagne lunch. Birders, look out for the orange-breasted falcon (which nests here), the king vulture and the Stygian owl, as well as heaps of colorful and less-rare species.

The rooms, situated amid well-tended gardens, are clean-cut and pleasing, with new mahogany furniture, and the main building contains comfortable lounge areas as well as a restaurant. On-site bird and hiking guides await your call. The lodge is 4 miles off the Chiquibul Rd, along Cooma Cairn Rd.

Five Sisters Lodge (☎ 820-4005/4024; www.fivesis terslodge.com; s/d/tr/q incl breakfast US$101/125/149/173, breakfast/lunch/dinner US$7/7/19; P) This locally owned lodge located 2.5 miles west of Blancaneaux Lodge is named for five side-by-side cascades on the Privassion Creek at the bottom of its property (see p171). The open-air restaurant has a great view over the falls. A hydro-powered mini-tram and a 45-minute medicinal plant trail will both take you down to the river for swimming and sunbathing. The cozy standard cabanas have terraces with hammocks, polished wood floors, mosquito screens and hot showers.

Pine Ridge Lodge (☎ 606-4557, in US 800-316-0706; www.pineridgelodge.com; cottages for up to 4 incl breakfast US$104, lunch/dinner US$8/23; P) The most rustic of the Pine Ridge lodges, this one, 4 miles along the Chiquibul Rd from the warden post, provides neat, clean rooms with screened verandahs and hot-water bathrooms. A little creek runs across the bottom of the grassy gardens. There's no electricity, but you'll come to love your kerosene lantern's soft glow. The restaurant cooks up delicious meals using butane.

Southern Belize

The south is Belize's least touristy region. The south stretches from the peaks of the Maya Mountains down across miles of untouched rainforest and a broad coastal plain, and out to the Belize barrier reef and the outlying atoll Glover's Reef. Three main towns dotted down the coast – the Garifuna 'capital' Dangriga, the low-key beach resort of Placencia, and Punta Gorda in the far south – give access to dozens of offshore islands and some of Belize's most spectacular diving and snorkeling spots, from Glover's Reef's coral gardens and bottomless dropoffs to the haunts of the whale shark at Gladden Spit. Island lodges and resorts invite you to while away the days with far less human company than on Belize's better-known northern cayes.

Back on land, a host of cultural and natural adventures awaits. Soak up some Garifuna rhythm in Dangriga or in the beachside village of Hopkins. Enjoy the beach, good food and laid-back scene at Placencia, perched at the tip of a 16-mile peninsula strung with soft, sandy beaches. Head inland to the rainforests of Cockscomb Basin where jaguars find sanctuary, or the manatee-inhabited waters of Southern Lagoon, or the scarlet macaw–scattered forests near Red Bank. In the far south, investigate the Maya sites Nim Li Punit and Lubaantun, venture into remote wildlife sanctuaries and national parks, and grab the opportunity to experience Maya village life in Toledo District's well-established guesthouse program. A range of accommodations from luxury resorts down is found all over southern Belize. All of them are ready and willing to help you make the most of your time here.

HIGHLIGHTS

- Soaking up the beach scene at **Placencia** (p192)

- Snorkeling, diving and beachbumming the days away on **Glover's Reef** (p185)

- Walking the jungle trails of **Cockscomb Basin Wildlife Sanctuary** (p190) and **Mayflower Bocawina National Park** (p186)

- Getting in touch with Garifuna culture at **Hopkins** (p186) and **Dangriga** (p179)

- Exploring the ancient Maya ruins, modern Maya villages and remote rivers, lagoons and forests of the **deep south** (p203)

| ■ POPULATION: 57,000 | ■ MONTHLY RAINFALL: JAN/JUN 6.5IN/23.4IN (PUNTA GORDA) | ■ HIGHEST ELEVATION: 3687FT |

SOUTHERN BELIZE

History

Ancient Maya sites in the south were less important than in the north, but Lubaantun and Nim Li Punit are evidence of a society flourishing around AD 700–800. Later, the Maya of southern Belize resisted Spanish conquest, but were decimated by European diseases. Those who survived were driven out by the British to the Alta Verapaz region of Guatemala in the 18th and 19th centuries. In the late 19th century, Maya started moving back to Belize's far south where there are now more than 30 Maya villages.

English buccaneers and North American Puritans settled along the coasts in the 17th century, and the earliest Creole villages were established near river mouths in the 18th century. Runaway slaves from Belize City founded Gales Point Manatee (p176) around 1800. Garifuna people started arriving in southern Belize around the same time: their biggest single landing came on November 19, 1832, when some 200 arrived at Dangriga (p179) from Honduras in dugout canoes.

Small-scale agriculture, fishing and some logging have long been mainstays of the region's economy. Today, the growing and processing of citrus fruit in the Stann Creek Valley, situated west of Dangriga, is a major agro-industry.

Language

Virtually everyone speaks English, but the Garifuna language is spoken in places like

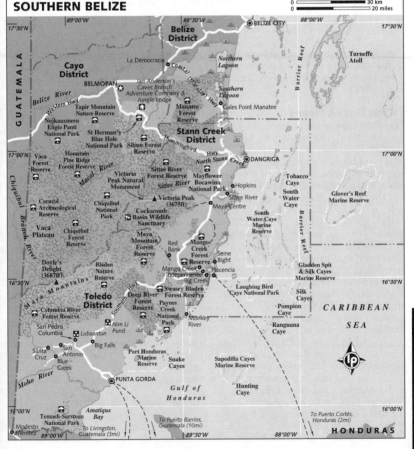

SOUTHERN BELIZE IN...

Two Days
Relax on the beach and eat a couple of good meals at **Placencia** (p192) and take a snorkeling day trip out to beautiful **Laughing Bird Caye** (p195) or the **Silk Cayes** (p194).

Four Days
Base yourself at Placencia and make one or two snorkel or dive trips and a day trip to **Cockscomb Basin** (p190).

One Week
Do the four-day itinerary with a spell out at **Tobacco Caye** (p183), **South Water Caye** (p184) or **Glover's Reef** (p185) in the middle.

Two Weeks
Spend three days imbibing some Garifuna ambience in **Hopkins** (p186) or **Dangriga** (p179), with outings to **Gales Point Manatee** (below) and **Mayflower Bocawina National Park** (p186), then plug in the one-week itinerary and round it off with a few days exploring the **Punta Gorda** area (p200 and p203).

Dangriga, Hopkins, Seine Bight and Punta Gorda, while Mopan and Kekchi Mayan are spoken by Maya groups in the southern Toledo District.

Getting There & Around
The main road to the south is the Hummingbird Hwy, running 50 miles from the Western Hwy near Belmopan to the start of the Southern Hwy near Dangriga – a gorgeous trip over the fringe of the Maya Mountains and down the Stann Creek Valley. The Southern Hwy then continues 100 miles south to Punta Gorda. Both these roads are well paved except for a 10-mile stretch of the Southern Hwy around Nim Li Punit. The mostly unpaved Coastal (or Manatee) Hwy provides an alternative route between the Western and Southern Hwys.

Buses from Belize City and Belmopan head down the Hummingbird Hwy to Dangriga then down the Southern Hwy to Independence and Punta Gorda. Other services run from Dangriga to Hopkins and Placencia, and from Punta Gorda to villages around the far south. Placencia can also be accessed by water-taxi service from Mango Creek, which adjoins Independence.

Daily flights head from Belize City to Dangriga, Placencia and Punta Gorda. Scheduled boat services link Dangriga and Placencia with Puerto Cortés in Honduras, and Punta Gorda with Puerto Barrios and

Lívingston in Guatemala. Boats cross to Tobacco Caye from Dangriga daily; boats to the other islands can be organized through tour operators, dive shops, accommodations or boat owners.

There is no land crossing point between southern Belize and Guatemala.

GALES POINT MANATEE
Population 500
This conservation-conscious Creole village is strung along a narrow peninsula jutting 2 miles into the Southern Lagoon, one of a series of interconnected lakes and waterways between Belize City and Dangriga. Apart from its friendly villagers and beautiful setting – ranks of jungle-clad limestone hills rise in the west – Gales Point Manatee has some superlative wildlife attractions. Chief among them is the presence in the lagoon of the highest concentration of West Indian manatees (an estimated 70 of these gentle aquatic giants) in the Caribbean. The 14-sq-mile Gales Point Wildlife Sanctuary covers the Southern and adjoining lagoons. Nearby beaches are the primary breeding ground for hawksbill turtles in Belize, and there's excellent bird-watching too.

Orientation & Information
The town's single street runs about 2.5 miles north from the Coastal Hwy to the tip of the peninsula. The landmarks along it in-

---

IBO ECHOES

Gales Point Manatee is believed to have been founded over 200 years ago by runaway slaves of Nigerian Ibo (or Ebo) origin from Belize City, and is probably the only place in Belize where the Ibo *sambai* dance rhythm – traditionally beaten out by drums under the full moon – survives. Creole rhythms such as the *sambai* are quite distinct from the Garifuna rhythms you hear in Dangriga or Hopkins.

---

clude Martha's Shop, after about 1.25 miles; the Belize Manatee Project, 0.9 miles further; and Manatee Lodge at the tip of the peninsula.

Few places in Gales Point Manatee have their own phone. You can attempt to get messages to villagers by calling the community phone ☎ 209-8031.

Activities

You will need a guide with a boat for most activities here; all accommodations can set you up with one if you like (your hosts may be guides themselves). Manatee Lodge (right) offers a wide range of trips at fixed prices; rates elsewhere can be lower. Established guides include John Moore, who can be contacted at Moore's Lodging, which is at the southern end of town, or through Manatee Lodge; Raymond Gentle, who runs Gentle's Cool Spot (p178) at the northern end of town; **Dana Myers** (☎ 209-8031), whose house is next door to the community phone; and Jerome and Carolita Samuel and Dean Myers, who are all contactable through Martha's Shop. Typical prices for a full-day boat outing range from US$100 to US$150.

MANATEE-WATCHING

Manatees graze on sea grass in the shallow, brackish Southern Lagoon, hanging out around the 'Manatee Hole,' a depression in the lagoon floor near its east side, fed by a warm freshwater spring. They rise about every 20 minutes for air, giving views of their heads and sometimes their backs and tails. A 1½-hour 'manatee watch' boat trip costs around US$50 for up to four people. Manatee-watching can also be combined with other activities.

TURTLE-WATCHING

Around 100 hawksbill turtles, which are protected in Belize, as well as loggerheads, which aren't, lay their eggs on the 21-mile beach straddling the mouth of the Bar River which connects the Southern Lagoon to the sea. For both species, this is the main nesting site in the country. Turtle-watch outings from Manatee Lodge (below) during the May-to-October nesting season involve a boat trip down the river then a 4-mile nocturnal beach walk looking for nesting turtles (US$175 for up to four people).

DRUMMING

The **Maroon Creole Drum School** (methos_drums@ hotmail.com; lessons per hr US$8) is run by talented and approachable drummer and drum-maker Emmeth Young, who has toured in North America and performs regularly with the village's percussion band, Talla Walla Vibrations, beating out *sambai*, *kunjai*, *bruk-down* and other Creole rhythms. Emmeth offers drumming lessons for any length of time from a couple of hours upwards, and you can find him at his Sugar Shack gift shop near the tip of the peninsula.

BIRD-WATCHING

Bird Caye, a small island in the Northern Lagoon about 45 minutes from Gales Point Manatee by boat, is home to many waterfowl. Gentle's Cool Spot (p178) combines trips here with a stop at the Manatee Hole for US$88.

FISHING

Large tarpon quite often break the surface of the Southern Lagoon. You can also fish for snook, snapper, jack and barracuda in the lagoon and rivers. A half-/full-day trip for up to three costs US$175/225 from Manatee Lodge.

Sleeping & Eating

Manatee Lodge (☎ 220-8040, from USA ☎ 877-462-6283; www.manateelodge.com; r US$95, breakfast/lunch/dinner US$11/9/16; ℗) The lodge is at the tip of the Gales Point peninsula, set in well-kept, grassy gardens with water on three sides. The eight rooms, on two floors, are spacious and comfortable, with bathtubs and lots of varnished wood, and there's a large sitting/reading room with a lovely breezy verandah. A wide range of activities is on offer, and canoes and a sailboat are free for guests.

Recommended budget lodgings include **Gentle's Cool Spot** (r US$10, s/d with private bathroom US$15/20, mains US$3; **P**) up near the north end of the village, where you can sample local cassava, cashew or berry wine as you eat, and **Ionie's B&B** (☎ 220-8066; r US$13-15, breakfast/lunch/dinner US$5/3.50/4; **P**), run by friendly Ionie Samuels opposite Martha's Shop. Ionie's good-size Belizean meals include a drink.

Getting There & Away

Gales Point Manatee is located about 1 mile off the Coastal (Manatee) Hwy: the turnoff is 22 miles off the Western Hwy and 14 miles from the Hummingbird Hwy. The Coastal Hwy and the road into the village are mostly unpaved, but quite drivable in a normal car.

One Novelo's bus per day passes through Gales Point Manatee en route from Dangriga to Belize City and vice versa. It will cost US$3 to Dangriga or Belize City from Gales Point Manatee. The bus leaves Dangriga at 5am, reaching Gales Point Manatee about 6am and arriving in Belize City around 7:30am. Returning to Dangriga, departure from Belize City is at 5pm (4pm Sunday) and from Gales Point Manatee around 6:30pm (5:30pm Sunday). The buses drive into Gales Point Manatee as far as Gentle's Cool Spot then turn around.

The best way to travel to or from Gales Point Manatee, if you can afford it, is by boat through a network of rivers, canals and lagoons that goes all the way to Belize City – a trip of about two hours costs around US$175 for up to four people. Arrangements can be made through Manatee Lodge, Gentle's Cool Spot and some agencies in Belize City.

HUMMINGBIRD HIGHWAY
St Herman's Blue Hole National Park

This 575-acre **national park** (admission US$4; ⏱ 8am-4:30pm) contains one of the few caves in Belize that you can visit independently, and a beautiful sapphire-blue cenote (limestone sinkhole) swimming hole. The visitors center (where flashlights can be rented for US$2.50) is 11 miles along the Hummingbird Hwy from Belmopan. From here a 500yd trail leads to St Herman's Cave. A path leads 300yd into the cave alongside an

underground river. To explore deeper in the extensive cave system, with its huge caverns and classic Maya ceremonial chambers containing calcified skeletons and artifacts, you must have a guide. Highly experienced **Marcos Cucul** (☎ 600-3116; www.mayaguide.bz) is often present at the visitors center. A three-hour route through the cave costs US$50 per person. Cucul also does cave-tubing here (US$60 per person). There's also a 1.5-mile above-ground jungle loop trail starting near the cave entrance, with a lookout tower on the area's highest point.

The **Blue Hole** is just off the highway, 1 mile east of the visitors center (an off-road trail connects the two). This is a 25ft-deep sapphire-blue swimming hole inside a 328ft-wide cenote that was formed when the roof caved in on one of the Sibun River's underground tributaries. A popular stop on the Hummingbird Hwy, the Blue Hole always makes for a refreshing dip, except after rain when it's murky and uninviting. An attendant at the Blue Hole parking area will collect your park fee if you don't have a ticket from the visitors center.

Buses along the Hummingbird Hwy will drop you at the visitors center or Blue Hole entrance (US$1, 20 minutes from Belmopan; US$2.25, 1¼ hours from Dangriga).

Ian Anderson's Caves Branch Adventure Company & Jungle Lodge

Canadian-born Ian Anderson is the pioneer of Belizean cave-tubing trips, and his **adventure company** (☎ 822-2800; www.cavesbranch.com; Mile 41½ Hummingbird Hwy) remains one of the best and most varied in Belize. Caves Branch operates on a 90-sq-mile private jungle estate, with its own jungle lodge. The tour leaders, local employees of the lodge, are highly trained, knowledgeable, attentive and enthusiastic.

Day trips (US$82 to US$114 per person) are tailored to various levels of strenuousness and adventure: you can choose a leisurely river-tube float down the Caves Branch River; float and climb through ceremonial caves to see evidence of the ancient Maya in pottery shards and other artifacts; or opt for a harder adventure where you'll hike, climb and even abseil to your destination. Horseback riding, nocturnal jungle walks and overnight cave, jungle and kayak expeditions are also available.

Showcasing the Caves Branch offerings is the **Black Hole Drop** (US$114), on which you'll get trussed up in a harness, then coaxed backward over a cliff to abseil down a seemingly bottomless, but actually 300ft, sinkhole named **Actun Loch Tunich**. The exhilarating descent takes you through the forest canopy, past the mouth of a sacred Maya cave and down into a tropical forest. The way to the cave is through steep, rough terrain; the hike in and out is harder on some people than the abseiling.

Ian Anderson's Jungle Lodge (☎ 822-2800; www .cavesbranch.com; Mile 41½ Hummingbird Hwy; camping per person US$5.35, dm US$16, d cabana/bungalow/ste US$82/116/137, breakfast/lunch/dinner US$13/13/19; P) is the starting point and nerve center of the Anderson activities. It provides a good balance of rusticity and comfort, making it popular with families as well as adult adventurers. The ethos of the place is to give tourists a busy, active and adventurous time without the hassle of planning it. Few stick around the lodge during the day.

The jungle beside the Caves Branch River has been cleared just enough to allow room for the buildings, giving the grounds an exotic feel, especially at night when the tiki torches are lit. You'll hear howler monkeys and see keel-billed toucans in the trees.

There are four classes of accommodation: bunk dorms for up to eight people, cabanas with shared bathrooms, and bungalows and deluxe jungle suites with private bathrooms. All are open to the sights and sounds of the forest but are equipped with fans and are well screened to keep bugs out. Bunkroom and cabana occupants will love their open-air warm-water jungle showers. During mealtimes, everyone sits at long tables overlooking the river and helps themselves to plentiful buffet meals.

Ian Anderson's is 1100yd off Hummingbird Hwy, 200yd west of the Blue Hole parking area. Buses along the highway will drop you at the turnoff (US$1, 20 minutes from Belmopan; US$2.25, 1¼ hours from Dangriga). The lodge offers transfers to/from points around central and southern Belize.

DANGRIGA
pop 10,400

Dangriga is the largest town in southern Belize and it's the 'capital' of the country's Garifuna people, who form the majority here (see the boxed text, p34 for more on the Garifuna). The town stretches along an untidy beach and is not exactly beautiful. Most travelers spend no more than one night here. But if you give Dangriga a bit more time you'll find it's a relaxed and friendly, but proud and often festive, town that does its best to make the most of its vibrant Garifuna heritage.

Dangriga – called Stann Creek Town until it got its current name (Garifuna for 'sweet' or 'still water') in the 1980s – was the birthplace of punta rock (a fusion of electric instruments and acoustic Garifuna instruments), and today is home to noted Garifuna artists, artisans, festivities and Belize's only Garifuna museum. Wander the streets in the early morning or late afternoon, hang out in the restaurants, buy something to eat or drink at a street stall, and talk to people. You'll walk with the ocean breeze on your skin, and the unfamiliar cadence of the Garifuna language in your ears.

Orientation

Dangriga stretches about 2.5 miles along the coast and up to 1000yd inland. North Stann Creek empties into the Caribbean roughly in the middle of town. The main street, stretching most of the length of the town, runs through the names Havana St, St Vincent St and Commerce St. The Novelo's bus station is toward its south end (Havana St); most boats to Tobacco Caye and other cayes dock on S Riverside Dr near the bridge over North Stann Creek. Most accommodations are in the southern half of town. The airstrip is at the north end.

Information

Belize Bank (☎ 522-2903; 24 St Vincent St; ☼ 8am-3pm Mon-Thu, 8am-4:30pm Fri) The ATM accepts international Visa, MasterCard, Plus and Cirrus cards.

First Caribbean International Bank (☎ 522-2015; Commerce St; ☼ 8am-2:30pm Mon-Thu, 8am-4:30pm Fri) ATM accepts international Visa cards.

Police (☎ 90, 911, 522-2022; Commerce St)

Post office (☎ 522-2035; Mahogany Rd; ☼ 8am-noon & 1-5pm Mon-Thu, 8am-noon & 1-4:30pm Fri)

Southern Regional Hospital (☎ 522-2078; Stann Creek Valley Rd) Good-standard public hospital.

Val's Laundry (☎ 502-3324; cnr Mahogany St & Sharp St; Internet per hr US$2.50, laundry wash & dry per lb US$1; ☼ 7:30am-7pm) Speedy Internet connections; washing machines in a separate room.

DANGRIGA

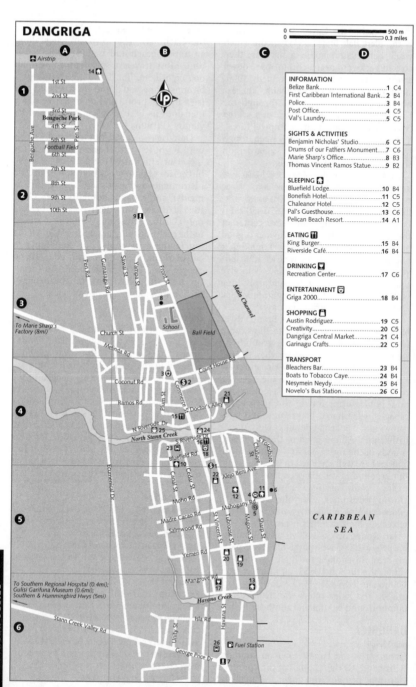

0 — 500 m
0 — 0.3 miles

INFORMATION
Belize Bank..1 C4
First Caribbean International Bank...2 B4
Police..3 B4
Post Office...4 C5
Val's Laundry..5 C5

SIGHTS & ACTIVITIES
Benjamin Nicholas' Studio..................6 C5
Drums of our Fathers Monument.....7 C6
Marie Sharp's Office.............................8 B3
Thomas Vincent Ramos Statue.........9 B2

SLEEPING
Bluefield Lodge...................................10 B4
Bonefish Hotel....................................11 C5
Chaleanor Hotel.................................12 C5
Pal's Guesthouse................................13 C6
Pelican Beach Resort.........................14 A1

EATING
King Burger...15 B4
Riverside Café.....................................16 B4

DRINKING
Recreation Center..............................17 C6

ENTERTAINMENT
Griga 2000..18 B4

SHOPPING
Austin Rodriguez................................19 C5
Creativity...20 C5
Dangriga Central Market...................21 C4
Garinagu Crafts..................................22 C5

TRANSPORT
Bleachers Bar......................................23 B4
Boats to Tobacco Caye.....................24 B4
Nesymein Neydy..................................25 B4
Novelo's Bus Station..........................26 C6

Sights & Activities

GULISI GARIFUNA MUSEUM

This new **museum** (Chuluhadiwa Park, Stann Creek Valley Rd; admission US$5; ☺ noon-7pm Tue-Fri, 8am-2pm Sat) opened in late 2004, and it's a must for anyone interested in the vibrant Garifuna people, though it's quite a hike from the town center. It brings together artifacts, pictures and documents on Garifuna history and culture – including film of the original punta rockers, Pen Cayetano and the Turtle Shell Band, in Dangriga back in 1983. Also hosting exhibitions, workshops and Garifuna language courses, the museum is about 1.5 miles inland along Stann Creek Valley Rd.

MARIE SHARP'S FACTORY

Habanero peppers, purchased from local farmers, are turned into the super-hot bottled sauces that adorn tables all over Belize and beyond at **Marie Sharp's Fine Foods** (☎ 520-2087; www.mariesharps-bz.com; ☺ 7am-4pm Mon-Fri), 8 miles northwest of town on Melinda Rd. Casual tours, often led by Marie herself, are offered during business hours, and the factory shop sells hot sauces and jams at outlet prices. If you can't make it to the factory but would still like to peruse the full line of sauces and jams, Marie Sharp's also has an **office** (☎ 522-2370; 3 Pier Rd; ☺ 8am-noon & 1-5pm Mon-Fri) in Dangriga. See the boxed text, p67 for more on the Marie Sharp phenomenon.

BENJAMIN NICHOLAS' STUDIO

Benjamin Nicholas' bright, primitivist scenes of wildlife, landscapes and Garifuna history and folklore have made him probably Belize's best-known painter. His art hangs in banks, hotels and public buildings throughout the country. Nicholas lives and works in Dangriga and visitors are usually welcome to stop by his **studio** (25 Howard St) to look at his work in progress.

MONUMENTS

The **Drums of our Fathers Monument**, in the traffic circle south of Novelo's bus station, underscores the importance of percussion in Garifuna (and Belizean) life with its large bronze representations of ritual *dügü* drums and *sisira* (maracas); it was sculpted by Stephen Okeke, a Nigerian resident in Dangriga. Up at the other end of town, at the meeting of Commerce and Front Sts, stands

---

GULISI

Dangriga's Garifuna museum is named for Gulisi, one of the original Garifuna settlers in Belize and a daughter of Joseph Chatoyer, a Garifuna leader who died fighting the British on St Vincent. Legend has it that Gulisi used to wake her grandchildren in the night to make them memorize her life story, so that they could pass their own people's history on to future generations.

---

a **statue of Thomas Vincent Ramos** (1887–1955), an early promoter of Garifuna culture who inaugurated Garifuna Settlement Day.

Festivals & Events

Dangriga explodes with celebrations to mark **Garifuna Settlement Day** (November 19), the Garifuna arrival here in 1832. Dangrigans living elsewhere flock home and drumming, dancing and drinking continue right through the night of the 18th to 19th, and canoes reenact the beach landing in the morning.

Dangrigans celebrate **Día de los Reyes** (Three Kings' Day; on nearest weekend to January 6) with the *wanaragua* or *jonkonu* (or John Canoe) dance: male dancers with bright feather-and-paper headdresses, painted masks representing European men, and rattling bands of shells around their knees move from house to house dancing to Garifuna drums. It's the culmination of two weeks of Christmas-season festivities and may also happen at other times between Christmas and January 6.

Sleeping

Bluefield Lodge (☎ 522-2742; www.toucantrail.com /Bluefield-Lodge.html; 6 Bluefield Rd; d with shared/private bathroom US$16/21.40, 2-bed d with shared/private bathroom US$21.40/32) This well-run small guesthouse fills up fast, so book ahead. With good, clean rooms in a pristine colonial-style building, it gets plenty of return visitors. All rooms have fans, some have cable TV. Single occupants may get discounts. The owner has a wealth of information about Dangriga.

Pelican Beach Resort (☎ 522-2044; www.pelican beachbelize.com; 1st St; s/d US$67/92, with sea-view porch US$82/108, with air-con US$91/116; Ⓟ ✖) Set in beachside gardens (with a sandy beach) at the far north end of town, Dangriga's one upmarket hotel has good, spacious rooms and the best restaurant in town. All rooms have phones and many are decorated with colorful art by Dangriga's Pen Cayetano. The owners also run the Pelican's Pouch (p185) on South Water Caye.

Chaleanor Hotel (☎ 522-2587; www.toucantrail.com /Chaleanor-Hotel.html; 35 Magoon St; s/d/tr with private bathroom US$27/43/54, with shared bathroom US$9/15/18; ✕ ✷) This friendly hotel on a residential street offers rooms with TV, fan and hot water. You can get air-con for an extra US$15 per night. There's free drinking water, and vehicle and boat charters and tours are available. The rooms with private facilities are clean, bright and spacious. Upstairs rooms catch more of the breeze. The economy rooms are small, board-partitioned affairs with cold-water bathrooms.

Pal's Guesthouse (☎ 522-2095; www.palsbelize .com; 868A Magoon St; s/d/tr with shared bathroom US$11/19/25, with private bathroom US$19/25/30, beachfront US$25/35/44) The beachfront rooms, across the street from the main building, are good-sized, with breezy balconies overlooking a good, clean stretch of beach. The rooms in the main building are more cell-like. All have fan and cable TV.

Bonefish Hotel (☎ 522-2243; www.bluemarlin lodge.com; 15 Mahogany St; r US$49-74; ✷) The rooms are charmless but all have two double beds, fan, air-con and cable TV. Price varies according to size and whether they're upstairs or down. Under the same ownership as Blue Marlin Lodge (p184) on South Water Caye, the hotel has a pleasant upstairs bar with a nice view of the sea.

Eating

Pelican Beach Resort (☎ 522-2044; 1st St; mains US$5-13; ✷ breakfast, lunch & dinner) The town's top hotel provides efficient service and a range of dependable Belizean and North American dishes – with a large indoor aquarium to gaze at while you eat. Full breakfasts run US$6 to US$10.

King Burger (☎ 522-2476; 135 Commerce St; dishes US$2-8; ✷ 7am-3pm & 5-10pm Mon-Sat) Better inside than its somewhat forbidding entrance suggests, this diner-style place does good-value breakfasts (US$3) and a heap of other straightforward foods from burgers and fried chicken to omelet's or shrimp – and healthy fresh juices.

Street Barbecues (meals around US$2.50) Do what the locals do in the evenings and enjoy tasty grilled chicken, beans, coleslaw and flour tortillas, cooked up in big tin drums set up on the streetside.

Riverside Café (☎ 502-3449; S Riverside Dr; mains US$3-10; ✷ breakfast, lunch & dinner) Just east of the Stann Creek bridge, this café is convenient if you're waiting for or asking about a boat. Some information about island accommodations and goings-on about town is posted on the walls. There's a large menu, but it's best to stick to the basics.

Drinking

Recreation Center (St Vincent St; ✷ 4pm-midnight) This piece of earth with a thatched roof, no walls and a mainly local clientele can be a lot of fun.

Pelican Beach Resort (☎ 522-2044; www.pelican beachbelize.com; 1st St) The Friday happy hour from 6pm to 8pm usually pulls in a crowd.

Entertainment

It's impossible to predict when you might hear **Garifuna drumming**, except around festivals such as Garifuna Settlement Day or Día de los Reyes (p181). Neighborhood kids may offer to perform for travelers. They're an entrepreneurial bunch: a cup will be passed around between numbers, and the big kids will usually keep the proceeds.

Griga 2000 (2 St Vincent St; ✷ from 9pm Tue-Thu & Sun, from 10pm Fri & Sat) The Club, as it's known, gets a bit of a crowd for midweek karaoke sessions, but things really start jumping at the Friday and Saturday dances, sometimes with live bands.

Shopping

Austin Rodriguez (☎ 502-3752; 32 Tubroose St) This master artisan carves Garifuna drums from mahogany, cedar and the mayflower tree; the surface is stretched deer, peccary or sheep skin. The people here are happy to answer questions on the drum-making process. The smaller 'primero' drums, which play the intricate cross patterns over the more fixed rhythm of the larger 'segunda,' sell for between US$25 and US$100.

Creativity (cnr St Vincent St & Yemeri Rd) This is a good place to pick up Garifuna art and drums and find out a bit about Garifuna culture. Hours vary, but there's usually someone around who can help you out.

Garinagu Crafts (☎ 522-2596; 44 St Vincent St) This place sells a range of Garifuna handicrafts, including drums, maracas, paintings and dolls, at reasonable prices.

Dangriga Central Market (Doctor's Alley) Traders sell shoes, clothes and crockery as well as fresh fish and vegetables. It's busiest in the morning.

Getting There & Away

AIR

From Dangriga airport (DGA), **Maya Island Air** (☎ 522-3475; www.mayaairways.com) and **Tropic Air** (☎ 522-2129; www.tropicair.com) both fly several times daily to Belize City and Placencia, and less often to Punta Gorda via Placencia.

BOAT

Most boats to the cayes leave from opposite the Riverside Café on S Riverside Dr. Regular passenger services to Tobacco Caye leave mid-morning and sometimes around lunchtime too. Stop by around 9am to 10am, or the afternoon before, to check when boats will be leaving. Some lodges on other islands will organize your boat for you, but if you need to arrange your own passage come down to S Riverside Dr and talk with the boat people.

The water taxi **Nesymein Neydy** (☎ 522-0082, 522-3227) departs N Riverside Dr at 9am Saturday for Puerto Cortés, Honduras (US$50, three to four hours). Be at the dock around 8am. The return trip from Puerto Cortés is on Tuesday.

BUS

Novelo's/Southern Transport (☎ 502-2160; 3 Havana St) has the following daily departures (subject to change):

Belize City (express/regular US$7/5, 2½/three hours, 107 miles) Eight buses via the Hummingbird Hwy and Belmopan between 5am and 5pm; one bus at 5am via the Coastal Hwy and Gales Point Manatee.

Belmopan (US$3, 1¾ hours, 55 miles) Eight buses, 5am to 5pm.

Gales Point Manatee (US$3, one hour, 23 miles) Bus at 5am.

Hopkins (US$2, 40 minutes, 20 miles) Buses at 12:15pm and 5:15pm; also KC's Bus Service (US$2.50) from Bleachers Bar, S Riverside Dr, at 10:30am Monday to Saturday, passing the Novelo's station two minutes later; or get a Punta Gorda–bound bus to the Hopkins junction on the Southern Hwy (US$1.50), and hitch or walk the final 4 miles.

Placencia (US$5, 2¼ hours, 65 miles) Buses at 10am Monday to Saturday and 12:15pm and 5:15pm daily – or get a Punta Gorda–bound bus to Independence then catch the Hokey Pokey Water Taxi (p199).

Punta Gorda (US$7, 3¾ hours, 105 miles) Three or four buses, 9am to 5pm.

James bus line (☎ 702-2049, 722-2625) comes through Dangriga en route between Belize City, Belmopan and Punta Gorda. Its buses halt at Bleachers Bar on S Riverside Dr and outside the Novelo's terminal, at (roughly) 8am, 1pm, 5:30pm and 6pm heading for Punta Gorda, and about 9:30am, 11:30am and 3:30pm heading for Belize City.

TOBACCO CAYE

Tiny Tobacco Caye, 200yd long, 100yd wide and mainly sandy, sits right on the barrier reef 12 miles off Dangriga. With half a dozen places to stay, it's popular with travelers on a limited budget who fancy an island experience. You can enjoy snorkeling, diving or fishing – or just bliss out in a hammock. The atmosphere is sociable and friendly. At most accommodations all guests eat at the same time, and three places have bars open to all. Just west is Man-O'-War Caye, an important nesting site for the brown booby and magnificent frigate bird, which you will very likely pass on the way to Tobacco Caye. Both islands are among the dozens within the World Heritage–listed South Water Caye Marine Reserve.

Activities

There's good snorkeling and diving to be done right off the island's shores, or you can take trips further afield. Organize dives through **Tobacco Caye Diving** (☎ 614-9907; www.tobaccocayediving.com), next to Reef's End Lodge. Local dives cost US$30 per dive, plus US$25 per day for equipment. Two-tank outings to Belize's atolls, usually requiring four people, are US$135 to Glover's Reef (p185), US$160 to Turneffe Atoll (p126) and US$200 to Lighthouse Reef (p127). Also in the vicinity is the Shark Hole (or Shark Cave), an underwater cave popular with fish, turtles and sharks. The entrance, 42ft down, is about 33ft wide but the cave opens up to about 150ft inside. In its center is a large sandhill around which the sharks circle.

There's good fishing for tarpon, bonefish and snook very close to the island.

Sleeping & Eating

Most accommodations do all-meals packages. The only restaurants are at the places to stay.

Tobacco Caye Lodge (☎ 520-5033, from Belize City ☎ 227-6247; www.tclodgebelize.com; s/d/tr incl meals US$85/128/192) This place on the east side of the island has six simple but clean and fairly spacious rooms with private bathroom, in sky-blue duplex cabins. The dining room serves good food and has a couple of useful marine life identification books. Snorkel gear rental is US$10 per day for guests; canoes are free. Day trips are offered to Glover's Reef, for US$150 to US$200 for a minimum of six people, and nearer spots. The lodge's open-air bar on the west side of the island is a great spot to watch the sun set over the mainland mountains.

Gaviota Reef Resort (☎ 509-5032, 502-0341; s/d US$30/60, with meals US$35/70) This perennial favorite has four rooms and five cabanas, all with shared bathrooms, on the east side of the island. The accommodations are nothing special, but service is friendly and the food pretty good. Snorkel gear is US$6 per day for guests.

Reef's End Lodge (☎ 520-5037, from Dangriga ☎ 522-2419; www.reefsendlodge.com; s/d incl meals US$65/130, d cabana incl meals US$162-194) At the south end of the island, Reef's End has eight sizable rooms (some not as fresh as you'd hope), plus a couple of better cabanas. All options have private bathroom. The popular restaurant and bar are built on stilts over the water. Meals are tasty and large. Snorkel gear here is US$8 per day.

There are three further options:

Lana's (☎ 520-5036; s/d incl meals US$43/86) On the west side of the island with four rather cramped rooms but good meals.

Ocean's Edge Lodge (☎ 601-8537; www2.symet.net /beltex; r per person incl/excl meals US$50/25) On the island's southeast edge, the lodge has seven good rooms, a deck over the water's edge, snorkel gear (US$3/5 a day for guests/nonguests) and boat outings to nearby islands.

Tobacco Caye Paradise (☎ 520-5101; r/cabana per person incl meals US$27/38) At the northern tip, this has the cheapest, most basic rooms and meals, but also two cabanas, with private bathrooms, built over the water (call ahead to secure one of these).

Getting There & Away

Passage to Tobacco Caye can be arranged along the river near the Riverside Café in Dangriga; show up around 9am to 9:30am to organize your trip. Boats usually leave mid-morning and often around lunchtime too. The 45-minute trip costs US$18 per person. If you need any help in organizing a passage, call your planned accommodation on the island. Returning to Dangriga, boats usually leave the island at 9am.

SOUTH WATER CAYE

Five miles south of Tobacco Caye, South Water Caye is three times as big, but home to just three more expensive resorts. The 15-acre island, often called Water Caye by locals, has excellent sandy beaches and an interesting combination of palm and pine trees, and, like Tobacco Caye, is part of the South Water Caye Marine Reserve. A seemingly bottomless 8-mile-long underwater cliff on the ocean side of the reef makes for excellent wall-diving, with usually good visibility. Snorkelers will find healthy coral reefs in the lagoon. Trips to Belize's offshore atolls are possible, and there's excellent fishing here too. Passage to South Water Caye is usually arranged through the resorts.

Sleeping & Eating

Blue Marlin Lodge (☎ 522-2243, from US ☎ 800-798-1558; www.bluemarlinlodge.com; 7-night diving package s/ d/tr US$1695/3190/4410, snorkeling US$1370/2500/3450; ✿) At the northern end of the island, Blue Marlin has its own full-service PADI dive center and a restaurant serving particularly good seafood. For an extra US$360 per cabin per week, you can upgrade to dome-shaped concrete igloos in the manicured grounds (weird but comfy) or cozy wooden beachfront cabanas. Fishing packages are available too and most diving packages are available in shorter four-night versions. All include transfers to/from Belize City International Airport.

International Zoological Expeditions (IZE; ☎ 520-5030, from US ☎ 800-548-5843; www.ize2belize .com; ize2belize@aol.com; package per person per night US$169, two-site packages 8-11 days US$1100-1200; 🖳) Massachusetts-based IZE's site here, in the middle of the island, has dorms for students and beautiful spacious wooden shoreline cottages for other guests. The main building incorporates a field station (with reference books and videos), an attractive wood-furnished dining room, Internet access and the swingin'est bar on the island!

The basic package (minimum three nights) includes meals, transfers to/from Dangriga, snorkeling and sightseeing boat trips, and use of kayaks and sports equipment. IZE also offers two-site eco-adventure and study packages combining South Water Caye with its Blue Creek Rainforest Lodge in Toledo District (p207).

Pelican's Pouch (☎ 522-2044; www.southwatercaye .com; s/d US$142/213, cottage US$180/240, all incl meals) The solar-powered Pelican's three comfortable wooden cottages at the south of the island are well spaced, giving a feeling of seclusion. Heron's Hideaway is probably the pick, with a big porch and two hammocks overlooking the surf crashing onto the reef. The main building (once an island retreat for Belize's Sisters of Mercy) houses the dining room and five guest rooms opening on long verandahs. If you want to dive from here, book at least a week ahead. Kayaks are available free of charge. Boat transfers to/from Dangriga are US$55 per person.

GLOVER'S REEF

Named after 18th-century English pirate John Glover, who attacked Spanish merchant ships from here, Glover's Reef is the southernmost of Belize's three atolls. It lies about 27 miles east-southeast of Dangriga, extending 16 miles north–south and up to 7 miles east–west. Half a dozen small cayes of white sand and palm trees are dotted along the atoll's southeastern rim, supporting a handful of low-key resorts and diving and kayaking bases.

The reef sits atop a submerged mountain ridge on the edge of the continental shelf, surrounded by enormous dropoffs with world-class dive sites. On the east side, where visibility is usually over 100ft, the ocean floor plummets away to 2700ft. Divers at Glover's regularly see spotted eagle rays, southern stingrays, turtles, moray eels, dolphins, several shark species, large groupers, barracudas and many tropical reef fish. In the shallow central lagoon 700 coral patches brim with marine life – brilliant for snorkelers. Turtles lay eggs on the beaches between June and August.

Glover's Reef is included in the Belize barrier reef World Heritage listing, and it's also a marine reserve with a no-take zone covering most of the southern third of the atoll.

You'll see signs all over Belize advertising **Glover's Atoll Resort** (☎ 520-5016, 614-8351; www .glovers.com.bz; per person per week camping US$106, dm or on-site tent US$160, cabin US$213-267), a ramshackle backpackers' resort on Northeast Caye. If you like getting back to basics – no electricity, no refrigeration, no running water (a well provides water for washing) – this could be for you. The weekly prices include cooking facilities and boat transfers on Sundays to/from the owners' mainland Glover's Guest House in the village of Sittee River (see p190), but you also need to think about the cost of water, food, equipment rentals and any excursions. Drinking water costs US$1.50 per gallon on the island (though water from the many coconuts is free).

The open-air thatched restaurant serves breakfast/lunch/dinner for US$9/7/12, or you can make your own meals – a few basic groceries plus fish, lobster and conch are available on the island, but the rest (including any alcohol) you must bring yourself. Snorkel gear rents for US$30 a week, kayaks from US$136 a week, and the resort has a PADI shop offering a range of courses and dives. There's a long list of rules to keep things running smoothly. If a Sunday-to-Sunday stay doesn't suit you, there are nightly accommodation rates but the boat trips there and back will push costs up. A one-way trip on the Sunday boat is US$40 per person. The resort may close from September to November.

On 13.5-acre Long Caye, just southwest of Northeast Caye, **Off the Wall** (☎ 614-6348; www.offthewallbelize.com; 7-night snorkeling/diving/ fishing package US$1295/1395/1595) is a small, professional, family-run operation focusing mainly on the terrific diving here. The beachfront wooden cabins are rustic but comfy, and PADI courses are available. The coral- and sponge-covered Long Caye Wall, with schools of brilliantly colored fish, was one of Jacques Cousteau's favorite dives. Just south of Long Caye are the Abyss, another wall site, Bev's Garden, with endless lettuce leaf and staghorn corals, and the Crack, a vertical cave entered at 45ft.

The atoll's southernmost caye, Southwest Caye, was split in two by Hurricane Hattie in 1961. On its southern half, the small **Isla Marisol Resort** (☎ 520-2056, 615-1485; www .islamarisol.com; 1-week snorkeling/kayaking/diving/fishing/ flyfishing package US$1100/1400/1750/2200/2499) provides sturdy, comfortable cabins with hot showers, a highly recommended PADI dive shop, excellent food and a bar on stilts over the water. In a week's diving you'll probably do around 17 dives, including some at other atolls. Prices include boat transfers to and from Dangriga.

Glover's Reef also houses camps/resorts for the excellent sea-kayak holidays of North American–based Slickrock Adventures and Island Expeditions (see the boxed text, p62), on Long Caye and the northern half of Southwest Caye respectively.

MAYFLOWER BOCAWINA NATIONAL PARK

This beautiful 11-sq-mile park of jungle, mountains, waterfalls, walking trails, swimming holes and small Maya sites lies about 16 miles southwest of Dangriga and 12 miles northwest of Hopkins. The walks are at least as good as the trails most people do at Cockscomb Basin (p190), and you'll encounter far fewer tourists. You'll see lots of birds, and the park is home to two troops of black howler monkeys.

A 4-mile unpaved access road, leaving the Southern Hwy 2 miles north of Silk Grass village, brings you to a small **visitors center** (8am-4pm) where you pay a US$5 park fee, and the partly-excavated **Mayflower Maya site**, with two pyramids and nine other structures, occupied in the late 9th and early 10th centuries. **Antelope Trail** leads down over Silk Grass Creek to the larger, unexcavated, partly tree-covered **Maintzunun temple mound**, 250yd away (built around 800). Continue on a further 1.7 miles – steep and strenuous in places – up to the beautiful 100ft-high **Antelope Falls**, with great panoramas. The less demanding **Bocawina Hill Trail** (1.4 miles) leads to the lower and upper **Bocawina Falls**: there's a cool swimming pool at the foot of the 50ft upper falls. Branch trails, for which a guide is recommended, lead to **Peck Falls** and **Big Drop Falls**.

On a beautiful, spacious plot 500yd past the visitors center along the Bocawina Hill Trail (drivable this far) is **Mama Noots Jungle Resort** (606-4353; www.mamanoots.com; s/d US$65/82, cabana for up to 4 US$93, breakfast/lunch/dinner US$8/10/15; P). Some 238 bird species have been identified on this property, which is run entirely on renewable energy but with 24-hour power. Mama Noots offers some adventurous guided hikes in the national park, and good

discounts for two- or three-night stays. Good Belizean and international food is served in the spacious, thatch-roofed restaurant, which welcomes drop-in customers. The colorfully decorated rooms sport artful paintings and ceramics, are wheelchair accessible and have good bathrooms.

Day tours to the park from Hopkins or Maya Centre cost around US$45 per person. A taxi from Dangriga is about US$30. If you're staying at Mama Noots, they can often pick you up at the highway junction if you call ahead.

HOPKINS
pop 1100

The Garifuna coastal village of Hopkins, south of Dangriga, is a cool place to base yourself for a few days, soaking up some Garifuna atmosphere and culture, exploring the area, meeting other travelers and enjoying those stretches of beach that are kept clean by the owners of the properties behind them. Dolphins and manatees are spotted regularly from the beach.

Founded in 1942 by people from Newtown, a nearby Garifuna settlement that was destroyed by a hurricane, the village is named for Frederick Charles Hopkins, a Catholic priest who drowned in the waters here in 1923. It's a friendly place, still mainly dedicated to farming and fishing but also with an emerging tourism industry. A growing trickle of North Americans are buying homes and plots in the area.

Orientation & Information

Hopkins stretches about 1.5 miles along the coast. The road in from the Southern Hwy reaches the village at King Cassava bar, roughly the village's mid-point. Most places to sleep and eat are south of here, on the beach or the single street. The northern half of the village, with two streets, is a little more densely populated and its Garifuna flavor is undiluted.

Hopkins Internet (per hr US$4; 9am-9pm Fri-Wed) is on the beach 650yd south of King Cassava. The nearest banks are in Dangriga.

Activities
WATER SPORTS

Hopkins affords quick and easy access to some of Belize's best dive sites. The barrier reef is less than a 40-minute boat ride

SOUTHERN BELIZE

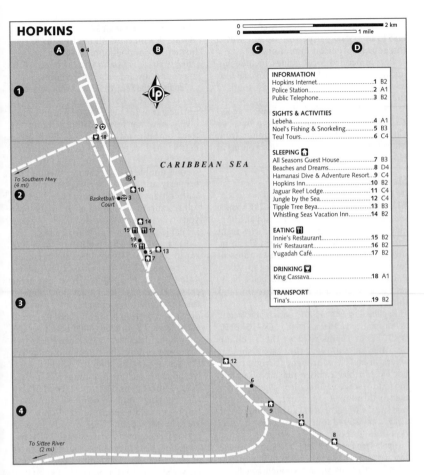

HOPKINS

away; Glover's Reef is about 1½ hours away. Diving can be arranged at **Hamanasi Dive & Adventure Resort** (see p188).

Hamanasi and Hopkins Inn (p188) offer reef snorkeling trips, as does **Noel's Fishing & Snorkeling** (☎ 523-7219, 609-1991) outside the Watering Hole Restaurant. Noel charges two people US$125 for a day outing. He also rents snorkel sets for US$5 a day.

Several accommodations have kayaks available for their guests.

DRUMMING
Lebeha (☎ 608-3143), at the north end of the village, is a Garifuna drumming school set up by local drummer Jabbar Lambey primarily as an education and culture center

for local kids, but also offering group drumming lessons at US$10 per person for two hours or US$13 for a one-hour private lesson. It's worth stopping by in any case if you're interested in learning more about Garifuna culture. They have drumming most nights from about 7pm (see p189).

Tours
Hopkins is handily placed for day trips to some of southern Belize's top natural attractions. Cockscomb Basin (p190) is the most popular inland trip: tours usually include early morning walks to see birds and nature, followed by a waterfall hike and a river-tube float. Other good trips are to Mayflower Bocawina National Park (opposite) and Gales

SOUTHERN BELIZE

Point Manatee (p176). All these cost around US$40 to US$60 per person, usually with a three- or four-person minimum.

Recommended local guides include Veluciano Teul of **Teul Tours** (☎ 522-0635, 603-6180; www.teultours.com), based on the coast south of the village (but contactable through several accommodations), and **Mark Nunez** (☎ 502-2277), contactable at King Cassava bar. For Cockscomb Basin, experienced guides from Maya Centre (see p191) can pick you up in Hopkins.

Sleeping

IN THE VILLAGE

Whistling Seas Vacation Inn (☎ 503-7203; whistling seas@btl.net; s/d/tr/q US$30/40/45/50) Solid and spacious concrete cabanas a stone's throw from the sea, a friendly welcome from Garifuna owners and one of the best restaurants in town make the Whistling Seas top value. Each cabana has two double beds, fans, refrigerator and a private bathroom, and they're spotlessly clean.

Hopkins Inn (☎ 523-7013; www.hopkinsinn.com; s/d/tr/q cabins incl continental breakfast US$43/54/80/96; P ✗) Four cabins right by the beach are on offer at this well-run establishment where breakfast is brought to your cabin. Each cabin has a coffee maker, verandah, mosquito screens and nice, clean, white-tiled bathroom. A catamaran, bicycles and free snorkeling gear are available, and owner Greg, a registered tour guide, takes snorkelers out in his boat.

Tipple Tree Beya (☎ /fax 520-7006; www.tippletree.com; camping per person US$5, d/tr US$43/50, d/q cabana US$54/70; P) This sturdy wooden beachside place rents three cosy, clean rooms sharing a sociable verandah beneath the owner's quarters upstairs. Two rooms have private hot-water bathroom; the third (cheaper at US$25 for two) has an unheated shower. The cabana, set a little further back, has a small kitchen. There are bikes (US$9 per day) and kayaks (US$20 per day), and the owner can set up tours and activities with local guides.

All Seasons Guest House (☎ 614-3328; www.all seasonsbelize.com; r US$43; P ✗) This modern guesthouse offers three bright, homey, spotless rooms with big private bathrooms and mosquito nets. All are different – one is zebra-striped – and two have air-con available for an extra US$7. There's a breezy upstairs sitting area with sea glimpses.

SOUTH OF THE VILLAGE

Within 1.5 miles south of Hopkins village, further accommodations make the most of a lovely stretch of palm-fringed beach curving round toward False Sittee Point.

Jungle by the Sea (☎ 523-7047; www.belize-beach -resort.com; cabanas US$30-50, cabins US$95-125) The northernmost of these places features three lovely new hardwood cabins among the trees but also with sea views. Each has a double bed, futon, bathroom, mosquito screens and verandah. One has a loft with a second double bed. At the north end of the property are a few older wooden cabanas, with similar amenities but more basic. A full restaurant should be open by the time you arrive, and a windsurfer and kayaks are available at a small charge for guests.

Hamanasi Dive & Adventure Resort (☎ 520-7073, from US ☎ 877-552-3483; www.hamanasi.com; r US$240, ste or treehouse US$280-300, prepaid meal packages lunch/dinner US$15/30; P ✗ ▢ ▣) Next down the coast, Hamanasi (Garifuna for 'almond tree') combines the amenities of a top-class dive resort with an array of inland tours and activities and a gorgeous 400ft beachfront. A continental breakfast is included and all 18 large, very comfortable rooms and suites face the sea, except the popular wood-floored treehouses, secluded among the foliage behind the beach. Attractive Guatemalan wall-hangings and colorful Mexican-tiled bathrooms add a special touch. Room rates are reduced by up to US$80 outside the peak seasons. Hamanasi's professional PADI dive operation can carry divers out to all three of Belize's atolls (Lighthouse, Turneffe and Glover's) as well as the barrier reef's best dive spots. Full-day, two- or three-tank dive trips cost US$140 to US$225, and PADI courses are available. A half-day barrier-reef snorkeling outing is US$45 to US$70. Kayaks and bikes are available free for guests.

Jaguar Reef Lodge (☎ 520-7040, US ☎ 800-289-5756; www.jaguarreef.com; s/d/tr/q cabana garden-view US$224/247/270/293, beachfront US$282/305/328/351, ste for up to 4 US$362-408, breakfast/lunch/dinner US$11/14/34; P ✗ ▢ ▣) A little further down the coast, Jaguar Reef is another luxury resort with a long, sandy beachfront and ample amenities and activities on land and water. It's good for families or wary adventurers. The cabanas are solidly built, with a conservative, familiar design that you would find in Hawaiian or Mexican resorts. As well as snorkeling, birding, diving, jungle hiking, fishing and river kayaking, guests can hang out at Jaguar Reef's day lodge on the nearby Sittee River or take a four-hour outing to their island lodge on Coco Plum Caye, 10 miles offshore. There's a three-night minimum stay and a range of packages is available.

Beaches and Dreams (☎ 523-7259; www.beaches anddreams.com; r incl continental breakfast US$136; **P** 🖳) This much smaller-scale inn sits on a palm-shaded beach, offering personal service, good food, and varied activities with an emphasis on fishing. Bikes and kayaks are available for guests. It's also a fine place just to relax with a *palapa* (thatched-roof shelter) out on the dock where you can enjoy your meals and drinks. There are just four rooms in two solid, octagonal wooden cabanas, with king-size beds, tiled bathrooms and futons for lounging.

Eating

The village has a number of straightforward, locally-run eateries, several of them serving up a good variety of fare, but if you want anything fancy you need to head down to the hotels south of the village. Some families will prepare special Garifuna meals in their homes: inquire at your lodging or at Tipple Tree Beya (opposite).

IN THE VILLAGE

Whistling Seas Vacation Inn (☎ 503-7203; mains US$6-8; ☒ breakfast, lunch & dinner) The restaurant here does pretty good Belizean and international food; try the tasty shrimp creole if available. Breakfasts are filling.

Yugadah Café (☎ 503-7255; mains US$5-9; ☒ breakfast, lunch & dinner, closed Wed) Hair-netted waitstaff-cum-cooks dole out a good range of Belizean dishes and seafood, plus burgers, burritos and desserts, at this neat restaurant.

Toward the south end of the village, **Innie's Restaurant** (☎ 523-7026) and **Iris' Restaurant** (☎ 523-7019) serve up dependable Belizean dishes, with mains ranging from US$4 to US$8.

SOUTH OF THE VILLAGE

Beaches and Dreams (☎ 523-7259; dishes US$5-15; ☒ breakfast, lunch & dinner) The experienced cooks here prepare great Caribbean, Mexican, North American and 'Carib-fusion' fare.

Hamanasi Dive & Adventure Resort (☎ 520-7073; lunch/dinner around US$15/30; ☒ breakfast, lunch & dinner) Hamanasi's indoor-outdoor restaurant is especially good for pasta, seafood and desserts; it also offers healthy light dishes.

Jaguar Reef Lodge (☎ 520-7040; lunch/dinner around US$15/30; ☒ breakfast, lunch & dinner) Caribbean and international dishes are served in a gorgeous open-air seafront setting. Sandwiches, pizza slices, salads and other light meals are available all day till 5pm.

Drinking & Entertainment

Lebeha (☎ 608-3143) The kids at the drumming school usually do a bit of a show around 7pm or 7:30pm for tips. You can get a beer and snack while you listen.

King Cassava (☎ 502-2277; ☒ till midnight) In the middle of town, this is a beer, pool and reggae hub for both locals and travelers.

The bars at Whistling Seas Vacation Inn, Hamanasi Dive & Adventure Resort, Jaguar Reef Lodge and Beaches and Dreams can all be fun depending on the night.

Getting There & Around

If there's no bus passing through Hopkins at a convenient time, it's quite common to hitch to the Southern Hwy junction and pick up a bus there. A taxi to Hopkins from Dangriga costs about US$50.

You can rent bicycles at **Lebeha** (☎ 608-3143) for US$8 a day, or at **Tina's** for US$1.50/5/10 per hour/half-day/day. **All Seasons Guest House** (☎ 614-3328) has scooters for US$38 a day.

SITTEE RIVER

The tranquil Creole village of Sittee River, with an increasing population of North American expats, straggles along the beautiful jungle-lined river of the same name about 3 miles by unpaved road southwest of Hopkins. It's a great bird-watching area, and a couple of good accommodations make excellent stress-free bases for a stay. Sittee River can be buggy, so make sure your accommodations are adequately screened or netted!

Sights & Activities

Nearby Boom Creek (inhabited by otters, a few crocodiles and plenty of birds) and Anderson's Lagoon make for good canoeing. One good birding spot is the ruined (but under-restoration) 19th-century Serpon Sugar Mill, 3 miles from the village toward the Southern Hwy.

Sleeping

Toucan Sittee (☎ 523-7039; www.toucansittee.info; dm US$12, d cabana with private bathroom US$25-50, d/tr/q apt US$77/88/99, breakfast US$6, dinner US$9-12; **P**) Set in beautiful, tropical, riverside gardens, friendly family-run Toucan Sittee has a range of cozy accommodations, mostly on stilts. Good meals, including vegetarian dishes, are available on request. The gardens are a birder's paradise, with hummingbirds, tanagers, orioles, parrots, woodpeckers and the eponymous toucans all commonly seen. You can rent bikes and canoes for US$10/14 per half-day/full day to explore the local roads, creeks and lagoons. Night trips up Boom Creek and to Cockscomb Basin Wildlife Sanctuary (below) are also offered.

River House Lodge (☎ 603-0298; www.riverhouse lodge.net; r incl continental breakfast US$74-107; **P** ✖ 🖥 🐾) With another lovely riverside setting about 1400yd nearer Hopkins than Toucan Sittee, River House Lodge provides very comfortable air-con rooms with screened verandahs in two-story wooden houses, plus a restaurant, bar and inviting indoor pool. Bikes and plenty of excursions are available.

Glover's Guest House (☎ 509-7099; www.glovers .com.bz; dm US$8, r with shared/private bathroom US$23/29, breakfast/lunch/dinner US$6/6/9; **P**) The boat to Glover's Atoll Resort (p185) leaves from this guesthouse in Sittee River. The accommodations are cramped and basic, but cheap.

Getting There & Away

The Novelo's buses that serve Hopkins (see p189) also go through Sittee River at about 1pm and 6pm heading out to the Southern Hwy and on to Placencia, and around 6:30am (7:45am Sunday) heading to Hopkins and Dangriga.

COCKSCOMB BASIN WILDLIFE SANCTUARY

The **Cockscomb Basin Wildlife Sanctuary** (admission US$5) is Belize's most famous and, at 200 sq miles, one of its biggest protected areas. Often known simply as the 'jaguar reserve,' this great swath of tropical forest became the world's first jaguar sanctuary in 1984, thanks to the efforts of American zoologist

Alan Rabinowitz. Today it's home to an estimated 40 to 50 jaguars and a vast array of other animal, bird and botanical life.

The sanctuary covers a large expanse of the eastern Maya Mountains as well as the Cockscomb Basin that spreads out below the mountains. Most visits are restricted to a small eastern pocket of the sanctuary where a visitors center, the sanctuary's accommodations and a network of walking trails are established. To avoid disappointment, disabuse yourself of any hopes that you might see a jaguar. What you can hope to see, especially in the early morning, are lots of birds, maybe fewer animals and, with luck, some jaguar pawprints. Later in the day most of the wildlife hides away, but walking the trails is still enjoyable.

Cockscomb became a forest reserve and no-hunting area in 1984. A small part of it was given sanctuary status in 1986, and the rest followed in 1990. The people of the small Maya village of Quan Bank were compulsorily relocated as part of the creation of the sanctuary. Many of them now live in **Maya Centre village**, a few miles east, and make a living from the sanctuary, running tourist accommodations or tours, or working as park staff.

The sanctuary itself is not big enough to support a healthy breeding population of jaguars, but it adjoins other reserves, which promises a hopeful future for this emblematic and threatened feline, the largest feline in the Western Hemisphere. Belize's four other wild cats – the puma, ocelot, margay and jaguarundi – also live here, as do tapirs, anteaters, armadillos (the jaguar's favorite prey hereabouts), brocket deer, coatimundis, kinkajous, otters, peccaries, tayras and birds galore – over 290 feathered species have been spotted including the keel-billed toucan, king vulture, great curassow and scarlet macaw. You may see, or at least hear, a thriving community of black howler monkeys close to the visitors center. They were reintroduced here from the Community Baboon Sanctuary (p94) in 1992. Snakes here include boa constrictors and the deadly poisonous fer-de-lance (tommygoff).

Orientation & Information

The unpaved, 6-mile road to the sanctuary starts at the village of Maya Centre, on the Southern Hwy 5 miles south of the Hopkins turnoff. Pay your admission fee at the crafts store of the Maya Centre Women's Group, on the corner of the Southern Hwy and the sanctuary road. Usually, the sanctuary road is perfectly drivable although it fords a couple of creeks so take care after rain. The road enters the sanctuary after 4 miles. The **sanctuary office** (7:30am-4:30pm), where you show your ticket, is 2 miles further. The office has trail maps (US$2.50) plus a few gifts, soft drinks and chocolate bars for sale, and binoculars for rent (US$2.50 per day), and there are worthwhile displays about the sanctuary in a nearby building. Some of Alan Rabinowitz' original jaguar traps, for capturing and tagging the animals, are on show nearby; nowadays jaguars are tracked by infrared cameras.

Activities

A well-maintained 12-mile network of trails fans out from the park office. Most of the walks are flat along the bottom of the basin, but the moderately strenuous **Ben's Bluff Trail** (1.25 miles and steep in parts) takes you up to a lookout point with fantastic views over the whole Cockscomb Basin and the Cockscomb Mountains. It's named for one of the original members of the Cockscomb Jaguar Sanctuary Project, who would make this climb daily to listen for signals from the radio transmitters attached to the jaguars.

An easy 1.4-mile **self-guided nature walk**, looping together the Curassow Trail, Rubber Tree Tail and River Path, can be followed with the trail map from the park office. The **River Path** (0.4 miles) and the **Wari Loop** (a 2.3-mile loop from the office) are good early morning bets for seeing a variety of birds. Jaguar tracks are often spotted on the Wari Loop and the Victoria Peak Path. The **Antelope Loop** (a 3.4-mile loop from the office) rises and falls through a variety of terrain and vegetation, and offers a good sample of the basin's geological features.

The office rents tubes (US$2.50) for half-hour river-tube floats down South Stann Creek from the River Overlook on Wari Loop.

Tours

Tours can be arranged in Maya Centre, and are usually conducted by Maya who were relocated there when the jaguar reserve was created. This is an interesting dynamic; not only do the guides show you the animals and the history of the park, they'll also show you where they lived just 20 years ago. Of course, they know the area pretty well and in general they're experienced and professional. The best include Ernesto Saqui of Nu'uk Che'il Cottages (below); Gregorio, Julian and Ouscal Chun of Tutzil Nah Cottages (p192); Julio Saqui of **Cockscomb Maya Tours** (www.cockscombmayatours.com), based at the Cockscomb Diner; and Eligorio Sho who works out of Greg's Bar, north of sanctuary turnoff on the Southern Hwy.

A typical day tour to the sanctuary from Maya Centre costs around US$45 to US$55 per person, including transportation, a walk or two (usually including a waterfall), lunch and maybe river-tubing on the river. An exciting option is a night tour (around US$25 per person), giving increased chances of seeing animals such as kinkajous, anteaters, peccaries and possibly even a feline. Guides can also lead tours for people who are staying in the sanctuary. Check whether your fee includes the sanctuary admission cost and, at night, whether flashlights are provided.

Sleeping & Eating

IN THE SANCTUARY

Staying in the sanctuary gives you easy access to the trails, and enables you to experience the sounds of the jungle at night and be up with the dawn when wildlife is most active. The disadvantage is that you have to bring all your food and drinks with you, unless you want to eat in Maya Centre or have meals brought from there. Maya Centre has a couple of grocery stores selling basic supplies. The accommodations options, most close to the sanctuary office, range from camping under *palapa* shelters (US$2.70 per person) through to a 'rustic cabin' with bunks and kerosene lamps (US$8 per person) and the clean 'new dorm,' with bunks, solar lighting and compost toilet (US$18 per person) to cabins sleeping up to eight people for US$48 to US$54. Use of a communal kitchen is included with all options except camping, where grill pits are available. You can rent kitchen utensils for up to five people for US$5 per day.

IN MAYA CENTRE

Nu'uk Che'il Cottages (615-2091, 520-3033; nuuk cheil@btl.net; camping per person US$3.50, dm US$10, d or

VICTORIA PEAK

Belize's second-highest mountain, Victoria Peak (3675ft), rises in the Cockscomb Mountains, which form the formidable northern flank of the wildlife sanctuary. A trek to its summit is a tough three- or five-day round-trip expedition, which surprisingly few people have accomplished. Anyone attempting it needs to be in excellent physical and mental condition. You'll have to carry all your food and other essentials in sometimes extreme humidity and heat, with four nights of camping and some steep ascents including some rope climbing to reach the summit. It is obligatory to be accompanied by a licensed tour guide. One recommended guide for this trip is **Marcos Cucul** (☎ 600-3116; www.mayaguide .bz), who charges US$250 per person for the five-day trip.

tr with shared/private bathroom US$23/30, dishes US$4-8; ⓨ restaurant 7am-8pm; Ⓟ) These accommodations, spread around a verdant garden about 500yd along the sanctuary road, are owned by Aurora Saqui, a niece and apprentice of the legendary Maya healer Eligio Panti (see boxed text, p166), and her husband Ernesto, a former Quan Bank villager who was director of the Cockscomb sanctuary from 1988 to 2004. The rooms are simple but clean, with hot-water bathrooms. Also here are a medicinal plant trail (US$2.50 per person with a self-guiding leaflet, US$10 per group for 30-minute guided tour), a large fan-cooled *palapa* restaurant with Maya dishes available, if ordered ahead, as well as more standard Belizean fare, lovely fresh fruit juices and a crafts shop.

Tutzil Nah Cottages (☎ 520-3044; www.maya center.com; s/d US$16/26, meals US$6-12; Ⓟ) On the Southern Hwy 100yd north of the Maya Centre junction, the three Chun brothers, also originally from Quan Bank, provide four neat, clean rooms with shared bathrooms: those in the wooden-stilt building at the rear are airier.

Cockscomb Diner (☎ 520-3042; mains US$4-5; ⓨ 6:30am-9pm) Well-prepared Belizean and Maya dishes and good fresh juices are served here, plus lighter eats like burgers and sandwiches. It adjoins a craft shop and the Maya Centre Women's Group.

Getting There & Away

Any bus along the Southern Hwy will drop you at Maya Centre, but there is no public transportation into the sanctuary. A taxi from Hopkins to Maya Centre or the sanctuary costs around US$50. Most of the Maya Centre tour guides (see p191) offer taxi service to the sanctuary for around US$18/30 one-way/return. To walk in takes about two hours (the terrain is relatively flat).

PLACENCIA

pop 600

Lucky Placencia (sometimes spelt Placentia) perches at the southern tip of a thin, 16-mile peninsula strung with definitely the best set of sandy beaches in southern Belize and arguably in the whole country. Once a fishing-village hideout known to few outsiders, Placencia is now firmly on the tourism map.

A varied, international bunch of travelers and tourists comes for the beaches, the beautiful location, the wide range of accommodations from budget guesthouses to luxury all-inclusive resorts, the good restaurants, a touch of nightlife – and, for those so inclined, plenty to do. Good diving, snorkeling, fishing, sailing and some of the country's prime inland attractions are all within easy reach.

Though it's gradually developing, Placencia is still a place where one of the two main streets is just a 3ft-wide sidewalk and the pace remains deeply unhurried. Its relaxed and friendly atmosphere, in a gorgeous setting between the turquoise Caribbean and a mangrove-fringed lagoon, makes it one of the finest places in Belize to kick back.

From the 17th to 19th centuries the peninsula had a population of Puritans hailing from Nova Scotia. Their settlement died out during the Central American independence wars of the 1820s. The current community goes back to five families who settled here in the late 19th and early 20th centuries, from origins as disparate as Scotland, Brazil and Roatan: the Garbutts, Westbys, Eileys, Cabrals and Leslies. Many villagers still bear these surnames today.

Orientation

Placencia village occupies the southern-most mile of the peninsula, with a sandy

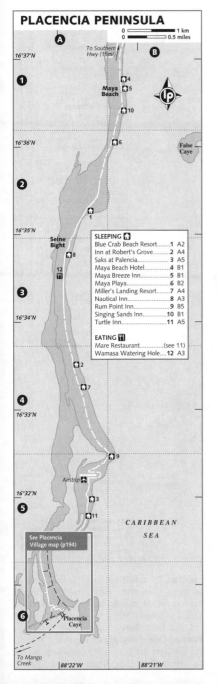

PLACENCIA PENINSULA

0   1 km
0   0.5 miles

To Southern Hwy (15mi)

Maya Beach

False Caye

Seine Bight

SLEEPING
Blue Crab Beach Resort........1 A2
Inn at Robert's Grove..........2 A4
Saks at Palencia................3 A5
Maya Beach Hotel..............4 B1
Maya Breeze Inn................5 B1
Maya Playa........................6 B2
Miller's Landing Resort.......7 A4
Nautical Inn......................8 A3
Rum Point Inn....................9 B5
Singing Sands Inn..............10 B1
Turtle Inn.........................11 A5

EATING
Mare Restaurant............(see 11)
Wamasa Watering Hole....12 A3

Airstrip

CARIBBEAN SEA

See Placencia Village map (p194)

Placencia Caye

To Mango Creek

88°22'W   88°21'W

16°37'N · 16°36'N · 16°35'N · 16°34'N · 16°33'N · 16°32'N

beach all along its eastern side. The road from the north runs down the western side of the village, ending at the Shell fuel station and the main boat dock (a handful of short piers). Parallel to the road and about 100yd east of it is the Sidewalk, a narrow pedestrians-only footway, with the beach about 100yd farther east. Anyone who was last here before October 8, 2001 will need to reorient themselves: on that date Hurricane Iris blew half the town away and much of it has been rebuilt differently.

Placencia's airport is about 1 mile north of the village; 3 miles further north is the Garifuna village of Seine Bight, and 3 miles beyond that is the North American–expat settlement of Maya Beach. A number of accommodations, including most of the luxury places, are dotted along the beach side of the peninsula as far as Maya Beach.

Information

INTERNET ACCESS

De-Tatch Café (Map p194; ☎ 503-3385; per hr US$5; ☒ 7am-9:30pm) This popular café sells lots of filling Belizean and Caribbean dishes.

Placencia Office Supply (Map p194; ☎ 523-3205; per hr US$5; ☒ 8:30am-7pm) High-speed Internet, CD burning, digital card readers.

Purple Space Monkey Village (Map p194; ☎ 523-4094; per hr US$5; ☒ 7am-2pm & 5-9:30pm) Internet, large breakfasts and burgers are the way to go at this café in a *palapa*.

INTERNET RESOURCES

Placencia Belize (www.placencia.com)
Placencia Breeze (www.placenciabreeze.com)

LAUNDRY

Julia's Laundry (Map p194; ☎ 503-3478; per load US$5-13; ☒ 7am-7pm) Located at the Julia & Lawrence Guesthouse in the heart of the popular beachfront, so you can head straight out for a swim when the laundry is done.

MONEY

Scotiabank (Map p194; ☒ 8:30am-2:30pm Mon-Thu, 8:30am-4pm Fri) Cash advances and currency and traveler's check exchange, but the ATM does not accept foreign cards.

TOURIST INFORMATION

Placencia Tourism Center (Map p194; ☎ 523-4045; ☒ 9-11:30am & 1-5pm Mon-Fri) Right by the bus stop and dock, friendly staff are ready to set travelers off on the right foot. Pick up the monthly *Placencia Breeze* to catch up on what's happening.

SOUTHERN BELIZE

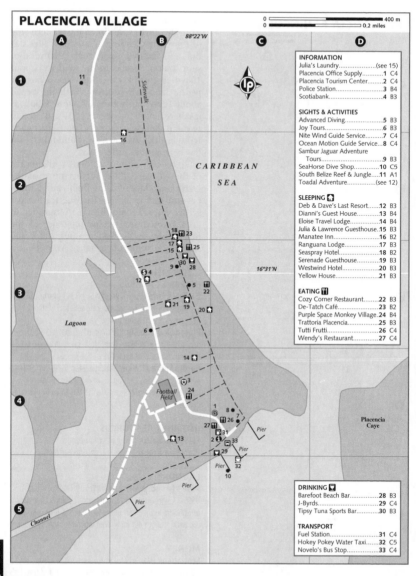

PLACENCIA VILLAGE

0 — 400 m
0 — 0.2 miles

88°22'W

CARIBBEAN
SEA

16°31'N

Lagoon

Football
Field

Channel

Pier

Pier

Pier

Placencia
Caye

INFORMATION
Julia's Laundry.......................(see 15)
Placencia Office Supply.............**1** C4
Placencia Tourism Center..........**2** C4
Police Station............................**3** B4
Scotiabank................................**4** B3

SIGHTS & ACTIVITIES
Advanced Diving......................**5** B3
Joy Tours.................................**6** B3
Nite Wind Guide Service..........**7** C4
Ocean Motion Guide Service....**8** C4
Sambur Jaguar Adventure
  Tours....................................**9** B3
SeaHorse Dive Shop................**10** C5
South Belize Reef & Jungle.....**11** A1
Toadal Adventure................(see 12)

SLEEPING
Deb & Dave's Last Resort.......**12** B3
Dianni's Guest House..............**13** B4
Eloise Travel Lodge.................**14** B4
Julia & Lawrence Guesthouse..**15** B3
Manatee Inn...........................**16** B2
Ranguana Lodge......................**17** B3
Seaspray Hotel........................**18** B2
Serenade Guesthouse..............**19** B3
Westwind Hotel.......................**20** B3
Yellow House...........................**21** B3

EATING
Cozy Corner Restaurant.........**22** B3
De-Tatch Café.........................**23** B2
Purple Space Monkey Village...**24** B4
Trattoria Placencia..................**25** B3
Tutti Frutti...............................**26** C4
Wendy's Restaurant................**27** C4

DRINKING
Barefoot Beach Bar.................**28** B3
J-Byrds....................................**29** C4
Tipsy Tuna Sports Bar.............**30** B3

TRANSPORT
Fuel Station.............................**31** C4
Hokey Pokey Water Taxi.........**32** C5
Novelo's Bus Stop....................**33** C4

Activities

The beach is sandy, fringed with palms and fine for swimming and a bit of snorkeling in nice, warm, usually clear waters.

DIVING & SNORKELING

The barrier reef is a little further offshore from Placencia (20 miles-plus, around 45 minutes in a fast-ish boat from dock to plunge) than it is from more northerly points, but it still has plenty of dramatic canyons, swim-throughs and walls. Myriad sea life lives here relatively undisturbed. **Pompion Caye**, **Ranguana Caye** and the beautiful **Silk Cayes** are good for snorkeling as well as dives of varying degrees of difficulty.

There's also some good snorkeling and novice diving inshore of the reef, especially at **Laughing Bird Caye** (www.laughingbird.org), with its sandy beaches, 12 miles from Placencia. The coral around Laughing Bird Caye has suffered damage from hurricanes and careless snorkelers, but there's still plenty of other marine life in the waters, from stoplight and queen parrotfish to spotted eagle rays, hawksbill turtles and the semi-tame lemon sharks that feed off barbecue leftovers chucked into the sea.

Other fine dive sites within two to three hours of Placencia include Glover's Reef (p185), the Shark Hole near Tobacco Caye (p183) and the lovely Sapodilla Cayes, 30 miles south.

About 25 miles east of Placencia is The Elbow at **Gladden Spit**, where for up to 10 days after the full moon, March through June (especially April and May), awesome but gentle whale sharks (the world's largest fish, up to 60ft long) gather to feast on the eggs of cubera snapper and other fish that spawn in huge quantities at these times. Whale sharks can also be seen some days from August to January.

SeaHorse Dive Shop (Map p194; ☎ 523-3166, 523-3466; www.belizescuba.com) at the docks and **South Belize Reef & Jungle** (Map p194; ☎ 523-3330; southbelize@yahoo.com) with an office on the road at the north end of town, are two of the best dive operators in Placencia, both offering PADI certification courses as well as dives for certified divers. North of the village, the Turtle Inn (p197), Rum Point Inn (p197), the Inn at Robert's Grove (p197) and the Nautical Inn (p198) all have professional dive shops. All the above offer snorkeling trips too, as do other operators including **Nite Wind Guide Service** (Map p194; ☎ 523-3487, 609-6845), in front of the boat dock, and **Ocean Motion Guide Service** (Map p194; ☎ 523-3162, 512-3363) and **Advanced Diving** (Map p194; ☎ 523-4037, 615-1233), both on the Sidewalk.

Regular two-tank dive trips cost around US$85 to US$100, longer outings to the Shark Hole, Glover's Reef or the Sapodilla Cayes about US$125 to US$150, and whale shark trips around US$150 to US$170. For some sites you may need to add admission fees of between US$4 and US$15.

A snorkeling day trip, often with a beach barbecue included, costs around US$30 to US$45 to Laughing Bird Caye, US$45 to US$55 to the barrier reef, or US$70 to US$80 to the whale sharks.

SAILING
Anyone from beginners to experts can enjoy sailing from Placencia. As well as Belize's cayes and other ports, Río Dulce in Guatemala and Honduras' Bay Islands are close. **Next Wave Sailing** (☎ 523-3391, 610-5592; www.nextwavesailing.com) does day sails on a 50ft catamaran out to sandy islands where you can snorkel, swim and lunch (adult/under-12s US$87/44) and also offers popular sunset cruises (US$49/27) and full-moon cruises (US$27). Departures are from Placencia docks: you can book at the Purple Space Monkey Village. **Sailing Belize** (☎ 523-3138; http://sailingbelize.com) does day sails on a 50ft monohull (US$132 per person), plus a whole range of crewed, skippered and bareboat charters on catamarans and monohulls.

KAYAKING & CANOEING
Toadal Adventure (Map p194; ☎ 523-3207; www .toadaladventure.com; Deb & Dave's Last Resort), led by highly experienced local guide Dave Vernon, does popular multi-day sea-kayaking trips. A five-night package, with three nights camping out on the beautiful Silk Cayes, is US$920 (no experience necessary). They also rent kayaks for US$35 per day.

Many beachside accommodations north of the village have free kayaks or canoes for guests' use.

FISHING
Southern Belize is an angler's paradise and in the waters off Placencia you can troll for barracuda, kingfish or tuna, spincast or fly-fish for tarpon, bonefish or snook, and bottom-fish for snapper or jack.

Ocean Motion Guide Service (Map p194; ☎ 523-3162, 512-3363) and **Advanced Diving** (Map p194; ☎ 523-4037, 615-1233), both on the Sidewalk, and **Joy Tours** (Map p194; ☎ 523-3325; www.belize withjoy.com), on the road, are among the operators who will take you out on fishing trips. You're looking at around US$300 a day per boat (maximum four people).

Tours
Apart from the many water-based options, Placencia is the starting point for some exciting terrestrial trips.

The forest fruits of Red Bank village, 14 miles west of Placencia as the crow flies, attract rare and beautiful scarlet macaws from January to March. On a good day you might see 30 of these spectacularly plumaged birds, plus plenty of other species. The trip costs around US$65 per person.

Placencia lagoon tours (US$25 to US$30) teach you about mangrove ecosystems and show you plenty of birds and, if you're lucky, manatees or dolphins.

A Monkey River trip (usually US$40 per person) includes a short sea cruise to Monkey River Town (a village), 14 miles southwest of Placencia, then a trip upriver to see howler monkeys, crocodiles and birds, broken by a couple of jungle walks and a swim or river-tube float, then often a Creole lunch in the village. The forests here are recovering from hurricane damage.

Day trips to **Cockscomb Basin Wildlife Sanctuary** (see p190) cost approximately US$55 to US$60.

Several local guide and tour services vie for your custom. Recommendable ones include the following:

Joy Tours (Map p194; ☎ 523-3325; www.belizewithjoy .com) North of football field.

Nite Wind Guide Service (Map p194; ☎ 523-3487, 609-6845) Opposite boat dock.

Sambur Jaguar Adventure Tours (Map p194; ☎ 523-3040, 600-2481; Sidewalk) Friendly little operation with colorful blackboard listing trips.

South Belize Reef & Jungle (Map p194; ☎ 523-3330; southbelize@yahoo.com) North end of town.

Festivals & Events

The **Sidewalk Art Festival** (mid-February, nearest weekend to Valentine's Day) features art, crafts and music, with scores of participants from all over Belize.

Lobsterfest (last weekend of June) celebrates the opening of the lobster-fishing season with music, boat races, a fishing contest, a huge variety of lobster dishes to eat and a lot of fun.

Sleeping

Lodgings in the village are nearly all budget or midrange. Many are small and family-run. There are plenty of beachside cabanas, but your neighbor may be just a couple of feet away! North of the village, a handful of top-end luxury resorts dot the coast as far as Seine Bight. Further north there's a clutch of

midrange beachfront places in Maya Beach. Most places north of the village offer free airport pickups and a full range of tours and activities, usually at slightly higher prices than the agencies in town.

Outside the high season of approximately November to May, many accommodations offer discounts.

PLACENCIA VILLAGE

Ranguana Lodge (Map p194; ☎ 523-3112, 610-2287; www.ranguanabelize.com; Sidewalk; r US$75-77; ⊠) This beachfront inn at Ranguana has five attractive, good-sized, mahogany cabins, although they are packed onto a small site. Two have kitchens; the others (smaller) have sea views and air-con. All have two double beds, hot-water bathroom and verandah. Management is especially friendly and helpful here.

Seaspray Hotel (Map p194; ☎ 523-3148; www .seasprayhotel.com; Sidewalk; r US$27-64; ⌨) The Seaspray's five grades of room, all with private hot-water bathroom, range from plain economy rooms (the only ones without any kind of sea view) up to 'Seaview' rooms with porch, deck, kitchenette and coffee-maker. The variety ensures that you'll meet travelers from all over and all budgets. A big plus is that one of Placencia's best restaurants, the De-Tatch Café (p198), is right on the premises.

Westwind Hotel (Map p194; ☎ 523-3255; www .westwindhotel.com; Sidewalk; r US$54-70) This funky two-story wooden building opening right onto the less crowded southern end of the beach is perfect for chilling out. Most rooms face the sea and all have a balcony, terrace or patio and hot-water bathroom. The six-hammock *palapa* out front on the sand is a popular feature; guests can also eat, play board games and socialize in the lobby area.

Julia & Lawrence Guesthouse (Map p194; ☎ 503-3478; Sidewalk; r with shared/private bathroom US$27/40) A sandfront place on the tightest packed part of the beach, J&L's has bright, clean rooms with private bathrooms, and rooms that share facilities are in a darker, older building behind.

Serenade Guesthouse (Map p194; ☎ 523-3380; www.belizecayes.com; Sidewalk; r US$69-75; ⊠ ⌨) This comfortable place occupies a beautiful, big, white wooden house on the Sidewalk. The nice, wood-floored rooms all have air-con, private bathroom and cable TV. The friendly local owners also run a small lodge on the idyllic Sapodilla Cayes and offer packages combining stays at their two places.

Dianni's Guest House (Map p194; ☎ 523-3159; dianni s@btl.net; s/d US$37/45, with air-con US$42/52; ✖ ☐) The clean, white rooms here, a stone's throw from Placencia's southern shore, are good value with their coffee-makers, microwaves, refrigerators and a nice wide verandah to sit out on. On-site gift shop, Internet access, bicycle rentals and tour and flight bookings enhance the deal.

Also recommended:

Deb & Dave's Last Resort (Map p194; ☎ 523-3207; debanddave@btl.net; r with shared bathroom US$25) Compact rooms with fans and coffee-makers, sharing a screened porch and very clean bathroom, in a leafy garden.

Manatee Inn (Map p194; ☎ 523-4083; www.manatee inn.com; Sidewalk; s/d with shared bathroom US$33/38, s/d/tr with private bathroom US$43/48/54) Charming, roomy, modern, wooden hotel with breezy verandahs.

Yellow House (Map p194; ☎ 523-3481; ctbze@btl.net; r US$25-35; ☐) Spotless rooms with kitchenette, bathroom and netted windows.

Eloise Travel Lodge (Map p194; ☎ 523-3299; d/tr with shared bathroom US$13/15, tr with private bathroom US$20) Sociable budget favorite. Recline in hammocks on the verandahs and cook your own meals in the equipped kitchen.

BETWEEN PLACENCIA VILLAGE & SEINE BIGHT

Saks at Palencia (Map p193; ☎ 523-3227; www.saksat palencia.com; r with shared bath US$47, standard US$174, deluxe US$221; pais) Saks has just the ambience you fantasize about for a Caribbean beach lodge. A variety of rooms and cabanas are scattered about lush gardens fronted by a beautiful sandy strip of beach, with a good restaurant and pool on site too. Many people return here year after year. The rooms run from luxurious, tile-floored, beachfront cabanas with large verandahs to cozy, cottage-style, garden rooms and just two fan-cooled budget rooms with shared bathroom. Most will hold at least four people, at a cost of US$18 per person above two. Saks also rents out self-catering houses and apartments close by (some on the lagoon side of the peninsula) with full access to the resort's amenities.

Inn at Robert's Grove (Map p193; ☎ 523-3565, from US ☎ 800-565-9757; www.robertsgrove.com; r US$209-233,

ste US$293-585; ☐ ✖ ☐ ☒) This very professionally run, top-end establishment provides everything needed for relaxing and fun vacations for those with deep enough pockets. It's very popular, including with Belize's elite. The 51 air-con rooms and suites, set in blocks around the ample grounds, are all spacious, comfortable, terracotta-floored and brightly decorated with colorful art and fabrics. They're complemented by a vast array of amenities including three pools, a PADI dive center, rooftop Jacuzzis, tennis, windsurfers, kayaks, Hobie Cats and a spa full of exotic body treatments.

Turtle Inn (Map p193; ☎ 523-3244, 824-4912, from US ☎ 800-746-3743; www.turtleinn.com; s/d/tr cottage from US$286/357/417, 2-bedroom d/tr/q villa from US$506/565/625; ☐ ☒) Francis Ford Coppola's beachside complement to his hill-country Blancaneaux Lodge (p173) combines luxury and attentive service with relaxation and an air of rusticity. Thickly thatched cottages and villas are arranged about the ample grounds, some right on the beach, others set back from it but elevated to help air circulation. The rich decor has a Balinese theme and nearly all units sport private gardens with outdoor showers. The resort also boasts a beachfront pool, PADI dive shop, spa and classy seaview restaurant. Continental breakfast is included in the room price.

Also recommended on this stretch of the peninsula:

Miller's Landing Resort (Map p193; ☎ 523-3010; www.millerslanding.net; s US$43-134, d US$54-145; ☐ ☒) A great location at affordable prices, with spotless rooms, pool, good restaurant and bar, and free bikes and kayaks.

Rum Point Inn (Map p193; ☎ 523-3239, from US ☎ 888-235-4031; www.rumpoint.com; d cabana/ste with continental breakfast US$210/245; ☐ ✖ ☒) Stay in mushroom-shaped stucco cabanas or 900-sq-ft, air-con suites. Amenities include a PADI dive shop, library and pool, and the staff are notably helpful.

SEINE BIGHT & MAYA BEACH

Maya Breeze Inn (Map p193; ☎ 523-8012, from US ☎ 888-458-8581; www.mayabreezeinn.com; Maya Beach; s or d US$98-161, tr US$132-178, q US$173-196, incl continental breakfast; ☐ ✖ ☐) A great place if you like to make the most of your time. Owners Buddy and Tressa Olson love the adventurous side of Belize and are keen for their guests to share the excitement, offering a full range of land and sea tours as far afield as Actun Tunichil Muknal in western Belize (p161) and Tikal in Guatemala, and activities with specially selected guides. Most of the bright, spacious, well appointed accommodations are in modern beachside cabins, with either a kitchen or kitchenette. Kayaks and bikes are free for guests.

Maya Beach Hotel (Map p193; ☎ 520-8040, from US ☎ 800-503-5124; www.mayabeachhotel.com; Maya Beach; r US$98-109; P ✗ 💻) Good, fresh, clean, air-con rooms with custom-made wooden furniture, and a highly popular bistro and bar. Kayaks and bikes are free for guests.

Also recommended:

Nautical Inn (Map p193; ☎ 523-3595; www.nauticalinn belize.com; Seine Bight; s US$127-138, d US$149-159; P ✗ 💻 🕾) Friendly small resort true to its name with its good-value, marine-theme restaurant and bar, PADI dive shop and fishers' tackle shop. The Wednesday night fun and games here draw visitors from up and down the peninsula (see opposite).

Blue Crab Beach Resort (Map p193; ☎ 523-3544; www.bluecrabbeach.com; Seine Bight; s/d cabana US$64/91, air-con room US$75/102; P ✗) Tranquil, family-run spot where a family of coatimundis roams the grounds, and endangered hawksbill turtles hatch on the palm-fringed beach in November. There's an excellent little restaurant here (see right).

Singing Sands Inn (Map p193; ☎ 520-8022, 523-8017; www.singingsands.com; Maya Beach; cabana incl continental breakfast US$100-125; P 🕾) Homey spot with the amenities of somewhere much bigger.

Maya Playa (Map p193; ☎ 523-8020; www.geocities .com/mayaplaya; Maya Beach; d/tr/q US$80/86/91; P) Imaginatively built rustic cabanas and a big open-air kitchen for guests.

Eating
PLACENCIA VILLAGE

De-Tatch Café (Map p194; ☎ 503-3385; Seaspray Hotel; breakfasts & lunch dishes US$2.50-6, dinner mains US$6-13; ✉ 7am-9:30pm Thu-Tue) Head to this popular, thatch-roofed, open-air, beachside place for satisfying Caribbean, Belizean and North American dishes (coconut shrimp curry, steaks, chicken in mango rum sauce…).

Trattoria Placencia (Map p194; ☎ 609-3143; mains US$10-13; ✉ from 5pm Mon-Sat) The trattoria serves great hand-made pasta, seafood and salads in a cozy wooden cabin with a terrace opening on the beach. The fettuccine with smoked chicken and broccoli is hard to beat. Located next to Julia & Lawrence Guesthouse, it is in the busy part of town. Get there by 6pm to 6:30pm to avoid a wait.

Cozy Corner Restaurant (Map p194; ☎ 523-3540; mains US$9-15; ✉ 11am-11pm) Another popular open-air beachside *palapa*, Cozy Corner scores with generous portions of seafood, steaks, chicken, burgers – and several types of enormous burritos for US$6 or less.

Purple Space Monkey Village (Map p194; ☎ 523-4094; breakfasts US$4-5, dinner mains US$10-18; ✉ breakfast, lunch & dinner) Dependable international fare is the recipe for success here, under a big *palapa* opposite the football field: large breakfasts; burgers and burritos for lunch; seafood, chicken and pork for dinner. Wednesday night there's a US$15 Belizean buffet.

Wendy's Restaurant (Map p194; ☎ 523-3335; breakfasts & lunch dishes US$2-7, dinner mains US$8-11; ✉ breakfast, lunch & dinner; ✗) Just up the road from the boat docks, Wendy's serves a long menu of reliable Mexican and Belizean food on stripey Guatemalan tablecloths. It's straightforward, clean and air-conditioned, and the prices are good.

Tutti Frutti (Map p194; 1/2 scoops US$1.40/1.75) Delicious multi-flavored Italian ice cream, opposite Wendy's.

NORTH OF THE VILLAGE

Mare Restaurant (Map p193; ☎ 523-3244; Turtle Inn; mains US$12-25; ✉ 6-10pm) A touch of Italy via northern California, this large beachside *palapa* at Placencia's most exotic resort is your best bet for upscale pastas, seafood, wood-fire pizzas and Placencia's best wine list. Reservations suggested.

Blue Crab (Map p193; ☎ 523-3544; Blue Crab Beach Resort, Seine Bight; mains US$17-20; ✉ 7-9am, noon-2pm, 6:30-8pm, closed lunch & dinner Wed & Sun) Blue Crab serves up unusual hand-crafted, Caribbean-cum-Asian dishes in a tiny, charming dining room. Be sure to book by 1pm for dinner.

Maya Beach Hotel (Map p193; ☎ 520-8040; Maya Beach; mains US$12-26; ✉ restaurant 7am-noon & 5:30-9pm, bar snacks & meals all day, closed Tue) Australian owner-chef John Lee concocts some really creative international dishes from top local ingredients for his very popular bistro-style restaurant, such as the spicy 'sassy shrimp pot,' with tequila-flambé caramelized pineapple tossed in coconut curry!

The sea-view restaurants at **Kitty's Place Beach Resort** (Map p193; ☎ 523-3227) and the **Inn at Robert's Grove** (Map p193; ☎ 523-3565) both serve quality Caribbean/Mediterranean fare.

They're open for all meals, with dinner mains starting from around US$13. Kitty's Place does a special US$18 Maya *pibil* dinner (pit-baked spiced chicken and pork) on Sundays. Robert's Grove offers free transportation for dinner guests.

Wamasa Watering Hole (Map p193; ☎ 523-3532; Seine Bight; mains US$5-8; ☺ 9am-3pm, 6-10pm) This friendly little Garifuna-run eatery in downtown Seine Bight serves up tasty quesadillas, salads and grilled shrimp. Or just stop by for a beer at the outdoor bar.

Drinking & Entertainment

Tipsy Tuna Sports Bar (Map p194; ☺ 7pm-midnight Sun-Wed, 7pm-2am Thu-Sat) Occasional live bands spice up the program at Placencia's shiniest bar, with pool tables, big-screen TV and a concrete apron spreading onto the sands. A fun-loving crowd gathers most nights. Happy hour is 7pm to 8pm.

Barefoot Beach Bar (Map p194; ☎ 523-3515; ☺ 10am-8pm Thu-Tue) Stroll in for a cooler or light eats. Happy hour is 5pm to 6pm.

J-Byrds (Map p194; ☎ 523-3412; ☺ 10am-midnight or 2am; ☒) This dockside bar can get pretty lively with locals and visitors, especially at the Friday dance party (9pm to 2am).

Nautical Inn (Map p193; ☎ 523-3595; Seine Bight; adult/under-12 US$19/10; ☺ 6-9pm Wed) The weekly beach barbecue here, preceded by Garifuna drumming and punta dancing, and followed by the tantalizing sport of coconut bowling, is real fun and pulls in visitors from up and down the peninsula. You need to book by 6pm Tuesday.

Getting There & Away

AIR

From Placencia airport (PLJ), **Maya Island Air** (☎ 523-3475; www.mayaairways.com) and **Tropic Air** (☎ 523-3410; www.tropicair.com) between them fly around 16 times daily to Belize City (US$64 to US$75, 35 minutes), 12 times to Dangriga (US$36, 15 minutes) and eight times to Punta Gorda (US$37, 15 to 20 minutes) – big time savings over the bus rides.

BOAT

The **Hokey Pokey Water Taxi** (Map p194; ☎ 601-0271, 523-2376) leaves Placencia dock at 10am, 12:30pm, 4pm and 5pm for the village of Mango Creek (US$5, 10 minutes) on the west side of Placencia Lagoon. Return trips leave Mango Creek at 6:30am, 7:30am, 8am,

11am, 2:30pm and 4:30pm. This service enables both departing and arriving travelers to connect with buses on the Southern Hwy in the small town of Independence, which adjoins Mango Creek, an alternative to using the few buses in and out of Placencia itself. From the dock at Mango Creek, walk 700m straight up the street ahead. Novelo's (Southern Transport) stops at the Hotel Hello, and James Bus Line stops at Sherl's Restaurant, behind the fuel station opposite. There should be southbound buses to Punta Gorda (US$4.50, two hours) every hour or two till about 7pm, and northbound services to Dangriga (US$4, 1¾ hours) and Belize City (US$9, 4½ hours) until at least 2pm.

The 45-passenger **Gulf Cruza** (☎ 202-4506, 523-4045, 601-4453) sails from Placencia dock to Puerto Cortés, Honduras (US$50, 4½ hours) at 9:30am on Friday. Tickets are sold at Placencia Tourism Center (p193). The return trip leaves Puerto Cortés at 11am Monday.

BUS

Novelo's buses are scheduled to leave Placencia dock for Dangriga (US$5, 2¼ hours) at 6am Monday to Saturday, 7am Sunday and 1:30pm daily. Double-check schedules with the tourist office. At least one of the morning buses passes through Sittee River and Hopkins.

CAR & MOTORCYCLE

The 24-mile road into Placencia from the Southern Hwy is unpaved except for a short stretch through Seine Bight and the last 2 miles into Placencia. Auto rentals are available at the **Nautical Inn** (Map p193; ☎ 523-3595; Seine Bight; per day US$75-90).

Getting Around

Many accommodations north of the village offer free airport transfers and free use of bicycles for guests.

Taxis meet many flights. The ride to or from the village costs US$2.50 per person (minimum US$5). A taxi from the village costs around US$3.50 per person to Seine Bight (minimum US$10) or US$5 per person to Maya Beach (minimum US$15).

Dianni's Guest House (Map p194; ☎ 523-3159) rents good bicycles for US$2.50/8/13 per hour/half-day/day.

SOUTHERN BELIZE

PUNTA GORDA

pop 4900

The southernmost town of size in Belize, and capital of Toledo District, Punta Gorda is a low-key, unpretentious place that for many travelers serves only as a gateway to Guatemala (daily boats cross the Gulf of Honduras to Puerto Barrios). Though on the coast, PG (as it's known throughout Belize) lacks beaches. But it's the center of an area with many and varied attractions – snorkeling, diving or kayaking the beautiful Snake Cayes or Sapodilla Cayes, investigating Maya ruins, visiting contemporary Maya villages, or exploring the caves, lagoons, rivers and waterfalls of a district still blessed with huge swaths of pristine jungle.

PG was founded by Garifuna settlers from Honduras in 1832 and nearly half its population is still Garifuna today. The town once served as an R&R center for the British Army, but that phase ended in 1992. Today, tourism is gradually getting back on its feet with a new emphasis on exploring the surrounding region.

Rainfall and humidity are at their highest down here in the south. From June through February, be ready for at least a short downpour almost daily and some sultry weather in between.

Orientation & Information

The town spreads along the Gulf of Honduras with the main built-up area stretching just over 1 mile parallel to the coast. The airport is on the inland edge of town. The town center is a triangular park with a distinctive blue-and-white clock tower. Wednesday, Saturday, and to a lesser extent Monday and Friday, are market mornings when local villagers come to town to buy, sell and barbecue around the central park and Front St. It's a fascinating and colorful mix.

Belize Bank (☎ 722-2324; 30 Main St; ☼ 8am-3pm Mon-Thu, 8am-4:30pm Fri) Exchanges cash and traveler's checks and the ATM accepts international Visa, MasterCard, Plus and Cirrus cards.

Belize Tourism Board (BTB; ☎ 722-2531; Front St; ☼ 8am-noon & 1-5pm Tue-Fri, 8am-noon Sat) Staff are knowledgeable and keen to enthuse visitors. The Toledo Ecotourism Association (TEA; see p206) shares the premises.

Emergency (☎ 911, 922)

Post office (Front St; ☼ 8am-noon & 1-5pm Mon-Thu, 8am-noon & 1-4:30pm Fri)

Punta Gorda Hospital (☎ 722-2026; Main St)

Punta Gorda Laundry Service (☎ 702-2273; Main St; wash & dry per lb US$0.75; ☼ 8:30am-12:30pm & 1:30-5pm Mon-Sat)

Southern Belize (www.southernbelize.com) Excellent website.

V-Comp Technologies (☎ 722-0093; 29 Main St; per hr US$4; ☼ 8am-8pm Mon-Sat) Internet access.

Activities

There's a lot to do around PG. Some operators plan to offer trips with per-person prices, but up to now they have dealt chiefly on a per-van or per-boat basis. Two well-equipped outfits are **TIDE Tours** (☎ 722-2129; www.tidetours.org; Prince St; ☼ 9am-noon & 2-6pm Mon-Wed & Fri, 9am-noon Thu & Sat) and **Wild Encounters** (☎ 722-2300; fax 722-2682; Sea Front Inn, 4 Front St). Contact them at least one day before you want to go. The BTB office can also direct you to recommended guides.

In the immediate environs of Punta Gorda, you can kayak on Joe Taylor Creek which enters the sea at the eastern end of town. Wild Encounters rents kayaks for US$13 per day and TIDE Tours for US$5/15/25 per hour/half-day/day. A three-hour guided trip is around US$50 for two people. Kayak trips on other rivers, where you may see monkeys, crocodiles and even manatees or dolphins off the river mouths, cost around US$150 to US$200 for up to four people.

Offshore, some of the islands of the Port Honduras Marine Reserve, northeast of Punta Gorda, present good snorkeling and diving, especially the Snake Cayes (named for their resident boa constrictors!) 16 miles out, with white sand beaches. The beautiful Sapodilla Cayes on the barrier reef, some 38 miles east of Punta Gorda, are even better, with healthy coral reefs, abundant marine life and sandy beaches. A day trip for four costs around US$250 to the Port Honduras Marine Reserve, or US$325 to the Sapodilla Cayes.

Fishing for bonefish, tarpon, permit, snook, barracuda, kingfish, jacks and snapper is superb in the offshore waters and some coastal lagoons and inland rivers: fly- and spin-fishing and trolling can be practiced all year round.

Tours

It is possible to explore the area on your own, but many sites around here will be more interesting with a guide. See Around

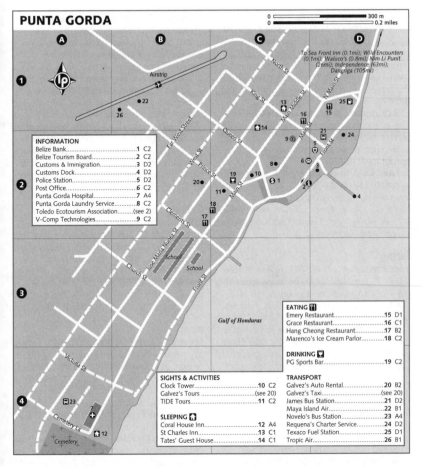

PUNTA GORDA

INFORMATION
Belize Bank..1 C2
Belize Tourism Board............................2 C2
Customs & Immigration.......................3 D2
Customs Dock...4 D2
Police Station...5 D2
Post Office..6 C2
Punta Gorda Hospital...........................7 A4
Punta Gorda Laundry Service............8 C2
Toledo Ecotourism Association.......(see 2)
V-Comp Technologies...........................9 C2

EATING
Emery Restaurant...............................15 D1
Grace Restaurant................................16 C1
Hang Cheong Restaurant..................17 B2
Marenco's Ice Cream Parlor.............18 C2

DRINKING
PG Sports Bar.......................................19 C2

SIGHTS & ACTIVITIES
Clock Tower..10 C2
Galvez's Tours..................................(see 20)
TIDE Tours..11 C2

SLEEPING
Coral House Inn..................................12 A4
St Charles Inn......................................13 C1
Tates' Guest House.............................14 C1

TRANSPORT
Galvez's Auto Rental..........................20 B2
Galvez's Taxi....................................(see 20)
James Bus Station...............................21 D2
Maya Island Air...................................22 B1
Novelo's Bus Station..........................23 A4
Requena's Charter Service................24 D2
Texaco Fuel Station............................25 D1
Tropic Air..26 B1

Gulf of Honduras

Punta Gorda, p203, for the best destinations. A typical day tour might take in Blue Creek and either or both of the main Maya sites, Lubaantun and Nim Li Punit, but guides and operators can take you almost anywhere you like. Most day tours cost US$150 to US$250 for up to four people. The services of a certified guide alone are around US$75 per day. Operators include **Wild Encounters** (☎ 722-2300; fax 722-2682; Sea Front Inn, 4 Front St), **TIDE Tours** (☎ 722-2129; www.tide tours.org; Prince St) and **Galvez's Tours** (☎ 722-2402; 61 Jose Maria Nunez St).

Festivals & Events

Two days of fishing, beer-drinking, punta-dancing, kayaking and volleyball contests, plus music, drumming and plenty to eat and drink add up to a big weekend at the **Toledo Fish Fest**, held close to Garifuna Settlement Day (November 19).

Sleeping

Sea Front Inn (☎ 722-2300; www.seafrontinn.com; 4 Front St; d/q US$64/80; ℗ ✕ ▯) A strong contender for the quirkiest-looking hotel in Belize, this four-story gabled construction in stone, wood and concrete was partly inspired by owner Larry Smith's travels in Europe. It's a comfortable and hospitable place where each of the good-sized, air-con rooms has a different theme – such as jaguar, blue morpho, manatee – try for the emperor angelfish with its exotic sculptures!

Coral House Inn (☎ 722-2878; www.coralhouseinn .com; south end Main St; d incl continental breakfast US$82-98; 🌊 🚲) This excellent inn, with garden swimming pool, opened in 2005 in a stylishly renovated house. Each of the tile-floored rooms has a spacious verandah overlooking the sea. A full range of tours is available and there are free bicycles for guests.

St Charles Inn (☎ 722-2149; 23 King St; s/d US$15/20) The aging, wooden, clean rooms here, with private bathroom and cable TV, are good value, and there are verandahs with hammocks to sit out on.

Tates' Guest House (☎ 722-0147; teach@btl.net; 34 Jose Maria Nunez St; r US$16-32; 🌊) The spotless rooms, on the ground floor of a family home on a quiet street, all have bath, cable TV and hot shower. The costlier rooms have air-con and kitchenettes.

Eating

Grace Restaurant (☎ 702-2414; 16 Main St; mains US$5-9; 🕑 6am-10pm; 🌊) The most consistent place in town for a good range of dependable food, Chinese as well as Belizean. Good-value breakfasts are US$2 to US$4.

Hang Cheong Restaurant (Main St; dishes US$3-9; 🕑 10:30am-2:30pm & 5pm-midnight; 🌊) Hang Cheong serves a wide range of well-prepared Chinese dishes in spick and span surroundings with shiny pine furnishings.

Emery Restaurant (Main St; mains US$5-11; 🕑 11:30-2pm & 6-10pm Mon-Fri, 6-10pm Sat) Daily fresh-fish specials, good curries, generous servings of delicious shrimp and quite possibly the best fried chicken in Belize, all in a relaxed outdoor atmosphere.

Sea Front Inn (☎ 722-2300; 4 Front St; breakfast US$4-6; 🕑 7-9:30am) This place has the best breakfasts in town – from the 'Hungry Man' down – with great 4th-floor ocean views.

Marenco's Ice Cream Parlor (☎ 722-2572; Main St; ice creams US$1-3, meals US$3-8; 🕑 11am-2pm & 5:30-10pm) A great spot to stop into for all ice-cream needs or meals from rice and beans to shrimp dishes. They do good juices and lemon pie too!

Drinking & Entertainment

PG is home to some top performers, such as *paranda* (serenading music) maestro Paul Nabor, *brukdown* (19th-century Creole music) queen Leela Vernon, and local punta rock favorites the Coolie Rebels. Don't miss a chance to hear any of these.

PG Sports Bar (☎ 722-2329; cnr Main & Prince Sts; 🕑 8pm-midnight Tue-Thu, 8pm-2am Fri & Sat) A good-sized, fairly standard bar, incongruously enhanced by a staggering collection of US sports photos and posters. There's usually a DJ or live music Friday and Saturday.

Waluco's (☎ 702-0073; Front St) If you're wondering where everybody is on Saturday or Sunday afternoon, they're probably out at this big breezy *palapa* a mile northeast of town, swimming off the pier, eating barbecue and knocking back a few Belikins. It's normally open Tuesday to Saturday evenings too and Garifuna drummers often play here.

Getting There & Away

AIR

Tropic Air (☎ 722-2008; www.tropicair.com) flies five times daily to Placencia (US$37, 20 minutes), Dangriga (US$60, 40 minutes) and Belize City (US$82 to US$97, one hour). **Maya Island Air** (☎ 722-2856; www.mayaairways.com) does the same trips three times daily. Ticket offices are at the airstrip (airport code PND).

BOAT

Requena's Charter Service (☎ 722-2070; 12 Front St) operates the *Mariestela,* departing Punta Gorda at 9am daily for Puerto Barrios, Guatemala (US$15, one hour), returning at 2pm. Tickets are sold at the office and the Customs Dock down the street. The Guatemalan **Pichilingo** (☎ 722-2870; one way US$18) sails from Puerto Barrios to Punta Gorda at 10am and returns from Punta Gorda at 2pm. From Puerto Barrios boats leave for Lívingston (US$1.50 to US$3.50, 30 to 90 minutes) until about 5pm. A Guatemalan-operated direct boat to Lívingston (US$15, one hour) leaves the Customs Dock about 10am Tuesday and Friday.

BUS

James Bus Line (☎ 722-2625, 702-2049; King St) departs for Independence (US$4.50, two hours), Dangriga (US$7, 3¾ hours), Belmopan (US$10, 5½ hours) and Belize City (US$11, seven hours) at 6am, 8am and noon daily. On Friday and Saturday there's a slightly quicker 3pm express (US$12 to Belize City). **Novelo's/Southern Transport** (☎ 702-2165; Jose Maria Nunez St) leaves for the same places at 4am, 5am and 10am, and some days at 9am.

CAR & MOTORCYCLE
Galvez's Auto Rental (☎ 722-2402; 61 Jose Maria Nunez St) rents Chevy Geo Trackers for around US$85 a day.

Getting Around
TIDE Tours (☎ 722-2129; Prince St; ☷ 9am-noon & 2-6pm Mon-Wed & Fri, 9am-noon Thu & Sat) rents bikes for US$1.50/6/10 per hour/half-day/day. **Galvez's Taxi** (☎ 722-2402; 61 Jose Maria Nunez St) is dependable.

AROUND PUNTA GORDA
The 1669-sq-mile Toledo District reaches from the Gulf of Honduras and its river-watered coastal lowlands up to the rugged ridges of the Maya Mountains. Only 27,000

people live in this huge area, perhaps the most pristine and undisturbed in the country. About half the district is under protection as national parks, wildlife sanctuaries, forest reserves or nature reserves.

Toledo's attractions – jungle trails, lagoons, wetlands, rivers, caves, waterfalls, countless birds – and its archaeological heritage are much less trumpeted than those of Belize's other districts, which makes them all the more magnetic to the interested traveler. Visitor facilities are increasing, and rural accommodations now range from a smattering of midrange and top-end lodges to an excellent guesthouse program.

The people of the district, two-thirds of them Maya, are dedicated primarily to

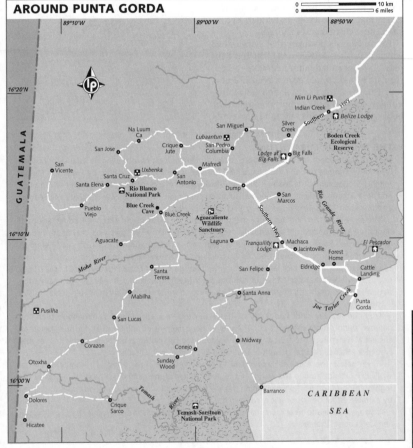

AROUND PUNTA GORDA

agriculture, and their traditional lifestyles provide a fascinating complement to the natural attractions.

Lubaantun

The Maya ruins at **Lubaantun** (admission US$5; 8am-5pm), 1.3 miles northwest of the village of San Pedro Columbia, are built on a natural hilltop and display a construction method unusual in the ancient Maya world (though typical of southern Belize) of neatly cut small limestone blocks. Belize's chief medical officer Thomas Gann, an amateur archaeologist, bestowed the name Lubaantun (Place of Fallen Stones) in 1924. History does not record whether Gann was inspired by his own practice of dynamiting temple tops to remove earth and rocks. More professional work has taken place since 1970 and much of the site is now cleared and restored.

Archaeologists postulate that Lubaantun, which flourished between AD 730 and 860, may have been an administrative center regulating trade, while nearby Nim Li Punit (opposite) was the local religious and ceremonial center. The site comprises a collection of five plazas, three ball courts and surround-

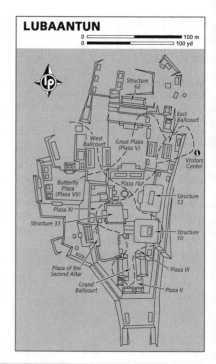

LUBAANTUN

THE SKULL OF LUBAANTUN

Some of the modern tales coming from Lubaantun are at least as intriguing as its ancient history. Dynamiter Thomas Gann was accompanied on one of his 1920s visits here by Frederick 'Midge' Mitchell-Hedges and Lady 'Mabs' Richmond-Brown, a pair of old-school British explorer-adventurers and avid Atlantis-seekers, who penned such travel memoirs as *Danger, My Ally* (Mitchell-Hedges) and *Unknown Tribes, Uncharted Waters* (Richmond-Brown).

The story goes that one day while messing around the excavations, Mitchell-Hedges' adopted daughter Anna uncovered a perfectly proportioned human skull that was carved from pure quartz crystal. So much has since been written and surmised about this 11.7lb skull, which is actually still in Anna Mitchell-Hedges' possession in Canada today, that there is probably no single uncontrovertible fact left concerning it. Its origins are a complete mystery. In the 1960s or 70s Hewlett-Packard scientists in California reportedly found that it was carved against the natural axis or 'grain' of the crystal – which under normal circumstances would have caused it to shatter.

Literature on the skull frequently quotes a Hewlett-Packard scientist commenting that 'The damned thing simply shouldn't be.' There is a strong current of opinion that, far from being an ancient Maya artifact, the skull wasn't actually found at Lubaantun at all. Some accounts aver that Frederick Mitchell-Hedges bought it at auction in London in the 1940s.

Nevertheless, the 'Mitchell-Hedges Skull' is considered one of the finest of a number of crystal skulls in existence around the world, and to some lovers of the paranormal is a cult object of the highest importance, possibly containing the key to human destiny or information codes implanted by extraterrestrial beings or a lost civilization.

If you would like to hear more, have a read of *The Mystery of the Crystal Skulls* by Chris Morton and Ceri Louise Thomas.

ing structures. Lubaantun is known for the many mold-made ceramic figurines found here, many of which represent ball players.

If making your own way to Lubaantun, head along the Southern Hwy for 15 miles from Punta Gorda. Continue straight along an unpaved road where the Southern Hwy turns sharp east at Dump junction, then turn right at a 'Lubaantun' sign after 2 miles. Go right again after 2.5 miles in San Pedro Columbia and then left at another 'Lubaantun' sign after 0.6 miles.

Nim Li Punit

The Maya ruins of **Nim Li Punit** (admission US$5; 9am-5pm) stand atop a natural hill 0.5 miles north of the Southern Hwy, 26 miles from Punta Gorda. Buses along the highway will drop you off or pick you up at the turnoff. Only discovered in 1976 by oil prospectors, Nim Li Punit was inhabited from some time in the middle Classic Period (400–700) until some time between 800 and 1000. It was probably a town of 5000 to 7000 people at its peak, a political and religious community of some importance in the region.

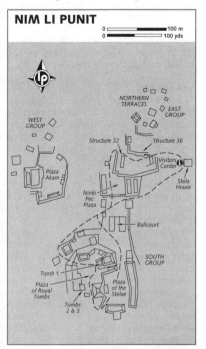

The site is notable for the 26 stelae found in its southern Plaza of the Stelae. Four of the finest are housed in the stela house beside the visitors center. Stela 14, at 33ft, is the second longest stela found anywhere in the Maya world (after Stela E from Quiri-gua, Guatemala). It shows the ruler of Nim Li Punit in an offering or incense-scattering ritual, wearing an enormous headdress which is responsible for the name Nim Li Punit ('Big Hat' in Kekchi Maya).

The most interesting part of the Nim Li Punit site is the south end, comprising the Plaza of the Stelae and the Plaza of Royal Tombs. The Plaza of the Stelae is thought to have acted as a calendrical observatory: seen from its western mound, three of the small stones in front of the long eastern mound align with sunrise on the equinoxes and solstices. The Plaza of Royal Tombs, with three open, excavated tombs, was a residential area for the ruling family, four of whom were uncovered in Tomb 1, along with several jadeite items and 37 ceramic vessels.

Villages of Toledo

Over 60% of the population of Toledo District is Maya and these people, with more than 30 villages, are the most culturally traditional in the area. Those Maya of southern Belize who survived European diseases were mostly driven into Guatemala by the British in the 18th and 19th centuries. But two groups crossed back from Guatemala to southern Belize in the late 19th and early 20th centuries, fleeing taxes, forced labor and land grabs by German coffee-growers. The Mopan Maya settled in the uplands of southern Belize, while the Kekchi Maya, from the Alta Verapaz area of Guatemala, settled in the lowlands. The Mopan and Kekchi speak distinct Mayan languages, as well as English and sometimes Spanish. The Kekchi's primary crops are rice and corn, while the Mopan farm beans and coffee, which thrive at higher elevations.

While Maya men generally adopt Western styles of dress, most women still wear plain, full-length dresses with bright trimmings, or calf-length skirts and embroidered blouses. Rituals and folklore still play an important role in Maya life, with masked dances such as the Cortés Dance and Deer Dance performed in some villages at festivals such as

SOUTHERN BELIZE

All Saints' and All Souls' Days (November 1 and 2), and Easter week. If your village visit coincides with one of these it will be all the more memorable.

A unique opportunity to be welcomed into local villages and experience village life firsthand is provided by the **Toledo Ecotourism Association** (TEA; ☎ 722-2096; ecoclub.com /toledo; Front St, Punta Gorda; ✆ 8am-noon Mon, Wed, Fri & Sat), which arranges stays in village guesthouses in eight Maya and one Garifuna village. This is probably the least-appreciated tourism possibility in Belize. The villages are gorgeous – simple, neat, clean, surrounded by lovely scenery and usually with a river or stream at their heart – and the villagers friendly without being overly so. Around the villages are waterfalls, caves and ancient Maya ruins that can be best experienced with a local guide.

The TEA office in Punta Gorda (shared with the BTB) is normally staffed from 8am to noon on Monday, Wednesday, Friday and Saturday, but the BTB staff can usually help at other times. The well-kept village guesthouses have been specially built for the program: outwardly they're long, plank-walled, thatch-roofed buildings like other Maya village houses; inside, broad bunks with good mattresses accommodate up to eight people. Showers (unheated water) and pit latrines are separate. The nightly cost, US$9 per person, includes sheets, blankets and mosquito nets. There's also a US$5 fee per visit.

Maya meals are prepared in local families' houses for US$3 to US$4 each, and a range of activities is on offer in each village to help you get to know the area and its way of life. Options range from guided hikes, caving, canoeing and bird-watching to classes in textiles or basket-weaving or cooking, village tours led by women and after-dinner storytelling. Most of these cost US$3.50 per person per hour. Performances of traditional dance (usually US$13) and music (harp in Kekchi villages, marimba among the Mopan; usually US$40) can also be arranged.

More than 80% of what you pay stays with the villagers. If possible, make your arrangements through the Punta Gorda office, a day or two ahead. This enables you to get advice, introductions and maybe help with transportation. Upon arrival in the village, guests are usually greeted immediately, and needs are sorted out easily.

When you visit village homes for your meals, it's unlikely that the family will eat with you. Instead they'll go about their family business while you're there. Some find this disconcerting at first, but it's still a great opportunity to ask questions and learn about Maya village and home life. Main meals usually consist of tortillas and *caldo* – a stew made from root vegetables and meat, usually chicken – although in Barranco you might luck onto some traditional Garifuna food. If you're vegetarian, specify this clearly and in advance.

LAGUNA

About 13 miles northwest of Punta Gorda, Laguna is just 2 miles off the Southern Hwy and quick and easy to get to. It's home to about 300 Kekchi Maya villagers. The lagoon the village is named for, about a two-hour walk away, is at the heart of the 8.6-sq-mile **Aguacaliente Wildlife Sanctuary**, an extensive wetland area. The area provides great bird-watching, with flocks of ibis and woodstork, many raptors including ospreys, plenty of kingfishers and herons and the odd jabiru stork. There's a visitor center on the trail from the village. The hike can be wet and muddy, and sometimes impassable at the height of the rains, but boardwalks are under construction, and canoes and kayaks are being made available.

SAN MIGUEL

This Kekchi village of 400 people is on the road close to the Lubaantun ruins and the Southern Hwy. You can walk to Lubaantun or make a little expedition to Tiger Cave, 1½ hours' walk away, and return by canoe along the Rio Grande.

NORTHWESTERN VILLAGES

With about 2500 people, **San Antonio** is the largest and probably the best-known and most-visited Maya village in Toledo, possibly the country. Arranged on roads winding through foothills, it's a picture-postcard sight, complete with brightly dressed villagers, thatched-roof buildings, roaming livestock, a church built from stones taken from Maya ruins and stained-glass windows from a church in St Louis, Missouri. The **Feast of San Luis**, a harvest festival where the famous Deer Dance is performed, is celebrated here from about August 15 to 25.

Santa Elena is another Mopan village, 6 miles west of San Antonio, with about 300 people. Just east is the little **Rio Blanco National Park**, containing the spectacular Rio Blanco Falls and one of the best swimming holes in the country. On the outskirts of the neighboring village of Santa Cruz are the Maya ruins of **Uxbenka**, visitable with a local guide.

Three miles beyond Santa Elena is **Pueblo Viejo** ('Old Town' in Spanish), the first Mopan settlement on their arrival from San Luis, Guatemala, and home to about 550 today. It's still an isolated place, without electricity. There are beautiful waterfalls close by and you can take jungle hikes or go horseback riding.

San Jose, also known as Hawaii, is a Mopan village of 700 in the foothills of the Maya Mountains known for practicing organic farming. The rainforest surrounding it is among the most pristine in Toledo. You can make jungle hikes to Gibnut Cave and a 200ft sinkhole. The village honors its patron saint with a three-day feast of eating and dancing to *marimba* and harp music around March 19.

BLUE CREEK

This village of some 250 people, part Kekchi and part Mopan, does indeed have a pretty, blue-tinted river running through the middle. Howler monkeys inhabit the surrounding hilly jungles, otters live along the creek, and green iguanas are plentiful. Blue Creek is a tourist stop for the **Blue Creek Cave** (Hokeb Ha Cave; admission US$1), a walk of about 0.75 miles along a marked jungle path from the bridge in the middle of the village. The cave has a 'wet side' in which you swim and wade up to an underground waterfall (about one hour in the cave), and a 'dry side' where you can try a more difficult venture involving some climbing and emerge from a different entrance. Guides are obligatory inside the cave. Another good hike here is the hill known as Jungle Height (about 1½ hours to the top) which affords great views.

In addition to the TEA guesthouse (one of the neat little cluster of plank-and-thatch houses on the south side of the creek), Blue Creek is home to **Blue Creek Rainforest Lodge** (International Zoological Expeditions Guesthouse; from US ☎ 800-548-5843; www.ize2belize.com; dm incl dinner & 1

activity US$45, breakfast US$8), 500yd along the trail toward the cave. Massachusetts-based International Zoological Expeditions (IZE) offers packages combining this lodge with its island location on South Water Caye (see p184), but independent travelers can stay here too. The five mosquito-screened cabanas hold bunks for between four and 10 people. You can swim in the river right here, and at night kinkajous can often be spotted in the trees.

BARRANCO

This oldest settlement in Toledo and only Garifuna village on the coast south of Punta Gorda can be reached by sea from PG in about 20 minutes, or by dirt road in 45 minutes. Barranco now supports itself by fishing, but in the past the area was heavily farmed; you'll see plenty of fruit trees. The village's population is about 150 and dwindling, as men of working age head for the cities and better economic opportunities. But the villagers are proud of their home and Barranco is a starting point for visits to the **Temash-Sarstoon National Park** bordering Guatemala. The park is a remote, 64-sq-mile area of rainforests, wetlands, estuaries and rivers lined by towering mangroves.

The park harbors a huge variety of wildlife from jaguar, tapir and ocelot on land to ospreys in the air, large snook and tarpon in the rivers and manatees in the estuaries. Trails for visitors, developed by the locally run Sarstoon Temash Institute for Indigenous Management (SATIIM), should be ready by the time you read this.

GETTING THERE & AWAY

Laguna can be accessed by any James or Southern Transport bus along the Southern Hwy. San Antonio is served by **Chun's Bus Service** (☎ 606-4257, 600-1016) leaving the village at 6am daily, except Sunday, and heading back from PG at noon (US$1.50, one hour). All the villages are served by 'market buses' to Punta Gorda on Monday, Wednesday, Friday and Saturday, leaving the villages between 3am and 6am, and setting off back from Punta Gorda's central park or market area between 11:30am and noon. Check with the TEA or BTB in Punta Gorda for current schedules and departure points. One-way fares range from US$1.25 to US$2.50.

It is possible to arrange for a taxi to the villages; the price will be around US$50 to

US$75 depending on the distance. Hitch-hiking is a common way to get around: this should be done with caution, and no-one, especially women, should hitch alone, but most feel comfortable hitchhiking in pairs or groups around here.

To return to Punta Gorda, be prepared to rise early – the farther from PG the village is, the earlier you'll leave. Luckily everyone in your village will be aware of your presence, so you'll have plenty of help making your connection!

Lodges Near the Southern Hwy

Lodge at Big Falls (☎ 614-2888; www.thelodgeatbig falls.com; s/d/tr US$115/145/170, breakfast/packed lunch/dinner US$9/8/27; P ⬜) At the village of Big Falls, 20 miles from Punta Gorda, spacious, tile-floored, palm-thatched cabins are spread about beautifully tended gardens on a loop of the jungle-clad Rio Grande River. There's first-class birding and butterfly and moth hunting here: 168 bird species have been recorded at the lodge, and a further 182 within 5 miles. Owners Rob and Marta Hirons are right in touch with all the best things to do and places to go in southern Belize, offering a host of activities from snorkeling the cayes to caving, fly-fishing, kayaking, excursions to archaeological sites and visits to local Maya harpist, Santiago Moh. Transfers to or from PG are US$50 for up to four people.

El Pescador (☎ 722-0050; www.elpescadorpg.com; r US$193, 4-night package for 2 incl/excl fishing US$3500/2600; P ⬕ ⬜ ⬛) This is a marvelous rainforest and fishing lodge with a superb hilltop setting overlooking miles of protected jungle stretching down to the Gulf of Honduras. Experienced fishing guides take anglers out on eight-hour fishing trips and the lodge has a well-stocked fly shop, and

fly-fishing gear for rent. On land, there's excellent birding here, trails to walk, and trips to southern Belize attractions. The 12 beautiful rooms boast solid wood furniture, ceramic-lined bathrooms, two queen-size beds and verandahs overlooking the jungle and sea. Packages include transfers to and from Belize City International Airport. The lodge is 2.4 miles off the Southern Hwy, from a turnoff 3 miles out of PG.

Tranquility Lodge (www.tranquility-lodge.com; tr/f incl breakfast US$50/70; P ⬕) Just north of Jacintoville, 8 miles from PG, this little lodge lives up to its name as a tranquil retreat perfect for relaxing for a couple of days or more. Set amid pretty gardens, the clean, tidy, air-conditioned rooms are equipped with hot water and colorful fabrics and there's a spacious upstairs dining/hangout area where you can enjoy good three-course dinners for US$15. Birds abound on the 20-acre grounds and there's a pretty swimming hole on the Jacinto River. Free rides are available to and from PG most days.

Belize Lodge (☎ 223-6324, from US ☎ 888-292-2462; www.belizelodge.com; 3-night package for 2 US$1660; P) You can't miss this luxury lodge (part of the privately owned, 51-sq-mile, Boden Creek Ecological Reserve) spreading over a small hill almost opposite the Nim Li Punit turnoff. The super-comfortable cabanas have airy verandahs overlooking a pair of lakes, and a 2-mile track leads down to a wildlife center with two captive-born jaguars donated by Mexico's Xcaret ecopark. The luxurious set-up also includes Jungle Camp, a 5-mile kayak or canoe trip away, with comfortable riverside safari-style cabins 16ft above ground and its own restaurant and bar. Packages combine stays in the main lodge and Jungle Camp, tours and all meals, including five-course dinners.

Tikal & Flores, Guatemala

A favorite excursion for visitors to Belize is to hop the Guatemalan border and head to Tikal. The monumental ceremonial center at Tikal is, for many people, the most impressive of all Maya archaeological sites. Set in the dense jungle of Guatemala's vast northern department of El Petén, Tikal has a touch of magic. As you explore the site you will hear the squawk of parrots, the chatter of monkeys and the rustlings of exotic animals moving through the bush.

While many tourists fly in from Belize City or come here overland on one-day or overnight package tours, it's a great idea to stay over at least one night, whether in Flores, Santa Elena, El Remate or Tikal itself. Tikal is so big you need two days to do it justice. Day trips from Belize are best taken from western Belize.

Tikal is in the 3906-sq-mile (10,000-sq-km) Reserva de la Biósfera Maya, which includes most of northern El Petén. The adjoining towns of Flores, Santa Elena and San Benito, on the shores of Lago de Petén Itzá, 42 miles (68km) south of Tikal, are the region's tourism bases. The tiny island/town of Flores is the best of the three. It's picturesque and has a laid-back international travelers' vibe, good restaurants and some appealing accommodations.

HIGHLIGHTS

- Climbing Tikal's stupendous **Templo IV** (October to March; p214) at sunrise
- Spotting parrots and monkeys at **Tikal** (p210)
- Taking a *lancha* (motor boat) from Flores on **Lago de Petén Itzá** (p219)
- Enjoying good food and the traveler ambience of **Flores** (p216)
- Lingering lakeside at low-key **El Remate** (p219)

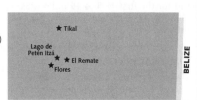

- POPULATION: 59,000
- MONTHLY RAINFALL: JAN/JUN 17IN/30IN (430MM/760MM; TIKAL)
- HIGHEST ELEVATION: 984FT (TIKAL)

Climate

From December to February, nights and mornings are cool. March and April are the hottest and driest months of the year, followed by rains – and mosquitoes – in May or June. July to November is humid, though by October the rains taper off and the temperature begins to cool down.

Language

Spanish is the main language of Guatemala; only a few people speak much English.

Dangers & Annoyances

A few years ago, Tikal and the area around El Remate were the scene of an unfortunate slew of assaults and rapes, most often perpetrated in the more isolated areas of the ruins, such as Templo VI (Templo de las Inscripciones). The criminals were caught and tranquility was restored to the area. However, caution is still recommended. Avoid going to remote ruins alone.

Getting There & Away

You can fly to Flores from Belize City and then take a taxi to Tikal, or take a day or overnight trip offered by many Belizean agencies and lodges. Independent adventurers can take through-buses to Flores from Belize City (p88), or a bus to Benque Viejo del Carmen or San Ignacio and then local transportation for the 2 miles (3.2km) to the border (p168).

From the border and Melchor de Mencos, which is just over the border into Guatemala, there is onward transportation to Flores and Santa Elena via Puente Ixlú (El Cruce), near El Remate. On the Guatemalan side of the border, the road is unpaved for the first 15.5 to 19 miles (25km to 30km). At El Cruce it meets the fast main road from Flores to Tikal. El Cruce is located 22 miles from Tikal and 18 miles from Flores.

For further details, see p215.

> **GUATEMALAN VISAS**
>
> Citizens of the USA, Canada, EU countries, Norway, Switzerland, Australia, New Zealand, Israel, Iceland, South Africa and Japan are among those who do not currently need visas for tourist visits to Guatemala. Regulations can change: check with your travel agent or a Guatemalan embassy or consulate well before travel.

> **CALLING GUATEMALA**
>
> Guatemala has no regional, area or city telephone codes. To call Guatemala from another country, dial the international access code (☎ 00 in most countries), followed by Guatemala's country code, ☎ 502, then the eight-digit local number.
>
> To call a Guatemalan number from anywhere within Guatemala, just dial the eight-digit local number.

TIKAL

Towering pyramids pierce the jungle's green canopy and catch the sun. Howler monkeys swing noisily through the branches of trees as brightly colored parrots and toucans dart from perch to perch amid a cacophony of squawks. When the warbling song of some mysterious jungle bird tapers off, the buzz of tree frogs fills the background.

Certainly the most striking feature of **Tikal** (☎ 2361-1399; admission US$7; ⏰ 6am-6pm) is its steep-sided temples, rising to heights of over 200ft (61m). But Tikal is different from most other great Maya sites because it is deep in the jungle. Its many plazas have been cleared of trees and vines, its temples uncovered and partially restored, but as you walk around you pass beneath the dense rainforest canopy.

History

The Maya began settling Tikal, situated on a small hill above low-lying swampy ground, around 700 BC. Within 200 years, they began to build stone ceremonial structures, and by 200 BC a complex of buildings stood on the site of the Acrópolis del Norte (North Acropolis). By about AD 250, Tikal had become an important religious, cultural and commercial city, ruled by King Yax Moch Xoc, whose reign began around AD 230.

In the middle of the 4th century, under King Great Jaguar Paw, Tikal became the dominant kingdom in the region. By the mid-6th century, Tikal sprawled across 11.5 sq miles (30 sq km) and had a population of perhaps 100,000. In 562, Lord Water, who had ascended to the throne of Caracol in southwestern Belize in 553, conquered and sacrificed Tikal's king. Tikal suffered under Caracol's rule until the late 7th century.

Around AD 700, Moon Double Comb (682–734), also called Ah Cacau (Lord Chocolate), ascended Tikal's throne, restoring the center's military strength and its primacy in the Maya world. He and his successors were responsible for building most of the temples around the Gran Plaza that survive today. The greatness of Tikal waned around 900, part of the mysterious general collapse of lowland Maya civilization.

During the late 19th century and the 20th century, archaeological and scientific interest in Tikal grew, starting with an 1848 expedition sponsored by the Guatemalan government. Since 1956, the University of Pennsylvania and the Guatemalan Instituto de Antropología e Historia have conducted archaeological research and restoration of Tikal, which was declared a Unesco World Heritage site in 1979.

Orientation & Information

Parque Nacional Tikal contains thousands of separate ruined structures. The central area of the city occupied about 6 sq miles (16 sq km).

The road from Flores enters the national park 10.5 miles (17km) south of the ruins. Here you pay the entrance fee; if you enter after 3pm your ticket will be stamped with the following day's date, meaning that it will be valid for the next day, too. Multilingual guides are available at the visitors center (US$50 per half-day, for up to five people). Also in the visitors center is a museum.

Near the visitors center are Tikal's hotels, a camping area, a **tourist information center** (✆ 8am-4pm), a few small *comedores* (basic eateries), another museum and a car park. From the visitors center it's a 0.9-mile (1.5km) walk southwest to the Gran Plaza. To visit all the major building complexes, you must walk at least 6 miles (10km), so you wear comfortable shoes with good rubber treads, as the ruins can be very slick from rain and organic material. Bring plenty of water, as dehydration is a real danger if you're walking around all day in the heat.

For more complete information on the monuments at Tikal, pick up a copy of *Tikal –*

A Handbook of the Ancient Maya Ruins, by William R Coe, available at Tikal and in Flores.

Sights
GRAN PLAZA

The path leading to the plaza goes around **Templo I**, the Templo del Gran Jaguar (Temple of the Great Jaguar), built to honor – and bury – King Moon Double Comb. The king's rich burial goods included 180 jade objects, 90 bits of bone carved with hieroglyphs, pearls and stingray spines, which were used for ritual bloodletting.

At the top of the 144ft (44m) temple is a small enclosure of three rooms that is covered by a corbeled arch. The lofty roof comb (ornamental structure) that crowned the temple was originally adorned with reliefs and bright paint, and may have symbolized the 13 realms of the Maya heaven.

Since at least two people tumbled to their deaths, the stairs up Templo I have been closed. But the views from **Templo II** just across the way are nearly as awe-inspiring. Templo II was once almost as high as Templo I, but now measures 124ft (38m) without its roof comb.

The **Acrópolis del Norte** (North Acropolis), while not as impressive as the two temples, is of great significance. Archaeologists have uncovered about 100 structures, with evidence of occupation as far back as 400 BC. The Maya rebuilt on top of older structures, and the many layers, combined with the elaborate burials, added sanctity and power to their temples. Look for the two huge, powerful wall masks. The final version of the acropolis, as it stood around AD 800, had more than 12 temples atop a vast platform.

ACRÓPOLIS CENTRAL

On the southeast side of the Gran Plaza, this maze of courtyards, little rooms and small temples is thought by some to have been a residential palace for Tikal's nobility. Others believe the tiny rooms may have been used for sacred rites.

PLAZA OESTE

North of Templo II is **Plaza Oeste** (West Plaza). To its north is a late-Classic temple. To the south, across the Calzada Tozzer (Tozzer Causeway), is **Templo III**, which is 181ft (55m) high and yet to be uncovered.

TIKAL

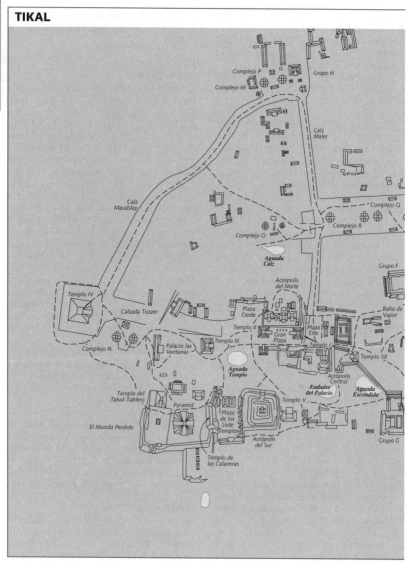

Calzada Tozzer, the causeway leading to Templo IV, was one of several sacred ways built among the complexes for astronomical and aesthetic reasons.

ACRÓPOLIS DEL SUR & TEMPLO V

Due south of the Gran Plaza is **Acrópolis del Sur** (South Acropolis). Excavation has just begun on this 2-hectare mass of masonry. The palaces on top are from late Classic times, but earlier constructions probably go back a thousand years.

Templo V, just east of the Acrópolis del Sur, is 190ft (58m) high and was built around AD 700. Unlike the other great temples, it has rounded corners and one tiny room at

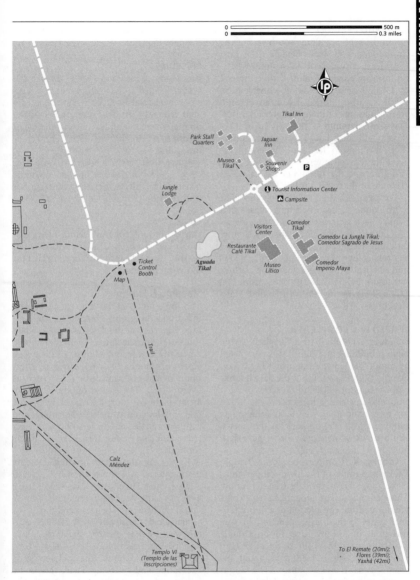

the top, less than 1m deep, but with walls up to 4.5m thick. Restoration of this temple took from 1991 to 2004. You can now climb a wooden stairway to the top.

PLAZA DE LOS SIETE TEMPLOS

Located on the other side of the Acrópolis del Sur is the **Plaza de los Siete Templos** (Plaza of the Seven Temples). The little temples, which are clustered together, were built in late Classic times. Note the skull and crossbones on the central temple.

On the plaza's northern side is an unusual triple ball court; another, larger version in the same design stands just south of Templo I.

TIKAL & FLORES, GUATEMALA

EL MUNDO PERDIDO

About 0.25 miles (400m) southwest of the Gran Plaza is **El Mundo Perdido** (The Lost World), a complex of 38 structures surrounding a huge pyramid. Unlike the rest of Tikal, where late-Classic construction overlays earlier work, El Mundo Perdido holds buildings of many different periods. The large pyramid is thought to be Preclassic with some later repairs and renovations, the Templo del Talud-Tablero (Temple of the Three Rooms) is an early-Classic structure, and the Templo de las Calaveras (Temple of the Skulls) is late Classic.

The pyramid, 105ft (32m) high and 262ft (80m) along its base, had huge masks that flanked each stairway but no temple structure at the top. Each side displays a slightly different architectural style. Tunnels dug by archaeologists reveal four similar pyramids beneath the outer face; the earliest (Structure 5C-54 Sub 2B) dates from 700 BC, making the pyramid the oldest Maya structure in Tikal.

TEMPLO IV & COMPLEJO N

Standing at 210ft (64m), **Templo IV** is the highest building at Tikal. It was completed by about 741, in the reign of King Moon Double Comb's son. From the base it looks like a precipitous little hill. A series of steep wooden steps and ladders takes you to the top for a panoramic view across the jungle canopy. If you stay up here for the sunset, climb down immediately, as it gets dark quickly.

Complejo N (Complex N), near Templo IV, is an example of the 'twin-temple' complexes popular in the late Classic Period. These complexes are thought to have commemorated the completion of a *katun* (20-year cycle) in the Maya calendar. This one was built in 711 by King Moon Double Comb to mark the 14th *katun* of Baktun 9. (A *baktun* – ie 144,000 days, about 394 years – consisted of 20 *katun*.) The king is portrayed on Stela 16, one of Tikal's finest.

TEMPLO VI (TEMPLO DE LAS INSCRIPCIONES)

Tikal sports relatively few inscriptions. The exception is **Templo VI**, 0.75 miles (1.2km) southeast of the Gran Plaza. On the rear of the 39ft-high roof comb is a long inscription; the sides and cornice of the roof comb bear glyphs as well. The inscriptions give the date 766.

MUSEUMS

Museo Lítico (admission US$1.50; ☉ 9am-noon & 1-4:30pm), located at the visitors center, houses a number of stelae and carved stones excavated from the ruins. Photographs of the jungle-covered temples in various stages of discovery in the late 19th century are intriguing.

Museo Tikal (free with ticket from Museo Lítico; ☉ 9am-5pm Mon-Fri, 9am-4pm Sat & Sun) has some fascinating exhibits, including burial goods of King Moon Double Comb (see p211).

Tours

Day tours to Tikal from Santa Elena and Flores cost between US$45 and US$60 per person. Contact Martsam Travel (p216) for more information.

Sleeping & Eating

The three hotels at Tikal are often booked in advance by groups, but staying here allows you to savor the dawn and dusk, when most of the jungle fauna is active. Do book, especially in July and August, and between Christmas and Easter. Arrive by early afternoon in case of any difficulties, such as overbooking. The easiest option is to take an all-inclusive tour; ask travel agents for one with lodging at the site. The hotels and campsites all depend on generators for electricity and hot water; they have set hours for both.

By the entrance road an **official campsite** (tent space per person US$4; tents for rent US$7) is set in a large, open lawn with some shady trees. You can hang your hammock under a *palapa* (thatched-roof shelter) here, too.

Jungle Lodge (Guatemala City ☎ 2477-0754, 2477-0570; www.junglelodge.guate.com; s/d with private bathroom US$69/86, breakfast US$6, lunch & dinner US$12; Ⓟ Ⓡ) Built to house the archaeologists excavating and restoring Tikal, this is the largest and most attractive of the hotels. The agreeable rooms in modern duplex bungalows come with two double beds; the older section was being renovated at the time of research. Amenities include large gardens, a restaurant-bar and a pool with milky-colored water. Bookings for the Jungle Lodge can also be made at **Hotel Isla de Flores** (☎ 7926-0614; ☉ 7am-4pm Mon-Fri) in Flores.

Tikal Inn (☎ 7926-1917, 7926-0065; hoteltikalinn @itelgua.com; s/d with private bathroom & fan US$50/75, incl breakfast & dinner US$73/100, breakfast & lunch items US$2-4, dinner mains US$7.50; P ⛽) This is the second-most attractive place to stay at Tikal. It has rooms in the main building, as well as slightly better thatched-roof bungalows, plus gardens and a characterless restaurant. The accommodations are simple but clean and quite large, and have hot water. The pool could be cleaner.

Jaguar Inn (☎ 7926-0002; www.jaguartikal.com; camping US$3.50, hammock, locker & net US$5.50, s/d with private bathroom & fan US$33/53, lunch & dinner mains US$8-9; P ⛽) Jaguar Inn has the feel of a travelers' place. You can camp on a small site or rent a bungalow room. The spacious restaurant with outdoor tables serves up good meals from a long menu. It also serves wine. Internet is available for US$5 per hour.

As you arrive at Tikal, you'll see the little **comedores** (⛽ breakfast, lunch & dinner) on the right-hand side of the road. Comedor Tikal seems to be the most popular. These places offer rustic and agreeable surroundings and huge plates of fairly tasty food. Chicken or meat dishes cost around US$5, pasta and burgers are cheaper, and a fruit platter is US$3.50. At the **Restaurante Café Tikal** (visitors center; mains US$6.50-12) you can dine on fancier food to the hum of the generator.

Picnic tables beneath shelters are located just off Tikal's Gran Plaza, with soft-drink and water peddlers standing by. If you want to spend all day at the ruins, carry food and water with you.

Getting There & Away

For details of transportation to Tikal and Flores from the Belize border, see p168. For Tikal or El Remate, get off at Puente Ixlú (El Cruce) and switch to northbound transportation for the remaining 22 miles (36km) to Tikal and 1.2 miles (2km) to El Remate. There is little northbound traffic after lunch.

Heading from Tikal to Belize, start early in the morning and get off at Puente Ixlú to catch a bus or minibus eastward. Shuttles to Belize advertised at Tikal may detour to Flores to pick up passengers. The Jungle Lodge (opposite) has a bus going to the Belize border at 5am (US$25).

From Flores and Santa Elena, **San Juan Travel** (☎ 7926-0042, 7926-2146; 2a Calle, Santa Elena

& Calle Sur, Flores) operates shuttle minibuses to Tikal (US$5 roundtrip, 1¼ hours each way), picking up passengers in front of their hotels (at 5am, 6am, 7am, 8am, 9am, 10am and 2pm). Any hotel or travel agent can arrange this.

Return minibuses to Flores and Santa Elena depart Tikal at 12:30pm, 2pm, 3pm, 4pm, 5pm and 6pm. If you're staying the night at Tikal, it's best to reserve your seat for the return bus journey from Tikal to Flores/Santa Elena. Buses are heavily used and you may not get a seat if you don't reserve. Failing that, get to the bus stop at Tikal half an hour before departure. Outside the normal timetable, you can rent a whole minibus for US$40. A taxi from Flores airport to Tikal also costs US$40.

YAXHÁ

A beautiful and quite large Classic Maya **ceremonial site** (admission free during restoration; ⛽ 7am-5pm), Yaxhá is 6.8 miles (11km) north of the Puente Ixlú–Melchor de Mencos road, from a turnoff around 20 miles (32km) from Puente Ixlú and 20.5 miles (33km) from Melchor de Mencos. The access road is unpaved.

Yaxhá's setting, on a hill overlooking two sizable lakes, Laguna Yaxhá and Laguna Sacnab, makes it particularly worth visiting, but don't swim in the lakes – there are crocodiles!

It takes about 1½ hours to look around the main groups of ruins, which are gradually being cleared and restored. The high point (literally), towering above all else, is **Templo 216** in the Acrópolis Este (Eastern Acropolis), which affords magnificent views in every direction. On an island near the far (south) shore of Laguna Yaxhá is a separate, late-Postclassic archaeological site, called Topoxté, whose dense covering of ruined temples and dwellings may date back to the Itzá culture that occupied Flores island when the Spanish came.

Campamento Ecológico El Sombrero (☎ 5800-0179; sombrero@guate.net; s/d US$18/29, with private bathroom US$29/46; P) is on the southern shore of the pristine lake, 273yd (250m) off the approach road. It is an excellent place to stay, and has good-sized, neat and clean rooms in mosquito-netted bungalows. There's also a fine restaurant here. *Lancha* (motor boat) tours to Topoxté are offered

(US$20 for one to three people), as well as horseback riding.

Agencies in Flores and El Remate offer organized trips to Yaxhá (US$30 to US$60). **Café Arqueológico Yax-há** (☎ 7926-3289; caféyax_ha @yahoo.com; Av Santa Ana, Flores; per person US$30) specializes in these trips.

FLORES & SANTA ELENA

Because it's the main service center near Tikal, many travelers visit Flores (population 2000) as part of a trip to Tikal. Imbibing the ambience in this Guatemalan departmental capital is worth an extra day or two. It's dignified and tranquil, with red-roofed houses and cool lake breezes. Flores is more expensive than its twin town Santa Elena (population 25,000), a rumpled place of dusty streets, with a hot, chaotic market and a main street strung with bus depots, banks and some hotels and restaurants.

History

Flores was founded on a *petén* (island) by a Maya people named the Itzáes, sometime between 1200 and 1500, after their expulsion from Chichén Itzá on the Yucatán Peninsula. They named the place Tayasal. Hernán Cortés peaceably dropped in on King Canek of Tayasal in 1524. Only in March 1697 did the Spaniards finally bring Tayasal forcibly under their control.

Orientation & Information

A 1600ft (500m) causeway connects Flores to Santa Elena. The airport is located 1.2 miles (2km) east of the causeway. Arriving long-distance buses drop passengers on or just off Santa Elena's main drag, 4a Calle.

There's a bank on the main plaza in Flores but for ATMs you will need to go to Santa Elena's 4a Calle.

Banco Banrural Flores (Flores Plaza; ☽ 8:30am-5pm Mon-Fri)

Banco G&T Continental Santa Elena (4a Calle, Santa Elena; ☽ 9am-7pm Mon-Fri, 9am-1pm Sat) Has a Visa ATM.

Banco Industrial Santa Elena (4a Calle, Santa Elena; ☽ 9am-4pm Mon-Fri, 10am-2pm Sat) Has a Visa ATM.

Inguat Tourist Office Flores (☎ 7926-0669; Parque Central, Flores; ☽ 8am-4:30pm, Mon-Fri, 8am-noon & 1-4:30pm Sat) Has helpful tourist information.

Martsam Travel Flores (☎ 7926-0346; www.martsam .com; Calle Centroamérica, Flores) Offers domestic and international telephone and fax services and a full range of tours; it also books buses and flights.

Tikal Net Flores (Calle Centroamérica, Flores; ☽ 8am-10pm Mon-Sat, 9am-9pm Sun; Internet per hr US$1.40); Santa Elena (4a Calle, Santa Elena; ☽ 8am-8pm Mon-Sat, 9am-5pm Sun; Internet per hr US$1.60) Also offers domestic and international phone calls.

Sleeping
FLORES
Flores offers plenty of choice.

Hotel La Casona de la Isla (☎ 7926-0593; www .hotelesdepeten.com; Calle 30 de Junio; s/d/t US$37/43/56; 🅿 💻 🐾) This romantic place has a pool with a waterfall and an open-air restaurant-bar overlooking the west side of Lago de Petén Itzá. The decor is pretty, with tones of blue and orange, and cane furniture. Rooms have all mod-cons; some have lake views.

Hotel Isla de Flores (☎ 7926-0614; www.jungle lodge.guate.com; Av La Reforma; s/d US$40/46; 🐾) In the same class as La Casona, but a street back from the lake and without a pool, this is an attractive choice. The large, well-equipped rooms have a bathroom with tub. Many rooms have balconies with lake views.

Hotel Casazul (☎ 7926-1138; www.hotelesdepeten .com; Calle Unión; s/d/tr US$33/35/45; 🐾) On the north shore, Casazul (Blue House) is a comfortable, quiet place. It takes the blue theme seriously, from the brightly painted exterior to the bed covers, as well as staff uniforms. Each room is unique, spotless and well-appointed; most have a balcony.

Hotel La Mesa de los Mayas (☎ /fax 7926-1240; mesamayas@hotmail.com; Av La Reforma; s/d US$15/25/ 35, with air-con US$20/30/40; 🐾) This place on three levels is welcoming, secure and good value. The clean, well-kept rooms have faded cerise walls, colorful (but scratchy) bedspreads, bathrooms with hot water, and TVs.

Hospedaje Doña Goya (☎ 7926-3538; Calle Unión; dm US$3.50, d with shared/private bathroom US$11/13.50, breakfast US$2-3.30) A popular, family-run guesthouse with a couple of dormitories, this place is often full. The beds are comfortable, the water's hot and there's a roof terrace with a palm-thatched shelter from which to enjoy lake views. There's a safe for valuables, too.

Youth Hostel Los Amigos (☎ 5584-8795, 5716-7702; mcdehoogh@hotmail.com; Calle Central; hammock/dm US$2.75/3.50, d with shared bathroom US$8) Head to this fun place, which is run by a Dutch/Flores couple, if you're on a tight budget or if you want information. Accommodations are packed onto a long narrow property. The restaurant and barbecue are in the garden.

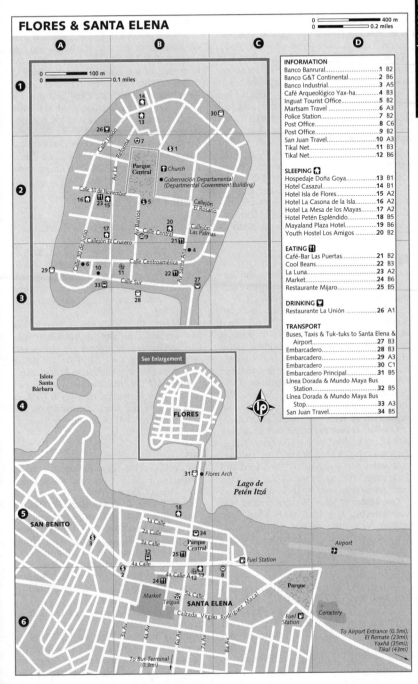

FLORES & SANTA ELENA

0 — 400 m
0 — 0.2 miles

INFORMATION
Banco Banrural..........................1 B2
Banco G&T Continental.............2 B6
Banco Industrial........................3 A5
Café Arqueológico Yax-ha.........4 B3
Inguat Tourist Office.................5 B2
Martsam Travel 6 A3
Police Station............................7 B2
Post Office.................................8 C6
Post Office.................................9 B2
San Juan Travel.......................10 A3
Tikal Net.................................11 B3
Tikal Net.................................12 B6

SLEEPING
Hospedaje Doña Goya..............13 B1
Hotel Casazul..........................14 B1
Hotel Isla de Flores..................15 A2
Hotel La Casona de la Isla........16 A2
Hotel La Mesa de los Mayas.....17 A2
Hotel Petén Espléndido.............18 B5
Mayaland Plaza Hotel...............19 B6
Youth Hostel Los Amigos 20 B2

EATING
Café-Bar Las Puertas................21 B2
Cool Beans..............................22 B3
La Luna....................................23 A2
Market.....................................24 B6
Restaurante Mijaro...................25 B5

DRINKING
Restaurante La Unión 26 A1

TRANSPORT
Buses, Taxis & Tuk-tuks to Santa Elena &
   Airport................................27 B3
Embarcadero............................28 B3
Embarcadero............................29 A3
Embarcadero............................30 C1
Embarcadero Principal..............31 B5
Línea Dorada & Mundo Maya Bus
   Station................................32 B5
Línea Dorada & Mundo Maya Bus
   Stop....................................33 A3
San Juan Travel.......................34 B5

SANTA ELENA

Hotel Petén Espléndido (☎ 7926-0880; www.peten esplendido.com; 1a Calle 5-01; s/d US$98/110; ℗ ⊠ 🖳 🕿) This glitzy waterside fun palace may have the only elevator in El Petén. Its amenities include a lakeside pool, a poolside bar and a restaurant. The spotless rooms have cable TV, safe, phone, computer jacks and little balconies, and are wheelchair accessible. Staff sport garish tropical shirts.

Mayaland Plaza Hotel (☎ 7926-4976; mayaland plaza@yahoo.com; 4a Calle; s/d/tr US$35/49/63; ℗ ⊠ 🖳 🕿) This is a terrific option. It's brand new, with clean lines and stylish decor. There is a travel agent out the front, a peaceful courtyard restaurant with delicious food, and a pool out the back. The spacious, comfortable rooms are set colonial-style around the courtyard.

Eating

Most restaurants keep long hours and prepare international foods. Local game animals do appear on some menus.

La Luna (☎ 7926-3346; cnr Calle 30 de Junio & Calle 10 de Noviembre, Flores; mains US$4-14; 🕑 lunch & dinner Mon-Sat) In a class by itself, this very popular restaurant cultivates an arty tropical ambience, with potted palms, carved wooden-framed mirrors, a decorated tree and other funky details. The food is continental and delectable, with innovative chicken, fish and beef dishes and flavorsome pasta and vegetarian options – the falafel is terrific.

Café-Bar Las Puertas (☎ 7926-1061; cnr Calle Central & Av Santa Ana, Flores; breakfast US$2-3, mains US$8-10; 🕑 breakfast, lunch & dinner Mon-Sat) This fashionable restaurant and bar has good food and great coffee. It's an arty sort of place with the walls painted Jackson Pollock–style.

Cool Beans (☎ 5690-6355; coffees, breakfast items & sandwiches US$2-3; 🕑 6am-8pm) On a little lane leading from the local bus stop in Flores, this low-key, friendly café serves full breakfasts, excellent coffee and snacks, and sells homemade bread, muffins and cinnamon rolls.

Restaurante Mijaro (☎ 7926-1615; 6a Av, Santa Elena; breakfast US$1.60-2.70, mains US$3.30-6; 🕑 7am-10pm) Cool off at this friendly *comedor* on the main street up from the causeway. It has fans inside and in its little thatched-roof garden area. It does long *limonadas* (a drink made from lime juice) and snacks as well as weightier food.

Drinking

Flores doesn't exactly jive at night, but start off with sunset drinks at the hotels and restaurants that have terraces, located on the west side of the island. Head for **Hotel La Casona de la Isla** (☎ 7926-0593; Calle 30 de Junio) or **Restaurante La Unión** (Calle Unión) and down a *Cuba libre* (rum and coke; US$1.30). Later on, restaurants such as **La Luna** (☎ 7926-3346; cnr Calle 30 de Junio & Calle 10 de Noviembre) and **Café-Bar Las Puertas** (☎ 7926-1061; cnr Calle Central & Av Santa Ana) are places suitable for just a drink. Café-Bar Las Puertas has live music some nights (mainly weekends).

Getting There & Away

AIR

International departure tax at Flores airport (FRS) is US$30.

Two Belizean airlines, **Tropic Air** (☎ 7926-0348; www.tropicair.com) and **Maya Island Air** (☎ 7926-3386; www.mayaairways.com), fly twice a day each between Belize City and Flores airport (one hour), both charging one-way/roundtrip US$98/193.

Tikal Jets (☎ 7926-0386; www.tikaljets.com) flies Monday and Thursday between Guatemala City and Belize City, stopping in Flores, and returning on the same day. Flores to Belize City costs one-way/roundtrip US$95/126.

Grupo TACA (www.taca.com) flies from Guatemala City to Flores and then on to Cancún four days of the week, returning on the same day (Flores–Cancún one-way/roundtrip US$253/349).

BUS

For details on bus services from the Belize border, see p168. For information on buses from Belize City, see p88.

Línea Dorada & Mundo Maya Bus Station (☎ 7926-0070/1741; 4a Calle) is in Santa Elena and there is also a bus stop on Calle Sur. Many long-distance buses and minivans leave from the new bus terminal in the south of Santa Elena, though some pass through Santa Elena's crowded market area. Buses of **San Juan Travel** (☎ 7926-0041/2, 7926-2146) leave from its office on 2a Calle, Santa Elena.

Buses from Flores and Santa Elena go to the following places:

Belize City Línea Dorada & Mundo Maya (US$15-16, 6am & 10pm); San Juan Travel (US$20, 5am & 7:30am) The 220km trip takes between four and five hours. Buses connect with boats to Caye Caulker and Ambergris Caye. It's cheaper but slower to take local buses from Flores to the border and go on from there.

Chetumal, Mexico Línea Dorada & Mundo Maya (US$23, 6am); San Juan Travel (US$25, 5am) The 350km trip takes seven to eight hours.

El Remate Bus Station (US$2, minibuses half-hourly 8am-5pm) The 29km trip takes 40 minutes. Alternatively, buses and minibuses to/from Melchor de Mencos will drop you at Puente Ixlú junction, 2km south of El Remate.

Melchor de Mencos, Belize border Bus Station (US$2.70, minibuses half-hourly 5am-6pm, four buses daily at 5am, 11am, 2pm & 4pm, three minivans daily at 9am, noon & 5pm) The 100km trip takes two hours.

Tikal See p215.

Getting Around

Flores, Santa Elena and the airport are connected by buses, taxis and *tuk-tuks* (open-air, three-wheeler vans). From the Flores end of the causeway, buses and *tuk-tuks* to Santa Elena cost US$0.20 and US$0.70, respectively; buses and taxis to the airport cost US$0.20 and US$2.70, respectively.

You can take a boat ride (one hour, US$14) in a *lancha* from one of several *embarcaderos* (piers) on Flores. The main *embarcadero (embarcadero principal)* is half-way across the causeway.

Rental-car companies are in the arrivals hall at the airport. A basic car with unlimited *kilometraje* (distance allowance) costs a minimum of US$47 per day. Fill your fuel tank in Santa Elena; no fuel is available at Tikal.

EL REMATE

A quiet alternative to Flores is the small lakeshore village of El Remate, which is 22 miles (35km) northeast of Santa Elena on the Tikal road. Here, you can arrange transportation to Tikal and rent bicycles, canoes, kayaks and horses.

Located around 1.8 miles (3km) west of El Remate is the **Biotopo Cerro Cahuí** (admission US$2.75; 7am-4pm), which protects 2.5 sq miles (4 sq km) of subtropical forest. Among the animals within the reserve are spider and howler monkeys, ocelots, white-tailed deer, raccoons, armadillos, turtles, snakes and Morelet's crocodiles. Depending upon the season and migration patterns, you may see kingfishers, ducks, herons, hawks, parrots, toucans, woodpeckers and the ocellated (or Petén) turkey, which resembles a peacock. The reserve has a series of trails. A guided walk costs US$6.75.

Sleeping & Eating

Several accommodations are strung along the main road and along the road around the lake's north side.

La Casa de Don David (7928-8469, 5306-2190; www.lacasadedondavid.com; s/d US$23/32, with verandah & hammock US$27/40, with air-con US$32/52, breakfast US$2-4, lunch & dinner US$4-8; restaurant 6:30am-9pm; P X X) Located just 50m along the north-shore road from the main road, this inviting place is American/Guatemalan-operated. The clean, simple rooms have hot water and overlook large tidy gardens that stretch toward the lake. The restaurant serves reliable meals and has a rack of good local-interest reading material.

Hotel La Mansión del Pájaro Serpiente (5702-9434; s/d US$23/40/50, d & tr with cable TV & air-con US$60, ste US$75; X X) On the main road coming from the south, this friendly American/Guatemalan establishment has the loveliest accommodations in El Remate village. The bungalows are dotted about beautiful hillside gardens and all have lake views, colorful textiles, tiled floors, fans, netted windows, sitting rooms and hot-water bathrooms. There's a gorgeous pool and a reasonably priced restaurant-bar.

La Lancha (7928-8331; www.blancaneaux.com; Aldea Jobompiche, San José; s/d casitas with lake views US$146/226, with rainforest views US$84/146; P X) About 13km west of El Remate, Francis Ford Coppola has created beautiful rustic accommodations overlooking the lake, and there are more tucked in the rainforest. The lake-view rooms are bigger and combine Balinese and Guatemalan furnishings. All room prices include breakfast.

Las Orquideas (pastas US$5-8, fish & pizzas US$7-11) On the north-shore road, Las Orquideas has a genial Italian owner-chef cooking up genuine Italian fare. Bottles of wine can be purchased (US$11).

Getting There & Away

Any bus or minibus going north from Santa Elena to Tikal can drop you at El Remate. For direct buses, see opposite. Buses between Flores and Melchor de Mencos stop at Puente Ixlú. A taxi from Puente Ixlú to El Remate is US$1.30. Taxis from Flores airport to El Remate cost around US$20. Once you're in El Remate, you can hail any passing bus or minibus on the Flores–Tikal road, but traffic is light after midmorning.

Directory

CONTENTS

ACCOMMODATIONS

Accommodations in Belize range from tents to palm-roofed shacks to guesthouses to luxury seaside resorts and jungle lodges on acres of lush grounds. Even many of the most luxurious places maintain a casual, relaxed atmosphere and a rustic style with (albeit very elegant) wood-and-thatch cabanas.

Belize is more costly than other Central American destinations, so the budget bracket in this book goes up to US$45 for a typical double (two-person) room. Within this range the best value is usually provided by small, often family-run guesthouses. These places will be well looked after and you'll usually get friendly attention. Only at the cheapest budget places will you be sharing bathrooms or showering with cold water. A few places provide dorm accommodations.

PRACTICALITIES

- The electrical current in Belize is 110V, 60Hz, with plugs of two flat prongs, the same as in the USA and Canada.

- Belize uses mainly non-metric measurements, with distances nearly always measured in miles, gasoline sold by the (US) gallon, and laundry weighed by the pound. Occasionally a metric measurement might pop up – most likely kilometers on the odometers of some rental cars.

- Prerecorded videos sold here normally use the NTSC image registration system, which is incompatible with the PAL and Secam systems.

Budget and lower midrange travelers will find the website Toucan Trail (www.toucan trail.com) useful. Put together by the Belize Tourism Board, this site details over 160 accommodations that have rooms for US$60 or less.

Midrange prices range from US$45 to US$120 for a typical double room. This spectrum embraces many hotels, the better and more comfortable guesthouses and most of the smaller-scale lodges and resorts. Many places in this range have their own restaurants and bars, and offer, or will arrange for you, a variety of activities, tours and other services. Within this range you'll encounter quite a variety in terms of luxuriousness and facilities, but all places will be comfortable and provide decent service.

Above US$120 you move into the top-end bracket, where accommodations start to get seriously luxurious (the fanciest rooms run over US$300 – and that's without thinking about suites, cottages and other costlier options). These are resorts, lodges and classy hotels with large, well-appointed rooms and plenty of other facilities, from restaurants and bars to private beaches, spas, pools, horse stables, dive shops and walking trails. Many have unique styles and atmospheres created with the help of architecture, decor, location and layout.

Peak tourist seasons in Belize are the couple of weeks each side of Christmas and Easter. Some accommodations get fully booked at these times, especially around Christmas and New Year's. The period between New Year's and Easter is fairly busy, too. Many establishments, especially in the top end and upper midrange, have high- and low-season prices: high is typically from December to May. Some also have 'extra' seasons (ie extra-high prices) that cover the Christmas–New Year's and Easter periods.

Prices in this book are high-season prices and include hotel room tax, which went up from 7% to 9% in 2005, and any service charges that are obligatorily included in your bill (some top-end places automatically add on 10% for service).

Cabanas & Cabins

These two terms are pretty well interchangeable and can refer to any kind of free-standing, individual accommodation structure. You'll find cabanas/cabins in every class of accommodations: they can be made of wood, concrete or brick and be roofed with palm thatch, tin or tiles. They may be small, bare and cheap or they may be super-luxurious and stylish, with Balinese screens, Japanese bathrooms and Thai wall-hangings. They may be beachside, riverside, surrounded by jungle or on the grounds of a hotel along with other types of accommodations.

Camping

Belize does not have many dedicated campsites, but there are a few (mainly budget) accommodations that provide camping space on their grounds, and just a few of those have gear for rent.

Guesthouses

Many budget accommodations, and some in the midrange, are guesthouses – places with just a few rooms and usually fairly personal attention from your hosts. Many of these are friendly and pleasant places to stay. Most are plain and simple, but well kept and quite comfortable, and the rooms will usually have a private bathroom with hot water. You'll find guesthouses in towns or on the coast or cayes. Some guesthouses provide breakfast and a few of these call themselves B&Bs.

Located in the southern Toledo District, the Toledo Ecotourism Association (p206) runs an excellent village guesthouse program that enables travelers to stay in the area's Maya villages.

Hotels

A hotel is, more or less, any accommodation that doesn't give itself another name. A hotel might sit on a gorgeous beach and have lovely rooms, a great restaurant and its own pool, or it may be a more functional town place. Hotels generally don't offer a vast range of tours and activities to their guests, but every generalization has its exceptions. Some smaller hotels call themselves inns.

Lodges & Resorts

In Belize the term 'lodge' usually means a pretty comfortable hotel in a fairly remote location, be it in the Cayo jungles or the offshore cayes. Most lodges focus on activities such as diving, fishing, horseback riding, or jungle or river adventures, aiming to provide comfortable accommodations and good meals to sustain their guests between outings. Many lodges have gorgeous island, beach or forest settings, and they tend to be on the expensive side due mainly to their high standards, wide range of amenities and often their remote locations.

Resorts have a great deal in common with lodges – again they tend to be among the more expensive options and can be found both inland and by the sea. If there is any real distinction, it's that the emphasis in resorts tends to be marginally less on activities and slightly more on relaxation and fun.

Rental Accommodations

In main tourist destinations such as San Pedro, Caye Caulker and Placencia, there are houses and apartments for rent by the week, month or even for periods as short as three days. If you plan a long stay you'll certainly cut costs by renting your own place. Try to plan ahead: these places can get booked up.

BUSINESS HOURS

Shops typically open from 9am to 5pm Monday to Saturday, often with a one-hour closure for lunch from noon to 1pm.

DIRECTORY

Businesses dealing with the public, such as travel agencies and airline offices, have similar hours but are likely to be closed on Saturday afternoon. Banks have varied hours but most are open from 8am to 2pm or 3pm Monday to Thursday, and till 4pm or 4:30pm on Friday. A few also open from 8am or 9am to noon on Saturday.

For typical restaurant hours, see p226. Opening hours of bars are very diverse. Some open from about noon to midnight, others just for a few evening hours, and others from early morning to early evening.

CHILDREN

Children are highly regarded in Belize and can often break down barriers and open doors to local hospitality. Most hotels, lodges and resorts are child-friendly. Some of the more expensive places allow children to stay free, or at a big discount, and also offer discounts on meals. Additionally, there are plenty of self-catering accommodations that can help to keep down the cost of a family holiday. These self-catering options are referred to as condos, suites, villas or casitas; they're available for short-term rentals and all provide pretty much the same thing, the main distinction between them being whether they have one or two bedrooms.

Belize has some special ingredients for a family holiday. You won't have to think too hard about entertaining your kids. Most of the attractions in the country – sea life, exploring caves and ruins, watching for birds, wildlife and bugs – are as delightful for kids as they are for grown-ups, and most activities are set up to accommodate children (see p24).

A few places even have holidays set up for families, for example, the **Oceanic Society** (www.oceanic-society.org) has a family education program to help families get to know atoll ecosystems, such as Turneffe Atoll (p126), while **International Zoological Expeditions** (www.ize2belize.com) does eco-adventure and study packages for families, which combine South Water Caye (p184) and Blue Creek (p207).

You'll find plenty of traveling families all over the country, especially during North American school breaks. Most do the rounds of the wildlife sanctuaries and major ruins, spend a little time on the cayes or in Placencia, and visit a jungle lodge. These cayes are safe enough to let your children loose on. Ambergris Caye and Caye Caulker are good spots for teenagers as there's a bit of town life to distract as well as the outdoors stuff. Adolescents like to hang out a bit, check out the shops and meet other kids. English is spoken so there's no language barrier to mixing with local kids. Your children will probably experience a touch of culture shock, but they'll soon adapt to Belize's captivating ways.

Local bus journeys will amuse if they're not too long. Bus drivers in Belize often play their favorite music, and reggae and Latin rhythms can make even a tedious journey quite enjoyable. Teenagers whose minds are open to music will get into the variety of music they hear in Belize. It's great fun.

Food is no problem in Belize (see p69).

Traveling with toddlers and young children can be challenging. You need to be organized. Be cautious concerning insect bites, sunburn, and, of course, water and sanitation. If you're staying in good accommodations and not moving around too much, you should have no major difficulties. For tried and tested general advice, check out Lonely Planet's *Travel with Children* by Cathy Lanigan and Maureen Wheeler.

CLIMATE CHARTS

Belize is typically hot and humid day and night for most of the year. Temperatures vary by only about 4°C between the coolest part of the year (December to March) and the hottest (May to September). The daily temperature range is around 10°C from the hottest part of the day to the coolest part of the night. In the uplands (Mountain Pine Ridge and the Maya Mountains) you can expect temperatures to fall by about 3°C for every 1000ft rise in altitude, making things noticeably more comfortable.

Belize has distinct wet and dry seasons. The wet season runs from mid-May to November in the south and from mid-June to November in the north. November to February is a transitional period, with the year's coolest temperatures and a limited amount of rain. The true dry season is February to April. There's quite a large difference in rainfall between the north of the country (around 1500mm or 60in a year)

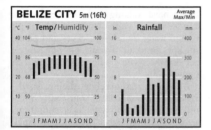

BELIZE CITY 5m (16ft)

and the south (about 4000mm or 160in). In the north and center of the country there's a dip in rainfall in August, between peaks in July and September.

For advice on the best seasons to visit Belize, see p17.

Hurricanes

While hurricane season officially lasts from June to November, Belize has traditionally been struck by its most damaging hurricanes in September and November. The worst hurricanes of the 20th century happened in 1931 (before hurricanes were named) and 1961 (Hurricane Hattie). In 2001, Hurricane Iris, with winds over 150mph, brought severe damage to Placencia, Monkey River and the Maya villages around Toledo, continuing the 'year ending in 1' bogey.

If you are in Belize when a hurricane threatens, the best advice is to head inland. There is usually plenty of warning as hurricanes are well reported as they make their way across the Caribbean. If it is not possible to get inland, you should shelter in the sturdiest concrete building you can find, as far as possible from the coast and away from windows. Most villages and towns now have official hurricane shelters.

Hurricanes are ranked from category 1 (with winds of at least 74mph) to category 5 (winds exceeding 155mph). A category 3 hurricane will blow down wooden houses and take the tin roofs off concrete houses, and the rains and floods that hurricanes bring can do as much damage as the winds. The **Belize National Meteorological Service** (www.hydromet.gov.bz) provides copious information on weather.

CUSTOMS

Duty-free allowances on entering Belize are 1L of wine or spirits and 200 cigarettes or 250g of tobacco or 50 cigars. It is illegal to take firearms or ammunition into or out of Belize, and it is illegal to leave the country with fish (unless you have obtained a free export permit from the Fisheries Department), ancient Maya artifacts, turtle shells and unprocessed coral.

DANGERS & ANNOYANCES

On the whole Belize is a pretty safe country. It certainly feels markedly safer than neighboring Guatemala, but there are a couple of areas where you need to take care. Occasional incidents of armed robbery and rape of tourists happen in regularly visited but isolated spots, mostly in the west not far from the Guatemalan border. In late 2004 and early 2005 there was a flurry of armed robberies here against people canoeing without guides on the Macal River (see p160). Some victims were forced to remove clothing but no sexual assaults were reported.

About the same time there were a couple of armed holdups of cars on the Hummingbird Hwy and of village buses traveling on country roads in the west of Belize. The perpetrators of these crimes are often reportedly Guatemalans or Hondurans.

Such incidents are very much the exception rather than the rule – the vast majority of visitors to Belize have trouble-free trips – and it's impossible to tell where the next incident will crop up. What you should do is keep your ear to the ground, talk to other travelers and locals, check bulletin boards such as **Belize Forums** (www.belizeforum.com) and look at the travel advisories issued by your own and other governments (see p224). A few foreign embassies in Belize maintain websites with useful information (see p225).

The other main trouble spot is Belize City, where some tourists fall victim to muggers and hustlers. You can greatly reduce this risk by a few straightforward steps (see p75).

To avoid becoming a victim of petty theft, take normal travelers' precautions:

- Don't make a big display of obvious signs of wealth (such as an expensive camera, computer equipment or jewelry).
- Don't flash thick wallets or wads of cash.
- Don't leave valuables lying around your room or in a car, especially in plain view.
- Keep an eye on your bags when you're traveling by bus.

DIRECTORY

DIRECTORY

Travelers can also help themselves by not getting involved with drugs. Signs bearing the northern cayes' celebrated catchphrase 'No Shirt, No Shoes – No Problem' have recently had a new line added, to read 'No Shirt, No Shoes, No Drugs – No Problem,' and police are enforcing this policy with fines and even jailings. Possessing just a small amount of marijuana, however, is unlikely to get you into trouble – the country's police commissioner announced in 2004 that people would not be prosecuted for possessing small amounts. (It is still officially illegal, however.)

Getting off your head on drugs or alcohol means your guard slips, you become less aware of your surroundings and people around you, and you make yourself more vulnerable.

Take care who you drink and eat with – we have heard of cases of mind-altering drugs such as scopolamine (which turns its victims temporarily into compliant zombies who will do virtually anything they are told) being slipped into travelers' drinks or food in Belize.

Belize's jungles can be dangerous places. As obvious as this may sound, it's easy to forget in one's enthusiasm for exploring the tropical environment. Apart from the possibility of getting lost, the country has its share of venomous snakes (see p49) and other possibly dangerous wildlife and some poisonous plants. Some parks, reserves and lodges have walking trails where you can wander off on your own (preferably with a map, water, hat, long sleeves and pants, bug spray and all of your common sense), but elsewhere you are better off going with a guide.

At sea, start snorkeling, diving, kayaking or sailing well within your ability limits and get acquainted with local conditions before taking on bigger challenges. See p60 for specific safety hints.

Belize has a system of licensed guides, whose licenses are granted by the Belize Tourism Board only after they have gained certain competencies in safety, first aid as well as other aspects of guiding, and it's worth making sure that your guide is a licensed one.

Belizeans on the whole are remarkably easygoing and travelers experience little hustle. Local men can be very direct about making advances to women, and ganja peddlers in seaside tourist spots can sometimes be a little over-persistent, but such people will take no for an answer.

Nationwide emergency numbers for the police are ☎ 90 and ☎ 911.

Belizean police are not always as cooperative as you might hope if you do want to report a crime of which you have been a victim. They may try to discourage you with, for example, stories of how long you'll have to stay in the country to see a matter resolved. If you want to report a crime, be persistent and if necessary seek help from locals (eg your hotel) or from your embassy or consulate.

DISABLED TRAVELERS

Belize lacks accessibility regulations and many buildings are on stilts or have uneven wooden steps. You won't see many ramps for wheelchair access. More difficulties for wheelchair users come from the lack of footpaths, as well as plentiful rough and sandy ground. Bus travel, with assistance, is feasible; small planes and water taxis might be a problem though. Visitors with limited mobility do come to Belize. Places to stay that are suitable for wheelchair users include the Radisson Fort George Hotel (p83), the Sun Breeze Beach Hotel (p110) on Ambergris Caye, Mama Noots Jungle Resort (p186) near Dangriga, and the little Hok'ol K'in Guest House (p142) in Corozal.

There are a number of useful organizations and websites for disabled travelers, though there's little information that is specific to Belize.

Access-Able Travel Source (www.access-able.com) Has good general information.

Allgohere Airline Directory (www.everybody.co.uk/airindex.htm) This site lists, by airline, services available to disabled passengers.

Global Access Disabled Travel Network (www.geocities.com/Paris/1502/index.html) Good website with interesting general travel information.

Mobility International (www.miusa.org) US-based website that advises disabled travelers on mobility issues; you can organize a mentor and someone to help you plan your travels.

Royal Association for Disability and Rehabilitation (Radar; www.radar.org.uk) Gives information on scuba diving for people with disabilities.

EMBASSIES & CONSULATES
Belizean Embassies & Consulates

Belize has limited diplomatic representation in other countries. The honorary consulates mentioned below can usually issue visas, but they may refer more complicated matters elsewhere. For full listings of Belizean embassies and consulates, visit the website of the **Government of Belize** (www.belize.gov.bz).

Australia Honorary consul (☎ 02-9880-7160; outcast@acon.com.au; 5/1 Oliver Rd, Roseville, NSW)

Canada Honorary consul general (☎ 604-730-1224; dwsmiling@hotmail.com; 2321 Trafalgar St, Vancouver BC V6K 3T1); Honorary consul (☎ 514-288-1687; dbellemare@cmmtl.com; 1800 McGill College, Suite 2480, Montreal, QC H3A 3J6); Honorary consul (☎ 416-865-7000; mpeterson@mcbinch.com; Suite 3800, South Tower, Royal Bank Plaza, Toronto, ON M5J 2J7)

Germany Honorary consul general (☎ 0711-90-710-920; wolfkahles@t-online.de; Breitscheidstrasse 10, D-70174 Stuttgart); Honorary consul (☎ 069-219313-80; holtermann@belize.de; Börsenstrasse 14; 60313 Frankfurt am Main)

Guatemala Embassy (☎ 334-5531, 331-1137; embelguat@guate.net; Avenida La Reforma 1-50, Zona 9, Edificio El Reformador, Oficina 801 & 802, Guatemala City)

Honduras Honorary consul general (☎ 220-5070; fax 220-5071; Hoteles de Honduras, R/do Hotel Honduras Maya, Tegucigalpa); Honorary consul (☎ 551-6191; fax 551-6460; 2 Avenida 7 Calle No 102, Colonia Bella Vista, San Pedro Sula)

Ireland Honorary consul (☎ 01-454-4333; accountancy@vfnathan.ie; Christchurch Sq, Dublin 8)

Mexico Embassy (☎ 55-5520-1274; embelize@prodigy.net.mx; Calle Bernardo de Gálvez 215, Colonia Lomas de Chapultepec, México DF 11000); Consulate (☎ 983-

832-18-03; bzeconsulate@prodigy.net.mx; Avenida de México 91, Chetumal); Consulate (☎ 998-887-84-17; nelbel@prodigy.net.mx; Avenida Náder 34, 1st Fl, Cancún)

Netherlands Honorary consul (☎ 020-6178858; roos@ebr.nl; Sloterkade 84, 1058 HF Amsterdam)

UK High commission (☎ 020-7499-9728; bzhc-lon@btconnect.com; 22 Harcourt House, 19 Cavendish Sq, London W1G 0PL)

USA Embassy (☎ 202-332-9636; www.embassyofbelize.org; 2535 Massachusetts Ave NW, Washington, DC 20008); Consulate general (☎ 323-469-7343; belizeconsul@earthlink.net; 5825 Sunset Blvd, Suite 206, Hollywood, CA 90028); Honorary consul general (☎ 281-999-4484; fax 281-999-0855; 7101 Breen, Houston TX 77086) There are also honorary consuls in several other cities.

Embassies & Consulates in Belize

A few countries have embassies in Belize. Many others handle relations with Belize from their embassies in countries such as Mexico or Guatemala, but may have an honorary consul in Belize to whom travelers can turn to as a first point of contact. Some embassies and consulates are open all day (from about 9am to 4pm or 5pm), Monday to Friday. Some close for lunch from noon to 1pm and others are only open in the morning.

Australia Embassy (☎ 55-1101-2200; www.mexico.embassy.gov.au) The Australian embassy in Mexico City handles relations with Belize.

Canada Honorary consul (Map p73; ☎ 223-1060; cdncon.bze@btl.net; 80 Princess Margaret Dr, Belize City)

France Honorary consul (Map pp76-7; ☎ 223-2708; 109 New Rd, Belize City)

Germany Honorary consul (Map pp76-7; ☎ 222-4369; seni@cisco.com.bz; 57 Southern Foreshore, Belize City)

Guatemala Embassy (Map p73; ☎ 223-3150; embbelice1@minex.gob.gt; 8 A St, Belize City)

Honduras Embassy (☎ 224-5889; 114 Bella Vista, Belize City)

Mexico Embassy (Map pp76-7; ☎ 223-0194; www.sre.gob.mx/belice; 18 N Park St, Belize City); Embassy (Map p151; ☎ 822-0497; Embassy Sq, Belmopan)

Netherlands Honorary consul (Map p73; ☎ 223-2953; mchulseca@btl.net; cnr Baymen Av & Calle Al Mar, Belize City)

UK High commission (Map p151; ☎ 822-2146; www.britishhighbze.com; Embassy Sq, Belmopan)

USA Embassy (Map pp76-7; ☎ 227-7161/2; usembassy.state.gov/belize; 29 Gabourel Lane, Belize City)

FESTIVALS & EVENTS
January

Krem New Year's Cycling Classic (January 1) Cycle race from Corozal to Belize City.

Horse Races (January 1) Horse racing at Burrell Boom.

February, March & April

Belize International Film Festival (Last week of February) See p81.

Fiesta de Carnaval (February or March; Sunday to Tuesday before the beginning of Lent, 49 to 47 days before Easter Sunday) Celebrated most in northern Belize.

Baron Bliss Day (March 9) Varied celebrations around the country honoring one of the country's great benefactors (see p78). Festivities include the four-day La Ruta Maya Belize River Challenge (see p157).

Holy Week (March or April) Various services and processions are held in the week leading up to Easter Sunday.

Holy Saturday Cycling Classic (Easter Saturday) Cycle race from Belize City to San Ignacio and back.

May

Labor Day (May 1) Parades.

Sovereign's Day (May 24) Celebrations include horse races in Belize City and Orange Walk.

August

Costa Maya Festival (Date varies) Celebration of Maya coastal culture at San Pedro, Ambergris Caye, with participants from Belize and the Yucatán.

September

National Day (September 10) Ceremonies and celebrations around the country.

September Celebrations (September 10–21) Festivities in Belize City (see p81).

Independence Day (September 21) Ceremonies, parades and celebrations.

November

Garifuna Settlement Day (November 19) Celebration of Garifuna culture, with lots of drumming, dancing and drinking, especially in Dangriga (see p181), Hopkins and Punta Gorda; celebrations may last several days.

December

Christmas Day (December 25) Belizeans decorate their houses weeks ahead with colorful lights and get together to eat and drink with family and friends; in some places Garifuna *jonkonu* dancers (see p181) go from house to house.

FOOD

See the Food & Drink chapter (p66) for an introduction to what and where to eat in Belize. Eating sections for each town select recommended restaurants. Where these are divided into budget, midrange and top-end categories, the midrange is places where typical main dishes cost between US$5 and US$15, with budget and top-end below and above that range, respectively. Standard res-

taurant hours are 7am to 9:30am for breakfast, 11:30am to 2pm for lunch and 6pm to 8pm for dinner. In Belize City and the main tourist destinations, many places don't close between meals and may stay open later at night.

GAY & LESBIAN TRAVELERS

Homosexuality for men and women is legal (since 1988) and the age of consent is 16. However, there isn't much of a gay scene in Belize. People aren't secretive or closeted, just low-key. While it's an incredibly tolerant society, and that Belizean attitude of live-and-let-live extends to homosexuality, the underlying Central American machismo and traditional religious beliefs make Belize a place where same-sex couples might want to forget about displaying affection in public.

San Pedro is the place that has the most gay- and lesbian-friendly accommodations. **Purple Roofs** (www.purpleroofs.com) has some listings in San Pedro and Placencia. Also try **Gay-Destinations** (www.gay-destinations.com).

Many gays and lesbians visit Belize from the USA, and businesses cater for them. **Maya Travel Services** (www.mayatravelservices.com) has Belize-specific information and can arrange your trip. The website **gaytimes** (www.gaytimes.co.uk) has a travel link to Belize. For dive trips to Belize from the US, try the **World's Gay & Lesbian Dive Travel Experts** (www.underseax.com).

The website www.gay.com/travel has a comprehensive list of gay and lesbian tour operators, plus links to other gay travel sites and a list of recommended travel agencies.

Further general information on gay and lesbian travel in Latin America can be obtained through the US and Australian offices of the **International Gay & Lesbian Travel Association** (www.iglta.com).

HOLIDAYS

Many of Belize's public holidays are moved to the Monday nearest the given date in order to make a long weekend. You'll find banks and most shops and businesses shut on these days. Belizeans themselves travel most around Christmas, New Year's and Easter and it's worth booking ahead for transportation and accommodation at these times.

New Year's Day January 1
Baron Bliss Day March 9
Good Friday March or April

Holy Saturday March or April
Easter Monday March or April
Labor Day May 1
Sovereign's Day May 24
National Day September 10
Independence Day September 21
Day of the Americas October 12
Garifuna Settlement Day November 19
Christmas Day December 25
Boxing Day December 26

See p225 for information on how some of the above holidays are celebrated.

INSURANCE

A travel insurance policy to cover theft, loss and medical problems is a very good idea. Some policies specifically exclude 'dangerous activities,' which can include scuba diving, motorcycling and even trekking. Check that the policy you are considering covers ambulances as well as emergency flights home.

You may prefer a policy that pays doctors or hospitals directly rather than requiring you to pay on the spot and claim later. If you have to claim later, make sure you keep all documentation. For further information on medical insurance see the Health chapter (p239). For information on motor insurance see p234 and p237.

INTERNET ACCESS

Most travelers make constant use of Internet cafés and free Web-based email such as Yahoo (www.yahoo.com) and Hotmail (http://hotmail.com). Belize has plenty of Internet cafés with typical rates of around US$3 per hour, and high-speed access is widely available. Some Internet cafés can burn CDs with your digital photos, usually for around US$2. If you have a USB cable for connecting your camera to a computer, you can't lose by taking it along.

A few accommodations have computer jacks in their rooms, which enable travelers with their own computers to connect to the Internet. If you're traveling with a notebook or hand-held computer, be aware that your modem may not work once you leave your home country. The safest option is to buy a reputable 'global' modem before you leave home, or buy a local PC-card modem if you're spending extended time in any one country. For more information

on traveling with a portable computer, see www.teleadapt.com.

For recommended websites about Belize, see p20.

LANGUAGE

Travelers in Belize don't need to use anything other than English to get by, but the topic of language is an interesting one in Belize. In addition to English, there are three different Mayan languages (Yucatec, Mopan and Kekchi), Garifuna (which has roots in African and Caribbean languages), and Kriol/Creole. The last is the subject of a campaign to get it recognized as a language in its own right, rather than just a dialect of English. For more information look for the *Bileez Kriol Glossary an Spellin Gide* in bookstores in Belize, or visit www.kriol.org.bz.

LEGAL MATTERS

Drug possession and use is officially illegal and, in general, offenders if caught will be arrested and prosecuted. In practice, possession of small amounts of marijuana compatible with purely personal use is unlikely to lead to prosecution. Possession or use of other drugs, or larger amounts of marijuana, are arrestable offences.

Persons found having sex with a minor will be prosecuted – the age of consent for both sexes is 16.

You are not required to carry ID in Belize but it's advisable to do so. If arrested you have the right to make a phone call. If you want to know more about your rights if arrested, check out www.belize.gov.bz/library and glance at 'Judge's Rules – A Police Guide to Interviewing Persons in Custody'.

The police force does not have a reputation for bribery and corruption as in many countries in Central America. A special **tourism police force** (☎ 227-6082) patrols tourist areas, including central Belize City, San Pedro, Caye Caulker and Placencia. The tourism police wear a special badge on their left shoulder.

MAPS

The maps in this book will enable you to find your way to all of the listed destinations, but if you'd like a larger-scale, more detailed travel map, you can't beat the 1:350,000 *Belize*, published by International Travel Maps of Vancouver. It's widely sold in Belize.

You can buy high-class 1:50,000 topographic sheets for US$20 each at the Ministry of Natural Resources in Belmopan (see p150). These maps cover the country, including the cayes, in 70 different sheets. Most of them were last updated in the 1990s.

Drivers will find *Emory King's Driver's Guide to Beautiful Belize* useful. Sold in bookstores and gift shops in Belize City, it's a compilation of route diagrams and user-friendly tips about turnoffs you might miss and speed bumps you might hit. A new edition is published annually.

MONEY

Belize's currency, the Belizean dollar (BZ$), has been fixed for many years at US$0.50, although talk of a devaluation is never far beneath the surface. For exchange rates see the Quick Reference page on the inside front cover. The currency bears the portrait of Queen Elizabeth II and the dollar is divided into 100 cents. Coins come in denominations of one, five, 10, 25 and 50 cents and one dollar; bills come in denominations of two, five, 10, 20, 50 and 100 dollars. The 25-cent coin is sometimes called a shilling, and you may hear the 100-dollar bill referred to as a 'bluenote.'

Prices are usually quoted in Belizean dollars, though you will sometimes – especially at the upper end of the price range – see prices quoted in US dollars. If in any doubt, ask which type of dollars people are talking about. Many businesses are happy to accept cash payments in US dollars.

For information about costs in Belize, see p18.

ATMs

Belize Bank ATMs, in Belize City, Belmopan, Corozal, Dangriga, Orange Walk, Punta Gorda, San Ignacio and San Pedro, accept international Visa, MasterCard, Plus and Cirrus cards. First Caribbean International Bank has a couple of ATMs in Belize City and Belmopan that take international Visa cards. Apart from that, at the time of writing other ATMs in Belize accept only Belizean cards. ATMs give only Belizean dollars. They are convenient but the exchange rate you get from ATMs is usually a cent or two under the BZ$2=US$1 rate used for cash or traveler's-check exchanges, and then you have the commissions and

handling fees that your card company may levy, which can amount to 5% of your transaction.

Cash

A few hundred US dollars in cash are handy to have. You can use them to pay for things in some places, and they are also easy to exchange informally, or in most banks, at the rate of BZ$2=US$1. Canadian dollars, pounds sterling and euros can also be exchanged at many banks but are harder to use as cash than US dollars.

Credit Cards

Visa and MasterCard are accepted by airlines, car-rental companies and at the larger hotels, restaurants and shops; American Express is often accepted at top-end places and is becoming more common among the smaller establishments. Some places levy a surcharge of around 5% if you pay by card.

You can also use a credit card to obtain an over-the-counter cash advance from most banks in Belize. The exchange rate is likely to be the same as for ATM withdrawals, and again you face commissions and handling charges imposed by your card issuer.

Taxes

Hotel room tax is 9%. Rates given in this guide also include the room tax. Restaurant meals are subject to an 8% sales tax. Prices given in this guide include all taxes to the best of our knowledge.

Tipping

Tipping is not obligatory but never goes amiss, especially if guides, drivers or waitstaff (for example) have provided you with genuinely good service. Rounding up the bill by somewhere between 5% and 10% is usually a suitable tip. Some upper-end hotels and restaurants add an obligatory service charge to your bill, in which case you definitely don't need to tip.

In highly touristed areas, tipping tour leaders, dive operators and waitstaff is becoming more common, but this should be done only if you feel the service warrants it. Tips need go no higher than 10%.

Traveler's Checks

It is handy to take some traveler's checks to Belize, preferably with a major well-known brand such as Visa or American Express and denominated in US dollars. You can exchange them at most banks and they usually attract the same advantageous exchange rate as cash, though there may be per-check fees to pay.

POST

There are post offices in the bigger towns. By airmail to Canada or the USA, a postcard costs US$0.15, a letter US$0.30. To Europe it's US$0.20 for a postcard and US$0.40 for a letter.

It is possible to receive incoming mail through the post offices of the major towns mentioned in this guide. Mail should be addressed to: your name, c/o General Delivery, town name, district name, Belize, Central America. It will be held for up to two months and must be claimed with a picture ID.

The courier services **DHL Express** (☎ 223-4350) and **Fedex Express** (☎ 224-5221) both have offices in Belize City.

SHOPPING

Belizeans do not trade in handicrafts at the level that Mexicans and Guatemalans do; instead, most gift shops in the country do a booming business in T-shirts, imported sarongs and beach gear, and Belikin beer paraphernalia. Popular regional handicrafts include folding mahogany deck chairs, *zericote* (ironwood) carvings of various sizes, baskets woven by Maya women in southern Belize, carved rosewood bowls, and striped wooden breadboards. These make good souvenirs, but they tend to be expensive when compared with similar items purchased in Guatemala or Mexico. For good handicraft shops, see under Shopping on p87 and p114, and Caesar's Place on p161. Drummers should head south to Dangriga if they want to pick up a Garifuna drum.

Some Belizean-made consumables are popular as souvenirs and useful when you're traveling. Among these are Rainforest Remedies, a line of all-natural health products – digestive aids, insect repellents, salves etc – from the **Ix Chel Centre** (www.arvigo massage.com/rainforest_remedies) near San Ignacio (see the boxed text, p166); Marie Sharp's hot sauces (see the boxed text, p67); and Rasta Pasta Rainforest Cafe spice packets (p124) for creating traditional Belizean dishes at home.

Books by Belizeans and books about Belize can be bought in many bookstores in the country and from **Cubola Productions** (www.belize business.com/cubola). **Belizean Perfumes** (☎ 226-0350; belizeperfumes@hotmail.com) creates products that are concocted from natural essences at the Lazy Iguana (p123) on Caye Caulker.

Belize City has a wide range of imported goods. The central shopping district can cater for most of your needs and you'll even find some local art there. Ambergris Caye has some good boutiques with exotic clothing and furnishings imported from Asia, as well as a number of art galleries with paintings by local artists. Local products on Ambergris Caye that are worth buying as gifts include handmade jewelry and clothing, fine coconut and wooden serving spoons, notebooks made from handcrafted paper, and brightly painted fish made from sheaths of coconut fronds. Caye Caulker has its share of tourist shops and a few small but excellent craft shops and art galleries (see p125).

TELEPHONE

Belize has no regional, area or city codes. Every number has seven digits and you just dial those seven digits from anywhere in the country. Belize's country code is ☎ 501. When calling Belize from other countries, follow the country code with the full seven-digit local number. The international access code for calling other countries from Belize is ☎ 00.

Public phones are fairly plentiful around the country – there are around 500 of them in all – and they're operated with cards that you can buy wherever you see the green signs announcing 'BTL's PrePaid Cards Sold Here.' (BTL is Belize Telecommunications Ltd.) The cards come in a range of denominations, from BZ$2 to BZ$50. You scratch the back of the card to reveal its PIN number, then to make a call you dial an access number given on the back of the card. Automated messages will ask you to key in your pin number, tell you how much credit is left on the card, then ask you to dial the number you want, followed by the pound (hash) key. Local calls are usually a flat rate of BZ$0.25. Long-distance calls within Belize can cost between BZ$0.10 and BZ$1 per minute.

DIRECTORY

Useful numbers (which can all be dialed without phone cards from public phones):

Ambulance ☎ 90
Directory assistance ☎ 113
Fire ☎ 90
Operator assistance ☎ 115
Police ☎ 90, 911

Cell Phones

You can rent cell phones from BTL only at the Philip Goldson International Airport in Belize City. The cost is US$5.40 per day, with a deposit of US$150 (credit cards accepted), and you can buy prepaid DigiCell phone cards (available where you see green signs announcing 'BTL's PrePaid Cards Sold Here,' in denominations from BZ$10 to BZ$50) to pay for your calls.

International cell phones can be used in Belize if they are GSM 1900 and unlocked. You can buy a Sim pack for US$25 from DigiCell distributors around the country.

International roaming is provided by T Mobil, Cingular and MexTel, but coverage is patchy – check with your service provider back home about coverage in Belize.

TIME

North American Central Standard Time (GMT/UTC minus six hours) is the basis of time in Belize, as in Guatemala and southern Mexico. Belize and Guatemala do not observe daylight saving, so there is never any time difference between them, but Mexico does observe daylight saving from the first Sunday in April to the last Sunday in October, so Belize is one hour behind Mexico during that period.

When it's noon in Belize, it's 1pm in New York, 6pm in London, 10am in San Francisco and 4am the next day in Sydney (add one hour to those times during daylight saving periods in those cities).

For world time zones, see p248.

TOURIST INFORMATION

The **Belize Tourism Board** (www.travelbelize.org) has tourist information offices in Belize City, Corozal and Punta Gorda and there are good local tourist information offices in San Pedro and Placencia.

The **Belize Tourism Industry Association** (www.btia.org) is an independent association of tourism businesses, with an office in Belize City (see p74) that can provide infor-

mation about what is offered by its many members.

VISAS

Information on visa requirements is available from Belizean embassies and consulates (see p225) and the **Belize Tourism Board** (www.travelbelize.org). During the time of writing visas were not required for citizens of EU or Caricom (Caribbean Community) countries, Australia, Canada, Hong Kong, Mexico, New Zealand, Norway, the USA or Venezuela. A visitor's permit valid for 30 days will be stamped in your passport when you enter the country. This can be extended by further periods of one month, up to a maximum of six months, by applying at an immigration office (there's at least one in each of Belize's six districts). The fee for each extension is US$12.50.

Visas for most other nationalities cost US$50 from a Belizean embassy or consulate and are valid for a 90-day stay.

For further information you can contact the **Immigration & Nationality Department** (☎ 822-2423; fax 822-2662), in Belmopan.

VOLUNTEERING

There are a lot of opportunities for volunteer work in Belize, especially on environmental projects. The US Peace Corps has been in Belize since the 1960s, but there are many other possibilities. Some of this work requires previous experience, some doesn't. You have to pay to participate in most cases (costs vary).

Belize Audubon Society (p79) Volunteers assist in the main office or in education and field programs. Volunteer birders are always required for the Christmas bird count.
Earthwatch (www.earthwatch.org) Paying volunteers are teamed with professional scientific researchers. Most projects are 10 to 14 days.
Elderhostel (www.elderhostel.org) One-week research assistance programs for seniors with Oceanic Society expeditions.
Explorations in Travel (www.volunteertravel.com) Places volunteers in wildlife rescue/rehabilitation centers, monkey sanctuaries and ecotourism projects.
Global Vision International (www.gvi.co.uk) Volunteer placements of over two months in conservation, research and education projects.
Help for Progress (www.helpforprogress.org) A Belizean NGO working with local community development organizations in fields such as education, gender issues, citizen participation and environment.

International Volunteer Programs Association
(www.volunteerinternational.org) A source for many
volunteer positions such as working in clinics, building
schools and helping conserve manatees.

Monkey Bay Wildlife Sanctuary (p96) Monkey Bay's
programs provide opportunities in conservation and community service. It also has many links to other conservation
organizations in Belize.

Oceanic Society (p127) Paying participants in the
society's expeditions assist scientists in marine research
projects at the society's field station on Blackbird Caye and
elsewhere.

Plenty International (www.plenty.org) Opportunities
for working with grassroots organizations (such as handicraft cooperatives) and schools, mostly in Toledo District.

ProWorld Service Corps (www.proworldsc.org) Much
like a privately run Peace Corps, ProWorld organizes small-
scale, sustainable projects in fields such as health care,
education, conservation, technology and construction.

Teachers for a Better Belize (www.twc.org/belize
/credits.html) US-based organization that sends volunteers
to schools in Toledo District to help train local teachers.

Trekforce Expeditions (www.trekforce.org.uk) Offers
one- to five-month programs that combine work such as
trail-cutting, visitor-center building in protected areas,
rural teaching or archaeological work, with optional jungle
treks, diving and Spanish courses.

Volunteer Abroad (www.volunteerabroad.com) Offers
scores of volunteer, study-abroad and internship opportunities (listed on the website by country), plus many useful
resources. Paid teaching jobs and opportunities for high-
school students are also available.

WOMEN TRAVELERS

Women can have a great time in Belize, even
traveling solo. You do need to keep your
wits about you and be vigilant, as does any
solo traveler.

Keep a clear head. Excessive alcohol will
make you vulnerable. For support and company, head for places where you're likely to
meet people, such as guesthouses that serve
breakfast, backpacker lodgings or popular
midrange or top-end hotels. Sign up for
excursions and if you're using Internet
cafés you're likely to run into other travelers. Being in an English-speaking country,
unlike elsewhere in Central America, can
be a confidence booster.

If you don't want attention, wear long
skirts or trousers and modest tops when
you're on public transportation and solo
explorations. You'll notice other savvy
women travelers dressed like this. Some of
them will be volunteers or other workers,
and are founts of information about the
country and how to safely move about it.

In Belize, especially on the cayes, many
men seem to think that unescorted women
are on the lookout for a man, and some men
in Belize, especially in the heavily touristed areas, can be quite forward with their
advances or even aggressive with their comments about your appearance.

In most cases advances are made light-
heartedly, although it can be disconcerting
if you're from a culture where men are less
overt in their attentions. Be direct, say no,
then ignore them – they're likely to go away.
A bicycle can be an asset in this scenario:
you can just scoot. If you're feeling particularly hassled, seek out company. Avoid
situations in which you might find yourself
alone with unknown men at remote archaeological sites, on empty city streets, or on
secluded stretches of beach.

Transportation

THINGS CHANGE...

The information in this chapter is particularly vulnerable to change. Check directly with the airline or a travel agent to make sure you understand how a fare (and ticket you may buy) works and be aware of the security requirements for international travel. Shop carefully. The details given in this chapter should be regarded as pointers and are not a substitute for your own careful, up-to-date research.

GETTING THERE & AWAY

ENTERING THE COUNTRY

You must present a passport that will be valid until you leave the country. It's advisable to have at least six months of validity remaining. Officially, visitors are also required to be in possession of an onward or return ticket from Belize and funds worth US$60 a day for their stay in the country, but it's rare for tourists to be required to show these.

Tourists are generally given a 30-day stay, extendable once you're in Belize. See p230 for information on visa requirements and extensions.

AIR
Airports & Airlines
Philip Goldson International Airport (BZE; ☎ 225-2014), at Ladyville, 11 miles northwest of Belize City center, handles all international flights. With Belize's short internal flying distances it's often possible to make a same-day connection at Belize City to or from other airports in the country.

Four US airlines, plus the Central American Grupo TACA from Houston, fly direct from the USA; Belize's Tropic Air and Maya Island Air and Guatemala's Tikal Jets fly from Flores, Guatemala (Tikal Jets also flies from Guatemala City); and Grupo TACA also flies from San Salvador (El Salvador) and San Pedro Sula (Honduras), with connections from other Central American cities.

AIRLINES FLYING TO & FROM BELIZE
American Airlines (code AA; ☎ 223-2522; www.aa.com) Hubs Dallas Fort Worth & Miami.
Continental Airlines (code CO; ☎ 227-8309; www.continental.com) Hub Houston.
Delta Air Lines (code DL; (☎ 225-3429; www.delta.com) Hub Atlanta.
Grupo TACA (code TA; ☎ 227-7363, 225-2163; www.taca.com) Hub San Salvador.
Maya Island Air (code MW; ☎ 225-2219; www.mayaairways.com) Hub Belize City.
Tikal Jets (code WU; ☎ 227-2583; www.tikaljets.com) Hub Guatemala City.
Tropic Air (code PM; ☎ 225-2302; www.tropicair.com) Hub Belize City.
US Airways (code US; ☎ 225-3589; www.usairways.com) Hub Charlotte, North Carolina.

Tickets
The Internet (airline websites as well as ticket-booking sites) is the obvious place to start looking for a flight to Belize, but in the search for a good deal it can also be worth checking out a couple of travel agencies and flight ads in the press. If you travel outside Belize's main tourist season of December to April, you may find cheaper fares are available. If you're planning to transfer straight on to a domestic flight on arrival in Belize City, you may well get a better deal by booking the domestic flight separately.

AIR DEPARTURE TAX

Non-Belizeans must pay fees that total US$35, in cash US dollars, when flying out of Belize City on international flights. Of this, US$3.75 is the PACT (Protected Areas Conservation Trust) fee, which helps to fund Belize's network of protected natural areas.

International online booking agencies that are worth a look include www.cheaptickets.com, www.expedia.com and www.sta.com (for travelers under the age of 26).

Australia & New Zealand

The cheapest way to get from Australia or New Zealand to Belize City is usually via the US (normally Los Angeles and at least one other airport). High-season roundtrip fares from Sydney start at around A$3200. Both **STA Travel** (☎ 1300-733-035; www.statravel.com.au) and **Flight Centre** (☎ 133-133; www.flightcentre.com.au) have offices throughout Australia. For online bookings, try www.travel.com.au.

In New Zealand, **Flight Centre** (☎ 0800-243-544; www.flightcentre.co.nz) and **STA Travel** (☎ 0508-782-872; www.statravel.co.nz) both have branches throughout the country. The site www.travel.co.nz is recommended for making online bookings.

Canada

From Canada you have to fly via one of the US airports that has flights to Belize. High-season roundtrip fares start at C$1100 to C$1200. **Travel Cuts** (☎ 800-667-2887; www.travelcuts.com) is Canada's national student travel agency. For online bookings you can try www.expedia.ca and www.travelocity.ca.

Central America, South America & Cuba

Grupo TACA can fly you to Belize City via San Salvador from all Central American capitals, plus San Pedro Sula, La Ceiba and Roatán in Honduras, Havana (Cuba) and several South American cities. Sample high-season one-way/roundtrip fares are about US$200/220 from Guatemala City, US$220/300 from San Salvador, US$230/320 from San Pedro Sula and US$240/470 from San José, Costa Rica, or Managua. Tikal Jets also flies from Guatemala City to Belize City (via Flores) and from Managua, Havana and San Pedro Sula to Guatemala City.

For information on flights to Belize City from Flores, see p218.

Continental Europe

You need to fly to Belize via the USA (high-season roundtrip fares start at €700 to €800 but you may have to pay considerably more), unless you want to fly to Cancún (Mexico) and then travel overland to Belize. Roundtrip fares to Cancún start at €600 to €700, but you're more likely to pay €800 to €900. Recommended agencies include the following.

FRANCE
Nouvelles Frontières (☎ 0825-000-747; www.nouvelles-frontieres.fr)
OTU Voyages (www.otu.fr) Specializes in student and youth travelers.

GERMANY
Just Travel (☎ 089-747-3330; www.justtravel.de)
Lastminute (☎ 01805-284-366; www.lastminute.de)

ITALY
CTS Viaggi (☎ 06-462-0431; www.cts.it) Specializes in student and youth travel.

THE NETHERLANDS
Airfair (☎ 020-620-5121; www.airfair.nl)

Mexico

There are currently no flights to Belize from anywhere in Mexico, but the domestic airport at Chetumal is just 8 miles from the Mexico/Belize border. You can fly from Mexico to Belize City via Guatemala City or Flores, or San Salvador. Grupo TACA and Mexican airlines fly from Mexico City to San Salvador and Guatemala City. Grupo TACA flies from Cancún to Flores.

UK & Ireland

You have to fly via the USA – high-season roundtrip fares from London start at around UK£650 – unless you want to fly to Cancún (Mexico) and make your way down to Belize overland. You can usually get a London–Cancún roundtrip ticket for between UK£500 and UK£650. Recommended travel agencies:

Bridge the World (☎ 0870-444-7474; www.b-t-w.co.uk)
Flightbookers (☎ 0870-010-7000; www.ebookers.com)
Journey Latin America (☎ 020-8747-3108; www.journeylatinamerica.co.uk)
Trailfinders (www.trailfinders.co.uk)

USA

Unless you're starting from a city with direct flights to Belize City (at research time Atlanta, Charlotte, Dallas, Houston and Miami), you'll be making a connection in one of those cities. Examples of typical high-season roundtrip fares to Belize City include US$450 to US$600 from Houston, US$675 to US$800 from New York and US$750 to US$950 from Los Angeles.

Discount travel agents in the USA are known as consolidators. San Francisco is the ticket consolidator capital of America, although some good deals can also be found in other big cities. Agencies recommended for online bookings include www.itn.net, www.lowestfare.com and www.orbitz.com.

LAND
Border Crossings

There are two official crossing points on the Belize/Mexico border. The more frequently used one is at Subteniente López (Mexico)/Santa Elena (Belize), 9 miles from Corozal (Belize) and 7 miles from Chetumal (Mexico). The all-paved Northern Hwy runs to Belize City. The other crossing is at La Unión (Mexico)/Blue Creek (Belize), a 34-mile drive southwest of Orange Walk. If you happened to be driving in from Mexico straight to La Milpa Field Station (p138) or Chan Chich Lodge (p139), you might consider using this crossing, as the road is paved all the way to the border on the Mexican side, whereas you face 28 unpaved miles on the road from Orange Walk to Blue Creek.

The only land crossing between Belize and Guatemala is 1 mile west of the Belizean town of Benque Viejo del Carmen at the end of the all-paved Western Hwy from Belize City. The town of Melchor de Mencos is on the Guatemalan side of the crossing. The border is 44 miles from the Puente Ixlú junction (also called El Cruce)

LAND DEPARTURE TAX

Non-Belizeans are required to pay fees that total US$18.75, in cash US or Belizean dollars, when departing Belize by land. Of this, US$3.75 is the PACT (Protected Areas Conservation Trust) fee, which helps to fund Belize's network of protected natural areas.

---

in Guatemala, where roads head north for Tikal (22 miles) and southwest to Flores (18 miles). The first 15 to 19 miles west from the border is unpaved.

Bus

Bus passengers crossing Belize's land borders have to disembark and carry their own luggage through immigration and customs. See p144 and p168 for further information on the two main crossing points.

In Chetumal, buses bound for Corozal (express/regular US$2/1, one/1¼ hours), Orange Walk (express/regular US$3.50/2.75, 1½/two hours) and Belize City (express/regular US$7/5, 3½/4½ hours) leave the north side of Nuevo Mercado, about 0.75 miles north of the city center, once or twice an hour from about 4:30am to 6pm. A few buses to the same places also go from the ADO intercity bus terminal, a further 0.6 miles north. The 6am Línea Dorada departure from the ADO goes to Belize City and then Flores (US$23, seven to eight hours).

For information on buses from Belize City to Flores, see p88. You can also use local services to and from both sides of the border (see p168, p218 and p215). There are plenty of buses and minibuses that link Flores with Guatemala City and other destinations around Guatemala.

Car & Motorcycle

To bring a vehicle into Belize, you need to obtain a temporary importation permit at the border. This obliges you to take the vehicle out of Belize again within the one-month validity of the permit. To get the permit you must present proof of ownership (vehicle registration) and purchase Belizean motor insurance (available for a few US dollars per day from agents at the borders). Permit extensions can be obtained by applying to the **Customs Department** (Belize City ☎ 227-7092). In the unlikely event that a Mexican or Guatemalan car-rental agency permits you to take one of their vehicles into Belize, you will also have to show the rental documents at the border.

It's not unusual to see US license plates on cars in Belize, as driving from the US through Mexico is pretty straightforward and car rental in Belize is expensive. The shortest route through Mexico to the crossing point between Chetumal and Corozal is from the

TRANSPORTATION

SEA DEPARTURE TAX

The only fee you have to pay when leaving Belize by sea is the US$3.75 PACT (Protected Areas Conservation Trust) fee. It's payable in US or Belizean dollars, in cash.

US/Mexico border points at Brownsville/ Matamoros (1257 miles) or McAllen/Reynosa (1267 miles), a solid three days of driving. The other main US/Mexico road borders are Laredo, Texas/Nuevo Laredo (1413 miles from the Belize border); El Paso/Ciudad Juárez (1988 miles) and Nogales, Arizona/ Nogales (2219 miles).

You are required to obtain a temporary import permit for your vehicle at the border when you enter Mexico: as well as the vehicle registration document you'll need to show your driver's license and pay a fee of around US$25 with a Visa, MasterCard or American Express credit card. And you'll have to buy Mexican motor insurance, also available at the border.

For information on driving within Belize, see p236.

SEA

The only scheduled boat services into Belize are from Puerto Cortés, Honduras, to Placencia (see p199) and Dangriga (p183), both once a week and taking around four to 4½ hours for US$50; from Puerto Barrios, Guatemala, to Punta Gorda daily, taking one hour for US$15 (p202); and from Lívingston, Guatemala, to Punta Gorda twice weekly, taking one hour for US$15 (p202).

GETTING AROUND

AIR

Belize's two domestic airlines, **Maya Island Air** (code MW; ☎ 226-2435; www.mayaairways.com) and **Tropic Air** (code PM; ☎ 225-2012; www.tropicair.com), provide an efficient and reasonably priced service in small planes on the routes Belize City–Dangriga–Placencia–Punta Gorda, Belize City–Caye Caulker–San Pedro and San Pedro–Sarteneja–Corozal, with plenty of flights daily by both airlines on all three routes.

Some domestic flights departing and arriving in Belize City use the international airport; some use the Municipal Airstrip, about 12 miles from the international airport; and some stop at both. Flights using the Municipal Airstrip are usually US$10 to US$20 cheaper than those using the international airport.

Since the year 2000 two Tropic Air passenger flights have crashed into the sea (apparently due to adverse weather conditions), and one Maya Island Air (nonscheduled) passenger flight crashed into a swamp, but neither airline has suffered fatalities. The oversight of air carrier operations in Belize by the country's civil aviation authority has been assessed as not in compliance with international aviation safety standards by the US's Federal Aviation Administration.

BICYCLE

Most of Belize, including all three of the main highways, is pretty flat, which makes for pleasant cycling, but other traffic on the main highways does tend to travel fairly fast. Make sure you're visible if riding along these roads. Belizeans use bicycles – often beach cruiser–type bikes on which you brake by pedaling backwards – for getting around locally, but you don't see them doing much long-distance cycling for fun unless they're into racing.

Bikes are available to rent in many of the main tourist destinations for around US$10 per day. Most are pretty well used. You don't usually have to give a deposit.

BOAT

The **Caye Caulker Water Taxi Association** (☎ 203-1969, 226-0992; www.cayecaulkerwatertaxi.com) operates speedy motor launches known as water taxis between Belize City, Caye Caulker and San Pedro (Ambergris Caye), with several daily services each way. It's one hour (US$10) from Belize City to Caye Caulker and 1½ hours (US$15) to San Pedro. The Caye Caulker Water Taxi Association also serves three smaller offshore islands: St George's Caye, Long Caye and Caye Chapel. Water taxis are open boats that can hold around 40 people each. Captains usually do their best to avoid traveling during rainstorms; when they can't, passengers huddle together under large tarps to stay dry.

The **Thunderbolt service** (☎ 226-2217/2904), with indoor seating, also operates the Belize City–Caye Caulker–San Pedro route and

TRANSPORTATION

provides a daily service linking Corozal, Sarteneja and San Pedro, too. Another regular service in open launches runs between Dangriga and Tobacco Caye (see p183), but apart from that getting to and around Belize's islands and reefs (unless you have your own boat) is a matter of taking tours or dive or snorkel trips, using boats organized by island accommodations that you are going to, or chartering a launch. As a rough rule of thumb, launch charters cost around US$100 per 10 miles. They're easy to arrange almost anywhere on the coast or the main islands visited by tourists.

Another useful boat service is the **Hokey Pokey Water Taxi** (☎ 601-0271, 523-2376) between Placencia and Mango Creek (US$5, 10 minutes), near Independence, which saves a long detour by road for travelers between Placencia and Punta Gorda. See p199 for further information.

BUS

Novelo's Bus Line (☎ 227-2025/7146), which has bought up most of Belize's other bus companies to attain almost a monopoly position, went into receivership in 2004. This put Belizean bus services into a state of some uncertainty, but at research time Novelo's was still operating frequent services (apart from a few cancellations and delays) along the country's three main routes:

- the Northern Hwy from Belize City to Orange Walk and Corozal (and on to Chetumal, Mexico)
- the Western Hwy from Belize City to Belmopan, San Ignacio and Benque Viejo del Carmen
- the Hummingbird and Southern Hwys from Belmopan to Dangriga, Independence and Punta Gorda (buses on this route use the Western Hwy between Belize City and Belmopan; from Dangriga there are separate buses to Hopkins and Placencia)

Most of Novelo's buses, like others in Belize, are US school buses. Regular Novelo's services will stop anywhere to drop and pick up passengers. Expresses, usually air-conditioned, have limited stops and as a result are quicker and usually less crowded. They also cost a bit more, but are still inexpensive and generally worth the extra dollar or two. The 86-mile run from Belize City to

Corozal, for example, takes about 2½ hours for US$6 on an express, and 3¼ hours for US$4.50 on a regular bus. In general you pay about US$2 to US$2.50 per hour on expresses and US$1 to US$1.50 per hour on regular buses. If you're traveling at a busy time, it's worth buying your ticket a day or two in advance.

The only other domestic long-distance bus company in operation at the time of writing is **James** (☎ 702-2049, 722-2625), which is a rival to Novelo's on the Belize City–Belmopan–Dangriga–Independence–Punta Gorda route.

A variety of smaller bus companies serve villages around the country. They often run to local work and school schedules, with buses going into a larger town in the morning and returning in the afternoon.

Occasional breakdowns and accidents happen with Belizean buses but their track record is at least as good as those in other Central American countries. Luggage pilfering has been a problem on some buses in the past. Carry valuables with you on the bus and give your stored baggage to the bus driver or conductor only, and watch as it is stored. Be there when the bus is unloaded and retrieve your luggage at once.

CAR & MOTORCYCLE

Having a vehicle in Belize gives you maximum travel flexibility and enables you to reach off-the-main-road destinations and attractions (of which there are many) without having to depend on tours and expensive transfers. Though car hire is costly in Belize compared to many other countries (you're normally looking at a minimum of US$80 per day plus fuel), it doesn't look so exorbitant when you consider the alternatives, especially if there are three or four people to share the expenses.

Belize has four good, asphalt-paved two-lane roads: the Northern Hwy between Belize City and the Mexican border north of Corozal; the Western Hwy between Belize City and the Guatemalan border near Benque Viejo del Carmen; the Hummingbird Hwy from Belmopan to Dangriga; and the Southern Hwy, which branches off the Hummingbird Hwy a few miles from Dangriga and heads south to Punta Gorda (it's all paved except for a 10-mile stretch around Nim Li Punit).

TRANSPORTATION

MAIN DRIVING ROUTES

- Northern Hwy: Belize City to Orange Walk (57 miles, 1½ hours), Corozal (86 miles, 2¼ hours) and Santa Elena (Mexican border; 95 miles, 2½ hours)

- Western Hwy: Belize City to Belmopan (52 miles, 1¼ hours), San Ignacio (72 miles, 1¾ hours), Benque Viejo del Carmen (80 miles, two hours) and the Guatemalan border (81 miles, two hours)

- Hummingbird and Southern Hwys: Belmopan to Dangriga (55 miles, 1½ hours), Hopkins (63 miles, two hours), Placencia (98 miles, 3½ hours) and Punta Gorda (148 miles, 4½ hours)

Most other roads are one- or two-lane unpaved roads. The most-used ones are maintained in fairly good condition, but heavy rains can make things challenging. Off the main roads you don't always need a 4WD vehicle but you do need one with high clearance, such as a Chevy Geo Tracker.

Driver's License
If you plan to drive in Belize, you'll need to bring a valid driver's license from your home country.

Fuel & Spare Parts
There are plenty of fuel stations in the larger towns and along the major roads. At last report, regular gasoline was going for just over US$4 per US gallon (US$1.05 per liter). Premium (unleaded) is a few cents more expensive. Spare parts and mechanics are most easily available in Belize City, although San Ignacio, Belmopan and Orange Walk also have parts suppliers. Check the telephone *Yellow Pages* under 'Automobile Parts & Supplies' and 'Automobile Repairing & Service'.

Hire
Generally, renters must be at least 25 years old, have a valid driver's license and pay by credit card.

Most car-rental companies have offices at Belize City's Philip Goldson International Airport as well as in the city (see p89 for details of recommended agencies); they will often also deliver or take return of cars at Belize City's municipal airstrip or in downtown Belize City. Rental possibilities are few outside Belize City, but it is possible to rent cars in San Ignacio (p159) and Punta Gorda (p203).

Rental rates including taxes, insurance and unlimited mileage generally start at around US$80 a day for a non-4WD, non-air-con vehicle. If you keep the car for six days of the week you'll often be given a seventh day free.

Most rental agencies will not allow you to take a vehicle out of the country. One that will allow cars to be taken in to Guatemala is Crystal Auto Rental (p89) in Belize City.

Insurance
Liability insurance is required in Belize, and there are occasional police checkpoints on the main highways, where you may be required to produce proof of it. You face possible arrest if you can't. Rental companies always organize the necessary insurance for you, and you won't be able to bring your own vehicle into Belize without buying Belizean insurance at the border.

Road Conditions & Hazards
Outside Belize City, traffic is wonderfully light throughout the country, but on the main roads you need to watch out for erratic and dangerously fast driving by others. Drive defensively. Also watch out very carefully for speed bumps ('sleeping policemen'): these are sometimes well signed, and sometimes not signed at all.

Off the major highways, most roads are unpaved and you need to watch out for potholes, but most of the roads you're likely to travel on are fairly well maintained. After a lot of rain, some roads may become impassable: make inquiries before you set out, and if you're in doubt about whether you'll get through a stretch, don't risk it. Always have water and a spare tire, and always fill your tank before you head off into the back country (and turn back before you've used half of it!).

Note that Belizean signposts give distances in miles.

TRANSPORTATION

Road Rules

Driving in Belize is on the right-hand side of the road. Speed limits are 55mph on the open highway, and either 40mph or 25mph in villages and towns. Use of seat belts is required for drivers and front-seat passengers. If you are caught not wearing yours, the fine is US$12.50.

Petty theft can be an issue – keep your vehicle locked at all times and do not leave valuables in it, especially not in plain view.

Mileposts and highway signs record distances in miles and speed limits in miles per hour, although many vehicles have odometers and speedometers that are calibrated in kilometers.

HITCHHIKING

Hitchhiking is never entirely safe in any country and in Belize, like anywhere, it's imperative that you listen to your instincts and travel smart. Travelers who decide to hitchhike should understand that they are taking a small but potentially serious risk. You're far better off traveling with another person, and never hitchhike at night. Also keep in mind that buses in Belize are cheap and fairly efficient; you might decide that a bus is a safer and more comfortable bet.

On the other hand hitchhiking is a fairly common way for Belizeans to get around. In a country where vehicle owners are a minority and public transportation is infrequent to places off the main roads, it's common to see people trying to catch a lift at bus stops or at speed bumps, where traffic slows down. If you too are trying to get some place where there's no bus for the next three hours, it's likely that you'll soon get a ride if you hold your hand up and look friendly. Offering to pay a share of the fuel costs at the end of your ride never goes amiss. But always be aware of the potential risks of hitchhiking.

LOCAL TRANSPORTATION

All of Belize's towns, including the parts of Belize City that most visitors frequent, are small enough to cover on foot, although for safety reasons you should take taxis for some trips within Belize City (see p75). Taxis are plentiful in all mainland towns and are also an option for getting to places out of town. Rates vary depending on where you are: the 7-mile ride from Corozal to Consejo costs US$10, but the 6-mile trip from Maya Centre to Cockscomb Basin Wildlife Sanctuary is US$18.

Bicycle is an enjoyable way of getting around local areas and bikes can be rented at around US$10 per day in many tourist haunts (and are free for guests at some accommodations).

On the cayes, of course, you get around by boat if you're going anywhere offshore. But Ambergris Caye and Caye Caulker have a mode of transportation all of their own for land trips: the golf-cart taxi!

Health Dr David Goldberg

Travelers to Central America need to be concerned about food- and mosquito-borne infections. While most infections are not life-threatening, they can certainly ruin your trip.

Besides getting the proper vaccinations, it's important that you pack a good insect repellent and exercise great care in what you eat and drink.

BEFORE YOU GO

INSURANCE

If your insurance doesn't cover medical expenses abroad, consider supplemental insurance. See the US State Department website (http://travel.state.gov/travel/tips/health /health_1185.html) for medical evacuation and travel-insurance companies.

Find out if your insurer will pay providers directly or reimburse you later for expenditures. You may prefer a policy that pays doctors or hospitals directly rather than requiring you to pay up front and claim later. If you have to claim later, keep all documentation. Some policies ask you to call collect to a center in your home country, where an assessment of your problem is made.

Check that the policy covers ambulances and an emergency flight home. Some policies offer lower and higher medical-expense options; the higher ones are for countries such as the USA, which have extremely high medical costs. There is a wide variety of policies available, so check the small print.

RECOMMENDED VACCINATIONS

Since most vaccines don't produce immunity until at least two weeks after they're

Vaccine	Recommended for	Dosage	Side effects
chickenpox	travelers who've never had chickenpox	2 doses 1 month apart	fever; mild case of chickenpox
hepatitis A	all travelers	one dose before trip with booster 6-12 months later	soreness at injection site; headaches; body aches
hepatitis B	long-term travelers in close contact with the local population	3 doses over a 6-month period	soreness at injection site; low-grade fever
measles	travelers born after 1956 who've had only 1 measles vaccination	1 dose	fever; rash; joint pain; allergic reaction
tetanus-diphtheria	all travelers who haven't had booster within 10 years	1 dose lasts 10 years	soreness at injection site
typhoid	all travelers	4 capsules by mouth, 1 taken every other day	abdominal pain; nausea; rash
yellow fever	required for travelers arriving from yellow fever–infected areas in Africa or South America	1 dose lasts 10 years	headaches; body aches; severe reactions are rare

given, visit a physician four to eight weeks before departure. Ask your doctor for an International Certificate of Vaccination (also known as a yellow booklet), which will list all the vaccinations you've received. This is mandatory for countries that require proof of yellow-fever vaccination upon entry, but it's a good idea to carry it wherever you travel. Note that some of the recommended vaccines are not approved for use by children and pregnant women; check with your physician.

The only required vaccine for Belize is yellow fever, and that's only if you're arriving from a yellow fever–infected country in Africa or South America. However, a number of vaccines are recommended (see the boxed text on p239).

MEDICAL CHECKLIST

It is a very good idea to carry a medical and first-aid kit with you, to help yourself in the case of minor illness or injury. Following is a list of items you should consider packing.

- antibiotics
- antidiarrheal drugs (eg loperamide)
- acetaminophen/paracetamol (Tylenol) or aspirin
- anti-inflammatory drugs (eg ibuprofen)
- antihistamines (for hay fever and allergic reactions)
- antibacterial ointment (eg Bactroban) for cuts and abrasions
- steroid cream or cortisone (for poison ivy and other allergic rashes)
- bandages, gauze, gauze rolls
- adhesive or paper tape
- scissors, safety pins, tweezers
- thermometer
- pocketknife
- DEET-containing insect repellent for the skin
- permethrin-containing insect spray for clothing, tents and bed nets
- sunblock
- oral rehydration salts
- iodine tablets (for water purification)
- syringes and sterile needles

Bring medications in their original containers, and clearly labeled. A signed, dated letter from your physician describing all medical conditions and medications, including generic names, is also a good idea.

If carrying syringes or needles, be sure to have a physician's letter documenting their medical necessity.

INTERNET RESOURCES

There is a wealth of travel health advice on the Internet. The Lonely Planet website at www.lonelyplanet.com is a good place to start. The World Health Organization publishes a superb book, *International Travel and Health,* which is revised annually and is available free online at www.who.int/ith.

It's a good idea to consult your government's travel health website before you depart:

Australia (www.dfat.gov.au/travel)
Canada (www.hc-sc.gc.ca/pphb-dgspsp/tmp-pmv/pub _e.html)
UK (www.doh.gov.uk/traveladvice/index.htm)
USA (www.cdc.gov/travel)

FURTHER READING

For more information, see Lonely Planet's *Healthy Travel Central & South America.* If you're traveling with children, Lonely Planet's *Travel with Children* may be useful. *ABC of Healthy Travel,* by Eric Walker et al, and *Medicine for the Outdoors,* by Paul S Auerbach, are other valuable resources.

IN TRANSIT

DEEP VEIN THROMBOSIS (DVT)

Blood clots may form in the legs (DVT) during plane flights, chiefly because of prolonged immobility. The main symptom of DVT is swelling or pain of the foot, ankle or calf, usually but not always on just one side. When a blood clot travels to the lungs, it may cause chest pain and difficulty breathing. Travelers with any of these symptoms should immediately seek medical attention.

To prevent DVT developing on long flights, you should walk about the cabin, contract your leg muscles while sitting, drink plenty of fluids and avoid alcohol.

JET LAG & MOTION SICKNESS

Jet lag is common when crossing more than five time zones and causes insomnia, fatigue, malaise or nausea. To avoid jet lag, drink plenty of fluids (non-alcoholic) and eat light meals. Upon arrival, get exposure to natural sunlight and readjust your schedule (for meals, sleep etc) as soon as it is possible.

Antihistamines such as dimenhydrinate (Dramamine) and meclizine (Antivert, Bonine) are usually the first choice for treating motion sickness. The main side effect caused is drowsiness. A herbal alternative is ginger, which works like a charm for some people.

IN BELIZE

AVAILABILITY & COST OF HEALTH CARE

Most doctors and hospitals in Belize expect payment in cash, regardless of whether you have travel health insurance. If you develop a life-threatening medical problem, you'll probably want to be evacuated to a country with state-of-the-art medical care. Since this may cost tens of thousands of dollars, be sure you have insurance to cover this before you depart.

Many pharmacies in Belize are well supplied, but important medications may not be consistently available. Be sure to bring along adequate supplies of all prescription drugs. While most prescription medications are available in Belize, they might be relatively expensive. You can obtain prescriptions from general practitioners, who will provide this service for a small fee. Some pharmacists, especially in smaller pharmacies, will dispense medications without a prescription.

Medical facilities in Belize are extremely limited and the number of doctors is quite small. Routine care is readily obtainable in Belize City and the larger towns, but facilities for complicated problems may be difficult to find. In rural areas, medical care may be unavailable. In Belize City there are two private hospitals that provide generally good care: **Belize Medical Associates** (☎ 223-0302/3/4) and **Universal Health Services** (☎ 223-7870; www.universalhealthbelize.com). In San Ignacio, **La Loma Luz Hospital** (☎ 804-2985, 824-2087) offers primary care as well as 24-hour emergency services. For divers, there is a hyperbaric chamber on Ambergris Caye.

In Belize, the phone number for an ambulance is ☎ 90, but this service is not available in many communities. For a private ambulance in Belize City, call ☎ 223-3292.

INFECTIOUS DISEASES

Chagas' Disease

Chagas' disease is a parasitic infection that is transmitted by triatomine insects (reduviid bugs), which inhabit crevices in the walls and roofs of traditional housing in South and Central America. In Belize, Chagas' disease occurs in rural areas. The triatomine insect lays its feces on human skin as it bites, usually at night. A person becomes infected when he or she unknowingly rubs the feces into the bite wound or an open sore. Chagas' disease is extremely rare in travelers. However, if you sleep in a poorly constructed house, especially one made of mud, adobe or thatch, be sure to protect yourself with a bed net and a good insecticide.

Dengue

Though relatively uncommon in Belize, dengue fever is a viral infection found throughout Central America and transmitted by aedes mosquitoes, which bite mostly during the daytime and are usually found close to human habitations, often indoors. They breed primarily in artificial water containers such as jars, barrels, cans, cisterns, metal drums, plastic containers and discarded tires. As a result, dengue is especially common in densely populated, urban environments.

Dengue usually causes flu-like symptoms, including fever, muscle aches, joint pains, headaches, nausea and vomiting, often followed by a rash. The body aches may be quite uncomfortable, but most cases resolve uneventfully in a few days. Severe cases usually occur in children under the age of 15 who are experiencing their second dengue infection.

There is no treatment available for dengue fever except to take analgesics such as acetaminophen/paracetamol (Tylenol) and drink plenty of fluids. Severe cases may require hospitalization for intravenous fluids and supportive care. There is no vaccine. The cornerstone of prevention is protection against insect bites (see p244).

Hepatitis A

Hepatitis A occurs throughout Belize. It's a viral infection of the liver that is usually acquired by ingestion of contaminated water, food or ice, though it may also be acquired by direct contact with infected persons. The illness occurs all over the world, but the incidence is higher in developing nations. Symptoms may include fever, malaise, jaundice, nausea, vomiting and abdominal pain. Most cases will resolve uneventfully, though hepatitis A occasionally causes severe liver damage. There is no treatment.

The vaccine for hepatitis A is extremely safe and highly effective. If you get a booster six to 12 months later, it lasts for at least 10 years. Vaccination is recommended for travelers visiting Belize. Because the safety of hepatitis A vaccine has not been established for pregnant women or children under age two, they should instead be given a gamma-globulin injection.

Hepatitis B

Like hepatitis A, hepatitis B is a liver infection that occurs worldwide but is more common in developing nations. Unlike hepatitis A, the disease is usually acquired by sexual contact or by exposure to infected blood, generally through blood transfusions or contaminated needles. The vaccine is recommended only for long-term travelers (on the road more than six months) who expect to live in rural areas or have close physical contact with the local population. Additionally, the vaccine is recommended for anyone who anticipates sexual contact with local people or the need for medical, dental or other treatments while abroad, especially transfusions or injections.

Hepatitis B vaccine is safe and highly effective. However, three injections are necessary to establish full immunity. Several countries added hepatitis B vaccine to the list of routine childhood immunizations in the 1980s, so many young adults are already protected.

Leishmaniasis

Leishmaniasis occurs in the mountains and jungles of Belize. The infection is transmitted by sand flies. To protect yourself, follow the same precautions for mosquitoes (p244), except that netting must be finer (at least 18 holes to the linear inch), and you should stay indoors during the early evening. There is no vaccine.

In Belize, the disease is generally limited to the skin, causing slow-growing ulcers over exposed parts of the body; less commonly, it may disseminate to the bone marrow, liver and spleen.

Leptospirosis

Leptospirosis is acquired by exposure to water that has been contaminated by the urine of infected animals. Outbreaks may occur as a result of flooding, when sewage overflow contaminates water sources. The initial symptoms, which resemble a mild flu, usually subside uneventfully in a few days, with or without treatment, but a minority of cases are complicated by jaundice or meningitis. There is no vaccine. Minimize your risk by staying out of bodies of fresh water that may be contaminated by animal urine. If you're engaging in high-risk activities in an area where an outbreak is in progress, you can take 200mg of doxycycline once weekly as a preventative measure. If you develop leptospirosis, the treatment is 100mg of doxycycline twice daily.

Malaria

Malaria occurs in every country in Central America. It's transmitted by mosquito bites, which usually occur between dusk and dawn. The main symptom is high, spiking fevers, which may be accompanied by chills, sweats, headache, body aches, weakness, vomiting or diarrhea. Severe cases may involve the central nervous system and lead to seizures, confusion, coma and death.

For Belize, malaria pills are recommended for travel to all areas except Belize City. The risk is highest in the western and southern regions.

The malaria pill of choice is chloroquine, taken once weekly in a dosage of 500mg, starting one to two weeks before arrival and continuing during the trip and for four weeks afterwards. Chloroquine is safe, inexpensive and highly effective. Side effects are typically mild and may include nausea, abdominal discomfort, headache, dizziness, blurred vision or itching. Severe reactions are uncommon.

Since no pills are 100% effective, protecting yourself against mosquito bites (p244) is just as important as taking malaria pills.

You may not have access to medical care while traveling, so you should bring along additional pills for emergency self-treatment, which you should take if you can't reach a doctor and you develop symptoms that suggest malaria, such as high, spiking fevers. One option is to take four tablets of Malarone once daily for three days. If you start self-medication, you should try to see a doctor at the earliest possible opportunity.

If you develop a fever after returning home, see a physician, as malaria symptoms may not occur for months.

Rabies

Rabies is a viral infection of the brain and spinal cord that is almost always fatal. The rabies virus is carried in the saliva of infected animals and is typically transmitted through an animal bite, though contamination of any break in the skin with infected saliva may result in rabies.

Rabies occurs in all Central American countries. The greatest risk is in the triangle where Belize, Guatemala and the Yucatán region meet. Most cases are related to bites from dogs or bats.

Rabies vaccine is safe, but requires three injections and is quite expensive. Those at high risk for rabies, such as spelunkers (ie cave explorers), should certainly be vaccinated. The treatment for a possibly rabid bite consists of vaccine with immune globulin. It's effective, but must be given promptly. Most travelers don't need to be vaccinated against rabies.

All animal bites and scratches must be promptly and thoroughly cleansed with large amounts of soap and water, and local health authorities should be contacted to determine whether or not further treatment is necessary (see right).

Typhoid

Typhoid fever is caused by the ingestion of contaminated food or water. Outbreaks sometimes occur at times of flooding, when sewage overflow may contaminate water sources. The initial symptoms, which resemble a mild flu, usually subside uneventfully in a few days, with or without treatment, but a minority of cases are complicated by jaundice or meningitis. Fever occurs in virtually all cases. Other symptoms may include headache, malaise, muscle aches, dizziness, loss of appetite, nausea and abdominal pain, and either diarrhea or constipation.

Unless you expect to take all your meals in major hotels and restaurants, vaccination for typhoid is a good idea. It's usually given orally, but is also available as an injection. Neither vaccine is approved for use in children under age two.

The drug of choice for typhoid fever is usually a quinolone antibiotic such as ciprofloxacin (Cipro) or levofloxacin (Levaquin), which many travelers carry for treatment of traveler's diarrhea. If you self-treat for typhoid fever, however, you may also need to self-treat for malaria, since the symptoms of the two diseases may be indistinguishable.

Yellow Fever

Yellow fever no longer occurs in Central America, but Belize, Guatemala and Mexico require yellow-fever vaccination before entry *only* if you're arriving from an infected country in Africa or South America. The vaccine is given only in approved yellow-fever vaccination centers, which provide validated International Certificates of Vaccination ('yellow booklets'). The vaccine should be given at least 10 days before leaving and remains effective for about 10 years.

Reactions to the vaccine are generally mild and may include headaches, muscle aches, low-grade fevers or discomfort at the injection site. Severe, life-threatening reactions are extremely rare. Vaccination is not recommended for pregnant women or children less than nine months old.

TRAVELER'S DIARRHEA

To prevent diarrhea, avoid tap water unless it's been boiled, filtered or chemically disinfected (with iodine tablets); only eat fresh fruit or vegetables if cooked or peeled; be wary of dairy products that might contain unpasteurized milk; and be highly selective when eating food from street vendors.

If you develop diarrhea, be sure to drink plenty of fluids, preferably an oral rehydration solution containing salt and sugar. A few loose stools don't require treatment, but if you start having more than four or five stools a day, you should start taking an antibiotic (usually a quinolone drug) and an antidiarrheal agent (such as loperamide). If diarrhea is bloody, persists for more than 72 hours or is accompanied by fever, shaking chills or severe abdominal pain, you should seek medical attention.

ENVIRONMENTAL HAZARDS
Animal Bites

Do not attempt to pet, handle or feed any animal, with the exception of domestic animals known to be free of infectious diseases.

HEALTH

Most animal injuries occur when people try to touch or feed animals.

Any bite or scratch by a mammal, including bats, should be promptly and thoroughly cleansed with large amounts of soap and water, and an antiseptic such as iodine or alcohol applied. The local health authorities should be contacted immediately for possible post-exposure rabies treatment, whether or not you've been immunized against rabies. It may also be advisable to take antibiotics, since wounds caused by animal bites and scratches frequently become infected. One of the newer quinolones, such as levofloxacin (Levaquin), which many travelers carry in case of diarrhea, would be an appropriate choice.

Mosquito Bites

To avoid mosquito bites, wear long sleeves, long pants, hats and shoes (rather than sandals). Pack insect repellent, preferably one containing DEET, which should be applied to exposed skin and clothing, but not to eyes, mouth, cuts, wounds or irritated skin. Products containing lower concentrations of DEET are as effective, but for shorter periods of time. In general, adults and children over 12 should use preparations containing 25% to 35% DEET, which lasts about six hours. Children between two and 12 years of age should use preparations containing no more than 10% DEET, applied sparingly, which will usually last about three hours.

Neurologic toxicity has been reported from using DEET, especially in children, but appears to be extremely uncommon and is generally related to overuse. DEET-containing compounds should not be used on children under age two.

Insect repellents containing certain botanical products, including eucalyptus and soybean oil, are effective but last only 1½ to two hours. DEET-containing repellents are preferable for areas where there is a high risk of malaria or yellow fever. Products based on citronella are not effective.

For additional protection, you can apply permethrin to clothing, shoes, tents and bed nets. Permethrin treatments are safe and remain effective for at least two weeks, even when items are laundered. Permethrin should not be applied directly to skin.

Don't sleep with windows open unless there is a screen. If sleeping outdoors or in accommodations that allow entry of mosquitoes, use a bed net, preferably treated with permethrin, with the edges tucked in under the mattress. The mesh size should be less than 1.5mm. If the sleeping area is not otherwise protected, use a mosquito coil, which will fill the room with insecticide through the night. Repellent-impregnated wristbands are not effective.

Snake Bites

Snakes are a hazard in Belize. The chief concern is *Bothrops asper,* the Central American or common lancehead, usually known in Belize as the yellow-jaw tommygoff, and also called the fer-de-lance, *barba amarilla* (yellow beard) or *terciopelo* (velvet skin). This heavy-bodied snake reaches up to 6.5ft in length and is found especially in the northern region. It is earth-toned and has a broadly triangular head with a pattern of Xs and triangles on its back. Others snakes to watch out for are the brightly striped coral snake and the tropical rattlesnake. All three snakes are deadly, though the coral snake is shyer than the 'irritable' rattlesnake.

In the event of a venomous snake bite, place the victim at rest, keep the bitten area immobilized, and move the victim immediately to the nearest medical facility. Avoid tourniquets, as they are are no longer recommended.

Tick Bites

To protect yourself from tick bites, follow the same precautions as for mosquitoes, except that boots are preferable to shoes, with pants tucked in. Be sure to perform a thorough tick check at the end of each day. You'll generally need the assistance of a friend or a mirror for a full examination. Remove ticks with tweezers, grasping them firmly by the head. Insect repellents based on botanical products (left) have not been adequately studied for insects other than mosquitoes and cannot be recommended to prevent tick bites.

Sun Exposure

To protect yourself from excessive exposure to the sun, you should stay out of the midday sun, wear sunglasses and a wide-brimmed hat, and apply sunscreen with SPF 15 or higher, with both UVA and UVB protection. Sunscreen should be generously applied to all exposed parts of the body approximately 30 minutes before sun exposure and should be reapplied after swimming or vigorous activities. Travelers should also drink plenty of fluids and avoid strenuous exercise when it is hot. Dehydration and salt deficiency can cause heat exhaustion, which can then progress to heatstroke.

Symptoms of this serious condition include a general feeling of unwellness, not sweating very much (or not at all) and a high body temperature (39°C to 41°C, or 102°F to 106°F). Severe, throbbing headaches and lack of coordination can also occur. Hospitalization is essential, but in the interim get victims out of the sun, remove their clothing, cover them with a wet sheet or towel and fan continually. Give fluids if they are conscious.

Water

Tap water is not safe to drink in Belize. Vigorous boiling for one minute is the most effective means of water purification. At altitudes greater than 3630ft, boil for three minutes.

Another option is to disinfect water with iodine pills. Follow the enclosed instructions carefully. Alternatively, you can add 2% tincture of iodine to one quart or liter of water (five drops to clear water, 10 drops to cloudy water) and let stand for 30 minutes. If the water is cold, longer times may be required. The taste of iodinated water may be improved by adding vitamin C (ascorbic acid). Iodinated water should not be consumed for more than a few weeks. Pregnant women, those with a history of thyroid disease and those allergic to iodine should not drink iodinated water.

Water filters with smaller pores (reverse osmosis filters) provide the broadest protection, but they are relatively large and are readily plugged by debris. Those with somewhat larger pores (microstrainer filters) are ineffective against viruses, although they remove other organisms. Follow manufacturers' instructions carefully.

Safe, inexpensive *agua pura* (purified water) is widely available in hotels, shops and restaurants.

CHILDREN & PREGNANT WOMEN

In general, it's safe for children and pregnant women to go to Belize. However, because some of the vaccines listed in this chapter are not approved for use in children and during pregnancy, these travelers should be particularly careful not to drink tap water or consume any questionable food or drink. Also, when traveling with children, make sure they're up to date on all routine immunizations. It's sometimes appropriate to give children some of their vaccines a little early before visiting a developing nation – discuss this with your pediatrician. If pregnant, bear in mind that should a complication, such as premature labor, develop while abroad, the quality of medical care may not be comparable to that in your home country.

Since yellow-fever vaccine is not recommended for pregnant women or children less than nine months old, these travelers, if arriving from a country with yellow fever, should obtain a waiver letter, preferably written on letterhead and bearing the stamp used by official immunization centers to validate the International Certificate of Vaccination.

HEALTH

Behind the Scenes

THIS BOOK

This 2nd edition of *Belize* was written by John Noble and Susan Forsyth. John, the coordinating author, wrote most of the front chapters plus Belize City, Northern Belize, Western Belize, Southern Belize, Directory and Transportation. Susan wrote the Northern Cayes and Tikal & Flores, Guatemala chapters. Food & Drink was coauthored by John and Susan. Dr Allen J Christenson wrote The Ancient Maya World chapter, and Mark Webster wrote the Diving & Snorkeling section of the Belize Outdoors chapter. The 1st edition of *Belize* was written by Carolyn Miller Carlstroem and Debra Miller.

THANKS FROM THE AUTHORS

John Noble Special thanks to Anita and George at the Coningsby Inn for their help and hospitality, and to Dirk Francisco at the Belize Audubon Society for his help and patience. Others whose assistance I am particularly grateful for include Maarten and Caspar Bijleveld van Lexmond at Shipstern Nature Reserve, Beatriz Guerra of the Casa Blanca in San Ignacio, and Rob Hirons of the Lodge at Big Falls.

Susan Forsyth Thanks to John, coordinating author and husband, for your hours of hard work. On Ambergris Caye, special thanks go to Jorge Santos of the tourist office, the staff of Ruby's Cafe for their big morning coffees, and Joe from the bicycle rental shop for his personal attention. (I did indeed have a great day cycling the north island.) Caye Caulker's village council greeted me warmly: thanks Berto, Irene and Mo for your hospitality and freeflowing tips. Also on Caye Caulker, Luciana Essenziale of

Seagull Adventures helped to track down some elusive details while the gentle folk, Al and Joanne of Jaguar Morning Star guesthouse, introduced me to Caulker's mellow mood and zesty orange juice. En route to Flores, Guatemala, my bus broke down a number of times. I thank fellow passenger and traveler, the English mechanic who cheerfully got the bus moving again so that we all arrived safely in Flores before nightfall. Finally, at home, thank you Isabella and Jack for your patience.

CREDITS

Commissioning Editors: Sam Benson & Heather Dickson
Coordinating Editor: Carolyn Boicos
Coordinating Cartographer: Daniel Fennessy
Coordinating Layout Designer: Jacqueline McLeod
Managing Cartographer: Shahara Ahmed
Assisting Editors: Adrienne Costanzo, Carly Hall & Helen Koehne
Assisting Cartographers: Malisa Plesa & Helen Rowley
Cover Designer: Candice Jacobus
Colour Designer: Kaitlin Beckett
Project Manager: Fabrice Rocher

Thanks to Yvonne Bischofberger, Sally Darmody, Alex Hershey, LPI, Alison Lyall, Adriana Mammarella, Wayne Murphy, Darren O'Connell & Sarah Sloane.

THANKS FROM LONELY PLANET

Many thanks to the travelers who used the last edition and wrote to us with helpful hints, useful advice and interesting anecdotes:

A Bruce Aisthorpe, Natasha Aisthorpe, Kim Albrecht, David R Anderson, Shawna Archa, Cather-

THE LONELY PLANET STORY

The story begins with a classic travel adventure: Tony and Maureen Wheeler's 1972 journey across Europe and Asia to Australia. There was no useful information about the overland trail then, so Tony and Maureen published the first Lonely Planet guidebook to meet a growing need.

From a kitchen table, Lonely Planet has grown to become the largest independent travel publisher in the world, with offices in Melbourne (Australia), Oakland (USA) and London (UK). Today Lonely Planet guidebooks cover the globe. There is an ever-growing list of books and information in a variety of media. Some things haven't changed. The main aim is still to make it possible for adventurous travelers to get out there – to explore and better understand the world.

At Lonely Planet we believe travelers can make a positive contribution to the countries they visit – if they respect their host communities and spend their money wisely. Every year 5% of company profit is donated to charities around the world.

ine Archibald, Sue Arnold, Santiago Ash, Christine Astaniou, Ray Auxillou **B** Hans Baekke Kristensen, David Barmettler, Lu Barnham, Hannah Bastiani, Steve Baxa, Alec Beardsell, Andrea Begel, Ronda Bernstein, Brendan Bietry, Philip Blackburn, Vashti Blacker, Munira Blacking, Sarah Blech, Duane Bong, Nancy Bouchard, Susan Brown, Linda Bufton, Steven J Burris, Ian Burton **C** Giovanni Capellini, Bonnie Carpenter, Mafalda Carvalho, Nelita Castillo, Chung-wah Chow, Philip Coebergh, Roger Conant, James Crooks, Damon Crowhurst, Emma Curnow **D** Marvin Darnell Coleman, Lindsay Dawes, Kevin Day, Emily Dean, Christian Debenath, Michael Dees, Elma de Jong, Maria De Keyser, Steph Dela, Igor De Ruitz, Jennifer Ditchburn, David Dodgson, Sue Doherty, Anouk Donker, Danielle Douglas, Marcel Driessen **E** Janet Edwards, Miriam Engeln, Tandi Erlmann, Nory Esteban, Chau Evans **F** Anat & Gil Feldman, Joseph Fette, Ian Fisher, Gary Fishman, Annelies Florquin, Ben Flynn, Chris Fox, Cynda Fuentes, Andreas Funke **G** Jonathon Gandy, Stuart Gardiner, A Geller, Janet Geller, Sandra Gennai, Raoul Genoud, Mark Goettel, Wendy Gonsalves, Caleb Goossen, Marilin Grahn, Randy Grahn, Anette Gram Madsen, Britney Grimes **H** Wolfgang Haertel, Marita Hagen, Evan Hall, Brian Hammond, Kate Harper, Jacob Hegner, Larry Heinlein, Mark Hermans, Sirpa Hillberg, Matthias Hillenkamp, Sara Hillman, Justin Hines, M Hoard, Tanya Hoeberechts, Jody Hoffmann, David Howard, Anja Huber, Sarah Hullah, Jayne Husband, Tasneem Hussain, Anna Huttenlauch **I** Nadler Ishay, Helga Itulah **J** Jan Jasiewicz, Erick Johns, Carlisle Johnson, David Johnson, Nick Jones, Peter Jones, Tammy Jorgensen, Vince Jorgensen, Greg Juhl **K** Amy Karon, Christoph Kilger, Jennifer Kim, Julie King, Simon King, Gregory Kipling, Constantine Kipnis, M Klein, C Klein Lataud, Elizabeth Knell, Aarnoud Kraan, Diane Kremer **L** Jean-Pierre Lamure, Jenny Lau, Seth Lazar, Antonia Learey, Michelle Legere, Joris Lenssens, Jeff Linwood, Laura Losee, Anne K Lowe, Stephen Lowe, Judith Lumb **M** Cedric Maizieres, Marsh Marcus, Birgit Maris, David Martin, Paul Martin, Malcom Massey, Stefan Mauersberger, Joanne Mauro, Paolo Mazzali, Beth McCall, Rory McCall, Tracey Mccosh, Robin McCutcheon, Fielding M McGehee, Joe Mehl, Ninfa Mendoza, Andrea Merschilz, John Miller, John Minichiello, Michelle Miranda, Brigitte Monfils, Diane Morrison, Donna Murray **N** Jim Nameny, Katharina Nothelfer, Soren Nyegaard **O** Shinji Okitsu, Justin Oliver, Katye Oliver **P** Jennifer Pacourek, Rosalyn Park, Trish Patrick, Ludovica & Pierpaolo Patroncini, Karin Pedersen, Christine Penn, Sam Pickering, Melissa Pike, Elisabeth Poetscher-Maerky, Cheri Powell, Natasha Pozo, Dimitri Prybylski, Juli Puryear **R** Terrell Rafferty, Jurgen Rahmer, Nyoka Rajah, Anthea Rawlence, Julia Rhodes, Kyle Richardson, Hilde Roelofsen, Jane Rose, Peter S Ross, Joan Rubin, Shimon Rumelt, Sarah Russell, Paul Rutten **S** Solomon Sandberg, Marilyn Sanders, Stephen Sandlos, Laura Sawyer, Susan Schroeder, Julia Seiders, BJ Semmes, Gavin Sexton, Alexander Sharman, Christa Shepherd, Daniel Sher, Noa Sher, Caesar Sherrard, Ian Sherriff, William Simons, Erica Smith, James Smith, Sarah Smith, James Squier, Steve & Marion Squire, Karen Stammer, Jennifer Stiff, Andy Stock, Melissa Sulivan **T** Achim Talmon, Edward Timpson, Julia Timpson, Lindsay Tomlinson, Karen Toohey, Bruno Stuart Torrie, Johnny Tran, Tom Triglone, David Truman, Christine Tuhy **V** Thomas van der Lijke, Eelco Van Geene, Rob Van Peer, Ron van Rooijen, Leonie van Rossum, Michel van Rossum, Judy van Veen, Bart Verlinden, Rolf Von Behrens **W** Chow Chung Wah, Katrin Wanner, Julian Wedgwood, Mark Weitz, Jonas Wernli, Ken Westmoreland, Philip Wiebe, Ellen Wijnand, Gretchen Wilhelm, Steve Wilson, Christopher & Tanda Wilson-Clarke, Irene Winterberger, Stephan Wolde, Dietmar Wuelfing **X** Liliane X **Y** Andrew Young **Z** Greg Zane, Jacqueline Zhang

ACKNOWLEDGMENTS

Globe on back cover © Mountain High Maps 1993 Digital Wisdom, Inc.

SEND US YOUR FEEDBACK

We love to hear from travelers – your comments keep us on our toes and help make our books better. Our well-traveled team reads every word on what you loved or loathed about this book. Although we cannot reply individually to postal submissions, we always guarantee that your feedback goes straight to the appropriate authors, in time for the next edition. Each person who sends us information is thanked in the next edition – and the most useful submissions are rewarded with a free book.

To send us your updates – and find out about Lonely Planet events, newsletters and travel news – visit our award-winning website: **www.lonelyplanet.com/feedback**.

Note: we may edit, reproduce and incorporate your comments in Lonely Planet products such as guidebooks, websites and digital products, so let us know if you don't want your comments reproduced or your name acknowledged. For a copy of our privacy policy visit www.lonelyplanet.com/privacy.

BEHIND THE SCENES

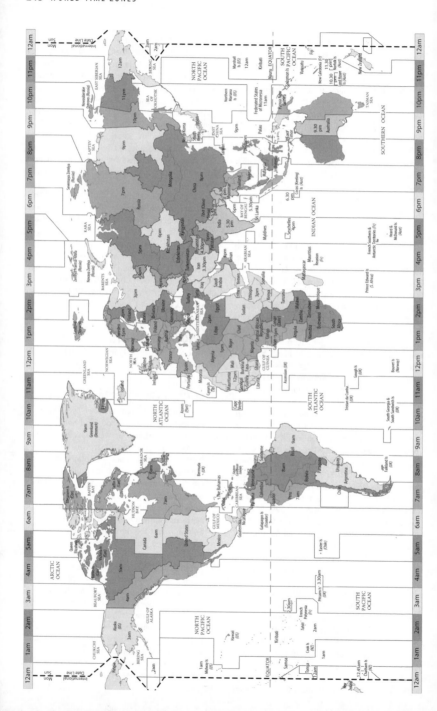

Index

000 Map pages
000 Location of colour photographs

INDEX

000 Map pages
000 Location of colour photogr

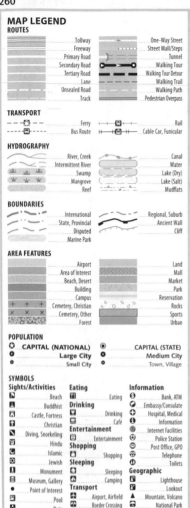

MAP LEGEND

ROUTES

Tollway	One-Way Street
Freeway	Street Mall/Steps
Primary Road	Tunnel
Secondary Road	Walking Tour
Tertiary Road	Walking Tour Detour
Lane	Walking Trail
Unsealed Road	Walking Path
Track	Pedestrian Overpass

TRANSPORT

Ferry	Rail
Bus Route	Cable Car, Funicular

HYDROGRAPHY

River, Creek	Canal
Intermittent River	Water
Swamp	Lake (Dry)
Mangrove	Lake (Salt)
Reef	Mudflats

BOUNDARIES

International	Regional, Suburb
State, Provincial	Ancient Wall
Disputed	Cliff
Marine Park	

AREA FEATURES

Airport	Land
Area of Interest	Mall
Beach, Desert	Market
Building	Park
Campus	Reservation
Cemetery, Christian	Rocks
Cemetery, Other	Sports
Forest	Urban

POPULATION

✪ CAPITAL (NATIONAL)	◉ CAPITAL (STATE)
● Large City	● Medium City
○ Small City	● Town, Village

SYMBOLS

Sights/Activities
- Beach
- Buddhist
- Castle, Fortress
- Christian
- Diving, Snorkeling
- Hindu
- Islamic
- Jewish
- Monument
- Museum, Gallery
- Point of Interest
- Pool
- Ruin
- Snorkeling
- Surfing, Surf Beach
- Trail Head
- Zoo, Bird Sanctuary

Eating
- Eating

Drinking
- Drinking
- Café

Entertainment
- Entertainment

Shopping
- Shopping

Sleeping
- Sleeping
- Camping

Transport
- Airport, Airfield
- Border Crossing
- Bus Station
- General Transport
- Parking Area
- Petrol Station
- Taxi Rank

Information
- Bank, ATM
- Embassy/Consulate
- Hospital, Medical
- Information
- Internet Facilities
- Police Station
- Post Office, GPO
- Telephone
- Toilets

Geographic
- Lighthouse
- Lookout
- Mountain, Volcano
- National Park
- Pass, Canyon
- Picnic Area
- River Flow
- Shelter, Hut
- Waterfall

LONELY PLANET OFFICES

Australia
Head Office
Locked Bag 1, Footscray, Victoria 3011
☎ 03 8379 8000, fax 03 8379 8111
talk2us@lonelyplanet.com.au

USA
150 Linden St, Oakland, CA 94607
☎ 510 893 8555, toll free 800 275 8555
fax 510 893 8572, info@lonelyplanet.com

UK
72–82 Rosebery Ave,
Clerkenwell, London EC1R 4RW
☎ 020 7841 9000, fax 020 7841 9001
go@lonelyplanet.co.uk

Published by Lonely Planet Publications Pty Ltd
ABN 36 005 607 983

© Lonely Planet 2005

© photographers as indicated 2005

Cover photographs: *Palapa* in shallow water, Belize, Mark Lewis/ Getty Images (front); Toucan Too Gift Shop, San Pedro, Ambergris Caye, Tony Wheeler/Lonely Planet Images (back). Many of the images in this guide are available for licensing from Lonely Planet Images: www.lonelyplanetimages.com.

Printed through Colorcraft Ltd, Hong Kong.
Printed in China.

INDEX